A Publisher and His Friends: Memoir and Correspondence of John Murray

Samuel Smiles

Edited by Thomas Mackay

A PUBLISHER AND HIS FRIENDS

MEMOIR AND CORRESPONDENCE OF JOHN MURRAY

WITH AN ACCOUNT OF THE ORIGIN AND PROGRESS OF THE
HOUSE, 1768-1843

BY THE LATE SAMUEL SMILES, LL. D.

CONDENSED AND EDITED BY THOMAS MACKAY

1911

PREFACE

When my Grandfather's Memoirs were published, twenty years ago, they met with a most favourable and gratifying reception at the hands of the public. Interest was aroused by the struggle and success of a man who had few advantages at the outset save his own shrewd sense and generous nature, and who, moreover, was thrown on his own resources to fight the battle of life when he was little more than a child.

The chief value of these volumes, however, consists in the fact that they supply an important, if not an indispensable, chapter in the literary history of England during the first half of the nineteenth century. Byron and Scott, Lockhart, Croker, George Borrow, Hallam, Canning, Gifford, Disraeli, Southey, Milman are but a few of the names occurring in these pages, the whole list of which it would be tedious to enumerate.

It may be admitted that a pious desire to do justice to the memory of John Murray the Second—"the Anax of Publishers, " as Byron called him—led to the inclusion in the original volumes of some material of minor importance which may now well be dispensed with.

I find, however, that the work is still so often quoted and referred to that I have asked my friend Mr. Thomas Mackay to prepare a new edition for the press. I am convinced that the way in which he has discharged his task will commend itself to the reading public. He has condensed the whole, has corrected errors, and has rewritten certain passages in a more concise form.

I desire to acknowledge my debt to him for what he has done, and to express a hope that the public may extend a fresh welcome to "an old friend with a new face. "

JOHN MURRAY.

December, 1910.

CONTENTS

CHAPTER I

JOHN MACMURRAY OR MURRAY

The first John Murray—An Officer of Marines—Retires from Active Service—His marriage—Correspondence with William Falconer—Falconer's death—Murray purchases Sandby's business—John Murray's first publications—His writings—Mr. Kerr—Thomas Cumming goes to Ireland on behalf of Murray—Prof. J. Millar—Mr. Whitaker—Defence of Sir R. Gordon—Ross estate—His controversy with Mr. Mason—The Edinburgh booksellers—Creech and Elliot—Dr. Cullen—The second John Murray—His education—Accident to his eye—Illness and death of the elder John Murray

CHAPTER II

JOHN MURRAY (II.)—BEGINNING OF HIS PUBLISHING CAREER—ISAAC D'ISRAELI, ETC.

John Murray the Second—"The Anax of Publishers"—His start in business—Murray and Highley—Dissolution of the partnership—Colman's "John Bull"—Mr. Joseph Hume—Archibald Constable—John Murray a Volunteer—The D'Israeli family—Isaac D'Israeli's early works—"Flim-Flams"—Birth of Benjamin D'Israeli—Projected periodical the "Institute"—The "Miniature"—Murray's acquaintance with Canning and Frere

CHAPTER III

MURRAY AND CONSTABLE—HUNTER AND THE FORFARSHIRE LAIRDS—MARRIAGE OF JOHN MURRAY

Archibald Constable & Co.—Alexander Gibson Hunter—The *Edinburgh Review*—Murray's early associations with Constable—Dispute between Longman and Constable—Murray appointed London Agent—He urges reconciliation between Constable and Longman—Mr. Murray visits Edinburgh—Engaged to Miss Elliot—Goes into Forfarshire—Rude Hospitality—Murray's marriage—The D'Israelis

CHAPTER IV

"MARMION" — CONSTABLES AND BALLANTYNES — THE "EDINBURGH REVIEW"

Murray's business prospects — Acquires a share of "Marmion" — Becomes London publisher of the *Edinburgh Review* — Acquaintance with Walter Scott — Constable's money transactions — Murray's remonstrance — He separates from Constable — The Ballantynes — Scott joins their printing business — Literary themes

CHAPTER V

ORIGIN OF THE "QUARTERLY REVIEW"

Canning's early schemes for a Penny Newspaper — The *Anti-Jacobin* — The *Edinburgh Review* — John Murray's letter to Mr. Canning — Walter Scott's assistance — Southey's letter to Scott — Review of "Marmion" in the *Edinburgh* — Murray's conditions — Meeting with James Ballantyne at Ferrybridge — Visit to Scott at Ashestiel — Letters to Scott — Scott's letters to Murray, Ellis, and Gifford on the *Quarterly* — Arrangements for the first number — Articles by Scott — James Mill — Mrs. Inchbald — Dr. Thomas Young

CHAPTER VI

THE "QUARTERLY" LAUNCHED

Meeting of Murray and Ballantyne at Boroughbridge — Walter Scott's interest in the new *Review* — Publication of the first number of the *Quarterly* — Scott's proposed "Secret History of the Court of James I." — *Portcullis* copies — "Old English Froissart" — Opinions of the *Quarterly* — Scott's energy and encouragement — Murray's correspondence with Mr. Stratford Canning — Murray's energy — Leigh Hunt — James Mill — Gifford's unpunctuality — Appearance of the second number — Mr. Canning's contributions — Appearance of No. 3 — Letters from Mr. Ellis to Isaac D'Israeli — John Barrow's first connection with the *Quarterly* — Robert Southey — Appearance of No. 4

CHAPTER VII

CONSTABLE AND BALLANTYNE

Murray's and Ballantyne's joint enterprises—Financial difficulties—
Murray's remonstrances—Ballantyne's reckless speculations—And
disregard of Murray's advice—Revival of Murray's business with
Constable—Publication of the "Lady of the Lake"—Murray excluded
from his promised share of it—Transfers his Edinburgh agency to
Mr. William Blackwood—Publication of No. 5 of the *Quarterly*—
Southey's articles and books—Unpunctuality of the *Review*—
Gifford's review of "The Daughters of Isenberg"—His letter to Miss
Palmer—Dispute between Murray and Gifford—Attacks on the
Edinburgh Review by the *Quarterly*—Murray's disapproval of them—
The Ballantynes and Constables applying for money—Nos. 8 and 9
of the *Review*—Southey's Publications—Letters from Scott—His
review of the "Curse of Kehama"—Southey's dependence on the
Quarterly—His letter to Mr. Wynn

CHAPTER VIII

MURRAY AND GIFFORD—RUPTURE WITH CONSTABLE—
PROSPERITY OF THE "QUARTERLY"

Increasing friendship between Murray and Gifford—Gifford's
opinion of humorous articles—Mr. Pillans—Gifford's feeble health—
Murray's financial difficulties—Remonstrates with Constable—
Correspondence with and dissociation from Constable—*Quarterly
Review* No. 12—Gifford's severe remarks on Charles Lamb—His
remorse—*Quarterly Review* No. 14—Murray's offer to Southey of
1,000 guineas for his poem

CHAPTER IX

LORD BYRON'S WORKS, 1811 TO 1814

Lord Byron's first acquaintance with Mr. Murray—Mr. Dallas's offer
to Cawthorn and Miller—Murray's acceptance of "Childe Harold"—
Byron's visits to Fleet Street—Murray's letters to Byron—Gifford's
opinion of the Poem—Publication of "Childe Harold"—Its
immediate success—Byron's presentation to the Prince of Wales—
Murray effects a reconciliation

between Byron and Scott—Letters to and from Scott—Publication of "The Giaour," "Bride of Abydos" and "Corsair"—Correspondence with Byron—"Ode to Napoleon"—"Lara" and "Jacqueline"

CHAPTER X

MR. MURRAY'S REMOVAL TO 50, ALBEMARLE STREET

Murray's removal to Albemarle Street—Miller's unfriendly behaviour—Progress of the *Quarterly*—Miscellaneous publications —D'Israeli's "Calamities of Authors"—Letters from Scott and Southey—Southey's opinions on the patronage of literature—Scott's embarrassments—Recklessness of the Ballantynes—Scott applies to Murray for a loan—Publication of "Waverley"—Mystery of the authorship—Mr. Murray's proposed trip to France—His letters to Mrs. Murray—Education of his son—Announcement of Lord Byron's engagement—Mr. Murray's visit to Newstead Abbey— Murray in Edinburgh—Mr. William Blackwood—Visit to Abbotsford—Letter to Lord Byron—Letters from Blackwood—The "Vision of Don Roderick"

CHAPTER XI

MURRAY'S DRAWING-ROOM—BYRON AND SCOTT—WORKS PUBLISHED IN 1815

Murray's drawing-room in Albemarle Street—A literary centre— George Ticknor's account of it—Letter from Gifford—Death of his housekeeper Nancy—First meeting of Byron and Scott— Recollections of John Murray III.—Napoleon's escape from Elba— Waterloo—Mr. Blackwood's letter—Suppression of an article written for the *Edinburgh*—Mr. Murray's collection of portraits of authors— Mr. Scott's visit to Brussels, Waterloo, etc.—Mr. Murray's visit to Paris—Return home—Important diplomatic correspondence offered by Miss Waldie—Miss Austen—"Emma"—Mr. Malthus's works— Letters from W. Scott

CHAPTER XII

VARIOUS   PUBLICATIONS—CHARLES   MATURIN—S.T.
COLERIDGE—LEIGH HUNT

Charles Maturin—His early career—His early publications—And
application to W. Scott—Performance of "Bertram" at Drury Lane—
Published by Murray—"Manuel, a Tragedy"—Murray's letter to
Byron—Death of Maturin—S.T. Coleridge—Correspondence about
his translation of "Faust"—"Glycine," "Remorse," "Christabel,"
"Zapolya," and other works—Further correspondence—Leigh
Hunt—Asked to contribute to the *Quarterly*—"Story of Rimini"—
Murray's letters to Byron and Hunt—Negotiations between Murray
and Leigh Hunt

CHAPTER XIII

THOMAS   CAMPBELL—JOHN   CAM   HOBHOUSE—J.W.
CROKER—JAMES HOGG, ETC.

Thomas Campbell—His early works—Acquaintance with Murray—
"Selections from the British Poets"—Letters to Murray—Proposed
Magazine—And Series of Ancient Classics—Close friendship
between Campbell and Murray—Murray undertakes to publish the
"Selections from British Poets"—Campbell's explanation of the
work—"Gertrude of Wyoming"—Scott reviews Campbell's poems
in the *Quarterly*—Campbell's Lectures at the Royal Institution—
Campbell's satisfaction with Murray's treatment of him—"Now
Barabbas was a publisher"—Increase of Murray's business—
Dealings with Gifford—Mr. J.C. Hobhouse—His "Journey to
Albania"—Isaac D'Israeli's "Character of James I."—Croker's
"Stories for Children"—The division of profits—Sir John Malcolm—
Increasing number of poems submitted to Mr. Murray—James
Hogg—His works—And letters to Murray—The "Repository"—
Correspondence with Murray—Hogg asks Murray to find a wife for
him

CHAPTER XIV

LORD BYRON'S DEALINGS WITH MR. MURRAY—*continued*

Lord Byron's marriage—Letters from Mr. Murray during the honeymoon—Mr. Fazakerly's interview with Bonaparte—Byron's pecuniary embarrassments—Murray's offers of assistance—"Siege of Corinth"—"Parisina"—Byron refuses remuneration—Pressed to give the money to Godwin, Maturin, and Coleridge—Murray's remonstrance —Gifford's opinion of the "Siege of Corinth" and Mr. D'Israeli's —Byron leaves England—Sale of his Library—The "Sketch from Private Life"—Mr. Sharon Turner's legal opinion—Murray's letter on the arrival of the MS. of "Childe Harold," CantoIII.

CHAPTER XIX

WORKS PUBLISHED IN 1817-18—CORRESPONDENCE, ETC.

Works published by Murray and Blackwood jointly—Illness of Scott—Efforts to help the Ettrick Shepherd—Murray's offers of assistance—Scott reviews the "Wake"—Hogg's house at Eltrive—Scott and the *Quarterly*—"Rob Roy"—The "Scottish Regalia"—"The Heart of Midlothian"—Appeal to Scott for an article—"Lord Orford's Letters"—Murray and James Hogg at Abbotsford—Conclusion of Hogg's correspondence—Robert Owen—Increased number of would-be poets—Sharon Turner—Gifford's illness—Croker and Barrow edit *Quarterly Review*

CHAPTER XX

HALLAM—BASIL HALL.—CRABBE—HOPE—HORACE AND JAMES SMITH

Mr. Hallam—Sir H. Ellis's "Embassy to China"—Correspondence with Lady Abercorn about new books—Proposed *Monthly Register*—Mr. Croker's condemnation of the scheme—Crabbe's Works—Mr. Murray's offer—Mr. Rogers's negotiations—Hope's "Anastasius"—"Rejected Addresses" —Colonel Macirone's action against the *Quarterly*—Murray's entertainments—Mrs. Bray's account of them

CHAPTER XXI

MEMOIRS OF LADY HERVEY AND HORACE WALPOLE—
BELZONI—MILMAN—SOUTHEY—MRS. RUNDELL, ETC.

Lady Hervey's Letters—Mr. Croker's letter about the editing of them—Horace Walpole's Memoirs—Mr. Murray's correspondence with Lord Holland—The Suffolk papers, edited by Mr. Croker—Mrs. Delany's Letters—Letter from Mr. Croker—Horace Walpole's "Reminiscences," edited by Miss Berry—Tomline's "Life of Pitt"— Giovanni Belzoni—His early career and works—His sensitiveness— His death—Examples of his strength—Rev. H.H. Milman's Works, "Fazio," "Samor," "The Fall of Jerusalem," "Martyr of Antioch," "Belshazzar"—Murray's dealings with Milman—Benjamin Disraeli—Letters from Southey about his articles on Cromwell—The New Churches, etc.—"The Book of the Church"—Warren Hastings, etc—The Carbonari—Mr. Eastlake—Mrs. Graham—Galignani's pirated edition of Byron—Mrs. Rundell's "Cookery Book"—Dispute with Longman's—An injunction obtained

CHAPTER XXII

WASHINGTON IRVING—UGO FOSCOLO—LADY CAROLINE
LAMB—"HAJJI BABA"—MRS. MARKHAM'S HISTORIES

Washington Irving—His early dealings with Murray—He comes to England—His description of a dinner at Murray's—"The Sketch Book"—Published in England by Miller—Afterwards undertaken by Murray—Terms of purchase—Irving's ill-success in business— "Bracebridge Hall"—James Fenimore Cooper—Ugo Foscolo—His early career—First article in the *Quarterly*—Letter from Mr. T. Mitchell—Foscolo's peculiarities—Digamma Cottage—His ectures—Death of Foscolo—Lady C. Lamb—"Glenarvon"— "Penruddock"—"Ada Reis"—Letter from the Hon. Wm. Lamb— Lord J. Russell—His proposed History of Europe—Mr. James Morier's "Hajji Baba"—Letter of Mirza Abul Hassan—Mrs. Markham's "History of England"—Allan Cunningham

CHAPTER XXIII

GIFFORD'S RETIREMENT FROM THE EDITORSHIP OF THE "QUARTERLY" — AND DEATH

Gifford's failing health—Difficulty of finding a successor—Barrow's assistance—Gifford's letter to Mr. Canning—Irregularity of the numbers—Southey's views as to the Editorship—Gifford's letter to Mr. Canning—Appointment of Mr. J.T. Coleridge—Murray's announcement of the appointment to Gifford—Close of Mr. Gifford's career—His correspondence with Murray—Letter from Mr. R. Hay to the present Mr. Murray about Gifford

CHAPTER XXIV

THE "REPRESENTATIVE"

Murray's desire to start a new periodical—Benjamin Disraeli—Projected morning paper—Benjamin Disraeli's early career and writings—Letters to Murray about "Aylmer Papillon"—Benjamin Disraeli's increasing intimacy with Murray—Origin of the scheme to start a daily paper—South American speculation—Messrs. Powles—Agreement to start a daily paper—the Representative—Benjamin Disraeli's journey to consult Sir W. Scott about the editorship—His letters to Murray—Visit to Chiefswood —Progress of the negotiation-Mr. Lockhart's reluctance to assume the editorship—Letter from Mr. I. D'Israeli to Murray—Mr. Lockhart's first introduction to Murray—His letter about the editorship—Sir W. Scott's letter to Murray—Editorship of Quarterly offered to Lockhart—Murray's letter to Sir W. Scott—Mr. Lockhart accepts the editorship of the Quarterly—Disraeli's activity in promoting the Representative—His letters to Murray—Premises taken—Arrangements for foreign correspondence—Letters to Mr. Maas—Engagement of Mr. Watts and Mr. S.C. Hall—Mr. Disraeli ceases to take part in the undertaking—Publication of the Representative—Dr. Maginn—Failure of the Representative—Effect of the strain on Murray's health—Letters from friends—The financial crisis—Failure of Constable and Ballantyne—The end of the Representative—Coolness between Murray and Mr. D'Israeli

CHAPTER XXV

MR. LOCKHART AS EDITOR OF THE "QUARTERLY"—HALLAM
WORDSWORTH—DEATH OF CONSTABLE

The editorship of the *Quarterly*—Mr. Lockhart appointed—Letter
from Sir W. Scott, giving his opinion of Lockhart's abilities and
character—Letters from Mr. Lockhart—Mr. Croker's article on
"Paroles d'un Croyant"—Charles Butler—Blanco White—
Controversies, etc.—Wordsworth's Works—Letter from Mr.
Lockhart—Renewed intercourse between Murray and Constable

CHAPTER XXVI

SIR WALTER'S LAST YEARS

South American speculation—Captain Head, R.E.—His rapid rides
across the Pampas—His return home and publication of his work—
Results of his mission—Mr. Disraeli and Mr. Powles—Letter from
Mr. B. Disraeli—Irving's "Life of Columbus"—His agent, Col.
Aspinwall—Letter of warning from Mr. Sharon Turner—Southey's
opinion—"The Conquest of Granada"—Lockhart's and Croker's
opinions—The financial result of their publication—Correspondence
between Irving and Murray—"Tales of the Alhambra"—Murray's
subsequent lawsuit with Bonn about the copyrights—Review of
Hallam's "Constitutional History" in the *Quarterly*—Mr. Hallam's
remonstrance—Letter from Murray—Letter from Mr. Mitchell—
Southey's discontent—Sir W. Scott and Lockhart—Scott's articles for
the *Quarterly*—Sir H. Davy's "Salmonia"—Anecdote of Lord
Nelson—The Duke of Wellington—Murray's offer to Scott for a
History of Scotland—Sale of Sir W. Scott's copyrights—Murray's
offer for "Tales of a Grandfather"—Scott's reply—Scott's closing
years—Murray's resignation of his one-fourth share of "Marmion"—
Scott's last contributions to the *Quarterly*—His death—Mr. John
Murray's account of the Theatrical Fund Dinner

CHAPTER XXVII

NAPIER'S "PENINSULAR WAR"—CROKER'S "BOSWELL"—
"THE FAMILY LIBRARY" ETC.

Napier's "History of the Peninsular War"—Origin of the work—Col.
Napier's correspondence with Murray—Publication of Vol. I.—
Controversy aroused by it—Murray ceases to publish the work—His
letter to the *Morning Chronicle*—The Duke of Wellington's
Despatches—Croker's edition of "Boswell's Johnson"—
Correspondence with Croker, Lockhart, etc.—Publication of the
book—Its value—Letter from Mrs. Shelley—Mr. Henry Taylor's
"Isaac Comnenus"—"Philip van Artevelde"—"The Family Library"
and the Society for the Diffusion of Useful Knowledge—The
progress of "The Family Library"—Milman's "History of the
Jews"—Controversy aroused by it—Opinion of the Jews

CHAPTER XXVIII

MOORE'S "LIFE OF BYRON"

Murray purchases the remainder of Byron's Poems—Leigh Hunt's
"Recollections"—Moore selected as the biographer of Byron—
Collection of Letters and Papers—Lockhart and Scott's opinion of the
work—Publication of the first volume of Byron's "Life"—Mrs.
Shelley's letter—Publication of the second volume—Letters from
Mrs. Somerville and Croker—Capt. Medwin's Conversations—
Pecuniary results of Lord Byron's "Life"—Reviews of Moore's works
in the *Quarterly*—Moore on Editors—Complete edition of "Byron's
Works"—Letters from Countess Guiccioli and Sir R. Peel—
Thorwaldsen's statue of Lord Byron—Refused at Westminster
Abbey, but erected in Trinity College Library, Cambridge

MEMOIRS OF JOHN MURRAY

CHAPTER I

JOHN MACMURRAY OR MURRAY

The publishing house of Murray dates from the year 1768, in which year John MacMurray, a lieutenant of Marines, having retired from the service on half-pay, purchased the bookselling business of William Sandby, at the sign of the "Ship, " No. 32, Fleet Street, opposite St. Dunstan's Church.

John MacMurray was descended from the Murrays of Athol. His uncle, Colonel Murray, was "out" in the rising of 1715, under the Earl of Mar, served under the Marquis of Tullibardine, the son of his chief, the Duke of Athol, and led a regiment in the abortive fight of Sheriffmuir. After the rebellion Colonel Murray retired to France, where he served under the exiled Duke of Ormonde, who had attached himself to the Stuart Court.

The Colonel's brother Robert followed a safer course. He prefixed the "Mac" to his name; settled in Edinburgh; adopted the law as a profession, and became a Writer to the Signet. He had a family of three daughters, Catherine, Robina, and Mary Anne; and two sons, Andrew and John.

John, the younger of Robert MacMurray's sons, was born at Edinburgh in 1745. After receiving a good general education, he entered the Royal Marines under the special patronage of Sir George Yonge, Bart., [Footnote: Sir George Yonge was Governor of the Cape of Good Hope, and subsequently Secretary at War; he died in 1812.] a well-known official of the last century, and his commission as second lieutenant was dated June 24, 1762. Peace was signed at the treaty of Paris in 1763, and young MacMurray found himself quartered at Chatham, where the monotony of the life to a young man of an active and energetic temperament became almost intolerable. He determined therefore to retire on half-pay at the age of twenty-three, and become a London bookseller!

It is not improbable that he was induced to embark on his proposed enterprise by his recent marriage with Nancy Wemyss, daughter of Captain Wemyss, then residing at Brompton, near Chatham.

While residing at Chatham, MacMurray renewed his acquaintance with William Falconer, the poet, and author of "The Shipwreck, " who, like himself, was a native of Edinburgh.

To this friend, who was then on the eve of sailing to India, he wrote:

BROMPTON, KENT, *October* 16, 1768.

DEAR WILL,

Since I saw you, I have had the intention of embarking in a scheme that I think will prove successful, and in the progress of which I had an eye towards your participating. Mr. Sandby, Bookseller, opposite St. Dunstan's Church, Fleet Street, has entered into company with Snow and Denne, Bankers. I was introduced to this gentleman about a week ago, upon an advantageous offer of succeeding him in his old business; which, by the advice of my friends, I propose to accept. Now, although I have little reason to fear success by myself in this undertaking, yet I think so many additional advantages would accrue to us both, were your forces and mine joined, that I cannot help mentioning it to you, and making you the offer of entering into company.

He resigns to me the lease of the house, the goodwill, etc. ; and I only take his bound stock, and fixtures, at a fair appraisement, which will not amount to much beyond £400, and which, if ever I mean to part with, cannot fail to bring in nearly the same sum. The shop has been long established in the Trade; it retains a good many old customers; and I am to be ushered immediately into public notice by the sale of a new edition of "Lord Lyttelton's Dialogues"; and afterwards by a like edition of his "History. " These Works I shall sell by commission, upon a certain profit, without risque; and Mr. Sandby has promised to continue to me, always, his good offices and recommendations.

These are the general outlines; and if you entertain a notion that the conjunction will suit you, advise me, and you shall be assumed upon equal terms; for I write to you before the affair is finally settled; not that I shall refuse it if you don't concur (for I am determined on the trial by myself); but that I think it will turn out better were we joined; and this consideration alone prompts me to write to you. Many Blockheads in the Trade are making fortunes; and did we not succeed as well as they, I think it must be imputed only to ourselves. Make Mrs. McMurray's compliments and mine to Mrs. Falconer; we hope she has reaped much benefit from the saltwater bath. Consider what I have proposed; and send me your answer soon. Be assured in the meantime, that I remain, Dear Sir,

Your affectionate and humble servant,

JOHN McMURRAY.

P. S.—My advisers and directors in this affair have been Thomas Cumming, Esq., Mr. Archibald Paxton, Mr. James Paterson of Essex House, and Messrs. J. and W. Richardson, Printers. These, after deliberate reflection, have unanimously thought that I should accept Mr. Sandby's offer.

Falconer's answer to this letter has not been preserved. It did not delay his departure from Dover in the *Aurora* frigate. The vessel touched at the Cape; set sail again, and was never afterwards heard of. It is supposed that she was either burnt at sea, or driven northward by a storm and wrecked on the Madagascar coast. Falconer intended to have prefixed some complimentary lines to Mr. Murray to the third edition of "The Shipwreck, " but they were omitted in the hurry of leaving London and England for India.

Notwithstanding the failure of MacMurray to obtain the aid of Falconer in his partnership, he completed alone his contract with Mr. Sandby. His father at Edinburgh supplied him with the necessary capital, and he began the bookselling business in November 1768. He dropped the prefix "Mac" from his surname; put a ship in full sail at the head of his invoices; and announced himself to the public in the following terms:

"John Murray (successor to Mr. Sandby), Bookseller and Stationer, at No. 32, over against St. Dunstan's Church, in Fleet Street, London, sells all new Books and Publications. Fits up Public or Private Libraries in the neatest manner with Books of the choicest Editions, the best Print, and the richest Bindings. Also, executes East India or foreign Commissions by an assortment of Books and Stationary suited to the Market or Purpose for which it is destined; all at the most reasonable rates. "

Among the first books he issued were new editions of Lord Lyttelton's "Dialogues of the Dead, " and of his "History of King Henry the Second, " in stately quarto volumes, as well as of

Walpole's "Castle of Otranto. " He was well supported by his friends, and especially by his old brother officers, and we find many letters from all parts of the world requesting him to send consignments of books and magazines, the choice of which was, in many cases, left entirely to his own discretion. In 1769 he received a letter from General Sir Robert Gordon, then in India, who informed him that he had recommended him to many of his comrades.

Sir R. Gordon to John Murray.

"Brigadier-General Wedderburn has not forgotten his old school-fellow, J. McMurray. Send me British news, and inform me of all political and other affairs at home. " [He also added that Colonel Mackenzie, another old friend, is to be his patron.] "I hope, " says Sir E. Gordon, in another letter, "that you find more profit and pleasure from your new employment than from that of the sword, which latter, you may remember, I endeavoured to dissuade you from returning to; but a little trial, and some further experience, at your time of life, cannot hurt you.... My best compliments to Mrs. Murray, who I suppose will not be sorry for your laying aside the wild Highland 'Mac' as unfashionable and even dangerous in the circuit of Wilkes's mob; but that, I am convinced, was your smallest consideration. "

The nature of Mr. Murray's business, and especially his consignments to distant lands, rendered it necessary for him to give long credit, while the expense and the risk of bringing out new books added a fresh strain on his resources. In these circumstances, he felt the need of fresh capital, and applied to his friend Mr. William Kerr, Surveyor of the General Post Office for Scotland, for a loan. Mr. Kerr responded in a kindly letter. Though he could not lend much at the time, he sent Mr. Murray £150, "lest he might be prejudiced for want of it, " and added a letter of kind and homely advice.

In order to extend his business to better advantage, Mr. Murray endeavoured to form connections with booksellers in Scotland and Ireland. In the first of these countries, as the sequel will show, the firm established permanent and important alliances. To push the trade in Ireland he employed Thomas Cumming, a Quaker mentioned in Boswell's "Life of Johnson, " who had been one of his advisers as to the purchase of Mr. Sandby's business.

Mr. T. Gumming to John Murray.

"On receipt of thine I constantly applied to Alderman Faulkener, and showed him the first Fable of Florian, but he told me that he would not give a shilling for any original copy whatever, as there is no law or even custom to secure any property in books in this kingdom [Ireland]. From him, I went directly to Smith and afterwards to Bradley, etc. They all gave me the same answer.... Sorry, and very sorry I am, that I cannot send a better account of the first commission thou hast favoured me with here. Thou may'st believe that I set about it with a perfect zeal, not lessened from the consideration of the troubles thou hast on my account, and the favours I so constantly receive from thee; nor certainly that my good friend Dr. Langhorne was not altogether out of the question. None of the trade here will transport books at their own risque. This is not a reading, but a hard-drinking city; 200 or 250 are as many as a bookseller, except it be an extraordinary work indeed, ever throws off at an impression. "

Mr. Murray not only published the works of others, but became an author himself. He wrote two letters in the *Morning Chronicle* in defence of his old friend Colonel (afterwards Sir) Robert Gordon, who had been censured for putting an officer under arrest during the siege of Broach, in which Gordon had led the attack. The Colonel's brother, Gordon of Gordonstown, wrote to Murray, saying, "Whether you succeed or not, your two letters are admirably written; and you have obtained great merit and reputation for the gallant stand you have made for your friend. " The Colonel himself wrote (August 20,1774): "I cannot sufficiently thank you, my dear sir, for the extraordinary zeal, activity, and warmth of friendship, with which you so strenuously supported and defended my cause, and my honour as a soldier, when attacked so injuriously by Colonel Stuart, especially when he was so powerfully supported. "

Up to this time Mr. Murray's success had been very moderate. He had brought out some successful works; but money came in slowly, and his chief difficulty was the want of capital. He was therefore under the necessity of refusing to publish works which might have done something to establish his reputation.

At this juncture, i.e. in 1771, an uncle died leaving a fortune of £17,000, of which Mr. Murray was entitled to a fourth share. On the strength of this, his friend Mr. Kerr advanced to him a further sum of £500. The additional capital was put into the business, but even then his prosperity did not advance with rapid strides; and in 1777 we find him writing to his friend Mr. Richardson at Oxford.

John Murray to Mr. Richardson.

DEAR JACK,

I am fatigued from morning till night about twopenny matters, if any of which is forgotten I am complained of as a man who minds not his business. I pray heaven for a lazy and lucrative office, and then I shall with alacrity turn my shop out of the window.

A curious controversy occurred in 1778 between Mr. Mason, executor of Thomas Gray the poet, and Mr. Murray, who had published a "Poetical Miscellany, " in which were quoted fifty lines from three passages in Gray's works.

Mr. Murray wrote a pamphlet in his own defence, and the incident is mentioned in the following passage from Boswell's "Life":

"Somebody mentioned the Rev. Mr. Mason's prosecution of Mr. Murray, the bookseller, for having inserted in a collection only fifty lines of Gray's Poems, of which Mr. Mason had still the exclusive property, under the Statute of Queen Anne; and that Mr. Mason had persevered, notwithstanding his being requested to name his own terms of compensation. Johnson signified his displeasure at Mr. Mason's conduct very strongly; but added, by way of showing that he was not surprised at it, 'Mason's a Whig. ' Mrs. Knowles (not hearing distinctly): 'What! a prig, Sir? ' Johnson: 'Worse, Madam; a Whig! But he is both! '"

Mr. Murray had considerable intercourse with the publishers of Edinburgh, among the chief of whom were Messrs. Creech & Elliot, and by their influence he soon established a connection with the professors of Edinburgh University. Creech, who succeeded Mr. Kincaid in his business in 1773, occupied a shop in the Luckenbooths, facing down the High Street, and commanding a prospect of Aberlady Bay and the north coast of Haddingtonshire. Being situated near the Parliament House—the centre of literary and antiquarian loungers, as well as lawyers—Creech's place of business was much frequented by the gossipers, and was known as *Creech's Levee*. Creech himself, dressed in black-silk breeches, with powdered hair and full of humorous talk, was one of the most conspicuous members of the group. He was also an author, though this was the least of his merits. He was an appreciative patron of literature, and gave large sums for the best books of the day.

Mr. Elliot, whose place of business was in the Parliament Close, and whose daughter subsequently married Mr. Murray's son the subject of this biography, was a publisher of medical and surgical works, and Mr. Murray was his agent for the sale of these in London. We find from Mr. Elliot's letters that he was accustomed to send his parcels of books to London by the Leith fleet, accompanied by an armed convoy. In June 1780 he wrote: "As the fleet sails this evening, and the schooner carries 20 guns, I hope the parcel will be in London in four or five days"; and shortly afterwards: "I am sending you four parcels of books by the *Carran*, which mounts 22 guns, and sails with the *Glasgow* of 20 guns. " The reason of the Edinburgh books being conveyed to London guarded by armed ships, was that war was then raging, and that Spain, France, and Holland were united against England. The American Colonies had also rebelled, and Paul Jones, holding their commission, was hovering along the East Coast with three small ships of war and an armed brigantine. It was therefore necessary to protect the goods passing between Leith and London by armed convoys. Sometimes the vessels on their return were quarantined for a time in Inverkeithing Bay.

The first Mrs. Murray died, leaving her husband childless, and he married again. By his second wife he had three sons and two daughters, two of the sons, born in 1779 and 1781 respectively, died in infancy, while the third, John, born in 1778, is the subject of this Memoir. In 1782 he writes to his friend the Rev. John Whitaker: "We have one son and daughter, the son above four years, and the daughter above two years, both healthy and good-natured. "

In June 1782 Mr. Murray had a paralytic stroke, by which he, for a time, lost the use of his left side, and though he shortly recovered, and continued his work as before, he was aware of his dangerous position. To a friend going to Madeira in September 1791 he wrote: "Whether we shall ever meet again is a matter not easily determined. The stroke by which I suffered in 1782 is only suspended; it will be repeated, and I must fall in the contest. "

In the meantime Mr. Murray made arrangements for the education of his son. He was first sent for a year to the High School of Edinburgh. While there he lived with Mr. Robert Kerr, author of several works on Chemistry and Natural History, published by Mr. Murray. Having passed a year in Edinburgh, the boy returned to London, and after a time was sent to a school at Margate. There he seems to have made some progress. To a friend Mr. Murray wrote: "He promises, I think, to write well, although his master complains a little of his indolence, which I am afraid he inherits from me. If he does not overcome it, *it* will overcome him. " In a later letter he said: "The school is not the best, but the people are kind to him, and his health leaves no alternative. He writes a good hand, is fond of figures, and is coming forward both in Latin and French. Yet he inherits a spice of indolence, and is a little impatient in his temper. His appearance—open, modest, and manly—is much in his favour. He is grown a good deal, and left us for Margate (after his holiday) as happy as could be expected. "

In the course of the following year Mr. Murray sent the boy to a well-known school at Gosport, kept by Dr. Burney, one of his old Mends. Burney was a native of the North of Ireland, and had originally been called MacBurney, but, like Murray, he dropped the Mac.

While at Dr. Burney's school, young Murray had the misfortune to lose the sight of his right eye. The writing-master was holding his penknife awkwardly in his hand, point downwards, and while the boy, who was showing up an exercise, stooped to pick up the book which had fallen, the blade ran into his eye and entirely destroyed the sight. To a friend about to proceed to Gosport, Mr. Murray wrote: "Poor John has met with a sad accident, which you will be too soon acquainted with when you reach Gosport. His mother is yet ignorant of it, and I dare not tell her. "

Eventually the boy was brought to London for the purpose of ascertaining whether something might be done by an oculist for the restoration of his sight. But the cornea had been too deeply wounded; the fluid of the eye had escaped; nothing could be done for his relief, and he remained blind in that eye to the end of his life. [Footnote: Long afterwards Chantrey the sculptor, who had suffered a similar misfortune, exclaimed, "What! are you too a brother Cyclops? " but, as the narrator of the story used to add, Mr. Murray could see better with one eye than most people with two.] His father withdrew him from Dr. Burney's school, and sent him in July 1793 to the Rev. Dr. Roberts, at Loughborough House, Kennington. In committing him to the schoolmaster's charge, Mr. Murray sent the following introduction:

"Agreeable to my promise, I commit to you the charge of my son, and, as I mentioned to you in person, I agree to the terms of fifty guineas. The youth has been hitherto well spoken of by the gentleman he has been under. You will find him sensible and candid in the information you may want from him; and if you are kind enough to bestow pains upon him, the obligation on my part will be lasting. The branches to be learnt are these: Latin, French, Arithmetic, Mercantile Accounts, Elocution, History, Geography, Geometry, Astronomy, the Globes, Mathematics, Philosophy, Dancing, and Martial Exercise. "

Certainly, a goodly array of learning, knowledge, and physical training!

To return to the history of Mr. Murray's publications. Some of his best books were published after the stroke of paralysis which he had sustained, and among them must be mentioned Mitford's "History of Greece, " Lavater's work on Physiognomy, and the first instalment of Isaac D'Israeli's "Curiosities of Literature. "

The following extract from a letter to the Rev. Mr. Whitaker, dated December 20, 1784, takes us back to an earlier age.

"Poor Dr. Johnson's remains passed my door for interment this afternoon. They were accompanied by thirteen mourning coaches with four horses each; and after these a cavalcade of the carriages of his friends. He was about to be buried in Westminster Abbey. "

In the same year the Rev. Alexander Fraser of Kirkhill, near Inverness, communicated to Mr. Murray his intention of publishing the Memoirs of Lord Lovat, the head of his clan. Mr. Eraser's father had received the Memoirs in manuscript from Lord Lovat, with an injunction to publish them after his death. "My father, " he said, "had occasion to see his Lordship a few nights before his execution, when he again enjoined him to publish the Memoirs. " General Fraser, a prisoner in the Castle of Edinburgh, had requested, for certain reasons, that the publication should be postponed; but the reasons no longer existed, and the Memoirs were soon after published by Mr. Murray, but did not meet with any success.

The distressed state of trade and the consequent anxieties of conducting his business hastened Mr. Murray's end. On November 6, 1793, Samuel Highley, his principal assistant, wrote to a correspondent: "Mr. Murray died this day after a long and painful illness, and appointed as executors Dr. G.A. Paxton, Mrs. Murray, and Samuel Highley. The business hereafter will be conducted by Mrs. Murray. " The Rev. Donald Grant, D.D., and George Noble, Esq., were also executors, but the latter did not act.

The income of the property was divided as follows: one half to the education and maintenance of Mr. Murray's three children, and the other half to his wife so long as she remained a widow. But in the event of her marrying again, her share was to be reduced by one-third and her executorship was to cease.

John Murray began his publishing career at the age of twenty-three. He was twenty-five years in business, and he died at the comparatively early age of forty-eight. That publishing books is not always a money-making business may be inferred from the fact that during these twenty-five years he did not, with all his industry, double his capital.

CHAPTER II

JOHN MURRAY (II.) — BEGINNING OF HIS PUBLISHING CAREER — ISAAC D'ISRAELI, ETC.

John Murray the Second — the "Anax of Publishers, " according to Lord Byron — was born on November 27, 1778. He was his father's only surviving son by his second marriage, and being only fifteen at his father's death, was too young to enter upon the business of the firm, which was carried on by Samuel Highley — the "faithful shopman" mentioned in the elder Murray's will — for the benefit of his widow and family. What his father thought of him, of his health, spirits, and good nature, will have been seen from the preceding chapter.

Young Murray returned to school, and remained there for about two years longer, until the marriage of his mother to Lieutenant Henry Paget, of the West Norfolk Militia, on September 28, 1795, when he returned to 32, Meet Street, to take part in the business. Mrs. Paget ceased to be an executor, retired from Fleet Street, and went to live at Bridgenorth with her husband, taking her two daughters — Jane and Mary Anne Murray — to live with her, and receiving from time to time the money necessary for their education.

The executors secured the tenancy of No. 32, Fleet Street, part of the stock and part of the copyrights, for the firm of Murray & Highley, between whom a partnership was concluded in 1795, though Murray was still a minor. In the circumstances Mr. Highley of course took the principal share of the management, but though a very respectable person, he was not much of a business man, and being possessed by an almost morbid fear of running any risks, he brought out no new works, took no share in the new books that were published, and it is doubtful whether he looked very sharply after the copyrights belonging to the firm. He was mainly occupied in selling books brought out by other publishers.

The late Mr. Murray had many good friends in India, who continued to send home their orders to the new firm of Murray & Highley. Amongst them were Warren Hastings and Joseph Hume. Hume had taken out with him an assortment of books from the late Mr. Murray, which had proved very useful; and he wrote to Murray and Highley for more. Indeed, he became a regular customer for books.

Meanwhile Murray fretted very much under the careless and indifferent management of Highley. The executors did not like to be troubled with his differences with his partner, and paid very little attention to him or his affairs. Since his mother's remarriage and removal to Bridgenorth, the young man had literally no one to advise with, and was compelled to buffet with the troubles and difficulties of life alone. Though inexperienced, he had, however, spirit and common sense enough to see that he had but little help to expect from his partner, and the difficulties of his position no doubt contributed to draw forth and develop his own mental energy. He was not a finished scholar, but had acquired a thorough love of knowledge and literature, and a keen perception of the beauties of our great English classics. By acquiring and cultivating a purity of taste, he laid the foundations of that quick discrimination which, combined with his rapidly growing knowledge of men and authors, rendered him afterwards so useful, and even powerful, in the pursuit of his profession.

Mr. Murray came of age on November 27, 1799; but he was prudent enough to continue with Highley for a few years longer. After four years more, he determined to set himself free to follow his own course, and the innumerable alterations and erasures in his own rough draft of the following letter testify to the pains and care which he bestowed on this momentous step.

John Murray to Mr. Highley.

GREAT QUEEN STREET, *Friday, November 19, 1802.*

MR. HIGHLEY,

I propose to you that our partnership should be dissolved on the twenty-fifth day of March next:

That the disposal of the lease of the house and every other matter of difference that may arise respecting our dissolution shall be determined by arbitrators—each of us to choose one—and that so chosen they shall appoint a third person as umpire whom they may mutually agree upon previous to their entering upon the business:

I am willing to sign a bond to this effect immediately, and I think that I shall be able to determine my arbitrator some day next week.

As I know this proposal to be as fair as one man could make to another in a like situation, and in order to prevent unpleasant altercation or unnecessary discussion, I declare it to be the last with which I intend to trouble you.

I take this opportunity of saying that, however much we may differ upon matters of business, I most sincerely wish you well.

JOHN MURRAY.

In the end they agreed to draw lots for the house, and Murray had the good fortune to remain at No. 32, Fleet Street. Mr. Highley removed to No. 24 in the same street, and took with him, by agreement, the principal part of the medical works of the firm. Mr. Murray now started on his own account, and began a career of publication almost unrivalled in the history of letters.

Before the dissolution of partnership, Mr. Murray had seen the first representation of Column's Comedy of "John Bull" at Covent Garden Theatre, and was so fascinated by its "union of wit, sentiment, and humour, " that the day after its representation he wrote to Mr. Colman, and offered him £300 for the copyright. No doubt Mr. Highley would have thought this a rash proceeding.

John Murray to Mr. Colman.

"The truth is that during my minority I have been shackled to a drone of a partner; but the day of emancipation is at hand. On the twenty-fifth of this month [March 1803] I plunge alone into the depths of literary speculation. I am therefore honestly ambitious that my first appearance before the public should be such as will at once stamp my character and respectability. On this account, therefore, I think that your Play would be more advantageous to me than to any other bookseller; and as 'I am not covetous of Gold, ' I should hope that no trifling consideration will be allowed to prevent my having the honour of being Mr. Colman's publisher. You see, sir, that I am endeavouring to interest your feelings, both as a Poet and as a Man."

Mr. Colman replied in a pleasant letter, thanking Mr. Murray for his liberal offer. The copyright, however, had been sold to the proprietor of the theatre, and Mr. Murray was disappointed in this, his first independent venture in business.

The times were very bad. Money was difficult to be had on any terms, and Mr. Murray had a hard task to call in the money due to Murray & Highley, as well as to collect the sums due to himself.

Mr. Joseph Hume, not yet the scrupulous financier which he grew to be, among others, was not very prompt in settling his accounts; and Mr. Murray wrote to him, on July 11, 1804:

"On the other side is a list of books (amount £92 8s. 6d.), containing all those for which you did me the favour to write: and I trust that they will reach you safely.... If in future you could so arrange that my account should be paid by some house in town within six months after the goods are shipped, I shall be perfectly satisfied, and shall execute your orders with much more despatch and pleasure. I mention this, not from any apprehension of not being paid, but because my circumstances will not permit me to give so large an extent of credit. It affords me great pleasure to hear of your advancement; and I trust that your health will enable you to enjoy all the success to which your talents entitle you. "

He was, for the same reason, under the necessity of declining to publish several new works offered to him, especially those dealing with medical and poetical subjects.

Mr. Archibald Constable of Edinburgh, and Messrs. Bell & Bradfute, Mr. Murray's agents in Edinburgh, were also communicated with as to the settlement of their accounts with Murray & Highley. "I expected, " he said, "to have been able to pay my respects to you both this summer [1803], but my *military duties*, and the serious aspect of the times, oblige me to remain at home. " It was the time of a patriotic volunteer movement, and Mr. Murray was enrolled as an ensign in the 3rd Regiment of Royal London Volunteers.

It cannot now be ascertained what was the origin of the acquaintance between the D'Israeli and Murray families, but it was of old standing. The first John Murray published the first volumes of Isaac D'Israeli's "Curiosities of Literature" (1791), and though no correspondence between them has been preserved, we find frequent mention of the founder of the house in Isaac D'Israeli's letters to John Murray the Second. His experiences are held up for his son's guidance, as for example, when Isaac, urging the young publisher to support some petition to the East India Company, writes, "It was a ground your father trod, and I suppose that connection cannot do you any harm"; or again, when dissuading him from undertaking some work submitted to him, "You can mention to Mr. Harley the fate of Professor Musaeus' 'Popular Tales, ' which never sold, and how much your father was disappointed. " On another occasion we find D'Israeli, in 1809, inviting his publisher to pay a visit to a yet older generation, "to my father, who will be very glad to see you at Margate. "

Besides the "Curiosities of Literature, " and "Flim-Flams, " the last a volume not mentioned by Lord Beaconsfield in the "Life" of his father prefixed to the 1865 edition of the "Curiosities of Literature, " Mr. D'Israeli published through Murray, in 1803, a small volume of "Narrative Poems" in 4to. They consisted of "An Ode to his Favourite Critic"; "The Carder and the Currier, a Story of Amorous Florence"; "Cominge, a Story of La Trappe"; and "A Tale addressed to a Sybarite. " The verses in these poems run smoothly, but they contain no wit, no poetry, nor even any story. They were never reprinted.

The following letter is of especial interest, as fixing the date of an event which has given rise to much discussion—the birth of Benjamin Disraeli.

Mr. Isaac D'Israeli to John Murray.

December 22, 1804. [Footnote: Mr. D'Israeli was living at this time in King's Road (now 1, John Street), Bedford Row, in a corner house overlooking Gray's Inn Gardens.]

MY DEAR SIR,

Mrs. D'Israeli will receive particular gratification from the interesting note you have sent us on the birth of our boy —when she shall have read it. In the meanwhile accept my thanks, and my best compliments to your sister. The mother and infant are both doing well.

Ever yours.

I. D'I.

Some extracts from their correspondence will afford an insight into the nature of the friendship and business relations which existed between Isaac D'Israeli and his young publisher as well as into the characters of the two men themselves.

From a letter dated Brighton, August 5, 1805, from Mr. D'Israeli to John Murray:

"Your letter is one of the repeated specimens I have seen of your happy art of giving interest even to commonplace correspondence, and I, who am so feelingly alive to the 'pains and penalties' of postage, must acknowledge that such letters, ten times repeated, would please me as often.

We should have been very happy to see you here, provided it occasioned no intermission in your more serious occupations, and could have added to your amusements.

With respect to the projected 'Institute, ' [Footnote: This was a work at one time projected by Mr. Murray, but other more pressing literary arrangements prevented the scheme being carried into effect.] if that title be English—doubtless the times are highly favourable to patronize a work skilfully executed, whose periodical pages would be at once useful information, and delightful for elegant composition, embellished by plates, such as have never yet been given, both for their subjects and their execution. Literature is a perpetual source opened to us; but the Fine Arts present an unploughed field, and an originality of character... But Money, Money must not be spared in respect to rich, beautiful, and interesting Engravings. On this I have something to communicate. Encourage Dagley, [Footnote: The engraver of the frontispiece of "Flim-Flams. "] whose busts of Seneca and Scarron are pleasingly executed; but you will also want artists of name. I have a friend, extremely attached to literature and the fine arts, a gentleman of opulent fortune; by what passed with him in conversation, I have reason to believe that he would be ready to assist by money to a considerable extent. Would that suit you? How would you arrange with him? Would you like to divide your work in *Shares*? He is an intimate friend of West's, and himself too an ingenious writer.

How came you to advertise 'Domestic Anecdotes'? Kearsley printed 1,250 copies. I desire that no notice of the authors of that work may be known from *your* side.

At this moment I receive your packet of poems, and Shee's letter. I perceive that he is impressed by your attentions and your ability. It will always afford me one of my best pleasures to forward your views; I claim no merit from this, but my discernment in discovering your talents, which, under the genius of Prudence (the best of all Genii for human affairs), must inevitably reach the goal. The literary productions of I. D['Israeli] and others may not augment the profits o£ your trade in any considerable degree; but to get the talents of such writers at your command is a prime object, and others will follow.

I had various conversations with Phillips [Footnote: Sir Richard Phillips, bookseller. This is the publisher whose book on philosophy George Borrow was set to translate into German, and who recommended him to produce something in the style of "The Dairyman's Daughter"!] here; he is equally active, but more *wise*. He owns his *belles-lettres* books have given no great profits; in my opinion he must have lost even by some. But he makes a fortune by juvenile and useful compilations. You know I always told you he wanted *literary taste*—like an atheist, who is usually a disappointed man, he thinks all *belles lettres* are nonsense, and denies the existence of *taste*; but it exists! and I flatter myself you will profit under that divinity. I have much to say on this subject and on him when we meet.

At length I have got through your poetry: it has been a weary task! The writer has a good deal of fire, but it is rarely a very bright flame. Here and there we see it just blaze, and then sink into mediocrity. He is too redundant and tiresome.... 'Tis a great disadvantage to read them in MS., as one cannot readily turn to passages; but life is too short to be peeping into other peoples' MSS. *I prefer your prose to your verse.* Let me know if you receive it safely, and pray give no notion to any one that I have seen the MS. "

Mr. D'Israeli to John Murray.

"It is a most disagreeable office to give opinions on MSS. ; one reads them at a moment when one has other things in one's head—then one is obliged to fatigue the brain with *thinking*; but if I can occasionally hinder you from publishing nugatory works, I do not grudge the pains. At the same time I surely need not add, how very *confidential* such communications ought to be. "

Mr. I. D'Israeli to John Murray.

I am delighted by your apology for not having called on me after I had taken my leave of you the day before; but you can make an unnecessary apology as agreeable as any other act of kindness....

You are sanguine in your hope of a good sale of "Curiosities, " it will afford us a mutual gratification; but when you consider it is not a new work, though considerably improved I confess, and that those kinds of works cannot boast of so much novelty as they did about ten years ago, I am somewhat more moderate in my hopes.

What you tell me of F. F. from Symond's, is *new* to me. I sometimes throw out in the shop *remote hints* about the sale of books, all the while meaning only *mine*; but they have no skill in construing the timid wishes of a modest author; they are not aware of his suppressed sighs, nor see the blushes of hope and fear tingling his cheek; they are provokingly silent, and petrify the imagination....

Believe me, with the truest regard,

Yours ever,

I. D'ISRAELI.

Mr. D'Israeli to John Murray. Saturday, May 31, 1806. KING'S ROAD.

MY DEAR FRIEND,

It is my wish to see you for five minutes this day, but as you must be much engaged, and I am likely to be prevented reaching you this morning, I shall only trouble you with a line.

Most warmly I must impress on your mind the *necessity* of taking the advice of a physician. Who? You know many. We have heard extraordinary accounts of Dr. Baillie, and that (what is more extraordinary) he is not mercenary....

I have written this to impress on your mind this point. Seeing you as we see you, and your friend at a fault, how to decide, and you without some relative or domestic friend about you, gives Mrs. D'I. and myself very serious concerns—for you know we do take the warmest interest in your welfare—and your talents and industry want nothing but health to make you yet what it has always been one of my most gratifying hopes to conceive of you.

Yours very affectionately,

I. D'ISRAELI.

A circumstance, not without influence on Murray's future, occurred about this time with respect to the "Miniature, " a volume of comparatively small importance, consisting of essays written by boys at Eton, and originally published at Windsor by Charles Knight. Through Dr. Kennell, Master of the Temple, his friend and neighbour, who lived close at hand, Murray became acquainted with the younger Kennell, Mr. Stratford Canning, Gally Knight, the two sons of the Marquis Wellesley, and other young Etonians, who had originated and conducted this School magazine. Thirty-four numbers appeared in the course of a year, and were then brought out in a volume by Mr. Knight at the expense of the authors. The transaction had involved them in debt. "Whatever chance of success our hopes may dictate, " wrote Stratford Canning, "yet our apprehensions teach us to tremble at the possibility of additional expenses, " and the sheets lay unsold on the bookseller's hands. Mr. Murray, who was consulted about the matter, said to Dr. Rennell, "Tell them to send the unsold sheets to me, and I will pay the debt due to the printer. " The whole of the unsold sheets were sent by the "Windsor Waggon" to Mr. Murray's at Fleet Street. He made waste-paper of the whole bundle—there were 6,376 numbers in all, — brought out a new edition of 750 copies, printed in good type, and neatly bound, and announced to Stratford Canning that he did this at his own cost and risk, and would make over to the above Etonians half the profits of the work. The young authors were highly pleased by this arrangement, and Stratford Canning wrote to Murray (October 20, 1805): "We cannot sufficiently thank you for your kind attention to our concerns, and only hope that the success of the *embryo* edition may be equal to your care. " How great was the importance of the venture in his eyes may be judged from the naïve allusion with which he proceeds: "It will be a week or two before we commit it to the press, for amidst our other occupations the business of the school must not be neglected, and that by itself is no trivial employment. "

By means of this transaction Murray had the sagacity to anticipate an opportunity of making friends of Canning and Frere, who were never tired of eulogizing the spirit and enterprise of the young Fleet Street publisher. Stratford Canning introduced him to his cousin George, the great minister, whose friendship and support had a very considerable influence in promoting and establishing his future prosperity. It is scarcely necessary to add that the new edition of the "Miniature" speedily became waste paper.

CHAPTER III

MURRAY AND CONSTABLE—HUNTER AND THE
FORFARSHIRE LAIRDS—MARRIAGE OF JOHN MURRAY

The most important publishing firm with which Mr. Murray was connected at the outset of his career was that of Archibald Constable & Co., of Edinburgh. This connection had a considerable influence upon Murray's future fortunes.

Constable, who was about four years older than Murray, was a man of great ability, full of spirit and enterprise. He was by nature generous, liberal, and far-seeing. The high prices which he gave for the best kind of literary work drew the best authors round him, and he raised the publishing trade of Scotland to a height that it had never before reached, and made Edinburgh a great centre of learning and literature.

In 1800 he commenced the *Farmer's Magazine,* and in the following year acquired the property of the *Scots Magazine,* a venerable repertory of literary, historical, and antiquarian matter; but it was not until the establishment of the *Edinburgh Review,* in October 1802, that Constable's name became a power in the publishing world.

In the year following the first issue of the *Review,* Constable took into partnership Alexander Gibson Hunter, eldest son of David Hunter, of Blackness, a Forfarshire laird. The new partner brought a considerable amount of capital into the firm, at a time when capital was greatly needed in that growing concern. His duties were to take charge of the ledger and account department, though he never took much interest in his work, but preferred to call in the help of a clever arithmetical clerk.

It is unnecessary to speak of the foundation of the *Edinburgh Review.* It appeared at the right time, and was mainly supported by the talents of Jeffrey, Brougham, Sydney Smith, Francis Horner, Dr. Thomas Brown, Lord Murray, and other distinguished writers. The first number immediately attracted public attention. Mr. Joseph Mawman was the London agent, but some dissatisfaction having arisen with respect to his management, the London sale was transferred to the Messrs. Longman, with one half share in the property of the work.

During the partnership of Murray and Highley, they had occasional business transactions with Constable of Edinburgh. Shortly after the partnership was dissolved in March 1803, Murray wrote as follows to Mr. Constable:

April 25, 1803.

"I have several works in the press which I should be willing to consign to your management in Edinburgh, but that I presume you have already sufficient business upon your hands, and that you would not find mine worth attending to. If so, I wish that you would tell me of some vigorous young bookseller, like myself, just starting into business, upon whose probity, punctuality, and exertion you think I might rely, and I would instantly open a correspondence with him; and in return it will give me much pleasure to do any civil office for you in London. I should be happy if any arrangement could be made wherein we might prove of reciprocal advantage; and were you from your superabundance to pick me out any work of merit of which you would either make me the publisher in London, or in which you would allow me to become a partner, I dare say the occasion would arise wherein I could return the compliment, and you would have the satisfaction of knowing that your book was in the hands of one who has not yet so much business as to cause him to neglect any part of it. "

Mr. Constable's answer was favourable. In October 1804 Mr. Murray, at the instance of Constable, took as his apprentice Charles Hunter, the younger brother of A. Gibson Hunter, Constable's partner. The apprenticeship was to be for four or seven years, at the option of Charles Hunter. These negotiations between the firms, and their increasing interchange of books, showed that they were gradually drawing nearer to each other, until their correspondence became quite friendly and even intimate. Walter Scott was now making his appearance as an author; Constable had published his "Sir Tristram" in May 1804, and his "Lay of the Last Minstrel" in January 1805. Large numbers of these works were forwarded to London and sold by Mr. Murray.

At the end of 1805 differences arose between the Constable and Longman firms as to the periodical works in which they were interested. The editor and proprietors of the *Edinburgh Review* were of opinion that the interest of the Longmans in two other works of a similar character — the *Annual Review* and the *Eclectic* — tended to lessen their exertions on behalf of the *Edinburgh*. It was a matter that might easily have been arranged; but the correspondents were men of hot tempers, and with pens in their hands, they sent stinging letters from London to Edinburgh, and from Edinburgh to London. Rees, Longman's partner, was as bitter in words on the one side as Hunter, Constable's partner, was on the other. At length a deadly breach took place, and it was resolved in Edinburgh that the publication of the *Edinburgh Review* should be transferred to John Murray, Fleet Street. Alexander Gibson Hunter, Constable's partner, wrote to Mr. Murray to tell of the rupture and to propose a closer alliance with him.

Mr. Murray replied:

John Murray to Mr. A.G. Hunter.

December 7, 1805.

"With regard to the important communication of your last letter, I confess the surprise with which I read it was not without some mixture of regret. The extensive connections betwixt your house and Longman's cannot be severed at once without mutual inconvenience, and perhaps mutual disadvantages, your share of which a more protracted dismemberment might have prevented. From what I had occasion to observe, I did not conceive that your concerns together would ever again move with a cordiality that would render them lasting; but still, I imagined that mutual interest and forbearance would allow them to subside into that indifference which, without animosity or mischief, would leave either party at liberty to enter upon such new arrangements as offered to their separate advantage. I do not, however, doubt but that all things have been properly considered, and perhaps finally settled for the best; but Time, the only arbitrator in these cases, must decide.

"In your proposed engagements with Mr. Davies, you will become better acquainted with a man of great natural talents, and thoroughly versed in business, which he regulates by the most honourable principles. As for myself, you will find me exceedingly assiduous in promoting your views, into which I shall enter with feelings higher than those of mere interest. Indeed, linked as our houses are at present, we have a natural tendency to mutual good understanding, which will both prevent and soften those asperities in business which might otherwise enlarge into disagreement.

Country orders [referring to Constable & Co. 's 'general order'] are a branch of business which I have ever totally declined as incompatible with my more serious plans as a publisher. But *your* commissions I shall undertake with pleasure, and the punctuality with which I have attempted to execute *your first order* you will, I hope, consider as a specimen of my disposition to give you satisfaction in every transaction in which we may hereafter be mutually engaged. "

It was a great chance for a young man entering life with a moderate amount of capital, to be virtually offered an intimate connection with one of the principal publishing houses of the day. It was one of those chances which, "taken at the flood, lead on to fortune, " but there was also the question of honour, and Mr. Murray, notwithstanding his desire for opening out a splendid new connection in business, would do nothing inconsistent with the strictest honour. He was most unwilling to thrust himself in between Constable and Longman. Instead, therefore, of jumping at Constable's advantageous offer, his feelings induced him to promote a reconciliation between the parties; and he continued to enjoin forbearance on the part of both firms, so that they might carry on their business transactions as before. Copies of the correspondence between Constable and the Longmans were submitted to referees (Murray and Davies), and the following was Mr. Murray's reply, addressed to Messrs. Constable & Co. :

John Murray to Messrs. Constable & Co.

December 14, 1805.

GENTLEMEN,

Mr. Hunter's obliging letter to me arrived this morning. That which he enclosed with yours to his brother last night, Charles gave me to read. The contents were very flattering. Indeed, I cannot but agree with Mr. H. that his brother has displayed very honourable feelings, upon hearing of the probable separation of your house, and that of Messrs. Longman & Co. Mr. Longman was the first who mentioned this to him, and indeed from the manner in which Charles related his conversation upon the affair, I could not but feel renewed sensations of regret at the unpleasant termination of a correspondence, which, had it been conducted upon Mr. Longman's own feelings, would have borne, I think, a very different aspect. Longman spoke of you both with kindness, and mildly complained that he had perceived a want of confidence on your part, ever since his junction with Messrs. Hurst & Orme. He confessed that the correspondence was too harsh for him to support any longer; but, he added, *"if we must part, let us part like friends. "* I am certain, from what Charles reported to me, that Mr. L. and I think Mr. R. [Rees] are hurt by this sudden disunion.

Recollect how serious every dispute becomes upon paper, when a man writes a thousand asperities merely to show or support his superior ability. Things that would not have been spoken, or perhaps even thought of in conversation, are stated and horribly magnified *upon paper*. Consider how many disputes have arisen in the world, in which both parties were so violent in what they believed to be the support of truth, and which to the public, and indeed to themselves a few years afterwards, appeared unwise, because the occasion or cause of it was not worth contending about. Consider that you are, all of you, men who can depend upon each other's probity and honour, and where these essentials are not wanting, surely in mere matters of business the rest may be palliated by mutual bearance and forbearance. Besides, you are so connected by various publications, your common property, and some of them such as will remain so until the termination of your lives, that you cannot effect an entire disunion, and must therefore be subject to eternal vexations and regrets which will embitter every transaction and settlement between you.

You know, moreover, that it is one of the misfortunes of our nature, that disputes are always the most bitter in proportion to former intimacy. And how much dissatisfaction will it occasion if either of you are desirous in a year or two of renewing that intimacy which you are now so anxious to dissolve—to say nothing of your relative utility to each other—a circumstance which is never properly estimated, except when the want of the means reminds us of what we have been at such pains to deprive ourselves. Pause, my dear sirs, whilst to choose be yet in your power; show yourselves superior to common prejudice, and by an immediate exercise of your acknowledged pre-eminence of intellect, suffer arrangements to be made for an accommodation and for a renewal of that connexion which has heretofore been productive of honour and profit. I am sure I have to apologize for having ventured to say so much to men so much my superiors in sense and knowledge of the world and their own interest; but sometimes the meanest bystander may perceive disadvantages in the movements of the most skilful players.

You will not, I am sure, attribute anything which I have said to an insensibility to the immediate advantages which will arise to myself from a determination opposite to that which I have taken the liberty of suggesting. It arises from a very different feeling. I should be very little worthy of your great confidence and attention to my interest upon this occasion, if I did not state freely the result of my humble consideration of this matter; and having done so, I do assure you that if the arrangements which you now propose are carried into effect, I will apply the most arduous attention to your interest, to which I will turn the channel of my own thoughts and business, which, I am proud to say, is rising in proportion to the industry and honourable principles which have been used in its establishment. I am every day adding to a most respectable circle of literary connexions, and I hope, a few months after the settlement of your present affairs, to offer shares to you of works in which you will feel it advantageous to engage. Besides, as I have at present no particular bias, no enormous works of my own which would need all my care, I am better qualified to attend to any that you may commit to my charge; and, being young, my business may be formed with a disposition, as it were, towards yours; and thus growing up with it, we are more likely to form a durable connexion than can be expected with persons whose views are imperceptibly but incessantly diverging from each other.

Should you be determined—*irrevocably* determined (but consider!) upon the disunion with Messrs. Longman, I will just observe that when persons have been intimate, they have discovered each other's vulnerable points; it therefore shows no great talent to direct at them shafts of resentment. It is easy both to write and to say ill-natured, harsh, and cutting things of each other. But remember that this power is *mutual*, and in proportion to the poignancy of the wound which you would inflict will be your own feelings when it is returned. It is therefore a maxim which I laid down soon after a separation which I *had*, never to say or do to my late colleague what he could say or do against me in return. I knew that I had the personal superiority, but what his own ingenuity could not suggest, others could write for him.

I must apologise again for having been so tedious, but I am sure that the same friendliness on your part which has produced these hasty but well-meant expostulations will excuse them. After this, I trust it is unnecessary for me to state with how much sincerity,

I am, dear sirs,

Your faithful friend,

JOHN MURRAY.

Ten days after this letter was written, Mr. Murray sent a copy of it to Messrs. Longman & Co., and wrote:

John Murray to Messrs. Longman & Co,

December 24, 1805.

GENTLEMEN,

The enclosed letter will show that I am not ignorant that a misunderstanding prevails betwixt your house and that of Messrs. Constable & Co. With the cause, however, I am as yet unacquainted; though I have attempted, but in vain, to obviate a disunion which I most sincerely regret. Whatever arrangements with regard to myself may take place in consequence will have arisen from circumstances which it was not in my power to prevent; and they will not therefore be suffered to interfere in any way with those friendly dispositions which will continue, I trust, to obtain between you and, gentlemen,

Your obedient servant,

J. MURRAY.

But the split was not to be avoided. It appears, however, that by the contract entered into by Constable with Longmans in 1803, the latter had acquired a legal right precluding the publication of the *Edinburgh Review* by another publisher without their express assent. Such assent was not given, and the London publication of the *Edinburgh* continued in Longman's hands for a time; but all the other works of Constable were at once transferred to Mr. Murray.

Mr. Constable invited Murray to come to Edinburgh to renew their personal friendship, the foundations of which had been laid during Mr. Murray's visit to Edinburgh in the previous year; and now that their union was likely to be much closer, he desired to repeat the visit. Mr. Murray had another, and, so far as regarded his personal happiness, a much more important object in view. This arose out of the affection which he had begun to entertain for Miss Elliot, daughter of the late Charles Elliot, publisher, with whom Mr. Murray's father had been in such constant correspondence. The affection was mutual, and it seemed probable that the attachment would ripen into a marriage.

Now that his reputation as a publisher was becoming established, Mr. Murray grew more particular as to the guise of the books which he issued. He employed the best makers of paper, the best printers, and the best book-binders. He attended to the size and tone of the paper, and quality of the type, the accuracy of the printing, and the excellence of the illustrations. All this involved a great deal of correspondence. We find his letters to the heads of departments full of details as to the turn-out of his books. Everything, from the beginning to the end of the issue of a work—the first inspection of the MS., the consultation with confidential friends as to its fitness for publication, the form in which it was to appear, the correction of the proofs, the binding, title, and final advertisement—engaged his closest attention. Besides the elegant appearance of his books, he also aimed at raising the standard of the literature which he published. He had to criticize as well as to select; to make suggestions as to improvements where the manuscript was regarded with favour, and finally to launch the book at the right time and under the best possible auspices. It might almost be said of the publisher, as it is of the poet, that he is born, not made. And Mr. Murray appears, from the beginning to the end of his career, to have been a born publisher.

In August 1806, during the slack season in London, Mr. Murray made his promised visit to Edinburgh. He was warmly received by Constable and Hunter, and enjoyed their hospitality for some days. After business matters had been disposed of, he was taken in hand by Hunter, the junior partner, and led off by him to enjoy the perilous hospitality of the Forfarshire lairds.

Those have been called the days of heroic drinking. Intemperance prevailed to an enormous extent. It was a time of greater licentiousness, perhaps, in all the capitals of Europe, and this northern one among the rest, than had been known for a long period. Men of the best education and social position drank like the Scandinavian barbarians of olden times. Tavern-drinking, now almost unknown among the educated and professional classes of Edinburgh, was then carried by all ranks to a dreadful excess.

Murray was conducted by Hunter to his father's house of Eskmount in Forfarshire, where he was most cordially received, and in accordance with the custom of the times the hospitality included invitations to drinking bouts at the neighbouring houses.

An unenviable notoriety in this respect attached to William Maule (created Baron Panmure 1831). He was the second son of the eighth Earl of Dalhousie, but on succeeding, through his grandmother, to the estates of the Earls of Panmure, he had assumed the name of Maule in lieu of that of Ramsay.

Much against his will, Murray was compelled to take part in some of these riotous festivities with the rollicking, hard-drinking Forfarshire lairds, and doubtless he was not sorry to make his escape at length uninjured, if not unscathed, and to return to more congenial society in Edinburgh. His attachment to Miss Elliot ended in an engagement.

In the course of his correspondence with Miss Elliot's trustees, Mr. Murray gave a statement of his actual financial position at the time:

"When I say, " he wrote, "that my capital in business amounts to five thousand pounds, I meant it to be understood that if I quitted business to-morrow, the whole of my property being sold, even disadvantageously, it would leave a balance in my favour, free from debt or any incumbrance, of the sum above specified. But you will observe that, continuing it as I shall do in business, I know it to be far more considerable and productive. I will hope that it has not been thought uncandid in me if I did not earlier specify the amount of my circumstances, for I considered that I had done this in the most delicate and satisfactory way when I took the liberty of referring you to Mr. Constable to whom I consequently disclosed my affairs, and whose knowledge of my connexions in business might I thought have operated more pleasingly to Miss Elliot's friends than any communication from myself. "

The correspondence with Miss Elliot went on, and at length it was arranged that Mr. Murray should proceed to Edinburgh for the marriage. He went by mail in the month of February. A tremendous snowstorm set in on his journey north. From a village near Doncaster he wrote to Constable: "The horses were twice blown quite round, unable to face the horrid blast of cold wind, the like of which I have never known before. There was at the same time a terrible fall of snow, which completely obscured everything that could be seen from the coach window. The snow became of great depth, and six strong horses could scarcely pull us through. We are four hours behind time. " From Doncaster he went to Durham in a postchaise; and pushing onward, he at last reached Edinburgh after six days' stormy travelling.

While at Edinburgh, Mr. Murray resided with Mr. Sands, one of the late Charles Elliot's trustees. The marriage took place on March 6, 1807, and the newly married pair at once started for Kelso, in spite of the roads being still very bad, and obstructed by snow. Near Blackshields the horses fell down and rolled over and over. The postboy's leg was broken, and the carriage was sadly damaged. A neighbouring blacksmith was called to the rescue, and after an hour and a half the carriage was sufficiently repaired to be able to proceed. A fresh pair of horses was obtained at the next stage, and the married couple reached Kelso in safety. They remained there a few days, waiting for Mrs. Elliot, who was to follow them; and on her arrival, they set out at once for the south.

The intimacy which existed between Mr. Murray and Mr. D'Israeli will be observed from the fact that the latter was selected as one of the marriage trustees. A few days after the arrival of the married pair in London, they were invited to dine with Mr. D'Israeli and his friends. Mr. Alexander Hunter, whom Mr. Murray had invited to stay with him during his visit to London, thus describes the event:

"Dressed, and went along with the Clan Murray to dine at Mr. D'Israeli's, where we had a most sumptuous banquet, and a very large party, in honour of the newly married folks. There was a very beautiful woman there, Mrs. Turner, wife of Sharon Turner, the Anglo-Saxon historian, who, I am told, was one of the Godwin school! If they be all as beautiful, accomplished, and agreeable as this lady, they must be a deuced dangerous set indeed, and I should not choose to trust myself amongst them.

"Our male part of the company consisted mostly of literary men— Cumberland, Turner, D'Israeli, Basevi, Prince Hoare, and Cervetto, the truly celebrated violoncello player. Turner was the most able and agreeable of the whole by far; Cumberland, the most talkative and eccentric perhaps, has a good sprinkling of learning and humour in his conversation and anecdote, from having lived so long amongst the eminent men of his day, such as Johnson, Foote, Garrick, and such like. But his conversation is sadly disgusting, from his tone of irony and detraction conveyed in a cunning sort of way and directed constantly against the *Edinburgh Review*, Walter Scott (who is a 'poor ignorant boy, and no poet, ' and never wrote a five-feet line in his life), and such other d — —d stuff. "

CHAPTER IV

"MARMION" — CONSTABLES AND BALLANTYNES — THE "EDINBURGH REVIEW"

Mr. Murray was twenty-nine years old at the time of his marriage. That he was full of contentment as well as hope at this time may be inferred from his letter to Constable three weeks after his marriage:

John Murray to Mr. Constable.

March 27, 1807.

"I declare to you that I am every day more content with my lot. Neither my wife nor I have any disposition for company or going out; and you may rest assured that I shall devote all my attention to business, and that your concerns will not be less the object of my regard merely because you have raised mine so high. Every moment, my dear Constable, I feel more grateful to you, and I trust that you will over find me your faithful friend. —J. M."

Some of the most important events in Murray's career occurred during the first year of his married life. Chief among them may perhaps be mentioned his part share in the publication of "Marmion" (in February 1808) — which brought him into intimate connection with Walter Scott — and his appointment for a time as publisher in London of the *Edinburgh Review*; for he was thus brought into direct personal contact with those forces which ultimately led to the chief literary enterprise of his life — the publication of the *Quarterly Review*.

Mr. Scott called upon Mr. Murray in London shortly after the return of the latter from his marriage in Edinburgh.

"Mr. Scott called upon me on Tuesday, and we conversed for an hour.... He appears very anxious that 'Marmion' should be published by the King's birthday.... He said he wished it to be ready by that time for very particular reasons; and yet he allows that the poem is not completed, and that he is yet undetermined if he shall make his hero happy or otherwise. "

The other important event, to which allusion has been made, was the transfer to Mr. Murray of part of the London agency for the

Edinburgh Review. At the beginning of 1806 Murray sold 1,000 copies of the *Review* on the day of its publication, and the circulation was steadily increasing. Constable proposed to transfer the entire London publication to Murray, but the Longmans protested, under the terms of their existing agreement. In April 1807 they employed as their attorney Mr. Sharon Turner, one of Murray's staunchest allies. Turner informed him, through a common friend, of his having been retained by the Longmans; but Murray said he could not in any way "feel hurt at so proper and indispensable a pursuit of his profession." The opinion of counsel was in favour of the Messrs. Longman's contention, and of their "undisputable rights to one-half of the *Edinburgh Review* so long as it continues to be published under that title. "

Longman & Co. accordingly obtained an injunction to prevent the publication of the *Edinburgh Review* by any other publisher in London without their express consent.

Matters were brought to a crisis by the following letter, written by the editor, Mr. Francis Jeffrey, to Messrs. Constable & Co. :

June 1, 1807.

GENTLEMEN,

I believe you understand already that neither I nor any of the original and regular writers in the *Review* will ever contribute a syllable to a work belonging to booksellers. It is proper, however, to announce this to you distinctly, that you may have no fear of hardship or disappointment in the event of Mr. Longman succeeding in his claim to the property of this work. If that claim be not speedily rejected or abandoned, it is our fixed resolution to withdraw entirely from the *Edinburgh Review*; to publish to all the world that the conductor and writers of the former numbers have no sort of connection with those that may afterwards appear; and probably to give notice of our intention to establish a new work of a similar nature under a different title.

I have the honour to be, gentlemen,

Your very obedient servant,

F. JEFFREY.

A copy of this letter was at once forwarded to Messrs. Longman. Constable, in his communication accompanying it, assured the publishers that, in the event of the editor and contributors to the *Edinburgh Review* withdrawing from the publication and establishing a new periodical, the existing *Review* would soon be of no value either to proprietors or publishers, and requested to be informed whether they would not be disposed to transfer their interest in the property, and, if so, on what considerations. Constable added: "We are apprehensive that the editors will not postpone for many days longer that public notification of their secession, which we cannot help anticipating as the death-blow of the publication. "

Jeffrey's decision seems to have settled the matter. Messrs. Longman agreed to accept £1,000 for their claim of property in the title and future publication of the *Edinburgh Review*. The injunction was removed, and the London publication of the *Review* was forthwith transferred to John Murray, 32, Fleet Street, under whose auspices No. 22 accordingly appeared.

Thus far all had gone on smoothly. But a little cloud, at first no bigger than a man's hand, made its appearance, and it grew and grew until it threw a dark shadow over the friendship of Constable and Murray, and eventually led to their complete separation. This was the system of persistent drawing of accommodation bills, renewals of bills, and promissory notes. Constable began to draw heavily upon Murray in April 1807, and the promissory notes went on accumulating until they constituted a mighty mass of paper money. Murray's banker cautioned him against the practice. But repeated expostulation was of no use against the impetuous needs of Constable & Co. Only two months after the transfer of the publication of the *Review* to Mr. Murray, we find him writing to "Dear Constable" as follows:

John Murray to Mr. Archd. Constable.

October 1, 1807.

"I should not have allowed myself time to write to you to-day, were not the occasion very urgent. Your people have so often of late omitted to give you timely notice of the day when my acceptances fell due, that I have suffered an inconvenience too great for me to have expressed to you, had it not occurred so often that it is impossible for me to undergo the anxiety which it occasions. A bill of yours for £200 was due yesterday, and I have been obliged to supply the means for paying it, without any notice for preparation.... I beg of you to insist upon this being regulated, as I am sure you must desire it to be, so that I may receive the cash for your bills two days at least before they are due. "

Mr. Murray then gives a list of debts of his own (including some of Constable's) amounting to £1,073, which he has to pay in the following week. From a cash account made out by Mr. Murray on October 3, it appears that the bill transactions with Constable had become enormous; they amounted to not less than £10,000.

The correspondence continued in the same strain, and it soon became evident that this state of things could not be allowed to continue. Reconciliations took place from time to time, but interruptions again occurred, mostly arising from the same source— a perpetual flood of bills and promissory notes, from one side and the other—until Murray found it necessary to put an end to it peremptorily. Towards the end of 1808 Messrs. Constable established at No. 10 Ludgate Street a London house for the sale of the *Edinburgh Review*, and the other works in which they were concerned, under the title of Constable, Hunter, Park & Hunter. This, doubtless, tended to widen the breach between Constable and Murray, though it left the latter free to enter into arrangements for establishing a Review of his own, an object which he had already contemplated.

There were many books in which the two houses had a joint interest, and, therefore, their relations could not be altogether discontinued. "Marmion" was coming out in successive editions; but the correspondence between the publishers grew cooler and cooler, and Constable had constant need to delay payments and renew bills.

Mr. Murray had also considerable bill transactions with Ballantyne & Co. of Edinburgh. James and John Ballantyne had been schoolfellows of Walter Scott at Kelso, and the acquaintance there formed was afterwards renewed. James Ballantyne established the *Kelso Mail* in 1796, but at the recommendation of Scott, for whom he had printed a collection of ballads, he removed to Edinburgh in 1802. There he printed the "Border Minstrelsy, " for Scott, who assisted him with money. Ballantyne was in frequent and intimate correspondence with Murray from the year 1806, and had printed for him Hogg's "Ettrick Shepherd, " and other works.

It was at this time that Scott committed the great error of his life. His professional income was about £1,000 a year, and with the profits of his works he might have built Abbotsford and lived in comfort and luxury. But in 1805 he sacrificed everything by entering into partnership with James Ballantyne, and embarking in his printing concern almost the whole of the capital which he possessed. He was bound to the firm for twenty years, and during that time he produced his greatest works. It is true that but for the difficulties in which he was latterly immersed, we might never have known the noble courage with which he met and rose superior to misfortune.

In 1808 a scheme of great magnitude was under contemplation by Murray and the Ballantynes. It was a uniform edition of the "British Novelists, " beginning with De Foe, and ending with the novelists at the close of last century; with biographical prefaces and illustrative notes by Walter Scott. A list of the novels, written in the hand of John Murray, includes thirty-six British, besides eighteen foreign authors. The collection could not have been completed in less than two hundred volumes. The scheme, if it did not originate with Walter Scott, had at least his cordial support.

Mr. Murray not unreasonably feared the cost of carrying such an undertaking to completion. It could not have amounted to less than twenty thousand pounds. Yet the Ballantynes urged him on. They furnished statements of the cost of printing and paper for each volume. "It really strikes me, " said James Ballantyne, "the more I think of and examine it, to be the happiest speculation that has ever been thought of. "

This undertaking eventually fell through. Only the works of De Foe were printed by the Messrs. Ballantyne, and published by Mr. Murray. The attention of the latter became absorbed by a subject of much greater importance to him—the establishment of the *Quarterly Review*. This for a time threw most of his other schemes into the shade.

CHAPTER V

ORIGIN OF THE "QUARTERLY REVIEW"

The publication of a Tory Review was not the result of a sudden inspiration. The scheme had long been pondered over. Mr. Canning had impressed upon Mr. Pitt the importance of securing the newspaper press, then almost entirely Whiggish or Revolutionary, on the side of his administration. To combat, in some measure, the democratic principles then in full swing, Mr. Canning, with others, started, in November 1797, the *Anti-Jacobin, or Weekly Examiner*.

The *Anti-Jacobin* ceased to be published in 1798, when Canning, having been appointed Under-Secretary of State for Foreign Affairs, found his time fully occupied by the business of his department, as well as by his parliamentary duties, and could no longer take part in that clever publication.

Four years later, in October 1802, the first number of the *Edinburgh Review* was published. It appeared at the right time, and, as the first quarterly organ of the higher criticism, evidently hit the mark at which it aimed. It was conducted by some of the cleverest literary young men in Edinburgh—Jeffrey, Brougham, Sydney Smith, Francis Horner, Dr. Thomas Brown, and others. Though Walter Scott was not a founder of the *Review*, he was a frequent contributor.

In its early days the criticism was rude, and wanting in delicate insight; for the most part too dictatorial, and often unfair. Thus Jeffrey could never appreciate the merits of Wordsworth, Southey, and Coleridge. "This will never do! " was the commencement of his review of Wordsworth's noblest poem. Jeffrey boasted that he had "crushed the 'Excursion. '" "He might as well say, " observed Southey, "that he could crush Skiddaw. " Ignorance also seems to have pervaded the article written by Brougham, in the second number of the *Edinburgh*, on Dr. Thomas Young's discovery of the true principles of interferences in the undulatory theory of light. Sir John Herschell, a more competent authority, said of Young's discovery, that it was sufficient of itself to have placed its author in the highest rank of scientific immortality.

The situation seemed to Mr. Murray to warrant the following letter:

John Murray to the Right Hon. George Canning.

September 25, 1807.

Sir,

I venture to address you upon a subject that is not, perhaps, undeserving of one moment of your attention. There is a work entitled the *Edinburgh Review*, written with such unquestionable talent that it has already attained an extent of circulation not equalled by any similar publication. The principles of this work are, however, so radically bad that I have been led to consider the effect that such sentiments, so generally diffused, are likely to produce, and to think that some means equally popular ought to be adopted to counteract their dangerous tendency. But the publication in question is conducted with so much ability, and is sanctioned with such high and decisive authority by the party of whose opinions it is the organ, that there is little hope of producing against it any effectual opposition, unless it arise from you, Sir, and your friends. Should you, Sir, think the idea worthy of encouragement, I should, with equal pride and willingness, engage my arduous exertions to promote its success; but as my object is nothing short of producing a work of the greatest talent and importance, I shall entertain it no longer if it be not so fortunate as to obtain the high patronage which I have thus taken the liberty to solicit.

Permit me, Sir, to add that the person who addresses you is no adventurer, but a man of some property, and inheriting a business that has been established for nearly a century. I therefore trust that my application will be attributed to its proper motives, and that your goodness will at least pardon its obtrusion.

I have the honour to be, Sir, Your must humble and obedient Servant,

John Murray.

So far as can be ascertained, Mr. Canning did not answer this letter in writing. But a communication was shortly after opened with him through Mr. Stratford Canning, whose acquaintance Mr. Murray had made through the publication of the "Miniature, " referred to in a preceding chapter. Mr. Canning was still acting as Secretary of State for Foreign Affairs, and was necessarily cautious, but Mr. Stratford Canning, his cousin, was not bound by any such official restraints. In January 1808 he introduced Mr. Gifford to Mr. Murray, and the starting of the proposed new periodical was the subject of many consultations between them.

Walter Scott still continued to write for the *Edinburgh*, notwithstanding the differences of opinion which existed between himself and the editor as to political questions. He was rather proud of the *Review*, inasmuch as it was an outgrowth of Scottish literature. Scott even endeavoured to enlist new contributors, for the purpose of strengthening the *Review*. He wrote to Robert Southey in 1807, inviting him to contribute to the *Edinburgh*. The honorarium was to be ten guineas per sheet of sixteen pages. This was a very tempting invitation to Southey, as he was by no means rich at the time, and the pay was more than he received for his contributions to the *Annual Register*, but he replied to Scott as follows:

Mr. Southey to Mr. Scott.

December, 1807.

"I have scarcely one opinion in common with it [the *Edinburgh Review*] upon any subject.... Whatever of any merit I might insert there would aid and abet opinions hostile to my own, and thus identify me with a system which I thoroughly disapprove. This is not said hastily. The emolument to be derived from writing at ten guineas a sheet, Scotch measure, instead of seven pounds for the *Annual*, would be considerable; the pecuniary advantage resulting from the different manner in which my future works would be handled [by the *Review*] probably still more so. But my moral feelings must not be compromised. To Jeffrey as an individual I shall ever be ready to show every kind of individual courtesy; but of Judge Jeffrey of the *Edinburgh Review* I must ever think and speak as of a bad politician, a worse moralist, and a critic, in matters of taste, equally incompetent and unjust. " [Footnote: "The Life and Correspondence of Robert Southey, " iii. pp. 124-5.] Walter Scott, before long, was led to entertain the same opinion of the *Edinburgh Review* as Southey. A severe and unjust review of "Marmion, " by Jeffrey, appeared in 1808, accusing Scott of a mercenary spirit in writing for money (though Jeffrey himself was writing for money in the same article), and further irritating Scott by asserting that he "had neglected Scottish feelings and Scottish characters." "Constable, " writes Scott to his brother Thomas, in November 1808, "or rather that Bear, his partner [Mr. Hunter], has behaved by me of late not very civilly, and I owe Jeffrey a flap with a foxtail on account of his review of 'Marmion, ' and thus doth the whirligig of time bring about my revenges. "

Murray, too, was greatly annoyed by the review of "Marmion. " "Scott, " he used to say, "may forgive but he can never forget this treatment"; and, to quote the words of Mr. Lockhart: "When he read the article on 'Marmion, ' and another on foreign politics, in the same number of the *Edinburgh Review*, Murray said to himself, 'Walter Scott has feelings, both as a gentleman and a Tory, which these people must now have wounded; the alliance between him and the whole clique of the *Edinburgh Review* is now shaken'"; and, as far at least as the political part of the affair was concerned, John Murray's sagacity was not at fault.

Mr. Murray at once took advantage of this opening to draw closer the bonds between himself and Ballantyne, for he well knew who was the leading spirit in the firm, and showed himself desirous of obtaining the London agency of the publishing business, which, as he rightly discerned, would soon be started in connection with the Canongate Press, and in opposition to Constable. The large increase of work which Murray was prepared to place in the hands of the printers induced Ballantyne to invite him to come as far as Ferrybridge in Yorkshire for a personal conference. At this interview various new projects were discussed—among them the proposed Novelists' Library—and from the information which he then obtained as to Scott's personal feelings and literary projects, Murray considered himself justified in at once proceeding to Ashestiel, in order to lay before Scott himself, in a personal interview, his great scheme for the new Review. He arrived there about the middle of October 1808, and was hospitably welcomed and entertained. He stated his plans, mentioned the proposed editor of the Review, the probable contributors, and earnestly invited the assistance of Scott himself.

During Murray's visit to Ashestiel No. 26 of the *Edinburgh Review* arrived. It contained an article entitled "Don Cevallos on the Occupation of Spain. " It was long supposed that the article was written by Brougham, but it has since been ascertained that Jeffrey himself was the author of it. This article gave great offence to the friends of rational liberty and limited monarchy in this country. Scott forthwith wrote to Constable: "The *Edinburgh Review had* become such as to render it impossible for me to become a contributor to it; *now* it is such as I can no longer continue to receive or read it. "

"The list of the then subscribers, " said Mr. Cadell to Mr. Lockhart, "exhibits, in an indignant dash of Constable's pen opposite Mr. Scott's name, the word 'STOPT! '"

Mr. Murray never forgot his visit to Ashestiel. Scott was kindness itself; Mrs. Scott was equally cordial and hospitable. Richard Heber was there at the time, and the three went out daily to explore the scenery of the neighbourhood. They visited Melrose Abbey, the Tweed, and Dryburgh Abbey, not very remote from Melrose, where Scott was himself to lie; they ascended the Eildon Hills, Scott on his sheltie often stopping by the way to point out to Murray and Heber, who were on foot, some broad meadow or heather-clad ground, as a spot where some legend held its seat, or some notable deed had been achieved during the wars of the Borders. Scott thus converted the barren hillside into a region of interest and delight. From the top of the Eildons he pointed out the scene of some twenty battles.

Very soon after his return to London, Murray addressed the following letter to Mr. Scott:

John Murray to Mr. Scott.

October 26, 1808.

DEAR SIR,

Although the pressure of business since my return to London has prevented me writing to you sooner, yet my thoughts have, I assure you, been almost completely employed upon the important subjects of the conversation with which you honoured me during the time I was experiencing the obliging hospitality of Mrs. Scott and yourself at Ashestiel.

Then, after a reference to the Novelists' Library mentioned in the last chapter, the letter continues:

"I have seen Mr. William Gifford, hinting distantly at a Review; he admitted the most imperious necessity for one, and that too in a way

41

that leads me to think that he has had very important communications upon the subject.... I feel more than ever confident that the higher powers are exceedingly desirous for the establishment of some counteracting publication; and it will, I suspect, remain only for your appearance in London to urge some very formidable plan into activity. "

This letter was crossed in transit by the following:

Mr. Scott to John Murray.

ASHESTIEL, BY SELKIRK, *October* 30, 1808.

DEAR SIR,

"Since I had the pleasure of seeing you I have the satisfaction to find that Mr. Gifford has accepted the task of editing the intended Review. This was communicated to me by the Lord Advocate, who at the same time requested me to write Mr. Gifford on the subject. I have done so at great length, pointing out whatever occurred to me on the facilities or difficulties of the work in general, as well as on the editorial department, offering at the same time all the assistance in my power to set matters upon a good footing and to keep them so. I presume he will have my letter by the time this reaches you, and that he will communicate with you fully upon the details. I am as certain as of my existence that the plan will answer, provided sufficient attention is used in procuring and selecting articles of merit. "

What Scott thought of Murray's visit to Ashestiel may be inferred from his letter to his political confidant, George Ellis, of which, as it has already appeared in Scott's Life, it is only necessary to give extracts here:

Mr. Scott to Mr. George Ellis.

November 2, 1808.

DEAR ELLIS,

"We had, equally to our joy and surprise, a flying visit from Heber about three weeks ago. He staid but three days, but, between old stories and new, we made them very merry in their passage. During his stay, John Murray, the bookseller in Fleet Street, who has more real knowledge of what concerns his business than any of his brethren—at least, than any of them that I know—came to canvass a most important plan, of which I am now, in "dern privacie, " to give you the outline. I had most strongly recommended to our Lord Advocate (the Right Hon. J.C. Colquhoun) to think of some counter measures against the *Edinburgh Review.* which, politically speaking, is doing incalculable damage. I do not mean this in a party way; the present ministry are not all I could wish them, for (Canning excepted) I doubt there is among them too much *self-seeking....* But their political principles are sound English principles, and, compared to the greedy and inefficient horde which preceded them, they are angels of light and purity. It is obvious, however, that they want defenders, both in and out of doors. Pitt's

"Love and fear glued many friends to him; And now he's fallen, those tough co-mixtures melt. "

Then, after a reference to the large circulation (9,000) and mischievous politics of the *Edinburgh Review*, he proceeds:

"Now, I think there is balm in Gilead for all this, and that the cure lies in instituting such a Review in London as should be conducted totally independent of bookselling influence, on a plan as liberal as that of the *Edinburgh*, its literature as well supported, and its principles English and constitutional. Accordingly, I have been given to understand that Mr. William Gifford is willing to become the conductor of such a work, and I have written to him, at the Lord Advocate's desire, a very voluminous letter on the subject. Now, should this plan succeed, you must hang your birding-piece on its hook, take down your old Anti-Jacobin armour, and "remember your swashing blow. " It is not that I think this projected Review ought to be exclusively or principally political; this would, in my opinion, absolutely counteract its purpose, which I think should be to offer to those who love their country, and to those whom we would wish to love it, a periodical work of criticism conducted with equal talent, but upon sounder principles. Is not this very possible? In point of learning, you Englishmen have ten times our scholarship; and, as for talent and genius, "Are not Abana and Pharpar, rivers of Damascus, better than any of the rivers in Israel? " Have we not yourself and your cousin, the Roses, Malthus, Matthias, Gifford, Heber, and his brother? Can I not procure you a score of blue-caps who would rather write for us than for the *Edinburgh Review* if they got as much pay by it? "A good plot, good friends, and full of expectation—an excellent plot, very good friends! "

Heber's fear was lest we should fail in procuring regular steady contributors; but I know so much of the interior discipline of reviewing as to have no apprehension of that. Provided we are once set a-going by a few dashing numbers, there would be no fear of enlisting regular contributors; but the amateurs must bestir themselves in the first instance. From the Government we should be entitled to expect confidential communications as to points of fact (so far as fit to be made public) in our political disquisitions. With this advantage, our good cause and St. George to boot, we may at least divide the field with our formidable competitors, who, after all, are much better at cutting than parrying, and whose uninterrupted triumph has as much unfitted them for resisting a serious attack as it has done Buonaparte for the Spanish war. Jeffrey is, to be sure, a man of the most uncommon versatility of talent, but what then?

"General Howe is a gallant commander,
There are others as gallant as he."

Think of all this, and let me hear from you very soon on the subject. Canning is, I have good reason to know, very anxious about the plan. I mentioned it to Robert Dundas, who was here with his lady for a few days on a pilgrimage to Melrose, and he highly approved of it. Though no literary man, he is judicious, *clair-voyant*, and uncommonly sound-headed, like his father, Lord Melville. With the exceptions I have mentioned, the thing continues a secret....

Ever yours,

Walter Scott. "

Mr. Scott to John Murray.

November 2, 1808.

I transmitted my letter to Mr. Gifford through the Lord Advocate, and left it open that Mr. Canning might read it if he thought it worth while. I have a letter from the Advocate highly approving my views, so I suppose you will very soon hear from Mr. Gifford specifically on the subject. It is a matter of immense consequence that something shall be set about, and that without delay....

The points on which I chiefly insisted with Mr. Gifford were that the Review should be independent both as to bookselling and ministerial influences—meaning that we were not to be advocates of party through thick and thin, but to maintain constitutional principles. Moreover, I stated as essential that the literary part of the work should be as sedulously attended to as the political, because it is by means of that alone that the work can acquire any firm and extended reputation.

Moreover yet, I submitted that each contributor should draw money for his article, be his rank what it may. This general rule has been of great use to the *Edinburgh Review*. Of terms I said nothing, except that your views on the subject seemed to me highly liberal. I do not add further particulars because I dare say Mr. Gifford will show you the letter, which is a very long one. Believe me, my dear Sir, with sincere regard,

Your faithful, humble Servant,

Walter Scott.

In a subsequent letter to Mr. Ellis, Scott again indicates what he considers should be the proper management of the proposed Review.

"Let me touch, " he says, "a string of much delicacy—the political character of the Review. It appears to me that this should be of a liberal and enlarged nature, resting upon principles—indulgent and conciliatory as far as possible upon mere party questions, but stern in detecting and exposing all attempts to sap our constitutional fabric. Religion is another slippery station; here also I would endeavour to be as impartial as the subject will admit of.... The truth is, there is policy, as well as morality, in keeping our swords clear as well as sharp, and not forgetting the Gentleman in the Critic. The public appetite is soon gorged with any particular style. The common Reviews, before the appearance of the *Edinburgh*, had become extremely mawkish; and, unless when prompted by the malice of the bookseller or reviewer, gave a dawdling, maudlin sort of applause to everything that reached even mediocrity. The *Edinburgh* folks squeezed into their sauce plenty of acid, and were popular from novelty as well as from merit. The minor Reviews, and other periodical publications, have *outré* the matter still further, and given us all abuse and no talent.... This, therefore, we have to trust to, that decent, lively, and reflecting criticism, teaching men not to abuse books, but to read and to judge them, will have the effect of novelty upon a public wearied with universal efforts at blackguard and indiscriminating satire. I have a long and very sensible letter [Footnote: Given below, under date November 15, 1808.] from John Murray, the bookseller, in which he touches upon this point very neatly. "

Scott was most assiduous in his preparations for the first number. He wrote to his brother, Thomas Scott, asking him to contribute an article; to Charles Kirkpatrick Sharpe, of Christ Church, Oxford; to Mr. Morritt, of Rokeby Park, Yorkshire; and to Robert Southey, of Keswick, asking them for contributions. To Mr. Sharpe he says:

"The Hebers are engaged, item Rogers, Southey, Moore (Anacreon), and others whose reputations Jeffrey has murdered, and who are rising to cry woe upon him, like the ghosts in 'King Richard. '"

Scott's letter to Gilford, the intended editor, was full of excellent advice. It was dated "Edinburgh, October 25, 1808. " We quote from it several important passages:

"John Murray, of Fleet Street, " says Scott, "a young bookseller of capital and enterprise, and with more good sense and propriety of sentiment than fall to the share of most of the trade, made me a visit at Ashestiel a few weeks ago; and as I found he had had some communication with you upon the subject, I did not hesitate to communicate my sentiments to him on this and some other points of the plan, and I thought his ideas were most liberal and satisfactory.

"The office of Editor is of such importance, that had you not been pleased to undertake it, I fear the plan would have fallen wholly to the ground. The full power of control must, of course, be vested in the editor for selecting, curtailing, and correcting the contributions to the Review. But this is not all; for, as he is the person immediately responsible to the bookseller that the work (amounting to a certain number of pages, more or less) shall be before the public at a certain time, it will be the editor's duty to consider in due turn the articles of which each number ought to consist, and to take measures for procuring them from the persons best qualified to write upon such and such subjects. But this is sometimes so troublesome, that I foresee with pleasure you will soon be obliged to abandon your resolution of writing nothing yourself. At the same time, if you will accept of my services as a sort of jackal or lion's provider, I will do all in my power to assist in this troublesome department of editorial duty.

"But there is still something behind, and that of the last consequence. One great resource to which the *Edinburgh* editor turns himself, and by which he gives popularity even to the duller articles of his *Review*, is accepting contributions from persons of inferior powers of writing, provided they understand the books to which their criticisms relate; and as such are often of stupefying mediocrity, he renders them palatable by throwing in a handful of spice, namely, any lively paragraph or entertaining illustration that occurs to him in reading them over. By this sort of veneering he converts, without loss of time or hindrance to business, articles, which in their original state might hang in the market, into such goods as are not likely to disgrace those among which they are placed. This seems to be a point in which an editor's assistance is of the last consequence, for those who possess the knowledge necessary to review books of research or abstruse disquisitions, are very often unable to put the criticisms into a readable, much more a pleasant and captivating form; and as their science cannot be attained 'for the nonce, ' the only remedy is to supply their deficiencies, and give their lucubrations a more popular turn.

"There is one opportunity possessed by you in a particular degree— that of access to the best sources of political information. It would not, certainly, be advisable that the work should assume, especially at the outset, a professed political character. On the contrary, the articles on science and miscellaneous literature ought to be of such a quality as might fairly challenge competition with the best of our contemporaries. But as the real reason of instituting the publication is the disgusting and deleterious doctrine with which the most popular of our Reviews disgraces its pages, it is essential to consider how this warfare should be managed. On this ground, I hope it is not too much to expect from those who have the power of assisting us, that they should on topics of great national interest furnish the reviewers, through the medium of their editor, with accurate views of points of fact, so far as they are fit to be made public. This is the most delicate and yet most essential part of our scheme.

"On the one hand, it is certainly not to be understood that we are to be held down to advocate upon all occasions the cause of administration. Such a dereliction of independence would render us entirely useless for the purpose we mean to serve. On the other hand, nothing will render the work more interesting than the public learning, not from any vaunt of ours, but from their own observation, that we have access to early and accurate information on points of fact. The *Edinburgh Review* has profited much by the pains which the Opposition party have taken to possess the writers of all the information they could give them on public matters. Let me repeat that you, my dear sir, from enjoying the confidence of Mr. Canning, and other persons in power, may easily obtain the confidential information necessary to give credit to the work, and communicate it to such as you may think proper to employ in laying it before the public. "

Mr. Scott further proceeded, in his letter to Mr. Gifford, to discuss the mode and time of publication, the choice of subjects, the persons to be employed as contributors, and the name of the proposed Review, thus thoroughly identifying himself with it.

"Let our forces, " he said, "for a number or two, consist of volunteers or amateurs, and when we have acquired some reputation, we shall soon levy and discipline our forces of the line. After all, the matter is become very serious—eight or nine thousand copies of the *Edinburgh Review* are regularly distributed, merely because there is no other respectable and independent publication of the kind. In this city (Edinburgh), where there is not one Whig out of twenty men who read the work, many hundreds are sold; and how long the generality of readers will continue to dislike politics, so artfully mingled with information and amusement, is worthy of deep consideration. But it is not yet too late to stand in the breach; the first number ought, if possible, to be out in January, and if it can burst among them like a bomb, without previous notice, the effect will be more striking.

"Of those who might be intrusted in the first instance you are a much better judge than I am. I think I can command the assistance of a friend or two here, particularly William Erskine, the Lord Advocate's brother-in-law and my most intimate friend. In London, you have Malthus, George Ellis, the Roses, *cum pluribus aliis*. Richard Heber was with me when Murray came to my farm, and, knowing his zeal for the good cause, I let him into our counsels. In Mr. Frere we have the hopes of a potent ally. The Rev. Reginald Heber would be an excellent coadjutor, and when I come to town I will sound Matthias. As strict secrecy would of course be observed, the diffidence of many might be overcome. For scholars you can be at no loss while Oxford stands where it did; and I think there will be no deficiency in the scientific articles. "

Thus instructed, Gifford proceeded to rally his forces. There was no want of contributors. Some came invited, some came unsought; but, as the matter was still a secret, the editor endeavoured to secure contributions through his personal friends. For instance, he called upon Mr. Rogers to request him to secure the help of Moore.

"I must confess, " said Rogers to Moore, "I heard of the new quarterly with pleasure, as I thought it might correct an evil we had long lamented together. Gifford wishes much for contributors, and is exceedingly anxious that you should assist him as often as you can afford time.... All this in *confidence* of course, as the secret is not my own. "

Gifford also endeavoured to secure the assistance of Southey, through his friend, Mr. Grosvenor Bedford. Southey was requested to write for the first number an article on the Affairs of Spain. This, however, he declined to do; but promised to send an article on the subject of Missionaries.

"Let not Gifford, " he wrote to Bedford, in reply to his letter, "suppose me a troublesome man to deal with, pertinacious about trifles, or standing upon punctilios of authorship. No, Grosvenor, I am a quiet, patient, easy-going hack of the mule breed; regular as clockwork in my pace, sure-footed, bearing the burden which is laid on me, and only obstinate in choosing my own path. If Gifford could see me by this fireside, where, like Nicodemus, one candle suffices me in a large room, he would see a man in a coat 'still more threadbare than his own' when he wrote his 'Imitation, ' working hard and getting little—a bare maintenance, and hardly that; writing poems and history for posterity with his whole heart and soul; one daily progressive in learning, not so learned as he is poor, not so poor as proud, not so proud as happy. "

Mr. James Ballantyne to John Murray.

October 28, 1808.

"Well, you have of course heard from Mr. Scott of the progress of the 'Great Plan. ' Canning bites at the hook eagerly. A review termed by Mr. Jeffrey *a tickler*, is to appear of Dryden in this No. of the

Edinburgh. By the Lord! they will rue it. You know Scott's present feelings, excited by the review of 'Marmion. ' What will they be when that of Dryden appears? "

It was some time, however, before arrangements could be finally made for bringing out the first number of the *Quarterly.* Scott could not as yet pay his intended visit to London, and after waiting for about a month, Murray sent him the following letter, giving his further opinion as to the scope and object of the proposed Review:

John Murray to Mr. Scott.

November 15, 1808.

DEAR SIR,

I have been desirous of writing to you for nearly a week past, as I never felt more the want of a personal conversation. I will endeavour, however, to explain myself to you, and will rely on your confidence and indulgence for secrecy and attention in what I have to communicate. I have before told you that the idea of a new Review has been revolving in my mind for nearly two years, and that more than twelve months ago I addressed Mr. Canning on the subject. The propriety, if not the necessity, of establishing a journal upon principles opposite to those of the *Edinburgh Review* has occurred to many men more enlightened than myself; and I believe the same reason has prevented others, as it has done myself, from attempting it, namely, the immense difficulty of obtaining talent of sufficient magnitude to render success even *doubtful.*

By degrees my plan has gradually floated up to this height. But there exists at least an equal difficulty yet—that peculiar talent in an editor of rendering our other great resources advantageous to the best possible degree. This, I think, may be accomplished, but it must be effected by your arduous assistance, at least for a little time. Our friend Mr. Gifford, whose writings show him to be both a man of learning and wit, has lived too little in the world lately to have obtained that delicacy and tact whereby he can feel at one instant, and habitually, whatever may gratify public desire and excite public attention and curiosity. But this you know to be a leading feature in the talents of Mr. Jeffrey and his friends; and that, without the most happy choice of subjects, as well as the ability to treat them well— catching the "manners living as they rise"—the *Edinburgh Review* could not have attained the success it has done; and no other Review, however preponderating in solid merit, will obtain sufficient attention without them. Entering the field too, as we shall do, against an army commanded by the most skilful generals, it will not do for us to leave any of our best officers behind as a reserve, for they would be of no use if we were defeated at first. We must enter with our most able commanders at once, and we shall then acquire confidence, if not reputation, and increase in numbers as we proceed.

Our first number must contain the most valuable and striking information in politics, and the most interesting articles of general literature and science, written by our most able friends. If our plan appears to be so advantageous to the ministers whose measures, to a certain extent, we intend to justify, to support, to recommend and assist, that they have promised their support; when might that support be so advantageously given, either for their own interests or ours, as at the commencement, when we are most weak, and have the most arduous onset to make, and when we do and must stand most in need of help? If our first number be not written with the greatest ability, upon the most interesting topics, it will not excite public attention. No man, even the friend of the principles we adopt, will leave the sprightly pages of the *Edinburgh Review* to read a dull detail of staid morality, or dissertations on subjects whose interest has long fled.

I do not say this from any, even the smallest doubt, of our having all that we desire in these respects in our power; but because I am apprehensive that without your assistance it will not be drawn into action, and my reason for this fear I will thus submit to you. You mentioned in your letter to Mr. Gifford, that our Review should open with a grand article on Spain—meaning a display of the political feeling of the people, and the probable results of this important contest. I suggested to Mr. Gifford that Mr. Frere should be written to, which he said was easy, and that he thought he would do it; for Frere could not only give the facts upon the subject, but could write them better than any other person. But having, in my project, given the name of Southey as a person who might assist occasionally in a number or two hence, I found at our next interview that Mr. Gifford, who does not know Mr. Southey, had spoken to a friend to ask Mr. S. to write the article upon Spain. It is true that Mr. Southey knows a great deal about Spain, and on another occasion would have given a good article upon the subject; but at present *his* is not the kind of knowledge which we want, and it is, moreover, trusting our secret to a stranger, who has, by the way, a directly opposite bias in politics.

Mr. Gifford also told me, with very great stress, that among the articles he had submitted to you was [one on] Hodgson's Translation of Juvenal, which at no time could be a very interesting article for us, and having been published more than six months ago, would probably be a very stupid one. Then, you must observe, that it would necessarily involve a comparison with Mr. Gifford's own translation, which must of course be praised, and thus show an *individual* feeling—the least spark of which, in our early numbers, would both betray and ruin us. He talks of reviewing *himself* a late translation of "Persius, " for (*entre nous*) a similar reason. He has himself nearly completed a translation, which will be published in a few months.

In what I have said upon this most exceedingly delicate point, and which I again submit to your most honourable confidence, I have no other object but just to show you without reserve how we stand, and to exemplify what I set out with—that without skilful and judicious management we shall totally mistake the road to the accomplishment of the arduous task which we have undertaken, and involve the cause and every individual in not merely defeat, but disgrace. I must at the same time observe that Mr. Gifford is the most obliging and well-meaning man alive, and that he is perfectly ready to be instructed in those points of which his seclusion renders him ignorant; and all that I wish and mean is, that we should strive to open clearly the view which is so obvious to us—that our first number must be a most brilliant one in every respect; and to effect this, we must avail ourselves of any valuable political information we can command. Those persons who have the most interest in supporting the Review must be called upon immediately for their strenuous personal help. The fact must be obvious to you, —that if Mr. Canning, Mr. Frere, Mr. Scott, Mr. Ellis, and Mr. Gifford, with their immediate and true friends, will exert themselves heartily in every respect, so as to produce with secrecy only *one* remarkably attractive number, their further labour would be comparatively light. With such a number in our hands, we might select and obtain every other help that we required; and then the persons named would only be called upon for their information, facts, hints, advice, and occasional articles. But without this—without producing a number that shall at least equal, if not excel, the best of the *Edinburgh Review*, it were better not to be attempted. We should do more harm to our cause by an unsuccessful attempt; and the reputation of the *Edinburgh Review* would be increased inversely to our fruitless opposition.... With respect to bookselling interference with the Review, I am equally convinced with yourself of its total incompatibility with a really respectable and valuable critical journal. I assure you that nothing can be more distant from my views, which are confined to the ardour which I feel for the cause and principles which it will be our object to support, and the honour of professional reputation which would obviously result to the publisher of so important a work. It were silly to suppress that I shall not be sorry to derive from it as much profit as I can satisfactorily enjoy, consistent with the liberal scale upon which it is my first desire to act towards every writer and friend concerned in the work. Respecting the terms upon which the editor shall be placed at first, I have proposed, and it appears to be satisfactory to Mr. Gifford, that he shall receive, either previous to, or immediately after, the publication of each number, the sum of 160 guineas, which he is to distribute as he thinks proper, without any question or interference on my part; and that in addition to this, he shall receive from me the sum of £200 annually, merely as the editor. This, Sir, is much more than I can flatter myself with the return of, for the first year at least; but it is my intention that his salary shall ever increase proportionately to the success of the work under his management. The editor has a most arduous office to perform, and the success of the publication must depend in a great measure upon his activity.

I am, dear Sir, Your obliged and faithful Servant,

John Murray.

It will be observed from this letter, that Mr. Murray was aware that, besides skilful editing, sound and practical business management was necessary to render the new Review a success. The way in which he informs Mr. Scott about Gifford's proposed review of "Juvenal" and "Persius, " shows that he fully comprehended the situation, and the dangers which would beset an editor like Gifford, who lived for the most part amongst his books, and was, to a large extent, secluded from the active world.

On the same day Scott was writing to Murray:

Mr. Scott to John Murray. Edinburgh, *November* 15, 1808.

Dear Sir,

I received two days ago a letter from Mr. Gifford highly approving of the particulars of the plan which I had sketched for the *Review*. But there are two points to be considered. In the first place, I cannot be in town as I proposed, for the Commissioners under the Judicial Bill, to whom I am to act as clerk, have resolved that their final sittings shall be held *here*, so that I have now no chance of being in London before spring. This is very unlucky, as Mr. Gifford proposes to wait for my arrival in town to set the great machine a-going. I shall write to him that this is impossible, and that I wish he would, with your assistance and that of his other friends, make up a list of the works which the first number is to contain, and consider what is the extent of the aid he will require from the North. The other circumstance is, that Mr. Gifford pleads the state of his health and his retired habits as sequestrating him from the world, and rendering him less capable of active exertion, and in the kindest and most polite manner he expresses his hope that he should receive very extensive assistance and support from me, without which he is pleased to say he would utterly despair of success. Now between ourselves (for this is strictly confidential) I am rather alarmed at this prospect. I am willing, and anxiously so, to do all in my power to serve the work; but, my dear sir, you know how many of our very ablest hands are engaged in the *Edinburgh Review*, and what a dismal work it will be to wring assistance from the few whose indolence has left them neutral. I can, to be sure, work like a horse myself, but then I have two heavy works on my hands already, namely, "Somers" and "Swift. " Constable had lately very nearly relinquished the latter work, and I now heartily wish it had never commenced; but two volumes are nearly printed, so I conclude it will now go on. If this work had not stood in the way, I should have liked Beaumont and Fletcher much better. It would not have required half the research, and occupied much less time. I plainly see that, according to Mr. Gifford's view, I should have almost all the trouble of a co-editor, both in collecting and revising the articles which are to come from Scotland, as well as in supplying all deficiencies from my own stores.

These considerations cannot, however, operate upon the first number, so pray send me a list of books, and perhaps you may send some on a venture. You know the department I had in the *Edinburgh Review*. I will sound Southey, agreeable to Mr. Gifford's wishes, on the Spanish affairs. The last number of the *Edinburgh Review* has given disgust beyond measure, owing to the tone of the article on Cevallos' *exposé*. Subscribers are falling off like withered leaves.

I retired my name among others, after explaining the reasons both to Mr. Jeffrey and Mr. Constable, so that there never was such an opening for a new *Review*. I shall be glad to hear what you think on the subject of terms, for my Northern troops will not move without pay; but there is no hurry about fixing this point, as most of the writers in the first number will be more or less indifferent on the subject. For my own share, I care not what the conditions are, unless the labour expected from me is to occupy a considerable portion of time, in which case they might become an object. While we are on this subject, I may as well mention that as you incur so large an outlay in the case of the Novels, I would not only be happy that my remuneration should depend on the profits of the work, but I also think I could command a few hundreds to assist in carrying it on.

By the way, I see "Notes on Don Quixote" advertised. This was a plan I had for enriching our collection, having many references by me for the purpose. I shall be sorry if I am powerfully anticipated. Perhaps the book would make a good article in the *Review*. Can you get me "Gaytoun's Festivous Notes on Don Quixote"?

I think our friend Ballantyne is grown an inch taller on the subjects of the "Romances. "

Believe me, dear Sir, Yours very truly, Walter Scott.

Gifford is much pleased with you personally.

John Murray to Mr. Scott.

November 19, 1808.

"Mr. Gifford has communicated to me an important piece of news. He met his friend, Lord Teignmouth, and learned from him that he and the Wilberforce party had some idea of starting a journal to oppose the *Edinburgh Review*, that Henry Thornton and Mr. [Zachary] Macaulay were to be the conductors, that they had met, and that some able men were mentioned. Upon sounding Lord T. as to their giving us their assistance, he thought this might be adopted in preference to their own plans.... It will happen fortunately that we intend opening with an article on the missionaries, which, as it will be written in opposition to the sentiments in the *Edinburgh Review*, is very likely to gain that large body of which Wilberforce is the head. I have collected from every Missionary Society in London, of which there are no less than five, all their curious reports, proceedings and history, which, I know, Sydney Smith never saw; and which I could only procure by personal application. Southey will give a complete view of the subject, and if he will enter heartily into it, and do it well, it will be as much as he can do for the first number. These transactions contain, amidst a great deal of fanaticism, the most curious information you can imagine upon the history, literature, topography and manners of nations and countries of which we are otherwise totally ignorant.... If you have occasion to write to Southey, pray urge the vast importance of this subject, and entreat him to give it all his ability. I find that a new volume of Burns' ('The Reliques') will be published by the end of this month, which will form the subject of another capital article under your hands. I presume 'Sir John Carr (Tour in Scotland)' will be another article, which even you, I fancy, will like; 'Mrs. Grant of Laggan, ' too, and perhaps your friend Mr. Cumberland's 'John de Lancaster' .... Are you not sufficiently well acquainted with Miss (Joanna) Baillie, both to confide in her, and command her talents? If so, you will probably think of what may suit her, and what may apply to her. Mr. Heber, too, would apply to his brother at your request, and his friend Coplestone, who will also be written to by a friend of Gifford's.... "

Scott was very desirous of enlisting George Canning among the contributors to the Quarterly. He wrote to his friend Ellis:

Mr. Scott to Mr. G. Ellis.

"As our start is of such immense consequence, don't you think Mr. Canning, though unquestionably our Atlas, might for a day find a Hercules on whom to devolve the burden of the globe, while he writes for us a review? I know what an audacious request this is, but suppose he should, as great statesmen sometimes do, take a political fit of the gout, and absent himself from a large ministerial dinner which might give it him in good earnest—dine at three on a chicken and pint of wine, and lay the foundation of at least one good article? Let us but once get afloat, and our labour is not worth talking about; but, till then, all hands must work hard. "

This suggestion was communicated by George Ellis to Gifford, the chosen editor, and on December 1, Murray informed Scott that the article on Spain was proceeding under Mr. Canning's immediate superintendence. Canning and Gifford went down to Mr. Ellis's house at Sunninghill, where the three remained together for four days, during which time the article was hatched and completed.

On receiving the celebrated "Declaration of Westminster" on the Spanish War, Scott wrote to Ellis:

"Tell Mr. Canning that the old women of Scotland will defend the country with their distaffs, rather than that troops enough be not sent to make good so noble a pledge. Were the thousands that have mouldered away in petty conquests or Lilliputian expeditions united to those we have now in that country, what a band would Sir John Moore have under him!... Jeffrey has offered terms of pacification, engaging that no party politics should again appear in his *Review*. I told him I thought it was now too late, and reminded him that I had often pointed out to him the consequences of letting his work become a party tool. He said 'he did not fear for the consequences — there were but four men he feared as opponents. ' 'Who are these? ' 'Yourself for one. ' 'Certainly you pay me a great compliment; depend upon it I will endeavour to deserve it. ' 'Why, you would not join against me? ' 'Yes, I would, if I saw a proper opportunity: not against you personally, but against your politics. ' 'You are privileged to be violent. ' 'I don't ask any privilege for undue violence. But who are your other foemen? ' 'George Ellis and Southey. ' The other he did not name. All this was in great good humour; and next day I had a very affecting note from him, in answer to an invitation to dinner. He has no suspicion of the *Review* whatever. "

In the meantime, Mr. Murray continued to look out for further contributors. Mr. James Mill, of the India House, in reply to a request for assistance, wrote:

"You do me a great deal of honour in the solicitude you express to have me engaged in laying the foundation stone of your new edifice, which I hope will be both splendid and durable; and it is no want of zeal or gratitude that delays me. But this ponderous Geography, a porter's, or rather a horse's load, bears me down to a degree you can hardly conceive. What I am now meditating from under it is to spare time to do well and leisurely the Indian article (my favourite subject) for your next number. Besides, I shall not reckon myself less a founder from its having been only the fault of my previous engagements that my first article for you appears only in the second number, and not in the first part of your work. "

Another contributor whom Mr. Murray was desirous to secure was Mrs. Inchbald, authoress of the "Simple Story. " The application was made to her through one of Murray's intimate friends, Mr. Hoppner, the artist. Her answer was as follows:

Mrs. Inchbald to Mr. Hoppner. December 31, 1808.

My dear Sir, As I wholly rely upon your judgment for the excellency of the design in question, I wish you to be better acquainted with my abilities as a reviewer before I suffer my curiosity to be further gratified in respect to the plan of the work you have undertaken, or the names of those persons who, with yourself, have done me the very great honour to require my assistance. Before I see you, then, and possess myself of your further confidence, it is proper that I should acquaint you that there is only one department of a Review for which I am in the least qualified, and that one combines plays and novels. Yet the very few novels I have read, of later publications, incapacitates me again for detecting plagiary, or for making such comparisons as proper criticism may demand. You will, perhaps, be surprised when I tell you that I am not only wholly unacquainted with the book you have mentioned to me, but that I never heard of it before. If it be in French, there will be another insurmountable difficulty; for, though I read French, and have translated some French comedies, yet I am not so perfectly acquainted with the language as to dare to write remarks upon a French author. If Madame Cottin's "Malvina" be in English, you wish it speedily reviewed, and can possibly have any doubt of the truth of my present report, please to send it me; and whatever may be the contents, I will immediately essay my abilities on the work, or immediately return it as a hopeless case.

Yours very faithfully,

E. Inchbald.

On further consideration, however, Mrs. Inchbald modestly declined to become a contributor. Notwithstanding her great merits as an author, she had the extremest diffidence in her own abilities.

Mrs. Inchbald to John Murray.

"The more I reflect on the importance of the contributions intended for this work, the more I am convinced of my own inability to become a contributor. The productions in question must, I am convinced, be of a certain quality that will demand far more acquaintance with books, and much more general knowledge, than it has ever been my good fortune to attain. Under these circumstances, finding myself, upon mature consideration, wholly inadequate to the task proposed, I beg you will accept of this apology as a truth, and present it to Mr. Hoppner on the first opportunity; and assure him that it has been solely my reluctance to yield up the honour he intended me which has tempted me, for an instant, to be undecided in my reply to his overture. —I am, Sir, with sincere acknowledgments for the politeness of your letter to me,

"E. Inchbald. "

And here the correspondence dropped.

It is now difficult to understand the profound secrecy with which the projection of the new Review was carried on until within a fortnight of the day of its publication. In these modern times widespread advertisements announce the advent of a new periodical, whereas then both publisher and editor enjoined the utmost secrecy upon all with whom they were in correspondence. Still, the day of publication was very near, when the *Quarterly* was, according to Scott, to "burst like a bomb" among the Whigs of Edinburgh. The only explanation of the secrecy of the preliminary arrangements is that probably down to the last it was difficult to ascertain whether enough materials could be accumulated to form a sufficiently good number before the first *Quarterly Review* was launched into the world.

CHAPTER VI

THE "QUARTERLY" LAUNCHED

While Mr. Gifford was marshalling his forces and preparing for the issue of the first number of the *Quarterly*, Mr. Murray was corresponding with James Ballantyne of Edinburgh as to the works they were jointly engaged in bringing out, and also with respect to the northern agency of the new *Review*. An arrangement was made between them that they should meet at Boroughbridge, in Yorkshire, at the beginning of January 1809, for the purpose of concocting their plans. Ballantyne proposed to leave Edinburgh on January 5, and Murray was to set out from London on the same day, both making for Boroughbridge. A few days before Ballantyne left Edinburgh he wrote to Murray:

"I shall not let a living soul know of my intended journey. Entire secrecy seems necessary at present. I dined yesterday *tête-à-tête* with Mr. Scott, and had a great deal of highly important conversation with him. He showed me a letter bidding a final farewell to the house of Constable. "

It was mid-winter, and there were increasing indications of a heavy storm brewing. Notwithstanding the severity of the weather, however, both determined to set out for their place of meeting in Yorkshire. Two days before Ballantyne left Edinburgh, he wrote as follows:

Mr. Ballantyne to John Murray. January 4, 1809.

Dear Murray, It is blowing the devil's weather here; but no matter— if the mail goes, I go. I shall travel by the mail, and shall, instantly on arriving, go to the "Crown, " hoping to find you and an imperial dinner. By the bye, you had better, on your arrival, take places north and south for the following day. In four or five hours after your receiving this, I expect to shake your princely paw.

Thine, J.B.

Scott also sent a note by the hand of Ballantyne to tell of his complete rupture with Constable owing to "Mr. Hunter's extreme incivility. "

As a result of these negotiations the Ballantynes were appointed publishers of the new Review in Edinburgh, and, with a view to a more central position, they took premises in South Hanover Street. Scott wrote with reference to this:

Mr. Scott to John Murray.

February, 1809.

I enclose the promised "Swift, " and am now, I think, personally out of your debt, though I will endeavour to stop up gaps if I do not receive the contributions I expect from others. Were I in the neighbourhood of your shop in London I could soon run up half a sheet of trifling articles with a page or two to each, but that is impossible here for lack of materials.

When the Ballantynes open shop you must take care to have them supplied with food for such a stop-gap sort of criticism. I think we will never again feel the pressure we have had for this number; the harvest has literally been great and the labourers few.

Yours truly,

W. S.

Mr. James Ballantyne. to John Murray.

January 27, 1809.

"I see or hear of nothing but good about the *Review*. Mr. Scott is at this moment busy with two articles, besides the one he has sent. In conversation a few days since, I heard a gentleman ask him, 'Pray, sir, do you think the *Quarterly Review* will be equal to the *Edinburgh*? ' His answer was, 'I won't be quite sure of the first number, because of course there are difficulties attending the commencement of every work which time and habit can alone smooth away. But I think the first number will be a good one, and in the course of three or four, *I think we'll sweat them!* '"

The first number of the *Quarterly Review* was published at the end of February, 1809. Like most first numbers, it did not entirely realize the sanguine views of its promoters. It did not burst like a thunderclap on the reading public; nor did it give promise to its friends that a new political power had been born into the world. The general tone was more literary than political; and though it contained much that was well worth reading, none of its articles were of first-rate quality.

Walter Scott was the principal contributor, and was keenly interested in its progress, though his mind was ever teeming with other new schemes. The allusion in the following letter to his publication of "many unauthenticated books, " if unintentional, seems little less than prophetic.

Mr. Scott to John Murray.

Edinburgh, *February* 25, 1809.

Dear Sir,

I see with pleasure that you will be out on the first. Yet I wish I could have seen my articles in proof, for I seldom read over my things in manuscript, and always find infinite room for improvement at the printer's expense. I hope our hurry will not be such another time as to deprive me of the chance of doing the best I can, which depends greatly on my seeing the proofs. Pray have the goodness to attend to this.

I have made for the Ballantynes a little selection of poetry, to be entitled "English Minstrelsy"; I also intend to arrange for them a first volume of English Memoirs, to be entitled—"Secret History of the Court of James I. " To consist of:

Osborne's "Traditional Memoirs. "

Sir Anthony Welldon's "Court and Character of James I. "

Heylin's "Aulicus Coquinariae. "

Sir Edward Peyton's "Rise and Fall of the House of Stewart. "

I will add a few explanatory notes to these curious memoirs, and hope to continue the collection, as (thanks to my constant labour on "Somers") it costs me no expense, and shall cost the proprietors none. You may advertise the publications, and Ballantyne, equally agreeable to his own wish and mine, will let you choose your own share in them. I have a commission for you in the way of art. I have published many unauthenticated books, as you know, and may probably bring forward many more. Now I wish to have it in my power to place on a few copies of each a decisive mark of appropriation. I have chosen for this purpose a device borne by a champion of my name in a tournament at Stirling! It was a gate and portcullis, with the motto CLAUSUS TUTUS ERO. I have it engraved on a seal, as you may remark on the enclosure, but it is done in a most blackguard style. Now what I want is to have this same gateway and this same portcullis and this same motto of *clausus tutus ero*, which is an anagram of *Walterus Scotus* (taking two single U's for the W), cut upon wood in the most elegant manner, so as to make a small vignette capable of being applied to a few copies of every work which I either write or publish. This fancy of making *portcullis* copies I have much at heart, and trust to you to get it accomplished for me in the most elegant manner. I don't mind the expense, and perhaps Mr. Westall might be disposed to make a sketch for me.

I am most anxious to see the *Review*. God grant we may lose no ground; I tremble when I think of my own articles, of two of which I have but an indefinite recollection.

What would you think of an edition of the "Old English Froissart, " say 500 in the small *antique quarto*, a beautiful size of book; the spelling must be brought to an uniformity, the work copied (as I could not promise my beautiful copy to go to press), notes added and illustrations, etc., and inaccuracies corrected. I think Johnes would be driven into most deserved disgrace, and I can get the use of a most curious MS. of the French Froissart in the Newbattle Library, probably the finest in existence after that of Berlin. I am an enthusiast about Berners' Froissart, and though I could not undertake the drudgery of preparing the whole for the press, yet Weber [Footnote: Henry Weber, Scott's amanuensis.] would do it under my eye upon the most reasonable terms. I would revise every part relating to English history.

I have several other literary schemes, but defer mentioning them till I come to London, which I sincerely hope will be in the course of a month or six weeks. I hear Mr. Canning is anxious about our *Review*. Constable says it is a Scotch job. I could not help quizzing Mr. Robert Miller, who asked me in an odd sort of way, as I thought, why it was not out? I said very indifferently I knew nothing about it, but heard a vague report that the Edition was to be much enlarged on account of the expected demand. I also inclose a few lines to my brother, and am, dear Sir,

Very truly yours,

W. Scott.

It is universally agreed here that Cumberland is five hundred degrees beneath contempt.

Ballantyne, Scott's partner, and publisher of the *Review* in Edinburgh, hastened to communicate to Murray their joint views as to the success of the work.

Mr. Ballantyne to John Murray.

February 28, 1809.

My dear Murray,

I received the *Quarterly* an hour ago. Before taking it to Mr. Scott, I had just time to look into the article on Burns, and at the general aspect of the book. It looks uncommonly well.... The view of Burns' character is better than Jeffrey's. It is written in a more congenial tone, with more tender, kindly feeling. Though not perhaps written with such elaborate eloquence as Jeffrey's, the thoughts are more original, and the style equally powerful. The two first articles (and perhaps the rest are not inferior) will confer a name on the *Review*. But why do I trouble you with *my* opinions, when I can give you Mr. Scott's? He has just been reading the Spanish article beside me, and he again and again interrupted himself with expressions of the strongest admiration.

Three days later, Ballantyne again wrote:

"I have now read 'Spain, ' 'Burns, ' 'Woman, ' 'Curran, ' 'Cid, ' 'Carr, ' 'Missionaries. ' Upon the whole, I think these articles most excellent. Mr. Scott is in high spirits; but he says there are evident marks of haste in most of them. With respect to his own articles, he much regrets not to have had the opportunity of revising them. He thinks the 'Missionaries' very clever; but he shakes his head at 'Sidney, ' 'Woman, ' and 'Public Characters. ' Our copies, which we expected this morning, have not made their appearance, which has given us no small anxiety. We are panting to hear the public voice. Depend upon it, *if* our exertions are continued, the thing will do. Would G. were as active as Scott and Murray! "

Murray had plenty of advisers. Gifford said he had too many. His friend, Sharon Turner, was ready with his criticism on No. 1. He deplored the appearance of the article by Scott on "Carr's Tour in Scotland. " [Footnote: Scott himself had written to Murray about this, which he calls "a whisky-frisky article, " on June 30. "I take the advantage of forwarding Sir John's *Review*, to send you back his letters under the same cover. He is an incomparable goose, but as he is innocent and good-natured, I would not like it to be publicly known that the flagellation comes from my hand. Secrecy therefore will oblige me. "]

Mr. Sharon Turner to John Murray.

"I cannot endure the idea of an individual being wounded merely because he has written a book. If, as in the case of the authors attacked in the 'Baviad, ' the works censured were vitiating our literature—or, as in the case of Moore's Poems, corrupting our morals—if they were denouncing our religious principles, or attacking those political principles on which our Government subsists—let them be criticised without mercy. The *salus publica* demands the sacrifice. But to make an individual ridiculous merely because he has written a foolish, if it be a harmless book, is not, I think, justifiable on any moral principle... I repeat my principle. Whatever tends to vitiate our literary taste, our morals, our religious or political principles, may be fairly at the mercy of criticism. So, whatever tends to introduce false science, false history, indeed, falsehood in any shape, exposes itself to the censor's rod. But harmless, inoffensive works should be passed by. Where is the bravery of treading on a worm or crushing a poor fly? Where the utility? Where the honour? "

An edition of 4,000 copies had been printed; this was soon exhausted, and a second edition was called for.

Mr. Scott was ample in his encouragements.

"I think, " he wrote to Murray, "a firm and stable sale will be settled here, to the extent of 1,000 or 1,500 even for the next number.... I am quite pleased with my ten guineas a sheet for my labour in writing, and for additional exertions. I will consider them as overpaid by success in the cause, especially while that success is doubtful. "

Ballantyne wrote to Murray in March:

"Constable, I am told, has consulted Sir Samuel Romilly, and means, after writing a book against me, to prosecute me for *stealing his plans!* Somebody has certainly stolen his brains! "

The confederates continued to encourage each other and to incite to greater effort the procrastinating Gifford. The following rather mysterious paragraph occurs in a letter from Scott to Murray dated March 19, 1809.

"I have found means to get at Mr. G., and have procured a letter to be written to him, which may possibly produce one to you signed Rutherford or Richardson, or some such name, and dated from the North of England; or, if he does not write to you, enquiry is to be made whether he would choose you should address him. The secrecy to be observed in this business must be most profound, even to Ballantyne and all the world. If you get articles from him (which will and must draw attention) you must throw out a false scent for enquirers. I believe this unfortunate man will soon be in London. "

In reply, Mr. Murray wrote on March 24 to Mr. Scott, urging him to come to London, and offering, "if there be no plea for charging your expenses to Government, " to "undertake that the *Review* shall pay them as far as one hundred guineas. " To this Scott replied:

Mr. Scott to John Murray.

Edinburgh, *March* 27, 1809.

I have only time to give a very short answer to your letter. Some very important business detains me here till Monday or Tuesday, on the last of which days at farthest I will set off for town, and will be with you of course at the end of the week. As to my travelling expenses, if Government pay me, good and well; if they do not, depend on it I will never take a farthing from you. You have, my good friend, enough of expense to incur in forwarding this great and dubious undertaking, and God forbid I should add so unreasonable a charge as your liberality points at. I am very frank in money matters, and always take my price when I think I can give money's worth for money, but this is quite extravagant, and you must think no more of it. Should I want money for any purpose I will readily make *you* my banker and give you value in reviews. John Ballantyne's last remittance continues to go off briskly; the devil's in you in London, you don't know good writing when you get it. All depends on our cutting in before the next *Edinburgh*, when instead of following their lead they shall follow ours.

Mrs. Scott is my fellow-traveller in virtue of an old promise. I am, dear Sir, yours truly,

Walter Scott.

April 4, at night.

I have been detained a day later than I intended, but set off to-morrow at mid-day. I believe I shall get *franked*, so will have my generosity for nothing. I hope to be in London on Monday.

In sending out copies of the first number, Mr. Murray was not forgetful of one friend who had taken a leading part in originating the *Review*.

In 1808 Mr. Stratford Canning, when only twenty years of age, had been selected to accompany Mr. Adair on a special mission to Constantinople. The following year, on Mr. Adair being appointed H. B.M. Minister to the Sublime Porte, Stratford Canning became Secretary of Legation. Mr. Murray wrote to him:

John Murray to Mr. Stratford Canning.

32, Fleet St., London, *March* 12, 1809.

Dear Sir,

It is with no small degree of pleasure that I send, for the favour of your acceptance, the first number of the *Quarterly Review*, a work which owes its birth to your obliging countenance and introduction of me to Mr. Gifford. I flatter myself that upon the whole you will not be dissatisfied with our first attempt, which is universally allowed to be so very respectable. Had you been in London during its progress, it would, I am confident, have been rendered more deserving of public attention.

The letter goes on to ask for information on foreign works of importance or interest.

Mr. Stratford Canning replied:

"With regard to the comission which you have given me, it is, I fear, completely out of my power to execute it. Literature neither resides at Constantinople nor passes through it. Even were I able to obtain the publications of France and Germany by way of Vienna, the road is so circuitous, that you would have them later than others who contrive to smuggle them across the North Sea. Every London newspaper that retails its daily sixpennyworth of false reports, publishes the French, the Hamburgh, the Vienna, the Frankfort, and other journals, full as soon as we receive any of them here. This is the case at all times; at present it is much worse. We are entirely insulated. The Russians block up the usual road through Bucharest, and the Servians prevent the passage of couriers through Bosnia. And in addition to these difficulties, the present state of the Continent must at least interrupt all literary works. You will not, I am sure, look upon these as idle excuses. Things may probably improve, and I will not quit this country without commissioning some one here to send you anything that may be of use to so promising a publication as your *Review*. "

No sooner was one number published, than preparations were made for the next. Every periodical is a continuous work—never ending, still beginning. New contributors must be gained; new books reviewed; new views criticised. Mr. Murray was, even more than the editor, the backbone of the enterprise: he was indefatigable in soliciting new writers for the *Quarterly*, and in finding the books fit for review, and the appropriate reviewers of the books. Sometimes the reviews were printed before the editor was consulted, but everything passed under the notice of Gifford, and received his emendations and final approval.

Mr. Murray went so far as to invite Leigh Hunt to contribute an article on Literature or Poetry for the *Quarterly*. The reply came from John Hunt, Leigh's brother. He said:

Mr. John Hunt to John Murray.
"My brother some days back requested me to present to you his thanks for the polite note you favoured him with on the subject of the *Review*, to which he should have been most willing to have contributed in the manner you propose, did he not perceive that the political sentiments contained in it are in direct opposition to his own. "

This was honest, and it did not interfere with the personal intercourse of the publisher and the poet. Murray afterwards wrote to Scott: "Hunt is most vilely wrong-headed in politics, which he has allowed to turn him away from the path of elegant criticism, which might have led him to eminence and respectability. "

James Mill, author of the "History of British India, " sent an article for the second number; but the sentiments and principles not being in accordance with those of the editor, it was not at once accepted. On learning this, he wrote to Mr. Murray as follows:

Mr. James Mill to John Murray.

My dear Sir,

I can have no objection in the world to your delaying the article I have sent you till it altogether suits your arrangements to make use of it. Besides this point, a few words of explanation may not be altogether useless with regard to another. I am half inclined to suspect that the objection of your Editor goes a little farther than you state. If so, I beg you will not hesitate a moment about what you are to do with it. I wrote it solely with a view to oblige and to benefit *you personally*, but with very little idea, as I told you at our first conversation on the subject, that it would be in my power to be of any use to you, as the views which I entertained respecting what is good for our country were very different from the views entertained by the gentlemen with whom in your projected concern you told me you were to be connected. To convince you, however, of my good-will, I am perfectly ready to give you a specimen, and if it appears to be such as likely to give offence to your friends, or not to harmonise with the general style of your work, commit it to the flames without the smallest scruple. Be assured that it will not make the smallest difference in my sentiments towards you, or render me in the smallest degree less disposed to lend you my aid (such as it is) on any other occasion when it may be better calculated to be of use to you.

Yours very truly,

J. Mill.

Gifford was not a man of business; he was unpunctual. The second number of the *Quarterly* appeared behind its time, and the publisher felt himself under the necessity of expostulating with the editor.

John Murray to Mr. Gifford.

May 11, 1809.

Dear Mr. Gifford,

I begin to suspect that you are not aware of the complete misery which is occasioned to me, and the certain ruin which must attend the *Review*, by our unfortunate procrastination. Long before this, every line of copy for the present number ought to have been in the hands of the printer. Yet the whole of the *Review* is yet to print. I know not what to do to facilitate your labour, for the articles which you have long had he scattered without attention, and those which I ventured to send to the printer undergo such retarding corrections, that even by this mode we do not advance. I entreat the favour of your exertion. For the last five months my most imperative concerns have yielded to this, without the hope of my anxiety or labour ceasing.

"Tanti miserere laboris, "

in my distress and with regret from

John Murray.

Mr. Gifford's reply was as follows:

"The delay and confusion which have arisen must be attributed to a want of confidential communication. In a word, you have too many advisers, and I too many masters. "

At last the second number of the *Quarterly* appeared, at the end of May instead of at the middle of April. The new contributors to this number were Dr. D'Oyley, the Rev. Mr. Walpole, and George Canning, who, in conjunction with Sharon Turner, contributed the last article on Austrian State Papers.

As soon as the second number was published, Mr. Gifford, whose health was hardly equal to the constant strain of preparing and editing the successive numbers, hastened away, as was his custom, to the seaside. He wrote to Mr. Murray from Ryde:

Mr. Gifford to John Murray.

June 18, 1809.

"I rejoice to hear of our success, and feel very anxious to carry it further. A fortnight's complete abstraction from all sublunary cares has done me much good, and I am now ready to put on my spectacles and look about me.... Hoppner is here, and has been at Death's door. The third day after his arrival, he had an apoplectic fit, from which blisters, etc., have miraculously recovered him.... This morning I received a letter from Mr. Erskine. He speaks very highly of the second number, and of the Austrian article, which is thought its chief attraction. Theology, he says, few people read or care about. On this, I wish to say a word seriously. I am sorry that Mr. E. has fallen into that notion, too general I fear in Scotland; but this is his own concern. I differ with him totally, however, as to the few readers which such subjects find; for as far as my knowledge reaches, the reverse is the fact. The strongest letter which I have received since I came down, in our favour, points out the two serious articles as masterly productions and of decided superiority. We have taught the truth I mention to the *Edinburgh Review,* and in their last number they have also attempted to be serious, and abstain from their flippant impiety. It is not done with the best grace, but it has done them credit, I hear.... When you make up your parcel, pray put in some small cheap 'Horace, ' which I can no more do without than

Parson Adams *ex* 'Aeschylus. ' I have left it somewhere on the road. Any common thing will do. "

Mr. Murray sent Gifford a splendid copy of "Horace" in the next parcel of books and manuscripts. In his reply Gifford, expostulating, "Why, my dear Sir, will you do these things? " thanked him warmly for his gift.

Mr. George Ellis was, as usual, ready with his criticism. Differing from Gifford, he wrote:

"I confess that, to my taste, the long article on the New Testament is very tedious, and that the progress of Socinianism is, to my apprehension, a bugbear which *we* have no immediate reason to be scared by; but it may alarm some people, and what I think a dull prosing piece of orthodoxy may have its admirers, and promote our sale. "

Even Constable had a good word to say of it. In a letter to his partner, Hunter, then in London, he said:

"I received the *Quarterly Review* yesterday, and immediately went and delivered it to Mr. Jeffrey himself. It really seems a respectable number, but what then? Unless theirs improves and ours falls off it cannot harm us, I think. I observe that Nos. 1 and 2 extend to merely twenty-nine sheets, so that, in fact, ours is still the cheaper of the two. Murray's waiting on you with it is one of the wisest things I ever knew him do: you will not be behindhand with him in civility. "

No. 3 of the *Quarterly* was also late, and was not published until the end of August. The contributors were behindhand; an article was expected from Canning on Spain, and the publication was postponed until this article had been received, printed and corrected. The foundations of it were laid by George Ellis, and it was completed by George Canning.

Of this article Mr. Gifford wrote:

"In consequence of my importunity, Mr. Canning has exerted himself and produced the best article that ever yet appeared in any Review. "

Although Mr. Gifford was sometimes the subject of opprobrium because of his supposed severity, we find that in many cases he softened down the tone of the reviewers. For instance, in communicating to Mr. Murray the first part of Dr. Thomson's article on the "Outlines of Mineralogy, " by Kidd, he observed:

Mr. Gifford to John Murray.

"It is very splenitick and very severe, and much too wantonly so. I hope, however, it is just. Some of the opprobrious language I shall soften, for the eternal repetitions of *ignorance, absurdity, surprising,* etc., are not wanted. I am sorry to observe so much Nationality in it. Let this be a secret between us, for I will not have my private opinions go beyond yourself. As for Kidd, he is a modest, unassuming man, and is not to be attacked with sticks and stones like a savage. Remember, it is only the epithets which I mean to soften; for as to the scientific part, it shall not be meddled with. "

His faithful correspondent, Mr. Ellis, wrote as to the quality of this third number of the *Quarterly*. He agreed with Mr. Murray, that though profound, it was "most notoriously and unequivocally *dull*.... We must veto ponderous articles; they will simply sink us. "

Isaac D'Israeli also tendered his advice. He was one of Mr. Murray's most intimate friends, and could speak freely and honestly to him as to the prospects of the *Review*. He was at Brighton, preparing his third volume of the "Curiosities of Literature. "

Mr. I. D'Israeli to John Murray.

"I have bought the complete collection of Memoirs written by individuals of the French nation, amounting to sixty-five volumes, for fifteen guineas.... What can I say about the *Q. R.?* Certainly nothing new; it has not yet invaded the country. Here it is totally unknown, though as usual the *Ed. Rev.* is here; but among private libraries, I find it equally unknown. It has yet its fortune to make. You must appeal to the *feelings* of Gifford! Has he none then? Can't you get a more active and vigilant Editor? But what can I say at this distance? The disastrous finale of the Austrians, received this morning, is felt here as deadly. Buonaparte is a tremendous Thaumaturgus!... I wish you had such a genius in the *Q. R.....* My son Ben assures me you are in Brighton. He saw you! Now, he never lies." [Footnote: Mr. Murray was in Brighton at the time.]

Thus pressed by his correspondents, Mr. Murray did his best to rescue the *Quarterly* from failure. Though it brought him into prominent notice as a publisher, it was not by any means paying its expenses. Some thought it doubtful whether "the play was worth the candle. " Yet Murray was not a man to be driven back by comparative want of success. He continued to enlist a band of competent contributors. Amongst these were some very eminent men: Mr. John Barrow of the Admiralty; the Rev. Reginald Heber, Mr. Robert Grant (afterwards Sir Robert, the Indian judge), Mr. Stephens, etc. How Mr. Barrow was induced to become a contributor is thus explained in his Autobiography. [Footnote: "Autobiographical Memoir of Sir John Barrow, " Murray, 1847.]

"One morning, in the summer of the year 1809, Mr. Canning looked in upon me at the Admiralty, said he had often troubled me on business, but he was now about to ask me a favour. 'I believe you are acquainted with my friend William Gifford? ' 'By reputation, ' I said, 'but not personally. ' 'Then, ' says he, 'I must make you personally acquainted; will you come and dine with me at Gloucester Lodge any day, the sooner the more agreeable—say to-morrow, if you are disengaged? ' On accepting, he said, 'I will send for Gifford to meet you; I know he will be too glad to come. '

"'Now, ' he continued, 'it is right I should tell you that, in the *Review* of which two numbers have appeared, under the name of the *Quarterly*, I am deeply, both publicly and personally, interested, and have taken a leading part with Mr. George Ellis, Hookham Frere, Walter Scott, Rose, Southey, and some others; our object in that work being to counteract the *virus* scattered among His Majesty's subjects through the pages of the *Edinburgh Review*. Now, I wish to enlist you in our corps, not as a mere advising idler, but as an efficient labourer in our friend Gifford's vineyard. '"

Mr. Barrow modestly expressed a doubt as to his competence, but in the sequel, he tells us, Mr. Canning carried his point, and "I may add, once for all, that what with Gifford's eager and urgent demands, and the exercise becoming habitual and not disagreeable, I did not cease writing for the *Quarterly Review* till I had supplied no less, rather more, than 190 articles. "

The fourth number of the *Quarterly*, which was due in November, was not published until the end of December 1809. Gifford's excuse was the want of copy. He wrote to Mr. Murray: "We must, upon the publication of this number, enter into some plan for ensuring regularity. "

Although it appeared late, the fourth number was the best that had yet been issued. It was more varied in its contents; containing articles by Scott, Southey, Barrow, and Heber. But the most important article was contributed by Robert Grant, on the "Character of the late C. J. Fox. " This was the first article in the *Quarterly*, according to Mr. Murray, which excited general admiration, concerning which we find a memorandum in Mr. Murray's own copy; and, what was an important test, it largely increased the demand for the *Review*.

CHAPTER VII

CONSTABLE AND BALLANTYNE

During the year in which the *Quarterly* was first given to the world, the alliance between Murray and the Ballantynes was close and intimate: their correspondence was not confined to business matters, but bears witness to warm personal friendship.

Murray was able to place much printing work in their hands, and amongst other books, "Mrs. Rundell's Cookery, " a valuable property, which had now reached a very large circulation, was printed at the Canongate Press.

They exerted themselves to promote the sale of one another's publications and engaged in various joint works, such, for example, as Grahame's "British Georgics" and Scott's "English Minstrelsy. "

In the midst of all these transactions, however, there were not wanting symptoms of financial difficulties, which, as in a previous instance, were destined in time to cause a severance between Murray and his Edinburgh agents. It was the old story—drawing bills for value *not* received. Murray seriously warned the Ballantynes of the risks they were running in trading beyond their capital. James Ballantyne replied on March 30, 1809:

Mr. James Ballantyne to John Murray.

"Suffer me to notice one part of your letter respecting which you will be happy to be put right. We are by no means trading beyond our capital. It requires no professional knowledge to enable us to avoid so fatal an error as that. For the few speculations we have entered into our means have been carefully calculated and are perfectly adequate. "

Yet at the close of the same letter, referring to the "British Novelists"—a vast scheme, to which Mr. Murray had by no means pledged himself—Ballantyne continues:

"For this work permit me to state I have ordered a font of types, cut expressly on purpose, at an expense of near £1,000, and have engaged a very large number of compositors for no other object. "

On June 14, James Ballantyne wrote to Murray:

"I can get no books out yet, without interfering in the printing office with business previously engaged for, and that puts me a little about for cash. Independent of *this* circumstance, upon which we reckoned, a sum of £1,500 payable to us at 25th May, yet waiting some cursed legal arrangements, but which we trust to have very shortly [*sic*]. This is all preliminary to the enclosures which I hope will not be disagreeable to you, and if not, I will trust to their receipt *accepted*, by return of post. "

Mr. Murray replied on June 20:

"I regret that I should be under the necessity of returning you the two bills which you enclosed, unaccepted; but having settled lately a very large amount with Mr. Constable, I had occasion to grant more bills than I think it proper to allow to be about at the same time. "

This was not the last application for acceptances, and it will be found that in the end it led to an entire separation between the firms.

The Ballantynes, however, were more sanguine than prudent. In spite of Mr. Murray's warning that they were proceeding too rapidly with the publication of new works, they informed him that they had a "gigantic scheme" in hand—the "Tales of the East, " translated by Henry Weber, Walter Scott's private secretary—besides the "Edinburgh Encyclopaedia, " and the "Secret Memoirs of the House of Stewart. " They said that Scott was interested in the "Tales of the East, " and in one of their hopeful letters they requested Mr. Murray to join in their speculations. His answer was as follows:

John Murray to Messrs. Ballantyne & Co.

October 31, 1809.

"I regret that I cannot accept a share in the 'Edinburgh Encyclopaedia. ' I am obliged to decline by motives of prudence. I do not know anything of the agreement made by the proprietors, except in the palpable mismanagement of a very exclusive and promising concern. I am therefore fearful to risk my property in an affair so extremely unsuitable.

"You distress me sadly by the announcement of having put the 'Secret Memoirs' to press, and that the paper for it was actually purchased six months ago! How can you, my good sirs, act in this way? How can you imagine that a bookseller can afford to pay eternal advances upon almost every work in which he takes a share with you? And how can you continue to destroy every speculation by entering upon new ones before the previous ones are properly completed?... Why, with your influence, will you not urge the completion of the 'Minstrelsy'? Why not go on with and complete the series of De Foe?... For myself, I really do not know what to do, for when I see that you will complete nothing of your own, I am unwillingly apprehensive of having any work of mine in your power. What I thus write is in serious friendship for you. I entreat you to let us complete what we have already in hand, before we begin upon any other speculation. You will have enough to do to sell those in which we are already engaged. As to your mode of exchange and so disposing of your shares, besides the universal obloquy which attends the practice in the mind of every respectable bookseller, and the certain damnation which it invariably causes both to the book and the author, as in the case of Grahame, if persisted in, it must end in serious loss to the bookseller.... If you cannot give me your solemn promise not to exchange a copy of Tasso, I trust you will allow me to withdraw the small share which I propose to take, for the least breath of this kind would blast the work and the author too—a most worthy man, upon whose account alone I engaged in the speculation. "

Constable, with whom Murray had never entirely broken, had always looked with jealousy at the operations of the house of Ballantyne. Their firm had indeed been started in opposition to himself; and it was not without a sort of gratification that he heard of their pecuniary difficulties, and of the friction between them and Murray. Scott's "Lady of the Lake" had been announced for publication. At the close of a letter to Murray, Constable rather maliciously remarks:

January 20, 1810.

"I have no particular anxiety about promulgating the folly (to say the least of it) of certain correspondents of yours in this quarter; but if you will ask our friend Mr. Miller if he had a letter from a shop nearly opposite the Royal Exchange the other day, he will, I dare say, tell you of the contents. I am mistaken if their game is not well up!

Indeed I doubt much if they will survive the 'Lady of the Lake. ' She will probably help to drown them! "

An arrangement had been made with the Ballantynes that, in consideration of their being the sole agents for Mr. Murray in Scotland, they should give him the opportunity of taking shares in any of their publications. Instead, however, of offering a share of the "Lady of the Lake" to Mr. Murray, according to the understanding between the firms, the Ballantynes had already parted with one fourth share of the work to Mr. Miller, of Albemarle Street, London, whose business was afterwards purchased by Mr. Murray. Mr. Murray's letter to Ballantyne & Co. thus describes the arrangement:

John Murray to Messrs. Ballantyne & Co.

March 26, 1810.

"Respecting my *Review*, you appear to forget that your engagement was that I should be your sole agent here, and that you were to publish nothing but what I was to have the offer of a share in. Your deviation from this must have led me to conclude that you did not desire or expect to continue my agent any longer. You cannot suppose that my estimation of Mr. Scott's genius can have rendered me indifferent to my exclusion from a share in the 'Lady of the Lake.' I mention this as well to testify that I am not indifferent to this conduct in you as to point it out to you, that if you mean to withhold from me that portion which you command of the advantages of our connexion, you must surely mean to resign any that might arise from me. The sole agency for my publications in Edinburgh is worth to any man who understands his business £300 a year; but this requires zealous activity and deference on one side, and great confidence on both, otherwise the connexion cannot be advantageous or satisfactory to either party. For this number of the *Review* I have continued your name solely in it, and propose to make you as before sole publisher in Scotland; but as you have yourself adopted the plan of drawing upon me for the amount of each transaction, you will do me the favour to consider what quantity you will need, and upon your remitting to me a note at six months for the amount, I shall immediately ship the quantity for you. "

Mr. James Ballantyne to John Murray.

"Your agency hitherto has been productive of little or no advantage to us, and the fault has not lain with us. We have persisted in offering you shares of everything begun by us, till we found the hopelessness of waiting any return; and in dividing Mr. Scott's poem, we found it our duty to give what share we had to part with to those by whom we were chiefly benefited both as booksellers and printers. "

This letter was accompanied with a heavy bill for printing the works of De Foe for Mr. Murray. A breach thus took place with the Ballantynes; the publisher of the *Quarterly* was compelled to look out for a new agent for Scotland, and met with a thoroughly competent one in Mr. William Blackwood, the founder of the well-known publishing house in Edinburgh.

To return to the progress of the *Quarterly*. The fifth number, which was due in February 1810, but did not appear until the end of March, contained many excellent articles, though, as Mr. Ellis said, some of them were contributed by "good and steady but marvellously heavy friends. " Yet he found it better than the *Edinburgh*, which on that occasion was "reasonably dull. "

It contained one article which became the foundation of an English classic, that of Southey on the "Life of Nelson. " Of this article Murray wrote to its author:

"I wish it to be made such a book as shall become the heroic text of every midshipman in the Navy, and the association of Nelson and Southey will not, I think, be ungrateful to you. If it be worth your attention in this way I am disposed to think that it will enable me to treble the sum I first offered as a slight remuneration. "

Mr. Murray, writing to Mr. Scott (August 28, 1810) as to the appearance of the new number, which did not appear till a month and a half after it was due, remarked on the fourth article. "This, " he said, "is a review of the 'Daughters of Isenberg, a Bavarian Romance,' by Mr. Gifford, to whom the authoress (Alicia T. Palmer) had the temerity to send three £1 notes! " Gifford, instead of sending back the money with indignation, as he at first proposed, reviewed the romance, and assumed that the authoress had sent him the money for charitable purposes.

Mr. Gifford to Miss A. T. Palmer.

"Our avocations leave us but little leisure for extra-official employment; and in the present case she has inadvertently added to our difficulties by forbearing to specify the precise objects of her bounty. We hesitated for some time between the Foundling and Lying in Hospitals: in finally determining for the latter, we humbly trust that we have not disappointed her expectations, nor misapplied her charity. Our publisher will transmit the proper receipt to her address. "

One of the principal objections of Mr. Murray to the manner in which Mr. Gifford edited the *Quarterly* was the war which he waged with the *Edinburgh*. This, he held, was not the way in which a respectable periodical should be conducted. It had a line of its own to pursue, without attacking its neighbours. "Publish, " he said, "the best information, the best science, the best literature; and leave the public to decide for themselves. " Relying on this opinion he warned Gifford and his friends against attacking Sydney Smith, and Leslie, and Jeffrey, because of their contributions to the *Edinburgh*. He thought that such attacks had only the effect of advertising the rival journal, and rendering it of greater importance. With reference to the article on Sydney Smith's "Visitation Sermon" in No. 5, Mr. George Ellis privately wrote to Mr. Murray:

"Gifford, though the best-tempered man alive, is *terribly* severe with his pen; but S. S. would suffer ten times more by being turned into ridicule (and never did man expose himself so much as he did in that sermon) than from being slashed and cauterized in that manner. "

The following refers to a difference of opinion between Mr. Murray and his editor. Mr. Gifford had resented some expression of his friend's as savouring of intimidation.

John Murray to Mr. Gifford.

September 25, 1810.

"I entreat you to be assured that the term 'intimidation' can never be applied to any part of my conduct towards you, for whom I entertain the highest esteem and regard, both as a writer and as a friend. If I am over-anxious, it is because I have let my hopes of fame as a bookseller rest upon the establishment and celebrity of this journal.

My character, as well with my professional brethren as with the public, is at stake upon it; for I would not be thought silly by the one, or a mere speculator by the other. I have a very large business, as you may conclude by the capital I have been able to throw into this one publication, and yet my mind is so entirely engrossed, my honour is so completely involved in this one thing, that I neither eat, drink, nor sleep upon anything else. I would rather it excelled all other journals and I gained nothing by it, than gain £300 a year by it without trouble if it were thought inferior to any other. This, sir, is true. "

Meanwhile, Mr. Murray was becoming hard pressed for money. To conduct his increasing business required a large floating capital, for long credits were the custom, and besides his own requirements, he had to bear the constant importunities of the Ballantynes to renew their bills. On July 25, 1810, he wrote to them: "This will be the last renewal of the bill (£300); when it becomes due, you will have the goodness to provide for it. " It was, however, becoming impossible to continue dealing with them, and he gradually transferred his printing business to other firms. We find him about this time ordering Messrs. George Ramsay & Co., Edinburgh, to print 8,000 of the "Domestic Cookery, " which was still having a large sale.

The Constables also were pressing him for renewals of bills. The correspondence of this date is full of remonstrances from Murray against the financial unpunctuality of his Edinburgh correspondents.

On March 21, 1811, he writes: "With regard to myself, I will engage in no new work of any kind"; and again, on April 4, 1811:

Dear Constable,

You know how much I have distressed myself by entering heedlessly upon too many engagements. You must not urge me to involve myself in renewed difficulties.

To return to the *Quarterly* No. 8. Owing to the repeated delay in publication, the circulation fell off from 5,000 to 4,000, and Mr. George Ellis had obviously reason when he wrote: "Hence I infer that *punctuality* is, in our present situation, our great and only desideratum. "

Accordingly, increased efforts were made to have the *Quarterly* published with greater punctuality, though it was a considerable time before success in this respect was finally reached. Gifford pruned and pared down to the last moment, and often held back the publication until an erasure or a correction could be finally inserted.

No. 9, due in February 1811, was not published until March. From this time Southey became an almost constant contributor to the *Review*. He wrote with ease, grace, and rapidity, and there was scarcely a number without one, and sometimes two and even three articles from his pen. His prose style was charming—clear, masculine, and to the point. The public eagerly read his prose, while his poetry remained unnoticed on the shelves. The poet could not accept this view of his merits. Of the "Curse of Kehama" he wrote:

"I was perfectly aware that I was planting acorns while my contemporaries were setting Turkey beans. The oak will grow, and though I may never sit under its shade, my children will. Of the 'Lady of the Lake, ' 25,000 copies have been printed; of 'Kehama', 500; and if they sell in seven years I shall be surprised. "

Scott wrote a kindly notice of Southey's poem. It was not his way to cut up his friend in a review. He pointed out the beauties of the poem, in order to invite purchasers and readers. Yet his private opinion to his friend George Ellis was this:

Mr. Scott to Mr. G. Ellis.

"I have run up an attempt on the 'Curse of Kehama' for the *Quarterly*: a strange thing it is—the 'Curse, ' I mean—and the critique is not, as the blackguards say, worth a damn; but what I could I did, which was to throw as much weight as possible upon the beautiful passages, of which there are many, and to slur over its absurdities, of which there are not a few. It is infinite pity for Southey, with genius almost to exuberance, so much learning and real good feeling of poetry, that, with the true obstinacy of a foolish papa, he *will* be most attached to the defects of his poetical offspring. This said 'Kehama' affords cruel openings to the quizzers, and I suppose will get it roundly in the *Edinburgh Review*. I could have made a very different hand of it indeed, had the order of the day been *pour déchirer*. "

It was a good thing for Southey that he could always depend upon his contributions to the *Quarterly* for his daily maintenance, for he could not at all rely upon the income from his poetry.

The failure of the *Edinburgh Annual Register*, published by Ballantyne, led to a diminution of Southey's income amounting to about £400 a year. He was thus led to write more and more for the *Quarterly*. His reputation, as well as his income, rose higher from his writings there than from any of his other works. In April 1812 he wrote to his friend Mr. Wynn:

Mr. Southey to Mr. Wynn.

"By God's blessing I may yet live to make all necessary provision myself. My means are now improving every year. I am up the hill of difficulty, and shall very soon get rid of the burthen which has impeded me in the ascent. I have some arrangements with Murray, which are likely to prove more profitable than any former speculations... Hitherto I have been highly favoured. A healthy body, an active mind, and a cheerful heart, are the three best boons Nature can bestow, and, God be praised, no man ever enjoyed these more perfectly. "

CHAPTER VIII

MURRAY AND GIFFORD—RUPTURE WITH CONSTABLE—
PROSPERITY OF THE "QUARTERLY"

A good understanding was now established between Mr. Murray
and his editor, and the *Quarterly* went on improving and gradually
increased in circulation. Though regular in the irregularity of its
publication, the subscribers seem to have become accustomed to the
delay, and when it did make its appearance it was read with
eagerness and avidity. The interest and variety of its contents, and
the skill of the editor in the arrangement of his materials, made up
for many shortcomings.

Murray and Gifford were in constant communication, and it is
interesting to remember that the writer of the following judicious
criticism had been editor of the *Anti-Jacobin* before he was editor of
the *Quarterly*.

Mr. Gifford to John Murray.

May 17, 1811.

"I have seldom been more pleased and vexed at a time than with the
perusal of the enclosed MS. It has wit, it has ingenuity, but both are
absolutely lost in a negligence of composition which mortifies me.
Why will your young friend fling away talent which might so
honourably distinguish him? He might, if be chose, be the ornament
of our *Review*, instead of creating in one mingled regret and
admiration. It is utterly impossible to insert such a composition as
the present; there are expressions which would not be borne; and if,
as you say, it will be sent to Jeffrey's if I do not admit it, however I
may grieve, I must submit to the alternative. Articles of pure humour
should be written with extraordinary attention. A vulgar laugh is
detestable. I never saw much merit in writing rapidly. You will
believe me when I tell you that I have been present at the production
of more genuine wit and humour than almost any person of my
time, and that it was revised and polished and arranged with a
scrupulous care which overlooked nothing. I have not often seen
fairer promises of excellence in this department than in your
correspondent; but I tell you frankly that they will all be blighted

and perish prematurely unless sedulously cultivated. It is a poor ambition to raise a casual laugh in the unreflecting.

The article did not appear in the *Quarterly*, and Mr. Pillans, the writer, afterwards became a contributor to the *Edinburgh Review*.

In a letter of August 25, 1811, we find Gifford writing to a correspondent: "Since the hour I was born I never enjoyed, as far as I can recollect, what you call *health* for a single day. " In November, after discussing in a letter the articles which were about to appear in the next *Review*, he concluded: "I write in pain and must break off. " In the following month Mr. Murray, no doubt in consideration of the start which his *Review* had made, sent him a present of £500. "I thank you, " he answered (December 6), "very sincerely for your magnificent present; but £500 is a vast sum. However, you know your own business. "

Yet Mr. Murray was by no means abounding in wealth. There were always those overdrawn bills from Edinburgh to be met, and Ballantyne and Constable were both tugging at him for accommodation at the same time.

The business arrangements with Constable & Co., which, save for the short interruption which has already been related, had extended over many years, were now about to come to an end. The following refers to the purchase of Mr. Miller's stock and the removal of Mr. Murray's business to Albemarle Street.

John Murray to Mr. Constable.

ALBEMARLE ST., *October* 27, 1812.

"I do not see any existing reason why we, who have so long been so very intimate, should now be placed in a situation of negative hostility. I am sure that we are well calculated to render to each other great services; you are the best judge whether your interests were ever before so well attended to as by me... The great connexion which I have for the last two years been maturing in Fleet Street I am now going to bring into action here; and it is not with any view to, or with any reliance upon, what Miller has done, but upon what I know I can do in such a situation, that I had long made up my mind to move. It is no sudden thing, but one long matured; and it is only from the accident of Miller's moving that I have taken his house; so that the notions which, I am told, you entertain respecting my plans are totally outside the ideas upon which it was formed.... I repeat, it is in my power to do you many services; and, certainly, I have bought very largely of you, and you never of me; and you know very well that I will serve you heartily if I can deal with you confidentially. "

A truce was, for a time, made between the firms, but it proved hollow. The never-ending imposition of accommodation bills sent for acceptance had now reached a point beyond endurance, having regard to Murray's credit. The last letter from Murray to Constable & Co. was as follows:

John Murray to Constable & Co.

April 30, 1813.

GENTLEMEN,

I did not answer the letter to which the enclosed alludes, because its impropriety in all respects rendered it impossible for me to do so without involving myself in a personal dispute, which it is my anxious resolution to avoid: and because my determination was fully taken to abide by what I told you in my former letter, to which alone I can or could have referred you. You made an express proposition to me, to which, as you have deviated from it, it is not my intention to accede. The books may remain with me upon sale or return, until you please to order them elsewhere; and in the meantime I shall continue to avail myself of every opportunity to sell them. I return, therefore, an account and bills, with which I have nothing to do, and desire to have a regular invoice.

I am, gentlemen, yours truly,

J. MURRAY.

Constable & Co. fired off a final shot on May 28 following, and the correspondence and business between the firms then terminated.

No. 12 of the *Quarterly* appeared in December 1811, and perhaps the most interesting article in the number was that by Canning and Ellis, on Trotter's "Life of Fox. " Gifford writes to Murray about this article:

"I have not seen Canning yet, but he is undoubtedly at work by this time. Pray take care that no one gets a sight of the slips. It will be a delightful article, but say not a word till it comes out. "

A pamphlet had been published by W. S. Landor, dedicated to the President of the United States, entitled, "Remarks upon Memoirs of Mr. Fox lately published. " Gifford was furious about it. He wrote to Murray:

Mr. Gifford to John Murray.

"I never read so rascally a thing as the Dedication. It is almost too bad for the Eatons and other publishers of mad democratic books. In the pamphlet itself there are many clever bits, but there is no taste and little judgment. His attacks on private men are very bad. Those on Mr. C. are too stupid to do much harm, or, indeed, any. The Dedication is the most abject piece of business that I ever read. It shows Landor to have a most rancorous and malicious heart. Nothing but a rooted hatred of his country could have made him dedicate his Jacobinical book to the most contemptible wretch that ever crept into authority, and whose only recommendation to him is his implacable enmity to his country. I think you might write to Southey; but I would not, on any account, have you publish such a scoundrel address. "

The only entire article ever contributed to the *Review* by Gifford himself was that which he wrote, in conjunction with Barron Field, on Ford's "Dramatic Works. " It was an able paper, but it contained a passage, the publication of which occasioned Gifford the deepest regret. Towards the conclusion of the article these words occurred: The Editor "has polluted his pages with the blasphemies of a poor maniac, who, it seems, once published some detached scenes of the 'Broken Heart. '" This referred to Charles Lamb, who likened the "transcendent scene [of the Spartan boy and Calantha] in imagination to Calvary and the Cross. " Now Gifford had never heard of the personal history of Lamb, nor of the occasional fits of lunacy to which his sister Mary was subject; and when the paragraph was brought to his notice by Southey, through Murray, it caused him unspeakable distress. He at once wrote to Southey [Footnote: When the subject of a memoir of Charles Lamb by Serjeant Talfourd was under consideration, Southey wrote to a friend: "I wish that I had looked out for Mr. Talfourd the letter which Gifford wrote in reply to one in which I remonstrated with him upon

88

his designation of Lamb as a poor maniac. The words were used in complete ignorance of their peculiar bearings, and I believe nothing in the course of Gifford's life ever occasioned him so much self-reproach. He was a man with whom I had no literary sympathies; perhaps there was nothing upon which we agreed, except great political questions; but I liked him the better ever after for his conduct on this occasion. "] the following letter:

Mr. W. Gifford to Mr. Southey.

February 13, 1812.

MY DEAR SIR,

I break off here to say that I have this moment received your last letter to Murray. It has grieved and shocked me beyond expression; but, my dear friend, I am innocent so far as the intent goes. I call God to witness that in the whole course of my life I never heard one syllable of Mr. Lamb or his family. I knew not that he ever had a sister, or that he had parents living, or that he or any person connected with him had ever manifested the slightest tendency to insanity. In a word, I declare to you *in the most solemn manner* that all I ever knew or ever heard of Mr. Lamb was merely his name. Had I been aware of one of the circumstances which you mention, I would have lost my right arm sooner than have written what I have. The truth is, that I was shocked at seeing him compare the sufferings and death of a person who just continues to dance after the death of his lover is announced (for this is all his merit) to the pangs of Mount Calvary; and not choosing to attribute it to folly, because I reserved that charge for Weber, I unhappily in the present case ascribed it to madness, for which I pray God to forgive me, since the blow has fallen heavily when I really thought it would not be felt. I considered Lamb as a thoughtless scribbler, who, in circumstances of ease, amused himself by writing on any subject. Why I thought so, I cannot tell, but it was the opinion I formed to myself, for I now regret to say I never made any inquiry upon the subject; nor by any accident in the whole course of my life did I hear him mentioned beyond the name.

I remain, my dear Sir,

Yours most sincerely,

W. GIFFORD.

It is unnecessary to describe in detail the further progress of the *Quarterly*. The venture was now fairly launched. Occasionally, when some friction arose from the editorial pruning of Southey's articles, or when Mr. Murray remonstrated with the exclusion or inclusion of some particular article, Mr. Gifford became depressed, or complained, "This business begins to get too heavy for me, and I must soon have done, I fear. " Such discouragement was only momentary. Gifford continued to edit the *Review* for many years, until and long after its complete success had become assured.

The following extract, from a letter of Southey's to his friend Bedford, describes very happily the position which Mr. Murray had now attained.

"Murray offers me a thousand guineas for my intended poem in blank verse, and begs it may not be a line longer than "Thomson's Seasons"! I rather think the poem will be a post obit, and in that case, twice that sum, at least, may be demanded for it. What his real feelings may be towards me, I cannot tell; but he is a happy fellow, living in the light of his own glory. The *Review* is the greatest of all works, and it is all his own creation; he prints 10,000, and fifty times ten thousand read its contents, in the East and in the West. Joy be with him and his journal! "

CHAPTER IX

LORD BYRON'S WORKS, 1811 TO 1814

The origin of Mr. Murray's connection with Lord Byron was as follows. Lord Byron had made Mr. Dallas [Footnote: Robert Charles Dallas (1754-1824). His sister married Captain George Anson Byron, and her descendants now hold the title.] a present of the MS. of the first two cantos of "Childe Harold, " and allowed him to make arrangements for their publication. Mr. Dallas's first intention was to offer them to the publisher of "English Bards and Scotch Reviewers, " but Cawthorn did not rank sufficiently high among his brethren of the trade. He was precluded from offering them to Longman & Co. because of their refusal to publish the Satire. He then went to Mr. Miller, of Albemarle Street, and left the manuscript with him, "enjoining the strictest secrecy as to the author. " After a few days' consideration Miller declined to publish the poem, principally because of the sceptical stanzas which it contained, and also because of its denunciation as a "plunderer" of his friend and patron the Earl of Elgin, who was mentioned by name in the original manuscript of the poem.

After hearing from Dallas that Miller had declined to publish "Childe Harold, " Lord Byron wrote to him from Reddish's Hotel:

Lord Byron to Mr. Miller.

July 30, 1811.

SIR,

I am perfectly aware of the justice of your remarks, and am convinced that if ever the poem is published the same objections will be made in much stronger terms. But, as it was intended to be a poem on *Ariosto's plan*, that is to say on *no plan* at all, and, as is usual in similar cases, having a predilection for the worst passages, I shall retain those parts, though I cannot venture to defend them. Under these circumstances I regret that you decline the publication, on my own account, as I think the book would have done better in your hands; the pecuniary part, you know, I have nothing to do with.... But I can perfectly conceive, and indeed approve your reasons, and assure you my sensations are not *Archiepiscopal* enough as yet to regret the rejection of my Homilies.

I am, Sir, your very obedient, humble servant,

BYRON.

"Next to these publishers, " proceeds Dallas, in his "Recollections of the Life of Lord Byron, " "I wished to oblige Mr. Murray, who had then a shop opposite St. Dunstan's Church, in Fleet Street. Both he and his father before him had published for myself. He had expressed to me his regret that I did not carry him the 'English Bards and Scotch Reviewers. ' But this was after its success; I think he would have refused it in its embryo state. After Lord Byron's arrival I had met him, and he said he wished I would obtain some work of his Lordship's for him. I now had it in my power, and I put 'Childe Harold's Pilgrimage' into his hands, telling him that Lord Byron had made me a present of it, and that I expected he would make a very liberal arrangement with me for it.

"He took some days to consider, during which time he consulted his literary advisers, among whom, no doubt, was Mr. Gifford, who was Editor of the *Quarterly Review*. That Mr. Gifford gave a favourable opinion I afterwards learned from Mr. Murray himself; but the objections I have stated stared him in the face, and he was kept in suspense between the desire of possessing a work of Lord Byron's and the fear of an unsuccessful speculation. We came to this conclusion: that he should print, at his expense, a handsome quarto edition, the profits of which I should share equally with him, and that the agreement for the copyright should depend upon the success of this edition. When I told this to Lord Byron he was highly pleased, but still doubted the copyright being worth my acceptance, promising, however, if the poem went through the edition, to give me other poems to annex to 'Childe Harold. '"

Mr. Murray had long desired to make Lord Byron's acquaintance, and now that Mr. Dallas had arranged with him for the publication of the first two cantos of "Childe Harold, " he had many opportunities of seeing Byron at his place of business. The first time that he saw him was when he called one day with Mr. Hobhouse in Fleet Street. He afterwards looked in from time to time, while the sheets were passing through the press, fresh from the fencing rooms of Angelo and Jackson, and used to amuse himself by renewing his practice of "Carte et Tierce, " with his walking-cane directed against the book-shelves, while Murray was reading passages from the poem, with occasional ejaculations of admiration; on which Byron would say, "You think that a good idea, do you, Murray? " Then he would fence and lunge with his walking-stick at some special book which he had picked out on the shelves before him. As Murray afterwards said, "I was often very glad to get rid of him! "

A correspondence took place with regard to certain omissions, alterations, and improvements which were strongly urged both by Mr. Dallas and the publisher. Mr. Murray wrote as follows:

John Murray to Lord Byron.

September 4, 1811.

MY LORD,

An absence of some days, passed in the country, has prevented me from writing earlier, in answer to your obliging letters. [Footnote: These letters are given in Moore's "Life and Letters of Lord Byron. "] I have now, however, the pleasure of sending you, under a separate cover, the first proof sheets of your poem; which is so good as to be entitled to all your care in rendering it perfect. Besides its general merits, there are parts which, I am tempted to believe, far excel anything that you have hitherto published; and it were therefore grievous indeed if you do not condescend to bestow upon it all the improvements of which your mind is so capable. Every correction already made is valuable, and this circumstance renders me more confident in soliciting your further attention. There are some expressions concerning Spain and Portugal which, however just at the time they were conceived, yet, as they do not harmonise with the now prevalent feeling, I am persuaded would so greatly interfere with the popularity which the poem is, in other respects, certainly calculated to excite, that, in compassion to your publisher, who does not presume to reason upon the subject, otherwise than as a mere matter of business, I hope your goodness will induce you to remove them; and with them perhaps some religious sentiments which may deprive me of some customers amongst the Orthodox. Could I flatter myself that these suggestions were not obtrusive, I would hazard another, —that you would add the two promised cantos, and complete the poem. It were cruel indeed not to perfect a work which contains so much that is excellent. Your fame, my Lord, demands it.

You are raising a monument that will outlive your present feelings; and it should therefore be constructed in such a manner as to excite no other association than that of respect and admiration for your character and genius. I trust that you will pardon the warmth of this address, when I assure you that it arises, in the greatest degree, from a sincere regard for your best reputation; with, however, some view to that portion of it which must attend the publisher of so beautiful a poem as you are capable of rendering in the 'Romaunt of Childe Harold. '"

In compliance with the suggestions of the publisher, Byron altered and improved the stanzas relating to Elgin and Wellington. With respect to the religious, or anti-religious sentiments, Byron wrote to Murray: "As for the 'orthodox, ' let us hope they will buy on purpose to abuse—you will forgive the one if they will do the other. " Yet he did alter Stanza VIII, and inserted what Moore calls a "magnificent stanza" in place of one that was churlish and sneering, and in all respects very much inferior.

Byron then proceeded to another point. "Tell me fairly, did you show the MS. to some of your corps? " "I will have no traps for applause, " he wrote to Mr. Murray, at the same time forbidding him to show the manuscript of "Childe Harold" to his Aristarchus, Mr. Gifford, though he had no objection to letting it be seen by any one else. But it was too late. Mr. Gifford had already seen the manuscript, and pronounced a favourable opinion as to its great poetic merits. Byron was not satisfied with this assurance, and seemed, in his next letter, to be very angry. He could not bear to have it thought that he was endeavouring to ensure a favourable review of his work in the *Quarterly*. To Mr. Dallas he wrote (September 23, 1811):

"I *will* be angry with Murray. It was a book-selling, back-shop, Paternoster Row, paltry proceeding; and if the experiment had turned out as it deserved, I would have raised all Fleet Street, and borrowed the giant's staff from St. Dunstan's Church, to immolate the betrayer of trust. I have written to him as he was never written to before by an author, I'll be sworn; and I hope you will amplify my wrath, till it has an effect upon him. "

Byron at first objected to allow the new poem to be published with his name, thinking that this would bring down upon him the enmity of his critics in the North, as well as the venom of the southern scribblers, whom he had enraged by his Satire. At last, on Mr. Murray's strong representation, he consented to allow his name to be published on the title-page as the author. Even to the last, however, his doubts were great as to the probable success of the poem; and he more than once talked of suppressing it.

In October 1811 Lord Byron wrote from Newstead Abbey to his friend Mr. Hodgson: [Footnote: The Rev. Francis Hodgson was then residing at Cambridge as Fellow and Tutor of King's College. He formed an intimate friendship with Byron, who communicated with him freely as to his poetical as well as his religious difficulties. Hodgson afterwards became Provost of Eton.]

"'Childe Harold's Pilgrimage' must wait till Murray's is finished. He is making a tour in Middlesex, and is to return soon, when high matter may be expected. He wants to have it in quarto, which is a cursed unsaleable size; but it is pestilent long, and one must obey one's publisher. "

The whole of the sheets were printed off in the following month of January; and the work was published on March 1, 1812. Of the first edition only 500 copies, demy quarto, were printed.

It is unnecessary to say with what applause the book was received. The impression it produced was as instantaneous as it proved to be lasting. Byron himself briefly described the result of the publication in his memoranda: "I awoke one morning and found myself famous." The publisher had already taken pains to spread abroad the merits of the poem. Many of his friends had re-echoed its praises. The attention of the public was fixed upon the work; and in three days after its appearance the whole edition was disposed of. When Mr. Dallas went to see Lord Byron at his house in St. James's Street, he found him loaded with letters from critics, poets, and authors, all lavish of their raptures. A handsome new edition, in octavo, was proposed, to which his Lordship agreed.

Eventually Mr. Murray consented to give Mr. Dallas £600 for the copyright of the poem; although Mr. Gifford and others were of opinion that it might prove a bad bargain at that price. There was, however, one exception, namely Mr. Rogers, who told Mr. Murray not to be disheartened, for he might rely upon its turning out the most fortunate purchase he had ever made; and so it proved. Three thousand copies of the second and third editions of the poem in octavo were printed; and these went off in rapid succession.

On the appearance of "Childe Harold's Pilgrimage" Lord Byron became an object of interest in the fashionable world of London. His poem was the subject of conversation everywhere, and many literary, noble, and royal personages desired to make his acquaintance. In the month of June he was invited to a party at Miss Johnson's, at which His Royal Highness the Prince Regent was present. As Lord Byron had not yet been to Court, it was not considered etiquette that he should appear before His Royal Highness. He accordingly retired to another room. But on the Prince being informed that Lord Byron was in the house, he expressed a desire to see him. Lord Byron was sent for, and the following is Mr. Murray's account of the conversation that took place.

John Murray to Mr. Scott.

June 27, 1812.

DEAR SIR,

I cannot refrain, notwithstanding my fears of intrusion, from mentioning to you a conversation which Lord Byron had with H. R.H. the Prince Regent, and of which you formed the leading subject. He was at an evening party at Miss Johnson's this week, when the Prince, hearing that Lord Byron was present, expressed a desire to be introduced to him; and for more than half an hour they conversed on poetry and poets, with which the Prince displayed an intimacy and critical taste which at once surprised and delighted Lord Byron. But the Prince's great delight was Walter Scott, whose name and writings he dwelt upon and recurred to incessantly. He preferred him far beyond any other poet of the time, repeated several passages with fervour, and criticized them faithfully. He spoke chiefly of the 'Lay of the Last Minstrel, ' which he expressed himself as admiring most of the three poems. He quoted Homer, and even some of the obscurer Greek poets, and appeared, as Lord Byron supposes, to have read more poetry than any prince in Europe. He paid, of course, many compliments to Lord Byron, but the greatest was "that he ought to be offended with Lord B., for that he had thought it impossible for any poet to equal Walter Scott, and that he had made him find himself mistaken. " Lord Byron called upon me, merely to let off the raptures of the Prince respecting you, thinking, as he said, that if I were likely to have occasion to write to you, it might not be ungrateful for you to hear of his praises.

In reply Scott wrote to Mr. Murray as follows, enclosing a letter to Lord Byron, which has already been published in the Lives of both authors:

Mr. Scott to John Murray.

EDINBURGH, *July* 2, 1812.

MY DEAR SIR,

I have been very silent, partly through pressure of business and partly from idleness and procrastination, but it would be very ungracious to delay returning my thanks for your kindness in transmitting the very flattering particulars of the Prince Regent's conversation with Lord Byron. I trouble you with a few lines to his Lordship expressive of my thanks for his very handsome and gratifying communication, and I hope he will not consider it as intrusive in a veteran author to pay my debt of gratitude for the high pleasure I have received from the perusal of 'Childe Harold, ' which is certainly the most original poem which we have had this many a day....

Your obliged, humble Servant,

WALTER SCOTT.

This episode led to the opening of an agreeable correspondence between Scott and Byron, and to a lasting friendship between the two poets.

The fit of inspiration was now on Lord Byron. In May 1813 appeared "The Giaour, " and in the midst of his corrections of successive editions of it, he wrote in four nights his second Turkish story, "Zuleika, " afterwards known as "The Bride of Abydos. "

With respect to the business arrangement as to the two poems, Mr. Murray wrote to Lord Byron as follows:

John Murray to Lord Byron.

November 18, 1813.

MY DEAR LORD,

I am very anxious that our business transactions should occur frequently, and that they should be settled immediately; for short accounts are favourable to long friendships.

I restore "The Giaour" to your Lordship entirely, and for it, the "Bride of Abydos, " and the miscellaneous poems intended to fill up the volume of the small edition, I beg leave to offer you the sum of One Thousand Guineas; and I shall be happy if you perceive that my estimation of your talents in my character of a man of business is not much under my admiration of them as a man.

I do most heartily accept the offer of your portrait, as the most noble mark of friendship with which you could in any way honour me. I do assure you that I am truly proud of being distinguished as your publisher, and that I shall ever continue,

Your Lordship's faithful Servant,

JOHN MURRAY.

With reference to the foregoing letter we read in Lord Byron's Diary:

"Mr. Murray has offered me one thousand guineas for 'The Giaour' and 'The Bride of Abydos. ' I won't. It is too much: though I am strongly tempted, merely for the say of it. No bad price for a fortnight's (a week each) what? —the gods know. It was intended to be called poetry. "

The "Bride of Abydos" was received with almost as much applause as the "Giaour. " "Lord Byron, " said Sir James Mackintosh, "is the author of the day; six thousand of his 'Bride of Abydos' have been sold within a month. "

"The Corsair" was Lord Byron's next poem, written with great vehemence, literally "struck off at a heat, " at the rate of about two hundred lines a day, —"a circumstance, " says Moore, "that is, perhaps, wholly without a parallel in the history of genius. " "The

Corsair" was begun on the 18th, and finished on the 31st of December, 1813.

A sudden impulse induced Lord Byron to present the copyright of this poem also to Mr. Dallas, with the single stipulation that he would offer it for publication to Mr. Murray, who eventually paid Mr. Dallas five hundred guineas for the copyright, and the work was published in February 1814. The following letters will give some idea of the reception it met with.

John Murray to Lord Byron.

February 3, 1814.

MY LORD,

I have been unwilling to write until I had something to say, an occasion to which I do not always restrict myself. I am most happy to tell you that your last poem *is*—what Mr. Southey's is *called*—*a Carmen Triumphale*. Never, in my recollection, has any work, since the "Letter of Burke to the Duke of Bedford, " excited such a ferment—a ferment which, I am happy to say, will subside into lasting fame. I sold, on the day of publication—a thing perfectly unprecedented—10,000 copies.... Gifford did what I never knew him do before—he repeated several passages from memory. "

The "Ode to Napoleon Bonaparte, " which appeared in April 1814, was on the whole a failure. It was known to be Lord Byron's, and its publication was seized upon by the press as the occasion for many bitter criticisms, mingled with personalities against the writer's genius and character. He was cut to the quick by these notices, and came to the determination to buy back the whole of the copyrights of his works, and suppress every line he had ever written. On April 29, 1814, he wrote to Mr. Murray:

Lord Byron to John Murray.

April 29, 1814.

I enclose a draft for the money; when paid, send the copyrights. I release you from the thousand pounds agreed on for "The Giaour" and "Bride, " and there's an end.... For all this, it might be well to assign some reason. I have none to give, except my own caprice, and

I do not consider the circumstance of consequence enough to require explanation.... It will give me great pleasure to preserve your acquaintance, and to consider you as my friend. Believe me very truly, and for much attention,

Yours, etc.,

BYRON.

Mr. Murray was of course very much concerned at this decision, and remonstrated. Three days later Lord Byron revoked his determination. To Mr. Murray he wrote (May 1, 1814):

"If your present note is serious, and it really would be inconvenient, there is an end of the matter; tear my draft, and go on as usual: in that case, we will recur to our former basis. "

Before the end of the month Lord Byron began the composition of his next poem, "Lara, " usually considered a continuation of "The Corsair. " It was published conjointly with Mr. Rogers's "Jacqueline. " "Rogers and I, " said Lord Byron to Moore, "have almost coalesced into a joint invasion of the public. Whether it will take place or not, I do not yet know, and I am afraid 'Jacqueline' (which is very beautiful) will be in bad company. But in this case, the lady will not be the sufferer. "

The two poems were published anonymously in the following August (1814): Murray allowed 500 guineas for the copyright of each.

CHAPTER X

MR. MURRAY'S REMOVAL TO 50, ALBEMARLE STREET

We must now revert to the beginning of 1812, at which time Mr. William Miller, who commenced business in Bond Street in 1791, and had in 1804 removed to 50, Albemarle Street, desired to retire from "the Trade. " He communicated his resolve to Mr. Murray, who had some time held the intention of moving westward from Fleet Street, and had been on the point of settling in Pall Mall. Murray at once entered into an arrangement with Miller, and in a letter to Mr. Constable of Edinburgh he observed:

John Murray to Mr. A. Constable.

May 1, 1812.

"You will probably have heard that Miller is about to retire, and that I have ventured to undertake to succeed him. I had for some time determined upon moving, and I did not very long hesitate about accepting his offer. I am to take no part of his stock but such as I may deem expedient, and for it and the rest I shall have very long credit. How far it may answer, I know not; but if I can judge of my own views, I think it may prove an advantageous opening. Miller's retirement is very extraordinary, for no one in the trade will believe that he has made a fortune; but from what he has laid open to me, it is clear that he has succeeded. In this arrangement, I propose of course to dispose of my present house, and my medical works, with other parts of my business. I have two offers for it, waiting my decision as to terms.... I am to enter at Miller's on September 29th next. " [Footnote: The Fleet Street business was eventually purchased by Thomas and George Underwood. It appears from the "Memoirs of Adam Black" that Black was for a short time a partner with the Underwoods. Adam Black quitted the business in 1813. Upon the failure of the Underwoods in 1831, Mr. Samuel Highley, son of Mr. Murray's former partner, took possession, and the name of Highley again appeared over the door.]

The terms arranged with Mr. Miller were as follows: The lease of the house, No. 50, Albemarle Street, was purchased by Mr. Murray, together with the copyrights, stock, etc., for the sum of £3,822 12s. 6d. ; Mr. Miller receiving as surety, during the time the purchase money remained unpaid, the copyright of "Domestic Cookery, " of the *Quarterly Review*, and the one-fourth share in "Marmion. " The debt was not finally paid off until the year 1821.

Amongst the miscellaneous works which Mr. Murray published shortly after his removal to Albemarle Street were William Sotheby's translation of the "Georgies of Virgil"—the most perfect translation, according to Lord Jeffrey, of a Latin classic which exists in our language; Robert Bland's "Collection from the Greek Anthology"; Prince Hoare's "Epochs of the Arts"; Lord Glenbervie's work on the "Cultivation of Timber"; Granville Penn's "Bioscope, or Dial of Life explained"; John Herman Merivale's "Orlando in Roncesvalles"; and Sir James Hall's splendid work on "Gothic Architecture. " Besides these, there was a very important contribution to our literature—in the "Miscellaneous Works of Gibbon" in 5 volumes, for the copyright of which Mr. Murray paid Lord Sheffield the sum of £1,000.

In 1812 he published Sir John Malcolm's "Sketch of the Sikhs, " and in the following year Mr. Macdonald Kinneir's "Persia. " Mr. D'Israeli's "Calamities of Authors" appeared in 1812, and Murray forwarded copies of the work to Scott and Southey.

Mr. Scott to John Murray.

July 2,1812.

I owe you best thanks for the 'Calamities of Authors, ' which has all the entertaining and lively features of the 'Amenities of Literature. ' I am just packing them up with a few other books for my hermitage at Abbotsford, where my present parlour is only 12 feet square, and my book-press in Lilliputian proportion. Poor Andrew Macdonald I knew in days of yore, and could have supplied some curious anecdotes respecting him. He died of a poet's consumption, viz. want of food.

"The present volume of 'Somers' [Footnote: Lord Somers' "Tracts, " a new edition in 12 volumes.] will be out immediately; with whom am I to correspond on this subject since the secession of Will. Miller? I shall be happy to hear you have succeeded to him in this department, as well as in Albemarle Street. What has moved Miller to retire? He is surely too young to have made a fortune, and it is

uncommon to quit a thriving trade. I have had a packet half finished for Gifford this many a day. "
Southey expressed himself as greatly interested in the "Calamities of Authors, " and proposed to make it the subject of an article for the *Quarterly*.

Mr. Southey to John Murray.

August 14, 1812.

"I should like to enlarge a little upon the subject of literary property, on which he has touched, in my opinion, with proper feeling. Certainly I am a party concerned. I should like to say something upon the absurd purposes of the Literary Fund, with its despicable ostentation of patronage, and to build a sort of National Academy in the air, in the hope that Canning might one day lay its foundation in a more solid manner. [Footnote: Canning had his own opinion on the subject. When the Royal Society of Literature was about to be established, an application was made to him to join the committee. He refused, for reasons "partly general, partly personal. " He added, "I am really of opinion, with Dr. Johnson, that the multitudinous personage, called The Public, is after all, the best patron of literature and learned men. "] And I could say something on the other side of the picture, showing that although literature in almost all cases is the worst trade to which a man can possibly betake himself, it is the best and wisest of all pursuits for those whose provision is already made, and of all amusements for those who have leisure to amuse themselves. It has long been my intention to leave behind me my own Memoirs, as a post-obit for my family—a wise intention no doubt, and one which it is not very prudent to procrastinate. Should this ever be completed, it would exhibit a case directly in contrast to D'Israeli's view of the subject. I chose literature for my own profession, with every advantage of education it is true, but under more disadvantages perhaps of any other kind than any of the persons in his catalogue. I have never repented the choice. The usual censure, ridicule, and even calumnies, which it has drawn on me never gave me a moment's pain; but on the other hand, literature has given me friends; among the best and wisest and most celebrated of my contemporaries it has given me distinction. If I live twenty years longer, I do not doubt that it will give me fortune, and if it pleases God to take me before my family are provided for, I doubt as little that in my name and in my works they will find a provision. I want to give you a 'Life of Wesley. ' The history of the Dissenters must be finished by that time, and it will afford me opportunity. "

During the year 1813 the recklessness of the younger Ballantyne, combined with the formation of the incipient estate at Abbotsford, were weighing heavily on Walter Scott. This led to a fresh alliance with Constable, "in which, " wrote Scott, "I am sensible he has gained a great advantage"; but in accordance with the agreement Constable, in return for a share in Scott's new works, was to relieve the Ballantynes of some of their heavy stock, and in May Scott was enabled "for the first time these many weeks to lay my head on a quiet pillow. " But nothing could check John Ballantyne. "I sometimes fear, " wrote Scott to him, "that between the long dates of your bills and the tardy settlements of the Edinburgh trade, some difficulties will occur even in June; and July I always regard with deep anxiety. " How true this forecast proved to be is shown by the following letter:

Mr. Scott to John Murray,

EDINBURGH, *July 5*, 1813.

I delayed answering your favour, thinking I could have overtaken the "Daemonology" for the *Review,* but I had no books in the country where it found me, and since that Swift, who is now nearly finished, has kept me incessantly labouring. When that is off my hand I will have plenty of leisure for reviewing, though you really have no need of my assistance. The volume of "Somers" being now out of my hands I take the liberty to draw at this date as usual for £105. Now I have a favour to ask which I do with the more confidence because, if it is convenient and agreeable to you to oblige me in the matter, it will be the means of putting our connection as author and publisher upon its former footing, which I trust will not be disagreeable to you. I am making up a large sum of money to pay for a late purchase, and as part of my funds is secured on an heritable bond which cannot be exacted till Martinmas, I find myself some hundreds short, which the circumstances of the money market here renders it not so easy to supply as formerly. Now if you will oblige me by giving me a lift with your credit and accepting the enclosed bills, [Footnote: Three bills for £300 each at three, four, and six months respectively.] it will accommodate me particularly at this moment, and as I shall have ample means of putting you in cash to replace them as they fall due, will not, I should hope, occasion you any inconvenience. Longmans' house on a former occasion obliged me in this way, and I hope found their account in it. But I entreat you will not stand on the least ceremony should you think you could not oblige me without inconveniencing yourself. The property I have purchased cost about £6,000, so it is no wonder I am a little out for the moment. Will you have the goodness to return an answer in course of post, as, failing your benevolent aid, I must look about elsewhere?

You will understand distinctly that I do not propose that you should advance any part of the money by way of loan or otherwise, but only the assistance of your credit, the bills being to be retired by cash remitted by me before they fall due.

Believe me, very truly,

Your obedient Servant,

WALTER SCOTT.

Mr. Murray at once replied:

John Murray to Mr. Scott.

July 8, 1813.

DEAR SIR,

I have the pleasure of returning accepted the bills which I received from you this morning. In thus availing myself of your confidential application, I trust that you will do me the justice to believe that it is done for kindness already received, and not with the remotest view towards prospective advantages. I shall at all times feel proud of being one of your publishers, but this must be allowed to arise solely out of your own feelings and convenience when the occasions shall present themselves. I am sufficiently content in the belief that even negative obstacles to our perfect confidence have now subsided.

When weightier concerns permit we hope that you will again appear in our *Review.* In confidence I may tell you that your long silence led us to avail ourselves of your friend Mr. Rose's offer to review Ferriar, [Footnote: Dr. Ferriar on "Apparitions. "] and his article is already printing.

I will send you a new edition of the "Giaour, " in which there are one or two stanzas added of peculiar beauty.

I trust that your family are well, and remain, dear Sir,

Your obliged and faithful Servant,

JOHN MURRAY.

Within a few months of this correspondence, Scott was looking into an old writing-desk in search of some fishing-tackle, when his eye chanced to light upon the Ashestiel fragment of "Waverley, " begun several years before. He read over the introductory chapters, and then determined to finish the story. It is said that he first offered it anonymously to Sir R. Phillips, London, who refused to publish it. "Waverley" was afterwards accepted by Constable & Co., and published on half profits, on July 7, 1814. When it came out, Murray got an early copy of the novel; he read it, and sent it to Mr. Canning, and wrote upon the title-page, "By Walter Scott. " The reason why he fixed upon Scott as the author was as follows. When he met Ballantyne at Boroughbridge, in 1809, to settle some arrangements as to the works which Walter Scott proposed to place in his hands for publication, he remembered that among those works were three — 1st, an edition of "Beaumont and Fletcher"; 2nd, a poem; and 3rd, a novel. Now, both the edition of "Beaumont and Fletcher" (though edited by Weber) and the poem, the "Lady of the Lake, " had been published; and now, at last, appeared *the novel*. [Footnote: Indeed, in Ballantyne & Co. 's printed list of "New Works and Publications for 1809-10, " issued August 1810 (now before us), we find the following entry: "Waverley; or, 'Tis Sixty Years Since; a novel in 3 vols. 12mo. " The work was not, however, published until July 1814.] He was confirmed in his idea that Walter Scott was the author after carefully reading the book. Canning called on Murray next day; said he had begun it, found it very dull, and concluded: "You are quite mistaken; it cannot be by Walter Scott. " But a few days later he wrote to Murray: "Yes, it is so; you are right: Walter Scott, and no one else. "

In the autumn of 1814 Mrs. Murray went to Leith by sailing-ship from the Thames, to visit her mother and friends in Edinburgh. She was accompanied by her son John and her two daughters. During her absence, Mr. Murray wrote to her two or three times a week, and kept her *au courant* with the news of the day. In his letter of August 9 he intimated that he had been dining with D'Israeli, and that he afterwards went with him to Sadler's Wells Theatre to see the "Corsair, " at which he was "woefully disappointed and enraged.... They have actually omitted his wife altogether, and made him a mere ruffian, ultimately overcome by the Sultan, and drowned in the New River! "

Mr. Blackwood, of Edinburgh, was then in London, spending several days with Mr. Murray over their accounts and future arrangements. The latter was thinking of making a visit to Paris, in the company of his friend D'Israeli, during the peace which followed the exile of Napoleon to Elba. D'Israeli had taken a house at Brighton, from which place the voyagers intended to set sail, and make the passage to Dieppe in about fourteen hours. On August 13 Mr. Murray informs his wife that "Lord Byron was here yesterday, and I introduced him to Blackwood, to whom he was very civil. They say," he added, "that Madame de Staël has been ordered to quit Paris, for writing lightly respecting the Bourbons. " Two days later he wrote to Mrs. Murray:

August 15, 1814.

"I dined yesterday with D'Israeli, and in the afternoon we partly walked and partly rode to Islington, to drink tea with Mrs. Lindo, who, with Mr. L. and her family, were well pleased to see me. Mr. Cervetto was induced to accompany the ladies at the piano with his violoncello, which he did delightfully. We walked home at 10 o'clock. On Saturday we passed a very pleasant day at Petersham with Turner and his family....

"I have got at last Mr. Eagle's 'Journal of Penrose, the Seaman, ' for which, as you may remember, I am to pay £200 in twelve months for 1,000 copies: too dear perhaps; but Lord Byron sent me word this morning by letter (for he borrowed the MS. last night): 'Penrose is most amusing. I never read so much of a book at one sitting in my life. He kept me up half the night, and made me dream of him the other half. It has all the air of truth, and is most entertaining and interesting in every point of view. '"

Writing again on August 24, 1814, he says:

"Lord Byron set out for Newstead on Sunday. It is finally settled to be his again, the proposed purchaser forfeiting £25,000. 'Lara' and 'Jacqueline' are nearly sold off, to the extent of 6,000, which leaves me £130, and the certain sale of 10,000 more in the 8vo form. Mr. Canning called upon Gifford yesterday, and from their conversation I infer very favourably for my *Review*. We shall now take a decided tone in Politics, and we are all in one boat. Croker has gone down to the Prince Regent, at Brighton, where I ought to have been last night, to have witnessed the rejoicings and splendour of the Duke of Clarence's birthday. But I am ever out of luck. 'O, indolence and indecision of mind! if not in yourselves vices, to how much exquisite misery do you frequently prepare the way! ' Have you come to this passage in 'Waverley' yet? Pray read 'Waverley'; it is excellent. "

On September 5, 1814, Mr. Murray communicated with Mrs. Murray as to the education of his son John, then six-and-a-half years old:

John Murray to Mrs. Murray.

"I am glad that you venture to say something about the children, for it is only by such minutiae that I can judge of the manner in which they amuse or behave themselves. I really do not see the least propriety in leaving John, at an age when the first impressions are so deep and lasting, to receive the rudiments and foundation of his education in Scotland. If learning English, his native language, mean anything, it is not merely to read it correctly and understand it grammatically, but to speak and pronounce it like the most polished native. But how can you expect this to be effected, even with the aid of the best teachers, when everybody around him, with whom he can practise his instructions, speaks in a totally different manner? No! I rather think it better that he should go to Edinburgh after he has passed through the schools here, and when he is sixteen or seventeen. He should certainly go to some school next spring, and I most confidingly trust that you are unremitting in your duty to give him daily lessons of preparation, or he may be so far behind children of his age when he does go to school, that the derision he may meet there may destroy emulation. All this, however, is matter for serious consideration and for future consultation, in which your voice shall have its rightful influence.... "

Mr. Murray was under the necessity of postponing his visit to France. He went to Brighton instead, and spent a few pleasant days with Mr. D'Israeli and his friends.

On September 24 Mr. Murray, having returned to London, informed his wife, still at Edinburgh, of an extraordinary piece of news.

John Murray to Mrs. Murray.

"I was much surprised to learn from Dallas, whom I accidentally met yesterday, that Lord Byron was expected in town every hour. I accordingly left my card at his house, with a notice that I would attend him as soon as he pleased; and it pleased him to summon my attendance about seven in the evening. He had come to town on business, and regretted that he would not be at Newstead until a fortnight, as he wished to have seen me there on my way to Scotland. Says he, 'Can you keep a secret? ' 'Certainly—positively— my wife's out of town! ' 'Then—I am going to be MARRIED! ' 'The devil! I shall have no poem this winter then? ' 'No. ' 'Who is the lady who is to do me this injury? ' 'Miss Milbanke—do you know her? ' 'No, my lord. '

"So here is news for you! I fancy the lady is rich, noble, and beautiful; but this shall be my day's business to enquire about. Oh! how he did curse poor Lady C—— as the fiend who had interrupted all his projects, and who would do so now if possible. I think he hinted that she had managed to interrupt this connexion two years ago. He thought she was abroad, and, to his torment and astonishment, he finds her not only in England, but in London. He says he has written some small poems which his friends think beautiful, particularly one of eight lines, his very best—all of which, I believe, I am to have; and, moreover, he gives me permission to publish the octavo edition of 'Lara' with his name, which secures, I think, £700 to you and me. So Scott's poem is announced ['Lord of the Isles'], and I am cut out. I wish I had been in Scotland six weeks ago, and I might have come in for a share. Should I apply for one to him, it would oblige me to be a partner with Constable, who is desperately in want of money. He has applied to Cadell & Davies (the latter told me in confidence) and they refused. "

At the beginning of October Mr. Murray set out for Edinburgh, journeying by Nottingham for the purpose of visiting Newstead Abbey.

The following is Mr. Murray's account of his visit to Newstead. His letter is dated Matlock, October 5, 1814:

"I got to Newstead about 11 o'clock yesterday and found the steward, my namesake, and the butler waiting for me. The first, who is good-looking and a respectable old man of about sixty-five years, showed me over the house and grounds, which occupied two hours, for I was anxious to examine everything. But never was I more disappointed, for my notions, I suppose, had been raised to the romantic. I had surmised the possibly easy restoration of this once famous abbey, the mere skeleton of which is now fast crumbling to ruin. Lord Byron's immediate predecessor stripped the whole place of all that was splendid and interesting; and you may judge of what he must have done to the mansion when inform you that he converted the ground, which used to be covered with the finest trees, like a forest, into an absolute desert. Not a tree is left standing, and the wood thus shamefully cut down was sold in one day for £60,000. The hall of entrance has about eighteen large niches, which had been filled with statues, and the side walls covered with family portraits and armour. All these have been mercilessly torn down, as well as the magnificent fireplace, and sold. All the beautiful paintings which filled the galleries—valued at that day at £80,000—have disappeared, and the whole place is crumbling into dust. No sum short of £100,000 would make the place habitable. Lord Byron's few apartments contain some modern upholstery, but serve only to show what ought to have been there. They are now digging round the cloisters for a traditionary cannon, and in their progress, about five days ago, they discovered a corpse in too decayed a state to admit of removal. I saw the drinking-skull [Footnote: When the father of the present Mr. Murray was a student in Edinburgh, he wrote to his father (April 10,1827): "I saw yesterday at a jeweller's shop in Edinburgh a great curiosity, no less than Lord Byron's skull cup, upon which he wrote the poem. It is for sale; the owner, whose name I could not learn (it appears he does not wish it known), wants £200 for it. "] and the marble mausoleum erected over Lord Byron's dog. I came away with my heart aching and full of melancholy reflections—producing a lowness of spirits which I did not get the better of until this morning, when the most enchanting scenery I have ever beheld has at length restored me. I am far more surprised that Lord Byron should ever have lived at Newstead, than that he should be inclined to part with it; for, as there is no possibility of his being able, by any reasonable amount of expense, to reinstate it, the place can present nothing but a perpetual memorial of the wickedness of his ancestors. There are three, or at most four, domestics at board wages. All that I was asked to taste was a piece of bread-and-butter. As my foot was on the step of the chaise, when about to enter it, I was informed that his lordship had ordered that I should take as much game as I liked. What makes the steward, Joe Murray, an interesting object to me, is that the old man has seen the abbey in all its vicissitudes of greatness and degradation. Once it was full of unbounded hospitality and splendour, and now it is simply miserable. If this man has feelings — of which, by the way, he betrays no symptom — he would possibly be miserable himself. He has seen three hundred of the first people in the county filling the gallery, and seen five hundred deer disporting themselves in the beautiful park, now covered with stunted offshoots of felled trees. Again I say it gave me the heartache to witness all this ruin, and I regret that my romantic picture has been destroyed by the reality. "

Among the friends that welcomed Mr. Murray to Edinburgh was Mr. William Blackwood, who then, and for a long time after, was closely connected with him in his business transactions. Blackwood was a native of Edinburgh; having served his apprenticeship with Messrs. Bell & Bradfute, booksellers, he was selected by Mundell & Company to take charge of a branch of their extensive publishing business in Glasgow. He returned to Edinburgh, and again entered the service of Bell et Bradfute; but after a time went to London to master the secrets of the old book trade under the well-known Mr. Cuthill. Returning to Edinburgh, he set up for himself in 1804, at the age of twenty-eight, at a shop in South Bridge Street — confining himself, for the most part, to old books. He was a man of great energy and decision of character, and his early education enabled him to conduct his correspondence with a remarkable degree of precision and accuracy. Mr. Murray seems to have done business with him as far back as June 1807, and was in the habit of calling upon Blackwood, who was about his own age, whenever he visited Edinburgh. The two became intimate, and corresponded frequently; and at last, when Murray withdrew from the Ballantynes, in August 1810 he transferred the whole of his Scottish agency to the house of William Blackwood. In return for the publishing business sent to him from London, Blackwood made Murray his agent for any new works published by him in Edinburgh. In this way Murray became the London publisher for Hogg's new poems, and "The Queen's Wake, " which had reached its fourth edition.

Mr. Murray paid at this time another visit to Abbotsford. Towards the end of 1814 Scott had surrounded the original farmhouse with a number of buildings — kitchen, laundry, and spare bedrooms — and was able to entertain company. He received Murray with great cordiality, and made many enquiries as to Lord Byron, to whom Murray wrote on his return to London:

John Murray to Lord Byron.

"Walter Scott commissioned me to be the bearer of his warmest greetings to you. His house was full the day I passed with him; and yet, both in corners and at the surrounded table, he talked incessantly of you. Unwilling that I should part without bearing some mark of his love (a poet's love) for you, he gave me a superb Turkish dagger to present to you, as the only remembrance which, at the moment, he could think of to offer you. He was greatly pleased with the engraving of your portrait, which I recollected to carry with me; and during the whole dinner—when all were admiring the taste with which Scott had fitted up a sort of Gothic cottage—he expressed his anxious wishes that you might honour him with a visit, which I ventured to assure him you would feel no less happy than certain in effecting when you should go to Scotland; and I am sure he would hail your lordship as 'a very brother.'"

After all his visits had been paid, and he had made his arrangements with his printers and publishers, Mr. Murray returned to London with his wife and family. Shortly after his arrival he received a letter from Mr. Blackwood.

Mr. Wm. Blackwood to John Murray.

November 8, 1814.

"I was much gratified by your letter informing me of your safe arrival. How much you must be overwhelmed just now, and your mind distracted by so many calls upon your attention at once. I hope that you are now in one of your best frames of mind, by which you are enabled, as you have told me, to go through, with more satisfaction to yourself, ten times the business you can do at other times. While you are so occupied with your great concerns, I feel doubly obliged to you for your remembrance of my small matters. "

After referring to his illness, he proceeds:

"Do not reflect upon your visit to the bard (Walter Scott). You would have blamed yourself much more if you had not gone. The advance was made by him through Ballantyne, and you only did what was open and candid. We shall be at the bottom of these peoples' views by-and-bye; at present I confess I only see very darkly—but let us have patience; a little time will develop all these mysteries. I have not seen Ballantyne since, and when I do see him I shall say very little indeed. If there really is a disappointment in not being connected with Scott's new poem, you should feel it much less than any man living—having such a poet as Lord Byron. "

Although Murray failed to obtain an interest in "The Lady of the Lake, " he was offered and accepted, at Scott's desire, a share in a new edition of "Don Roderick. "

CHAPTER XI

MURRAY'S DRAWING-ROOM—BYRON AND SCOTT—WORKS
PUBLISHED IN 1815

During Mrs. Murray's absence in Edinburgh, the dwelling-house at
50, Albemarle Street was made over to the carpenters, painters, and
house decorators. "I hope, " said Mr. Murray to his wife, "to leave
the drawing-room entirely at your ladyship's exclusive command. "
But the drawing-room was used for other purposes than the
reception of ordinary visitors. It became for some time the centre of
literary friendship and intercommunication at the West End. In those
days there was no Athenaeum Club for the association of gentlemen
known for their literary, artistic, or scientific attainments. That
institution was only established in 1823, through the instrumentality
of Croker, Lawrence, Chantrey, Sir Humphry Davy, and their
friends. Until then, Murray's drawing-room was the main centre of
literary intercourse in that quarter of London. Men of distinction,
from the Continent and America, presented their letters of
introduction to Mr. Murray, and were cordially and hospitably
entertained by him; meeting, in the course of their visits, many
distinguished and notable personages.

In these rooms, early in 1815, young George Ticknor, from Boston, in
America, then only twenty-three, met Moore, Campbell, D'Israeli,
Gifford, Humphry Davy, and others. He thus records his
impressions of Gifford:

"Among other persons, I brought letters to Gifford, the satirist, but
never saw him till yesterday. Never was I so mistaken in my
anticipations. Instead of a tall and handsome man, as I had supposed
him from his picture—a man of severe and bitter remarks in
conversation, such as I had good reason to believe him from his
books, I found him a short, deformed, and ugly little man, with a
large head sunk between his shoulders, and one of his eyes turned
outward, but withal, one of the best-natured, most open and well-
bred gentlemen I have ever met. He is editor of the *Quarterly Review*,
and was not a little surprised and pleased to hear that it was
reprinted with us, which I told him, with an indirect allusion to the
review of 'Inchiquen's United States. '.... He carried me to a
handsome room over Murray's book-store, which he has fitted up as
a sort of literary lounge, where authors resort to read newspapers,

and talk literary gossip. I found there Elmsley, Hallam, Lord Byron's 'Classic Hallam, much renowned for Greek, ' now as famous as being one of his lordship's friends, Boswell, a son of Johnson's biographer, etc., so that I finished a long forenoon very pleasantly. " [Footnote: "Life, Letters, and Journal of George Ticknor, " i. 48.]

The following letter and Ticknor's reference to Gifford only confirm the testimony of all who knew him that in private life the redoubtable editor and severe critic was an amiable and affectionate man.

Mr. Gifford to John Murray,

JAMES STREET, *October* 20, 1814.

My DEAR SIR,

What can I say in return for your interesting and amusing letter? I live here quite alone, and see nobody, so that I have not a word of news for you. I delight in your visit to Scotland, which I am sure would turn to good, and which I hope you will, as you say, periodically repeat. It makes me quite happy to find you beating up for recruits, and most ardently do I wish you success. Mention me kindly to Scott, and tell him how much I long to renew our wonted acquaintance. Southey's article is, I think, excellent. I have softened matters a little. Barrow is hard at work on Flinders [*Q. R.* 23]. I have still a most melancholy house. My poor housekeeper is going fast. Nothing can save her, and I lend all my care to soften her declining days. She has a physician every second day, and takes a world of medicines, more for their profit than her own, poor thing. She lives on fruit, grapes principally, and a little game, which is the only food she can digest. Guess at my expenses; but I owe in some measure the extension of my feeble life to her care through a long succession of years, and I would cheerfully divide my last farthing with her. I will not trouble you again on this subject, which is a mere concern of my own; but you have been very kind to her, and she is sensible of it. "

With respect to this worthy woman, it may be added that she died on February 6, 1815, carefully waited on to the last by her affectionate master. She was buried in South Audley Churchyard, where Gifford erected a tomb over her, and placed on it a very touching epitaph, concluding with these words: "Her deeply-affected master erected this stone to her memory, as a faithful testimony of her uncommon worth, and of his gratitude, respect, and affection for her long and meritorious services. " [Footnote: It will serve to connect the narrative with one of the famous literary quarrels of the day, if we remind the reader that Hazlitt published a cruel and libellous pamphlet in 1819, entitled "A Letter to William Gifford, " in which he hinted that some improper connection had subsisted between himself and his "frail memorial. " Hazlitt wrote this pamphlet because of a criticism on the "Round Table" in the *Quarterly*, which Gifford did not write, and of a criticism of Hunt's "Rimini, " published by Mr. Murray, which was also the work of another writer. But Gifford never took any notice of these libellous attacks upon him. He held that secrecy between himself and the contributors to the *Quarterly* was absolutely necessary. Hazlitt, in the above pamphlet, also attacks Murray, Croker, Canning, Southey, and others whom he supposed to be connected with the *Review*.]

Murray's own description of his famous drawing-room may also be given, from a letter to a relative:

"I have lately ventured on the bold step of quitting the old establishment to which I have been so long attached, and have moved to one of the best, in every respect, that is known in my business, where I have succeeded in a manner the most complete and flattering. My house is excellent; and I transact all the departments of my business in an elegant library, which my drawing-room becomes during the morning; and there I am in the habit of seeing persons of the highest rank in literature and talent, such as Canning, Frere, Mackintosh, Southey, Campbell, Walter Scott, Madame de Staël, Gifford, Croker, Barrow, Lord Byron, and others; thus leading the most delightful life, with means of prosecuting my business with the highest honour and emolument. "

It was in Murray's drawing-room that Walter Scott and Lord Byron first met. They had already had some friendly intercourse by letter and had exchanged gifts, but in the early part of 1815 Scott was summoned to London on matters connected with his works. Mr. Murray wrote to Lord Byron on April 7:

"Walter Scott has this moment arrived, and will call to-day between three and four, for the chance of having the pleasure of seeing you before he sets out for Scotland. I will show you a beautiful caricature of Buonaparte. "

Lord Byron called at the hour appointed, and was at once introduced to Mr. Scott, who was in waiting. They greeted each other in the most affectionate manner, and entered into a cordial conversation. How greatly Mr. Murray was gratified by a meeting which he had taken such pains to bring about, is shown by the following memorandum carefully preserved by him:

"1815. *Friday, April 7.* —This day Lord Byron and Walter Scott met for the first time and were introduced by me to each other. They conversed together for nearly two hours. There were present, at different times, Mr. William Gifford, James Boswell (son of the biographer of Johnson), William Sotheby, Robert Wilmot, Richard Heber, and Mr. Dusgate. "

Mr. Murray's son—then John Murray, Junior—gives his recollections as follows:

"I can recollect seeing Lord Byron in Albemarle Street. So far as I can remember, he appeared to me rather a short man, with a handsome countenance, remarkable for the fine blue veins which ran over his pale, marble temples. He wore many rings on his fingers, and a brooch in his shirt-front, which was embroidered. When he called, he used to be dressed in a black dress-coat (as we should now call it), with grey, and sometimes nankeen trousers, his shirt open at the neck. Lord Byron's deformity in his foot was very evident, especially as he walked downstairs. He carried a stick. After Scott and he had ended their conversation in the drawing-room, it was a curious sight to see the two greatest poets of the age—both lame—stumping downstairs side by side. They continued to meet in Albemarle Street nearly every day, and remained together for two or three hours at a time. Lord Byron dined several times at Albemarle Street, On one of these occasions, he met Sir John Malcolm—a most agreeable and accomplished man—who was all the more interesting to Lord Byron, because of his intimate knowledge of Persia and India. After dinner, Sir John observed to Lord Byron, how much gratified he had been to meet him, and how surprised he was to find him so full of gaiety and entertaining conversation. Byron replied, 'Perhaps you see me now at my best. ' Sometimes, though not often, Lord Byron read passages from his poems to my father. His voice and manner were very impressive. His voice, in the deeper tones, bore some resemblance to that of Mrs. Siddons. "

Shortly before this first interview between Scott and Byron the news had arrived that Bonaparte had escaped from Elba, and landed at Cannes on March 1, 1815.

A few days before—indeed on the day the battle was fought— Blackwood gave great praise to the new number of the *Quarterly*, containing the contrast of Bonaparte and Wellington. It happened that Southey wrote the article in No. 25, on the "Life and Achievements of Lord Wellington, " in order to influence public opinion as much as possible, and to encourage the hearts of men throughout the country for the great contest about to take place in the Low Countries. About the same time Sir James Mackintosh had written an able and elaborate article for the *Edinburgh*, to show that the war ought to have been avoided, and that the consequences to England could only be unfortunate and inglorious. The number was actually printed, stitched, and ready for distribution in June; but it was thought better to wait a little, for fear of accidents, and especially for the purpose of using it instantly after the first reverse should occur, and thus to give it the force of prophecy. The Battle of Waterloo came like a thunderclap. The article was suppressed, and one on "Gall and his Craniology" substituted. "I think, " says Ticknor, "Southey said he had seen the repudiated article. " [Footnote: "Life, Letters, and Journals of George Ticknor "(2nd ed.), i. p. 41.]

Lord Byron did not write another "Ode on Napoleon. " He was altogether disappointed in his expectations. Nevertheless, he still, like Hazlitt, admired Napoleon, and hated Wellington. When he heard of the result of the Battle of Waterloo, and that Bonaparte was in full retreat upon Paris, he said, "I'm d——d sorry for it! "

Mr. Murray, about this time, began to adorn his dining-room with portraits of the distinguished men who met at his table. His portraits include those of Gifford, [Footnote: This portrait was not painted for Mr. Murray, but was purchased by him.] by Hoppner, R.A. ; Byron and Southey, by Phillips; Scott and Washington Irving, by Stewart Newton; Croker, by Eddis, after Lawrence; Coleridge, Crabbe, Mrs. Somerville, Hallam, T. Moore, Lockhart, and others. In April 1815 we find Thomas Phillips, afterwards R. A., in communication with Mr. Murray, offering to paint for him a series of Kit-cat size at eighty guineas each, and in course of time his pictures, together with those of John Jackson, R.A., formed a most interesting gallery of the great literary men of the time, men and women of science, essayists, critics, Arctic voyagers, and discoverers in the regions of Central Africa.

Byron and Southey were asked to sit for their portraits to Phillips. Though Byron was willing, and even thought it an honour, Southey pretended to grumble. To Miss Barker he wrote (November 9, 1815):

"Here, in London, I can find time for nothing; and, to make things worse, the Devil, who owes me an old grudge, has made me sit to Phillips for a picture for Murray. I have in my time been tormented in this manner so often, and to such little purpose, that I am half tempted to suppose the Devil was the inventor of portrait painting. "

Meanwhile Mr. Murray was again in treaty for a share in a further work by Walter Scott. No sooner was the campaign of 1815 over, than a host of tourists visited France and the Low Countries, and amongst them Murray succeeded in making his long-intended trip to Paris, and Scott set out to visit the battlefields in Belgium. Before departing, Scott made an arrangement with John Ballantyne to publish the results of his travels, and he authorized him to offer the work to Murray, Constable, and the Longmans, in equal shares.

In 1815 a very remarkable collection of documents was offered to Mr. Murray for purchase and publication. They were in the possession of one of Napoleon's generals, a friend of Miss Waldie. [Footnote: Afterwards Mrs. Eaton, author of "Letters from Italy. "] The collection consisted of the personal correspondence of Bonaparte, when in the height of his power, with all the crowned heads and leading personages of Europe, upon subjects so strictly confidential that they had not even been communicated to their own ministers or private secretaries. They were consequently all written by their own hands.

As regards the contents of these letters, Mr. Murray had to depend upon his memory, after making a hurried perusal of them. He was not allowed to copy any of them, but merely took a rough list. No record was kept of the dates. Among them was a letter from the King of Bavaria, urging his claims as a true and faithful ally, and claiming for his reward the dominion of Wurtemberg.

There were several letters from the Prussian Royal family, including one from the King, insinuating that by the cession of Hanover to him his territorial frontier would be rendered more secure. The Emperor

Paul, in a letter written on a small scrap of paper, proposed to transfer his whole army to Napoleon, to be employed in turning the English out of India, provided he would prevent them passing the Gut and enclosing the Baltic.

The Empress of Austria wrote an apology for the uncultivated state of mind of her daughter, Marie Louise, about to become Napoleon's bride; but added that her imperfect education presented the advantage of allowing Napoleon to mould her opinions and principles in accordance with his own views and wishes.

This correspondence would probably have met with an immense sale, but Mr. Murray entertained doubts as to the propriety of publishing documents so confidential, and declined to purchase them for the sum proposed. The next day, after his refusal, he ascertained that Prince Lieven had given, on behalf of his government, not less than £10,000 for the letters emanating from the Court of Russia alone. Thus the public missed the perusal of an important series of international scandals.

In December 1815 Mr. Murray published "Emma" for Miss Jane Austen, and so connected his name with another English classic. Miss Austen's first novel had been "Northanger Abbey. " It remained long in manuscript, and eventually she had succeeded in selling it to a bookseller at Bath for £10. He had not the courage to publish it, and after it had remained in his possession for some years, Miss Austen bought it back for the same money he had paid for it. She next wrote "Sense and Sensibility, " and "Pride and Prejudice. " The latter book was summarily rejected by Mr. Cadell. At length these two books were published anonymously by Mr. Egerton, and though they did not make a sensation, they gradually attracted attention and obtained admirers. No one could be more surprised than the authoress, when she received no less than £150 from the profits of her first published work—"Sense and Sensibility. "

When Miss Austen had finished "Emma, " she put herself in communication with Mr. Murray, who read her "Pride and Prejudice, " and sent it to Gifford. Gifford replied as follows:

Mr. Gifford to John Murray.

"I have for the first time looked into 'Pride and Prejudice'; and it is really a very pretty thing. No dark passages; no secret chambers; no wind-howlings in long galleries; no drops of blood upon a rusty dagger—things that should now be left to ladies' maids and sentimental washerwomen. "

In a later letter he said:

September 29, 1815.

"I have read 'Pride and Prejudice' *again*—'tis very good—wretchedly printed, and so pointed as to be almost unintelligible. Make no apology for sending me anything to read or revise. I am always happy to do either, in the thought that it may be useful to you.

* * * * *

"Of 'Emma, ' I have nothing but good to say. I was sure of the writer before you mentioned her. The MS., though plainly written, has yet some, indeed many little omissions; and an expression may now and then be amended in passing through the press. I will readily undertake the revision. "

Miss Austen's two other novels, "Northanger Abbey" and "Persuasion, " were also published by Murray, but did not appear until after her death in 1818. The profits of the four novels which had been published before her death did not amount to more than seven hundred pounds.

Mr. Murray also published the works of Mr. Malthus on "Rent, " the "Corn Laws, " and the "Essay on Population. " His pamphlet on Rent appeared in March 1815.

Murray's correspondence with Scott continued. On December 25, 1815, he wrote:

"I was about to tell you that Croker was so pleased with the idea of a Caledonian article from you, that he could not refrain from mentioning it to the Prince Regent, who is very fond of the subject, and he said he would be delighted, and is really anxious about it. Now, it occurs to me, as our *Edinburgh* friends choose on many occasions to bring in the Prince's name to abuse it, this might offer an equally fair opportunity of giving him that praise which is so justly due to his knowledge of the history of his country....

"I was with Lord Byron yesterday. He enquired after you, and bid me say how much he was indebted to your introduction of your poor Irish friend Maturin, who had sent him a tragedy, which Lord Byron received late in the evening, and read through, without being able to stop. He was so delighted with it that he sent it immediately to his fellow-manager, the Hon. George Lamb, who, late as it came to him, could not go to bed without finishing it. The result is that they have laid it before the rest of the Committee; they, or rather Lord Byron, feels it his duty to the author to offer it himself to the managers of Covent Garden. The poor fellow says in his letter that his hope of subsistence for his family for the next year rests upon what he can get for this play. I expressed a desire of doing something, and Lord Byron then confessed that he had sent him fifty guineas. I shall write to him tomorrow, and I think if you could draw some case for him and exhibit his merits, particularly if his play succeeds, I could induce Croker and Peel to interest themselves in his behalf, and get him a living.

".... Have you any fancy to dash off an article on 'Emma'? It wants incident and romance, does it not? None of the author's other novels have been noticed, and surely 'Pride and Prejudice' merits high commendation. "

Scott immediately complied with Murray's request. He did "dash off an article on 'Emma, '" which appeared in No. 27 of the *Quarterly*. In enclosing his article to Murray, Scott wrote as follows:

Mr. Scott to John Murray.

January 19, 1816.

Dear Sir,

Enclosed is the article upon "Emma. " I have been spending my holidays in the country, where, besides constant labour in the fields during all the hours of daylight, the want of books has prevented my completing the Highland article. (The "Culloden Papers, " which appeared in next number.) It will be off, however, by Tuesday's post, as I must take Sunday and Monday into the account of finishing it. It will be quite unnecessary to send proofs of "Emma, " as Mr. Gifford will correct all obvious errors, and abridge it where necessary.

January, 25, 1816.

"My article is so long that I fancy you will think yourself in the condition of the conjuror, who after having a great deal of trouble in raising the devil, could not get rid of him after he had once made his appearance. But the Highlands is an immense field, and it would have been much more easy for me to have made a sketch twice as long than to make it shorter. There still wants eight or nine pages, which you will receive by tomorrow's or next day's post; but I fancy you will be glad to get on. "

The article on the "Culloden Papers, " which occupied fifty pages of the *Review* (No. 28), described the clans of the Highlands, their number, manners, and habits; and gave a summary history of the Rebellion of '45. It was graphically and vigorously written, and is considered one of Scott's best essays.

CHAPTER XII

VARIOUS PUBLICATIONS—CHARLES MATURIN—S. T.
COLERIDGE—LEIGH HUNT

Scott's "poor Irish friend Maturin, " referred to in the previous
chapter, was a young Irish clergyman, who was under the necessity
of depending upon his brains and pen for the maintenance of his
family. Charles Maturin, after completing his course of education at
Trinity College, married Miss Harriet Kinsburg. His family grew, but
not his income. He took orders, and obtained the curacy of St. Peter's
Church, Dublin, but owing to his father's affairs having become
embarrassed, he was compelled to open a boarding-school, with the
view of assisting the family. Unfortunately, he became bound for a
friend, who deceived him, and eventually he was obliged to sacrifice
his interest in the school. Being thus driven to extremities, he tried to
live by literature, and produced "The Fatal Revenge; or, the Family
of Montorio, " the first of a series of romances, in which he outdid
Mrs. Radcliffe and Monk Lewis. "The Fatal Revenge" was followed
by "The Wild Irish Boy, " for which Colburn gave him £80, and "The
Milesian Chief, " all full of horrors and misty grandeur. These works
did not bring him in much money; but, in 1815, he determined to
win the height of dramatic fame in his "Bertram; or, the Castle of St.
Aldebrand, " a tragedy. He submitted the drama to Walter Scott, as
from an "obscure Irishman, " telling him of his sufferings as an
author and the father of a family, and imploring his kind opinion.
Scott replied in the most friendly manner, gave him much good
advice, spoke of the work as "grand and powerful, the characters
being sketched with masterly enthusiasm"; and, what was
practically better, sent him £50 as a token of his esteem and
sympathy, and as a temporary stop-gap until better times came
round. He moreover called the attention of Lord Byron, then on the
Committee of Management of Drury Lane Theatre, to the play, and
his Lordship strongly recommended a performance of it. Thanks to
the splendid acting of Kean, it succeeded, and Maturin realized
about £1,000.

"Bertram" was published by Murray, a circumstance which brought
him into frequent communication with the unfortunate Maturin. The
latter offered more plays, more novels, and many articles for the
Quarterly. With reference to one of his articles—a review of Sheil's
"Apostate" —Gifford said, "A more potatoe-headed arrangement, or

rather derangement, I have never seen. I have endeavoured to bring some order out of the chaos. There is a sort of wild eloquence in it that makes it worth preserving. "

Maturin continued to press his literary work on Murray, who however, though he relieved him by the gift of several large sums of money, declined all further offers of publication save the tragedy of "Manuel. "

John Murray to Lord Byron.

March 15, 1817.

"Maturin's new tragedy, 'Manuel, ' appeared on Saturday last, and I am sorry to say that the opinion of Mr. Gifford was established by the impression made on the audience. The first act very fine, the rest exhibiting a want of judgment not to be endured. It was brought out with uncommon splendour, and was well acted. Kean's character as an old man—a warrior—was new and well sustained, for he had, of course, selected it, and professed to be—and he acted as if he were— really pleased with it.... I have undertaken to print the tragedy at my own expense, and to give the poor Author the whole of the profit. "

In 1824 Maturin died, in Dublin, in extreme poverty.

The following correspondence introduces another great name in English literature. It is not improbable that it was Southey who suggested to Murray the employment of his brother-in-law, Samuel Taylor Coleridge, from his thorough knowledge of German, as the translator of Goethe's "Faust. " The following is Mr. Coleridge's first letter to Murray:

Mr. Coleridge to John Murray.

JOSIAH WADE'S, Esq., 2, QUEEN'S SQUARE, BRISTOL. [*August* 23, 1814.]

Dear Sir,

I have heard, from my friend Mr. Charles Lamb, writing by desire of Mr. Robinson, that you wish to have the justly-celebrated "Faust" of Goethe translated, and that some one or other of my partial friends have induced you to consider me as the man most likely to execute the work adequately, those excepted, of course, whose higher power (established by the solid and satisfactory ordeal of the wide and rapid sale of their works) it might seem profanation to employ in any other manner than in the development of their own intellectual organization. I return my thanks to the recommender, whoever he be, and no less to you for your flattering faith in the recommendation; and thinking, as I do, that among many volumes of praiseworthy German poems, the "Louisa" of Voss, and the "Faust" of Goethe, are the two, if not the only ones, that are emphatically *original* in their conception, and characteristic of a new and peculiar sort of thinking and imagining, I should not be averse from exerting my best efforts in an attempt to import whatever is importable of either or of both into our own language.

But let me not be suspected of a presumption of which I am not consciously guilty, if I say that I feel two difficulties; one arising from long disuse of versification, added to what I know, better than the most hostile critic could inform me, of my comparative weakness; and the other, that *any* work in Poetry strikes me with more than common awe, as proposed for realization by myself, because from long habits of meditation on language, as the symbolic medium of the connection of Thought with Thought, and of Thoughts as affected and modified by Passion and Emotion, I should spend days in avoiding what I deemed faults, though with the full preknowledge that their admission would not have offended perhaps three of all my readers, and might be deemed Beauties by 300—if so many there were; and this not out of any respect for the Public (*i. e.* the persons who might happen to purchase and look over the Book), but from a hobby-horsical, superstitious regard to my own feelings and sense of Duty. Language is the sacred Fire in this Temple of Humanity, and the Muses are its especial and vestal Priestesses. Though I cannot prevent the vile drugs and counterfeit Frankincense, which render its flame at once pitchy, glowing, and unsteady, I would yet be no voluntary accomplice in the Sacrilege. With the commencement of a PUBLIC, commences the degradation of the GOOD and the BEAUTIFUL—both fade and retire before the accidentally AGREEABLE. "Othello" becomes a hollow lip-worship; and the "CASTLE SPECTRE, " or any more recent thing of Froth, Noise, and Impermanence, that may have overbillowed it on the restless sea of curiosity, is the *true* Prayer of Praise and Admiration.

I thought it right to state to you these opinions of mine, that you might know that I think the Translation of the "Faust" a task demanding (from *me*, I mean), no ordinary efforts—and why? This—that it is painful, very painful, and even odious to me, to attempt anything of a literary nature, with any motive of *pecuniary* advantage; but that I bow to the all-wise Providence, which has made me a *poor* man, and therefore compelled me by other duties inspiring feelings, to bring *even my Intellect to the Market*. And the finale is this. I should like to attempt the Translation. If you will mention your terms, at once and irrevocably (for I am an idiot at bargaining, and shrink from the very thought), I will return an answer by the next Post, whether in my present circumstances, I can or cannot undertake it. If I do, I will do it immediately; but I must have all Goethe's works, which I cannot procure in Bristol; for to give the "Faust" without a preliminary critical Essay would be worse than nothing, as far as regards the PUBLIC. If you were to ask me as a Friend, whether I think it would suit *the General Taste*, I should reply that I cannot calculate on caprice and accident (for instance, some fashionable man or review happening to take it up favourably), but that otherwise my fears would be stronger than my hopes. Men of genius will admire it, of necessity. Those most, who think deepest and most imaginatively. The "Louisa" would delight *all* of good hearts.

I remain, dear Sir, With due respect, S.T. COLERIDGE.

To this letter Mr. Murray replied as follows:

John Murray to Mr. Coleridge.

August 29, 1814.

Dear Sir,

I feel greatly obliged by the favour of your attention to the request which I had solicited our friend Mr. Robinson to make to you for the translation of Goethe's extraordinary drama of "Faust, " which I suspect that no one could do justice to besides yourself. It will be the first attempt to render into classical English a German work of peculiar but certainly of unquestionable Genius; and you must allow that its effects upon the public must be doubtful. I am desirous however of making the experiment, and this I would not do under a less skilful agent than the one to whom I have applied. I am no less anxious that you should receive, as far as I think the thing can admit, a fair remuneration; and trusting that you will not undertake it unless you feel disposed to execute the labour perfectly *con amore*, and in a style of versification equal to "Remorse, " I venture to propose to you the sum of One Hundred Pounds for the Translation and the preliminary Analysis, with such passages translated as you may judge proper of the works of Goethe, with a copy of which I will have the pleasure of supplying you as soon as I have your final determination. The sum which I mention shall be paid to you in two months from the day on which you place the complete Translation and Analysis in my hands; this will allow a reasonable time for your previous correction of the sheets through the press. I shall be glad to hear from you by return of Post, if convenient, as I propose to set out this week for the Continent. If this work succeeds, I am in hopes that it will lead to many similar undertakings.

With sincere esteem, I am, dear Sir, Your faithful Servant, J. Murray

I should hope that it might not prove inconvenient to you to complete the whole for Press in the course of November next.

Mr. Coleridge replied as follows, from the same address:

Mr. Coleridge to John Murray.

August 31, 1814.

Dear Sir,

I have received your letter. Considering the necessary labour, and (from the questionable nature of the original work, both as to its fair claims to Fame—the diction of the good and wise according to unchanging principles—and as to its chance for Reputation, as an accidental result of local and temporary taste), the risk of character on the part of the Translator, who will assuredly have to answer for any disappointment of the reader, the terms proposed are humiliatingly low; yet such as, under modifications, I accede to. I have received testimonials from men not merely of genius according to my belief, but of the highest accredited reputation, that my translation of "Wallenstein" was in language and in metre superior to the original, and the parts most admired were substitutions of my own, on a principle of compensation. Yet the whole work went for waste-paper. I was abused—nay, my own remarks in the Preface were transferred to a Review, as the Reviewer's sentiments *against* me, without even a hint that he had copied them from my own

Preface. Such was the fate of "Wallenstein"! And yet I dare appeal to any number of men of Genius—say, for instance, Mr. W. Scott, Mr. Southey, Mr. Wordsworth, Mr. Wilson, Mr. Sotheby, Sir G. Beaumont, etc., whether the "Wallenstein" with all its defects (and it has grievous defects), is not worth all Schiller's other plays put together. But I wonder not. It was *too* good, and not good enough; and the advice of the younger Pliny: "Aim at pleasing either *all*, or *the few*, " is as prudentially good as it is philosophically accurate. I wrote to Mr. Longman before the work was published, and foretold its fate, even to a detailed accuracy, and advised him to put up with the loss from the purchase of the MSS and of the Translation, as a much less evil than the publication. I went so far as to declare that its success was, in the state of public Taste, impossible; that the enthusiastic admirers of "The Robbers, " "Cabal and Love, " etc., would lay the blame on me; and that he himself would suspect that if he had only lit on *another* Translator then, etc. Everything took place as I had foretold, even his own feelings—so little do Prophets gain from the fulfilment of their Prophecies!

On the other hand, though I know that executed as alone I can or dare do it—that is, to the utmost of my power (for which the intolerable Pain, nay the far greater Toil and Effort of doing otherwise, is a far safer Pledge than any solicitude on my part concerning the approbation of the PUBLIC), the translation of so very difficult a work as the "Faustus, " will be most inadequately remunerated by the terms you propose; yet they very probably are the highest it may be worth your while to offer to *me*. I say this as a philosopher; for, though I have now been much talked of, and written of, for evil and not for good, but for suspected capability, yet none of my works have ever sold. The "Wallenstein" went to the waste. The "Remorse, " though acted twenty times, rests quietly on the shelves in the second edition, with copies enough for seven years' consumption, or seven times seven. I lost £200 by the non-payment, from forgetfulness, and under various pretences, by "The Friend"; [Footnote: Twenty-seven numbers of *The Friend* were published by Coleridge at Penrith in Cumberland in 1809-10, but the periodical proved a failure, principally from the irregularity of its appearance. It was about this time that he was addicted to opium-eating.] and for my poems I *did* get from £10 to £15. And yet, forsooth, the *Quarterly Review* attacks me for neglecting and misusing my powers! I do not quarrel with the Public—all is as it must be—but surely the Public (if there be such a Person) has no right to quarrel with *me* for not getting into jail by publishing what they will not read!

The "Faust, " you perhaps know, is only a *Fragment*. Whether Goethe ever will finish it, or whether it is ever his object to do so, is quite unknown. A large proportion of the work cannot be rendered in blank verse, but must be given in wild *lyrical* metres; and Mr. Lamb informs me that the Baroness de Staël has given a very unfavourable account of the work. Still, however, I will undertake it, and that instantly, so as to let you have the last sheet by the middle of November, on the following terms:

1. That on the delivery of the last MS. sheet you remit 100 guineas to Mrs. Coleridge, or Mr. Robert Southey, at a bill of five weeks. 2. That I, or my widow or family, may, any time after two years from the first publication, have the privilege of reprinting it in any collection of all my poetical writings, or of my works in general, which set off with a Life of me, might perhaps be made profitable to my widow. And 3rd, that if (as I long ago meditated) I should re-model the whole, give it a finale, and be able to bring it, thus re-written and re-cast, on the stage, it shall not be considered as a breach of the engagement between us, I on my part promising that you shall, for an equitable consideration, have the copy of this new work, either as a separate work, or forming a part of the same volume or both, as circumstances may dictate to you. When I say that I am confident that in this *possible* and not probable case, I should not repeat or retain one fifth of the original, you will perceive that I consult only my dread of appearing to act amiss, as it would be even more easy to compose the whole anew.

If these terms suit you I will commence the Task as soon as I receive Goethe's works from you. If you could procure Goethe's late Life of himself, which extends but a short way, or any German biographical work of the Germans living, it would enable me to render the preliminary Essay more entertaining.

Respectfully, dear Sir,

S. T. COLERIDGE.

Mr. Murray's reply to this letter has not been preserved. At all events, nothing further was done by Coleridge with respect to the translation of "Faust, " which is to be deplored, as his exquisite and original melody of versification might have produced a translation almost as great as the original.

Shortly after Coleridge took up his residence with the Gillmans at Highgate, and his intercourse with Murray recommenced. Lord Byron, while on the managing committee of Drury Lane Theatre, had been instrumental in getting Coleridge's "Remorse" played upon the stage, as he entertained a great respect for its author. He was now encouraging Mr. Murray to publish other works by Coleridge—among others, "Zapolya" and "Christabel. "

On April 12, 1816, Coleridge gave the following lines to Mr. Murray, written in his own hand: [Footnote: The "Song, by Glycine" was first published in "Zapolya: A Christmas Tale, " 1817, Part II., Act ii., Scene I. It was set to music by W. Patten in 1836; and again, with the title "May Song, " in 1879, by B. H. Loehr.]

GLYCINE: Song.

"A sunny shaft did I behold,
From sky to earth it slanted,
And pois'd therein a Bird so bold—
Sweet bird! thou wert enchanted!
He sank, he rose, he twinkled, he troll'd,
Within that shaft of sunny mist:
His Eyes of Fire, his Beak of Gold,
All else of Amethyst!
And thus he sang: Adieu! Adieu!
Love's dreams prove seldom true.
Sweet month of May! we must away!
Far, far away!
Today! today!"

In the following month (May 8, 1816) Mr. Coleridge offered Mr. Murray his "Remorse" for publication, with a Preface. He also offered his poem of "Christabel, " still unfinished. For the latter Mr. Murray agreed to give him seventy guineas, "until the other poems shall be completed, when the copyright shall revert to the author, " and also £20 for permission to publish the poem entitled "Kubla Khan. "

Next month (June 6) Murray allowed Coleridge £50 for an edition of "Zapolya: A Christmas Tale, " which was then in MS. ; and he also advanced him another £50 for a play which was still to be written. "Zapolya" was afterwards entrusted to another publisher (Rest Fenner), and Coleridge repaid Murray £50. Apparently (see *letter* of March 29, 1817) Murray very kindly forewent repayment of the second advance of £50. There was, of course, no obligation to excuse a just debt, but the three issues of "Christabel" had resulted in a net profit of a little over £100 to the publisher.

Mr. Coleridge to John Murray.

HIGHGATE, *July* 4, 1816.

I have often thought that there might be set on foot a review of old books, *i. e.*, of all works important or remarkable, the authors of which are deceased, with a probability of a tolerable sale, if only the original *plan* were a good one, and if no articles were admitted but from men who understood and recognized the Principles and Rules of Criticism, which should form the first number. I would not take the works chronologically, but according to the likeness or contrast of the *kind* of genius—*ex. gr.* Jeremy Taylor, Milton (his prose works), and Burke—Dante and Milton—Scaliger and Dr. Johnson. Secondly, if especial attention were paid to all men who had produced, or aided in producing, any great revolution in the Taste or opinions of an age, as Petrarch, Ulrich von Hutten, etc. (here I will dare risk the charge of self-conceit by referring to my own parallel of Voltaire and Erasmus, of Luther and Rousseau in the seventh number of "The Friend "). Lastly, if proper care was taken that in every number of the *Review* there should be a fair proportion of positively *amusing* matter, such as a review of Paracelsus, Cardan, Old Fuller; a review of Jest Books, tracing the various metempsychosis of the same joke through all ages and countries; a History of Court Fools, for which a laborious German has furnished ample and highly interesting materials; foreign writers, though alive, not to be excluded, if only their works are of established character in their own country, and scarcely heard of, much less translated, in English literature. Jean Paul Richter would supply two or three delightful articles.

Any works which should fall in your way respecting the Jews since the destruction of the Temple, I should of course be glad to look through. Above all, Mezeray's (no! that is not the name, I think) "History of the Jews, " that I *must* have.

I shall be impatient for the rest of Mr. Frere's sheets. Most unfeignedly can I declare that I am unable to decide whether the *admiration* which the *excellence* inspires, or the wonder which the knowledge of the countless *difficulties* so happily overcome, never ceases to excite in my mind during the re-perusal and collation of them with the original Greek, be the greater. I have not a moment's hesitation in fixing on Mr. Frere as the man of the correctest and most genial taste among all our contemporaries whom I have ever met with, personally or in their works. Should choice or chance lead you to sun and air yourself on Highgate Hill during any of your holiday excursions, my worthy friend and his amiable and accomplished wife will be happy to see you. We dine at four, and drink tea at six.

Yours, dear Sir, respectfully, S.T. COLERIDGE.

Mr. Murray did not accept Mr. Coleridge's proposal to publish his works in a collected form or his articles for the *Quarterly*, as appears from the following letter:

Mr. Coleridge to John Murray.

HIGHGATE, *March* 26, 1817.

DEAR SIR,

I cannot be offended by your opinion that my talents are not adequate to the requisites of matter and manner for the *Quarterly Review,* nor should I consider it as a disgrace to fall short of Robert Southey in any department of literature. I owe, however, an honest gratification to the conversation between you and Mr. Gillman, for I read Southey's article, on which Mr. Gillman and I have, it appears, formed very different opinions. It is, in my judgment, a very masterly article. [Footnote: This must have been Southey's article on Parliamentary Reform in No. 31, which, though due in October 1816, was not, published until February 1817.] I would to heaven, my dear sir, that the opinions of Southey, Walter Scott, Lord Byron, Mr. Frere, and of men like these in learning and genius, concerning my comparative claims to be a man of letters, were to be received as the criterion, instead of the wretched, and in deed and in truth mystical jargon of the *Examiner* and *Edinburgh Review*.

Mr. Randall will be so good as to repay you the £50, and I understand from Mr. Gillman that you are willing to receive this as a settlement respecting the "Zapolya. " The corrections and additions to the two first books of the "Christabel" may become of more value to you when the work is finished, as I trust it will be in the course of the spring, than they are at present. And let it not be forgotten, that while I had the utmost malignity of personal enmity to cry down the work, with the exception of Lord Byron, there was not one of the many who had so many years together spoken so warmly in its praise who gave it the least positive furtherance after its publication. It was openly asserted that the *Quarterly Review* did not wish to attack it, but was ashamed to say a word in its favor. Thank God! these things pass from me like drops from a duck's back, except as far as they take the bread out of my mouth; and this I can avoid by consenting to publish only for the *present* times whatever I may write. You will be so kind as to acknowledge the receipt of the £50 in such manner as to make all matters as clear between us as possible; for, though you, I am sure, could not have intended to injure my character, yet the misconceptions, and perhaps misrepresentations, of your words have had that tendency. By a letter from R. Southey I find that he will be in town on the 17th. The article in Tuesday's *Courier* was by me, and two other articles on Apostacy and Renegadoism, which will appear this week.

Believe me, with respect, your obliged,

S. T. COLERIDGE.

The following letter completes Coleridge's correspondence with Murray on this subject:

Mr. Coleridge to John Murray.

[Highgate], *March* 29, 1817.

Dear Sir,

From not referring to the paper dictated by yourself, and signed by me in your presence, you have wronged yourself in the receipt you have been so good as to send me, and on which I have therefore written as follows—"A mistake; I am still indebted to Mr. Murray £20 *legally* (which I shall pay the moment it is in my power), and £30 from whatever sum I may receive from the 'Christabel' when it is finished. Should Mr. Murray decline its publication, I conceive myself bound *in honor* to repay. " I strive in vain to discover any single act or expression of my own, or for which I could be directly or indirectly responsible as a moral being, that would account for the change in your mode of thinking respecting me. But with every due acknowledgment of the kindness and courtesy that I received from you on my first coming to town,

I remain, dear Sir, your obliged, S.T. COLERIDGE.

Leigh Hunt was another of Murray's correspondents. When the *Quarterly* was started, Hunt, in his Autography, says that "he had been invited, nay pressed by the publisher, to write in the new Review, which surprised me, considering its politics and the great difference of my own. " Hunt adds that he had no doubt that the invitation had been made at the instance of Gifford himself. Murray had a high opinion of Hunt as a critic, but not as a politician. Writing to Walter Scott in 1810 he said:

John Murray to Mr. Scott,

"Have you got or seen Hunt's critical essays, prefixed to a few novels that he edited. Lest you should not, I send them. Hunt is most vilely wrongheaded in politics, and has thereby been turned away from the path of elegant criticism, which might have led him to eminence and respectability. "

Hunt was then, with his brother, joint editor of the *Examiner*, and preferred writing for the newspaper to contributing articles to the *Quarterly*.

On Leigh Hunt's release from Horsemonger Lane Gaol, where he had been imprisoned for his libel on the Prince Regent, he proceeded, on the strength of his reputation, to compose the "Story of Rimini, " the publication of which gave the author a place among the poets of the day. He sent a portion of the manuscript to Mr. Murray before the poem was finished, saying that it would amount to about 1,400 lines. Hunt then proceeded (December 18, 1815) to mention the terms which he proposed to be paid for his work when finished. "Booksellers, " he said, "tell me that I ought not to ask less than £450 (which is a sum I happen to want just now); and my friends, not in the trade, say I ought not to ask less than £500, with such a trifling acknowledgment upon the various editions after the second and third, as shall enable me to say that I am still profiting by it. "

Mr. Murray sent his reply to Hunt through their common friend, Lord Byron:

John Murray to Lord Byron.

December 27, 1815.

"I wish your lordship to do me the favour to look at and to consider with your usual kindness the accompanying note to Mr. Leigh Hunt respecting his poem, for which he requests £450. This would presuppose a sale of, at least, 10,000 copies. Now, if I may trust to my own experience in these matters, I am by no means certain that the sale would do more than repay the expenses of paper and print. But the poem is peculiar, and may be more successful than I imagine, in which event the proposition which I have made to the author will secure to him all the advantages of such a result, I trust that you will see in this an anxious desire to serve Mr. Hunt, although as a mere matter of business I cannot avail myself of his offer. I would have preferred calling upon you today were I not confined by a temporary indisposition; but I think you will not be displeased at a determination founded upon the best judgment I can form of my own business. I am really uneasy at your feelings in this affair, but I think I may venture to assume that you know me sufficiently well to allow me to trust my decision entirely to your usual kindness. "

John Murray to Mr. Leigh Hunt.

December 27, 1815.

"I have now read the MS. poem, which you confided to me, with particular attention, and find that it differs so much from any that I have published that I am fearful of venturing upon the extensive speculation to which your estimate would carry it. I therefore wish that you would propose its publication and purchase to such houses as Cadell, Longman, Baldwin, Mawman, etc., who are capable of becoming and likely to become purchasers, and then, should you not have found any arrangement to your mind, I would undertake to print an edition of 500 or 750 copies as a trial at my own risk, and give you one half of the profits. After this edition the copyright shall be entirely your own property. By this arrangement, in case the work turn out a prize, as it may do, I mean that you should have every advantage of its success, for its popularity once ascertained, I am sure you will find no difficulty in procuring purchasers, even if you should be suspicious of my liberality from this specimen of fearfulness in the first instance. I shall be most happy to assist you with any advice which my experience in these matters may render serviceable to you. "

Leigh Hunt at once accepted the offer.

After the poem was printed and published, being pressed for money, he wished to sell the copyright. After a recitation of his pecuniary troubles, Hunt concluded a lengthy letter as follows:

"What I wanted to ask you then is simply this—whether, in the first instance, you think well enough of the "Story of Rimini" to make you bargain with me for the copyright at once; or, in the second instance, whether, if you would rather wait a little, as I myself would do, I confess, if it were convenient, you have still enough hopes of the work, and enough reliance on myself personally, to advance me £450 on security, to be repaid in case you do not conclude the bargain, or merged in the payment of the poem in case you do. "

Mr. Murray's reply was not satisfactory, as will be observed from the following letter of Leigh Hunt:

Mr. Leigh Hunt to John Murray,

April 12, 1816.

Dear Sir,

I just write to say something which I had omitted in my last, and to add a word or two on the subject of an expression in your answer to it. I mean the phrase "plan of assistance. " I do not suppose that you had the slightest intention of mortifying me by that phrase; but I should wish to impress upon you, that I did not consider my application to you as coming in the shape of what is ordinarily termed an application for assistance. Circumstances have certainly compelled me latterly to make requests, and resort to expedients, which, however proper in themselves, I would not willingly have been acquainted with; but I have very good prospects before me, and you are mistaken (I beg you to read this in the best and most friendly tone you can present to yourself) if you have at all apprehended that I should be in the habit of applying to you for assistance, or for anything whatsoever, for which I did not conceive the work in question to be more than a security.

I can only say, with regard to yourself, that I am quite contented and ought to be so, as long as you are sincere with me, and treat me in the same gentlemanly tone.

Very sincerely yours,

LEIGH HUNT.

This negotiation was ultimately brought to a conclusion by Mr. Hunt, at Mr. Murray's suggestion, disposing of the copyright of "Rimini" to another publisher.

CHAPTER XIII

THOMAS CAMPBELL—JOHN CAM HOBHOUSE—J. W. CROKER-
JAMES HOGG, ETC.

Thomas Campbell appeared like a meteor as early as 1799, when, in his twenty-second year, he published his "Pleasures of Hope. " The world was taken by surprise at the vigour of thought and richness of fancy displayed in the poem. Shortly after its publication, Campbell went to Germany, and saw, from the Benedictine monastery of Scottish monks at Ratisbon, a battle which was not, as has often been said, the Battle of Hohenlinden. What he saw, however, made a deep impression on his mind, and on his return to Scotland he published the beautiful lines beginning, "On Linden when the sun was low. " In 1801 he composed "The Exile of Erin" and "Ye Mariners of England. " The "Battle of the Baltic" and "Lochiel's Warning" followed; and in 1803 he published an edition of his poems. To have composed such noble lyrics was almost unprecedented in so young a man; for he was only twenty-six years of age when his collected edition appeared. He was treated as a lion, and became acquainted with Walter Scott and the leading men in Edinburgh. In December 1805 we find Constable writing to Murray, that Longman & Co. had offered the young poet £700 for a new volume of his poems.

One of the earliest results of the association of Campbell with Murray was a proposal to start a new magazine, which Murray had long contemplated. This, it will be observed, was some years before the communications took place between Walter Scott and Murray with respect to the starting of the *Quarterly*.

The projected magazine, however, dropped out of sight, and Campbell reverted to his proposed "Lives of the British Poets, with Selections from their Writings. " Toward the close of the year he addressed the following letter to Mr. Scott:

Mr. T. Campbell to Mr. Scott.

November 5, 1806.

My Dear Scott,

A very excellent and gentlemanlike man—albeit a bookseller—Murray, of Fleet Street, is willing to give for our joint "Lives of the Poets, " on the plan we proposed to the trade a twelvemonth ago, a thousand pounds. For my part, I think the engagement very desirable, and have no uneasiness on the subject, except my fear that you may be too much engaged to have to do with it, as five hundred pounds may not be to you the temptation that it appears to a poor devil like myself. Murray is the only gentleman, except Constable, in the trade; —I may also, perhaps, except Hood. I have seldom seen a pleasanter man to deal with. .... Our names are what Murray principally wants—*yours* in particular.... I will not wish, even in confidence, to say anything ill of the London booksellers *beyond their deserts*; but I assure you that, to compare this offer of Murray's with their usual offers, it is magnanimous indeed.... The fallen prices of literature-which is getting worse by the horrible complexion of the times-make me often rather gloomy at the life I am likely to lead.

Scott entered into Campbell's agreement with kindness and promptitude, and it was arranged, under certain stipulations, that the plan should have his zealous cooperation; but as the number and importance of his literary engagements increased, he declined to take an active part either in the magazine or the other undertaking. "I saw Campbell two days ago, " writes Murray to Constable, "and he told me that Mr. Scott had declined, and modestly asked if it would do by *himself* alone; but this I declined in a way that did not leave us the less friends. "

At length, after many communications and much personal intercourse, Murray agreed with Campbell to bring out his work, without the commanding name of Walter Scott, and with the name of Thomas Campbell alone as Editor of the "Selections from the British Poets. " The arrangement seems to have been made towards the end of 1808. In January 1809 Campbell writes of his intention "to devote a year exclusively to the work, " but the labour it involved was perhaps greater than he had anticipated. It was his first important prose work; and prose requires continuous labour. It cannot, like a piece of poetry, be thrown off at a heat while the fit is on. Campbell stopped occasionally in the midst of his work to write poems, among others, his "Gertrude of Wyoming, " which confirmed his poetical reputation. Murray sent a copy of the volume to Walter Scott, and requested a review for the *Quarterly*, which was then in its first year. What Campbell thought of the review will appear from the following letter:

Mr. T. Campbell to John Murray.

June 2, 1809.

My Dear Murray,

I received the review, for which I thank you, and beg leave through you to express my best acknowledgments to the unknown reviewer. I do not by this mean to say that I think every one of his censures just. On the contrary, if I had an opportunity of personal conference with so candid and sensible a man, I think I could in some degree acquit myself of a part of the faults he has found. But altogether I am pleased with his manner, and very proud of his approbation. He reviews like a gentleman, a Christian, and a scholar.

Although the "Lives of the Poets" had been promised within a year from January 1809, four years passed, and the work was still far from completion.

In the meantime Campbell undertook to give a course of eleven Lectures on Poetry at the Royal Institution, for which he received a hundred guineas. He enriched his Lectures with the Remarks and Selections collected for the "Specimens, " for which the publisher had agreed to pay a handsome sum. The result was a momentary hesitation on the part of Mr. Murray to risk the publication of the work. On this, says Campbell's biographer, a correspondence ensued between the poet and the publisher, which ended to the satisfaction of both. Mr. Murray only requested that Mr. Campbell should proceed with greater alacrity in finishing the long projected work.

At length, about the beginning of 1819, fourteen years after the project had been mentioned to Walter Scott, and about ten years after the book should have appeared, according to Campbell's original promise, the "Essays and Selections of English Poetry" were published by Mr. Murray. The work was well received. The poet was duly paid for it, and Dr. Beattie, Campbell's biographer, says he "found himself in the novel position of a man who has money to lay out at interest. " This statement must be received with considerable deduction, for, as the correspondence shows, Campbell's pecuniary difficulties were by no means at an end.

It appears that besides the £1,000, which was double the sum originally proposed to be paid to Campbell for the "Selections, " Mr.

Murray, in October 1819, paid him £200 "for books, " doubtless for those he had purchased for the "Collections, " and which he desired to retain.

We cannot conclude this account of Campbell's dealing with Murray without referring to an often-quoted story which has for many years sailed under false colours. It was Thomas Campbell who wrote "Now Barabbas was a publisher, " whether in a Bible or otherwise is not authentically recorded, and forwarded it to a friend; but Mr. Murray was not the publisher to whom it referred, nor was Lord Byron, as has been so frequently stated, the author of the joke.

The great burden of the correspondence entailed by the *Quarterly Review* now fell on Mr. Murray, for Gifford had become physically incapable of bearing it. Like the creaking gate that hangs long on its hinges, Gifford continued to live, though painfully. He became gradually better, and in October 1816 Mr. Murray presented him with a chariot, by means of which he might drive about and take exercise in the open air. Gifford answered:

"I have a thousand thanks to give you for the pains you have taken about the carriage, without which I should only have talked about it, and died of a cold. It came home yesterday, and I went to Fulham in it. It is everything that I could wish, neat, easy, and exceedingly comfortable. "

Among the other works published by Mr. Murray in 1816 may be mentioned, "The Last Reign of Napoleon, " by Mr. John Cam Hobhouse, afterwards Lord Broughton. Of this work the author wrote to Mr. Murray:

January, 1816.

"I must have the liberty of cancelling what sheets I please, for a reason that I now tell you in the strictest confidence: the letters are to go to Paris previously to publication, and are to be read carefully through by a most intimate friend of mine, who was entirely in the secrets of the late Imperial Ministry, and who will point out any statements as to facts, in which he could from his *knowledge* make any necessary change. "

The first edition, published without the author's name, was rapidly exhausted, and Hobhouse offered a second to Murray, proposing at the same time to insert his name as author on the title-page.

"If I do, " he said, "I shall present the book to Lord Byron in due form, not for his talents as a poet, but for his qualities as a companion and a friend. I should not write 'My dear Byron, ' *à la Hunt.* " [Footnote: Leigh Hunt had dedicated his "Rimini" to the noble poet, addressing him as "My dear Byron. "]

Mr. D'Israeli also was busy with his "Inquiry into the Literary and Political Character of James the First. " He wrote to his publisher as follows: "I am sorry to say every one, to whom I have mentioned the subject, revolts from it as a thing quite untenable, and cares nothing about 'James. ' This does not stop me from finishing. "

Mr. Croker, in the midst of his work at the Admiralty, his articles for the *Quarterly*, and his other literary labours, found time to write his "Stories for Children from the History of England. " In sending the later stories Mr. Croker wrote to Mr. Murray:

The Rt. Hon. J.W. Croker to John Murray.

"I send you seven stories, which, with eleven you had before, brings us down to Richard III., and as I do not intend to come down beyond the Revolution, there remain nine stories still. I think you told me that you gave the first stories to your little boy to read. Perhaps you or Mrs. Murray would be so kind as to make a mark over against such words as he may not have understood, and to favour me with any criticism the child may have made, for on this occasion I should prefer a critic of 6 years old to one of 60. "

Thus John Murray's son, John Murray the Third, was early initiated into the career of reading for the press. When the book came out it achieved a great success, and set the model for Walter Scott in his charming "Tales of a Grandfather. "

It may be mentioned that "Croker's Stories for Children" were published on the system of division of profits. Long after, when Mr. Murray was in correspondence with an author who wished him to pay a sum of money down before he had even seen the manuscript, the publisher recommended the author to publish his book on a division of profits, in like manner as Hallam, Milman, Mahon,

Croker, and others had done. "Under this system, " he said, "I have been very successful. For Mr. Croker's 'Stories from the History of England, ' selling for 2s. 6d., if I had offered the small sum of twenty guineas, he would have thought it liberal. However, I printed it to divide profits, and he has already received from me the moiety of £1,400. You will perhaps be startled at my assertion; for woeful experience convinces me that not more than one publication in fifty has a sale sufficient to defray its expenses. "

The success of Scott's, and still more of Byron's Poems, called into existence about this time a vast array of would-be poets, male and female, and from all ranks and professions. Some wrote for fame, some for money; but all were agreed on one point—namely, that if Mr. Murray would undertake the publication of the poems, the authors' fame was secured.

When in doubt about any manuscript, he usually conferred with Croker, Campbell, or Gifford, who always displayed the utmost kindness in helping him with their opinions. Croker was usually short and pithy. Of one poem he said: "Trash—the dullest stuff I ever read. " This was enough to ensure the condemnation of the manuscript. Campbell was more guarded, as when reporting on a poem entitled "Woman, " he wrote, "In my opinion, though there are many excellent lines in it, the poem is not such as will warrant a great sum being speculated upon it. But, as it is short, I think the public, not the author or publisher, will be in fault if it does not sell one edition. "

Of a poem sent for his opinion, Gifford wrote:

"Honestly, the MS. is totally unfit for the press. Do not deceive yourself: this MS. is not the production of a male. A man may write as great nonsense as a woman, and even greater; but a girl may pass through those execrable abodes of ignorance, called boarding schools, without learning whether the sun sets in the East or in the West, whereas a boy can hardly do this, even at Parson's Green. "

James Hogg, the Ettrick Shepherd, was another of Murray's correspondents.

The publication of "The Queen's Wake" in 1813 immediately brought Hogg into connection with the leading authors and publishers of the day, Hogg sent a copy of the volume to Lord

Byron, his "brother poet, " whose influence he desired to enlist on behalf of a work which Hogg wished Murray to publish.

The poem which the Ettrick Shepherd referred to was "The Pilgrims of the Sun, " and the result of Lord Byron's conversation with Mr. Murray was, that the latter undertook to publish Hogg's works. The first letter from him to Murray, December 26, 1814, begins:

"What the deuce have you made of my excellent poem that you are never publishing it, while I am starving for want of money, and cannot even afford a Christmas goose to my friends? "

To this and many similar enquiries Mr. Murray replied on April 10, 1815:

My Dear Friend,

I entreat you not to ascribe to inattention the delay which has occurred in my answer to your kind and interesting letter. Much more, I beg you not for a moment to entertain a doubt about the interest which I take in your writings, or the exertions which I shall ever make to promote their sale and popularity.... They are selling every day.

I have forgotten to tell you that Gifford tells me that he would receive, with every disposition to favour it, any critique which you like to send of new Scottish works. If I had been aware of it in time I certainly would have invited your remarks on "Mannering. " Our article is not good and our praise is by no means adequate, I allow, but I suspect you very greatly overrate the novel. "Meg Merrilies" is worthy of Shakespeare, but all the rest of the novel might have been written by Scott's brother or any other body.

The next letter from the Shepherd thanks Murray for some "timeous" aid, and asks a novel favour.

May 7, 1815.

I leave Edinburgh on Thursday for my little farm on Yarrow. I will have a confused summer, for I have as yet no home that I can dwell in; but I hope by-and-by to have some fine fun there with you, fishing in Saint Mary's Loch and the Yarrow, eating bull-trout, singing songs, and drinking whisky. This little possession is what I stood much in need of—a habitation among my native hills was what of all the world I desired; and if I had a little more money at command, I would just be as happy a man as I know of; but that is an article of which I am ever in want. I wish you or Mrs. Murray would speer me out a good wife with a few thousands. I dare say there is many a romantic girl about London who would think it a fine ploy to become a Yarrow Shepherdess! Believe me, dear Murray,

Very sincerely yours, JAMES HOGG.

Here, for the present, we come to an end of the Shepherd's letters; but we shall find him turning up again, and Mr. Murray still continuing his devoted friend and adviser.

CHAPTER XIV

LORD BYRON'S DEALINGS WITH MR. MURRAY—continued

On January 2, 1815, Lord Byron was married to Miss Milbanke, and during the honeymoon, while he was residing at Seaham, the residence of his father-in-law Sir Ralph Milbanke, he wrote to Murray desiring him to make occasional enquiry at his chambers in the Albany to see if they were kept in proper order.

John Murray to Lord Byron.

February 17, 1815.

MY LORD,

I have paid frequent attention to your wish that I should ascertain if all things appeared to be safe in your chambers, and I am happy in being able to report that the whole establishment carries an appearance of security, which is confirmed by the unceasing vigilance of your faithful and frigid Duenna [Mrs. Mule].

Every day I have been in expectation of receiving a copy of "Guy Mannering, " of which the reports of a friend of mine, who has read the first two volumes, is such as to create the most extravagant expectations of an extraordinary combination of wit, humour and pathos. I am certain of one of the first copies, and this you may rely upon receiving with the utmost expedition.

I hear many interesting letters read to me from the Continent, and one in particular from Mr. Fazakerly, describing his interview of four hours with Bonaparte, was particularly good. He acknowledged at once to the poisoning of the sick prisoners in Egypt; they had the plague, and would have communicated it to the rest of his army if he had carried them on with him, and he had only to determine if he should leave them to a cruel death by the Turks, or to an easy one by poison. When asked his motive for becoming a Mahomedan, he replied that there were great political reasons for this, and gave several; but he added, the Turks would not admit me at first unless I submitted to two indispensable ceremonies.... They agreed at length to remit the first and to commute the other for a solemn vow, for every offence to give expiation by the performance of some good action. "Oh, gentlemen, " says he, "for good actions, you know you may command me, " and his first good action was to put to instant death an hundred of their priests, whom he suspected of intrigues against him. Not aware of his summary justice, they sent a deputation to beg the lives of these people on the score of his engagement. He answered that nothing would have made him so happy as this opportunity of showing his zeal for their religion; but that they had arrived too late; their friends had been dead nearly an hour.

He asked Lord Ebrington of which party he was, in Politics. "The Opposition. " "The Opposition? Then can your Lordship tell me the reason why the Opposition are so unpopular in England? " With something like presence of mind on so delicate a question, Lord Ebrington instantly replied: "Because, sir, we always insisted upon it, that you would be successful in Spain. "

During the spring and summer of 1815 Byron was a frequent visitor at Albemarle Street, and in April, as has been already recorded, he first met Walter Scott in Murray's drawing-room.

In March, Lord and Lady Byron took up their residence at 13, Piccadilly Terrace. The following letter is undated, but was probably written in the autumn of 1815.

John Murray to Lord Byron.

My Lord,

I picked up, the other day, some of Napoleon's own writing paper, all the remainder of which has been burnt; it has his portrait and eagle, as you will perceive by holding a sheet to the light either of sun or candle: so I thought I would take a little for you, hoping that you will just write me a poem upon any twenty-four quires of it in return.

By the autumn of 1815 Lord Byron found himself involved in pecuniary embarrassments, which had, indeed, existed before his marriage, but were now considerably increased and demanded immediate settlement. His first thought was to part with his books, though they did not form a very valuable collection. He mentioned the matter to a book collector, who conferred with other dealers on the subject. The circumstances coming to the ears of Mr. Murray, he at once communicated with Lord Byron, and forwarded him a cheque for £1,500, with the assurance that an equal sum should be at his service in the course of a few weeks, offering, at the same time, to dispose of all the copyrights of his poems for his Lordship's use.

Lord Byron could not fail to be affected by this generous offer, and whilst returning the cheque, he wrote:

November 14, 1815.

"Your present offer is a favour which I would accept from you, if I accepted such from any man... The circumstances which induce me to part with my books, though sufficiently, are not *immediately*, pressing. I have made up my mind to this, and there's an end. Had I been disposed to trespass upon your kindness in this way, it would have been before now; but I am not sorry to have an opportunity of declining it, as it sets my opinion of you, and indeed of human nature, in a different light from that in which I have been accustomed to consider it. "

Meanwhile Lord Byron had completed his "Siege of Corinth" and "Parisina, " and sent the packet containing them to Mr. Murray. They had been copied in the legible hand of Lady Byron. On receiving the poems Mr. Murray wrote to Lord Byron as follows:

John Murray to Lord Byron.

December, 1815.

My Lord,

I tore open the packet you sent me, and have found in it a Pearl. It is very interesting, pathetic, beautiful—do you know, I would almost say moral. I am really writing to you before the billows of the passions you excited have subsided. I have been most agreeably disappointed (a word I cannot associate with the poem) at the story, which—what you hinted to me and wrote—had alarmed me; and I should not have read it aloud to my wife if my eye had not traced the delicate hand that transcribed it.

Mr. Murray enclosed to Lord Byron two notes, amounting to a thousand guineas, for the copyright of the poems, but Lord Byron refused the notes, declaring that the sum was too great.

"Your offer, " he answered (January 3, 1816), "is *liberal* in the extreme, and much more than the poems can possibly be worth; but I cannot accept it, and will not. You are most welcome to them as additions to the collected volumes, without any demand or expectation on my part whatever.... I am very glad that the handwriting was a favourable omen of the *morale* of the piece; but you must not trust to that, as my copyist would write out anything I desired in all the ignorance of innocence—I hope, however, in this instance, with no great peril to either. "

The money, therefore, which Murray thought the copyright of the "Siege of Corinth" and "Parisina" was worth, remained untouched in the publisher's hands. It was afterwards suggested, by Mr. Rogers and Sir James Mackintosh, to Lord Byron, that a portion of it (£600) might be applied to the relief of Mr. Godwin, the author of "An Enquiry into Political Justice, " who was then in difficulties; and Lord Byron himself proposed that the remainder should be divided between Mr. Maturin and Mr. Coleridge. This proposal caused the deepest vexation to Mr. Murray, who made the following remonstrance against such a proceeding.

John Murray to Lord Byron.

ALBEMARLE STREET, *Monday*, 4 o'clock.

My Lord,

I did not like to detain you this morning, but I confess to you that I came away impressed with a belief that you had already reconsidered this matter, as it refers to me—Your Lordship will pardon me if I cannot avoid looking upon it as a species of cruelty, after what has passed, to take from me so large a sum—offered with no reference to the marketable value of the poems, but out of personal friendship and gratitude alone, —to cast it away on the wanton and ungenerous interference of those who cannot enter into your Lordship's feelings for me, upon, persons who have so little claim upon you, and whom those who so interested themselves might more decently and honestly enrich from their own funds, than by endeavouring to be liberal at the cost of another, and by forcibly resuming from me a sum which you had generously and nobly resigned.

I am sure you will do me the justice to believe that I would strain every nerve in your service, but it is actually heartbreaking to throw away my earnings on others. I am no rich man, abounding, like Mr. Rogers, in superfluous thousands, but working hard for independence, and what would be the most grateful pleasure to me if likely to be useful to you personally, becomes merely painful if it causes me to work for others for whom I can have no such feelings.

This is a most painful subject for me to address you upon, and I am ill able to express my feelings about it. I commit them entirely to your liberal construction with a reference to your knowledge of my character.

I have the honour to be, etc.,

JOHN MURRAY.

This letter was submitted to Gifford before it was despatched, and he wrote:

Mr. Gifford to John Murray.

"I have made a scratch or two, and the letter now expresses my genuine sentiments on the matter. But should you not see Rogers? It is evident that Lord Byron is a little awkward about this matter, and his officious friends have got him into a most *unlordly* scrape, from which they can only relieve him by treading back their steps. The more I consider their conduct, the more I am astonished at their impudence. A downright robbery is honourable to it. If you see Rogers, do not be shy to speak: he trembles at report, and here is an evil one for him. "

In the end Lord Byron was compelled by the increasing pressure of his debts to accept the sum offered by Murray and use it for his own purposes.

It is not necessary here to touch upon the circumstances of Lord Byron's separation from his wife; suffice it to say that early in 1816 he determined to leave England, and resolved, as he had before contemplated doing, to sell off his books and furniture. He committed the arrangements to Mr. Murray, through Mr. Hanson, his solicitor, in Bloomsbury Square. A few months before, when

Lord Byron was in straits for money, Mr. Hanson communicated with Mr. Murray as follows:

Mr. Hanson to John Murray.

November 23, 1815.

"Mr. Hanson's compliments to Mr. Murray. He has seen Lord Byron, and his Lordship has no objection to his Library being taken at a valuation. Mr. Hanson submits to Mr. Murray whether it would not be best to name one respectable bookseller to set a value on them. In the meantime, Mr. Hanson has written to Messrs. Crook & Armstrong, in whose hands the books now are, not to proceed further in the sale. "

On December 28, 1815, Mr. Murray received the following valuation:

"Mr. Cochrane presents respectful compliments to Mr. Murray, and begs to inform him that upon carefully inspecting the books in Skinner Street, he judges the fair value of them to be £450. "

Mr. Murray sent Lord Byron a bill of £500 for the books as a temporary accommodation. But the books were traced and attached by the sheriff. On March 6, 1816, Lord Byron wrote to Murray:

"I send to you to-day for this reason: the books you purchased are again seized, and, as matters stand, had much better be sold at once by public auction. I wish to see you to-morrow to return your bill for them, which, thank Heaven, is neither due nor paid. *That* part, so far as *you* are concerned, being settled (which it can be, and shall be, when I see you tomorrow), I have no further delicacy about the matter. This is about the tenth execution in as many months; so I am pretty well hardened; but it is fit I should pay the forfeit of my forefathers' extravagance as well as my own; and whatever my faults may be, I suppose they will be pretty well expiated in time—or eternity. "

A letter was next received by Mr. Murray's solicitor, Mr. Turner, from Mr. Gunn, to the following effect:

Mr. Gunn to Mr. Turner.

March 16, 1816.

Sir,

Mr. Constable, the plaintiff's attorney, has written to say he will indemnify the sheriff to sell the books under the execution; as such, we must decline taking your indemnity.

The result was, that Lord Byron, on March 22, paid to Crook & Armstrong £231 15*s*., "being the amount of three levies, poundage, and expenses, " and also £25 13*s*. 6*d*., the amount of Crook & Armstrong's account. Crook & Armstrong settled with Levy, the Jew, who had lent Byron money; and also with the officer, who had been in possession twenty-three days, at 5*s*. a day. The books were afterwards sold by Mr. Evans at his house, 26, Pall Mall, on April 5, 1816, and the following day. The catalogue describes them as "A collection of books, late the property of a nobleman, about to leave England on a tour. "

Mr. Murray was present at the sale, and bought a selection of books for Mrs. Leigh, for Mr. Rogers, and for Mr. J.C. Hobhouse, as well as for himself. He bought the large screen, with the portraits of actors and pugilists, which is still at Albemarle Street. There was also a silver cup and cover, nearly thirty ounces in weight, elegantly chased. These articles realised £723 12*s*. 6*d*., and after charging the costs, commission, and Excise duty, against the sale of the books, the balance was handed over to Lord Byron.

The "Sketch from Private Life" was one of the most bitter and satirical things Byron had ever written. In sending it to Mr. Murray (March 30, 1816), he wrote: "I send you my last night's dream, and request to have fifty copies struck off for private distribution. I wish Mr. Gifford to look at it; it is from life. " Afterwards, when Lord Byron called upon Mr. Murray, he said: "I could not get to sleep last night, but lay rolling and tossing about until this morning, when I got up and wrote that; and it is very odd, Murray, after doing that, I went to bed again, and never slept sounder in my life. "

The lines were printed and sent to Lord Byron. But before publishing them, Mr. Murray took advice of his special literary adviser and solicitor, Mr. Sharon Turner. His reply was as follows:

Mr. Turner to John Murray.

April 3, 1816.

There are some expressions in the Poem that I think are libellous, and the severe tenor of the whole would induce a jury to find them to be so. The question only remains, to whom it is applicable. It certainly does not itself name the person. But the legal pleadings charge that innuendo must mean such a person. How far evidence extrinsic to the work might be brought or received to show that the author meant a particular person, I will not pretend to affirm. Some cases have gone so far on this point that I should not think it safe to risk. And if a libel, it is a libel not only by the author, but by the printer, the publisher, and every circulator.

I am, dear Murray, yours most faithfully,

SHN. TURNER.

Mr. Murray did not publish the poems, but after their appearance in the newspapers, they were announced by many booksellers as "Poems by Lord Byron on his Domestic Circumstances. " Among others, Constable printed and published them, whereupon Blackwood, as Murray's agent in Edinburgh, wrote to him, requesting the suppression of the verses, and threatening proceedings. Constable, in reply, said he had no wish to invade literary property, but the verses had come to him without either author's name, publisher's name, or printer's name, and that there was no literary property in publications to which neither author's, publisher's, nor printer's name was attached. Blackwood could proceed no farther. In his letter to Murray (April 17, 1816), he wrote:

"I have distributed copies of 'Fare Thee Well' and 'A Sketch' to Dr. Thomas Brown, Walter Scott, and Professor Playfair. One cannot read 'Fare Thee Well' without crying. The other is 'vigorous hate, ' as you say. Its power is really terrible; one's blood absolutely creeps while reading it. "

Byron left England in April 1816, and during his travels he corresponded frequently with Mr. Murray.

The MSS. of the third canto of "Childe Harold" and "The Prisoner of Chillon" duly reached the publisher. Mr. Murray acknowledged the MSS. :

Mr. Murray to Lord Byron.

September 12, 1816.

My Lord,

I have rarely addressed you with more pleasure than upon the present occasion. I was thrilled with delight yesterday by the announcement of Mr. Shelley with the MS. of "Childe Harold. " I had no sooner got the quiet possession of it than, trembling with auspicious hope about it, I carried it direct to Mr. Gifford. He has been exceedingly ill with jaundice, and unable to write or do anything. He was much pleased by my attention. I called upon him today. He said he was unable to leave off last night, and that he had sat up until he had finished every line of the canto. It had actually agitated him into a fever, and he was much worse when I called. He had persisted this morning in finishing the volume, and he pronounced himself infinitely more delighted than when he first wrote to me. He says that what you have heretofore published is nothing to this effort. He says also, besides its being the most original and interesting, it is the most finished of your writings; and he has undertaken to correct the press for you.

Never, since my intimacy with Mr. Gifford, did I see him so heartily pleased, or give one-fiftieth part of the praise, with one-thousandth part of the warmth. He speaks in ecstasy of the Dream—the whole volume beams with genius. I am sure he loves you in his heart; and when he called upon me some time ago, and I told him that you were gone, he instantly exclaimed in a full room, "Well! he has not left his equal behind him—that I will say! " Perhaps you will enclose a line for him....

Respecting the "Monody, " I extract from a letter which I received this morning from Sir James Mackintosh: "I presume that I have to thank you for a copy of the 'Monody' on Sheridan received this morning. I wish it had been accompanied by the additional favour of mentioning the name of the writer, at which I only guess: it is difficult to read the poem without desiring to know. "

Generally speaking it is not, I think, popular, and spoken of rather for fine passages than as a whole. How could you give so trite an image as in the last two lines? Gifford does not like it; Frere does. *A-propos* of Mr. Frere: he came to me while at breakfast this morning, and between some stanzas which he was repeating to me of a truly original poem of his own, he said carelessly,

"By the way, about *half-an-hour ago* I was so silly (taking an immense pinch of snuff and priming his nostrils with it) as to get *married I* "Perfectly true. He set out for Hastings about an hour after he left me, and upon my conscience I verily believe that, if I had had your MS. to have put into his hands, as sure as fate he would have sat with me reading it [Footnote: He had left his wife at the church so as to bring his poem to Murray.] all the morning and totally forgotten his little engagement.

I saw Lord Holland today looking very well. I wish I could send you Gifford's "Ben Jonson"; it is full of fun and interest, and allowed on all hands to be most ably done; would, I am sure, amuse you. I have very many new important and interesting works of all kinds in the press, which I should be happy to know any means of sending. My Review is improving in sale beyond my most sanguine expectations. I now sell nearly 9,000. Even Perry says the *Edinburgh, Review* is going to the devil. I was with Mrs. Leigh today, who is very well; she leaves town on Saturday. Her eldest daughter, I fancy, is a most engaging girl; but yours, my Lord, is unspeakably interesting and promising, and I am happy to add that Lady B. is looking well. God bless you! my best wishes and feelings are always with you, and I sincerely wish that your happiness may be as unbounded as your genius, which has rendered me so much,

My Lord, your obliged Servant,

J. M.

The negotiations for the purchase of the third canto were left in the hands of Mr. Kinnaird, who demurred to Mr. Murray's first offer of 1,500 guineas, and eventually £2,000 was fixed as the purchase price.

Mr. Murray wrote to Lord Byron on December 13, 1816, informing him that, at a dinner at the Albion Tavern, he had sold to the assembled booksellers 7,000 of his third canto of "Childe Harold" and 7,000 of his "Prisoner of Chillon. " He then proceeds:

John Murray to Lord Byron.

"In literary affairs I have taken the field in great force—opening with the Third Canto and "Chillon, " and, following up my blow, I have since published 'Tales of my Landlord, ' another novel, I believe (but I really don't know) by the author of 'Waverley'; but much superior to what has already appeared, excepting the character of Meg Merrilies. Every one is in ecstasy about it, and I would give a finger if I could send it you, but this I will contrive. Conversations with your friend Buonaparte at St. Helena, amusing, but scarce worth sending. Lord Holland has just put forth a very improved edition of the Life of Lope de Vega and Inez de Castro. ' Gifford's 'Ben Jonson' has put to death all former editions, and is very much liked. "

At Mr. Murray's earnest request, Scott had consented to review the third canto of "Childe Harold" in the *Quarterly*. In forwarding the MS. he wrote as follows:

Mr. Scott to John Murray.

EDINBURGH, *January* 10, 1817.

My Dear Sir,

I have this day sent under Croker's cover a review of Lord Byron's last poems. You know how high I hold his poetical reputation, but besides, one is naturally forced upon so many points of delicate consideration, that really I have begun and left off several times, and after all send the article to you with full power to cancel it if you think any part of it has the least chance of hurting his feelings. You know him better than I do, and you also know the public, and are aware that to make any successful impression on them the critic must appear to speak with perfect freedom. I trust I have not abused this discretion. I am sure I have not meant to do so, and yet during Lord Byron's absence, and under the present circumstances, I should feel more grieved than at anything that ever befell me if there should have slipped from my pen anything capable of giving him pain.

There are some things in the critique which are necessarily and unavoidably personal, and sure I am if he attends to it, which is unlikely, he will find advantage from doing so. I wish Mr. Gifford and you would consider every word carefully. If you think the general tenor is likely to make any impression on him, if you think it likely to hurt him either in his feelings or with the public, in God's name fling the sheets in the fire and let them be as *not written*. But if it appears, I should wish him to get an early copy, and that you would at the same time say I am the author, at your opportunity. No one can honour Lord Byron a genius more than I do, and no one had so great a wish to love him personally, though personally we had not the means of becoming very intimate. In his family distress (deeply to be deprecated, and in which probably he can yet be excused) I still looked to some moment of reflection when bad advisers (and, except you were one, I have heard of few whom I should call good) were distant from the side of one who is so much the child of feeling and emotion. An opportunity was once afforded me of interfering, but things appeared to me to have gone too far; yet, even after all, I wish I had tried it, for Lord Byron always seemed to give me credit for wishing him sincerely well, and knew me to be superior to what Commodore Trunnion would call "the trash of literary envy and petty rivalry. "

Lord Byron's opinion of the article forms so necessary a complement to Walter Scott's sympathetic criticism of the man and the poet, that we make no excuse for reproducing it, as conveyed in a letter to Mr. Murray (March 3, 1817).

"In acknowledging the arrival of the article from the *Quarterly*, which I received two days ago, I cannot express myself better than in the words of my sister Augusta, who (speaking of it) says, that it is written in a spirit 'of the most feeling and kind nature. '

"It is, however, something more. It seems to me (as far as the subject of it may be permitted to judge) to be very well written as a composition, and I think will do the journal no discredit, because even those who condemn its partiality, must praise its generosity. The temptations to take another and a less favourable view of the question have been so great and numerous, that, what with public opinion, politics, etc., he must be a gallant as well as a good man who has ventured in that place, and at this time, to write such an article, even anonymously. Such things, however, are their own reward; and I even flatter myself that the writer, whoever he may be (and I have no guess), will not regret that the perusal of this has given me as much gratification as any composition of that nature could give, and more than any has given—and I have had a good many in my time of one kind or the other. It is not the mere praise, but there is a *tact* and a *delicacy* throughout, not only with regard to me but to *others*, which, as it had not been observed *elsewhere*, I had till now doubted whether it could be observed *anywhere*. "

"When I tell you, " Lord Byron wrote to Moore a week later, "that Walter Scott is the author of the article in the *Quarterly*, you will agree with me that such an article is still more honourable to him than to myself. "

We conclude this episode with the following passage from a letter from Scott to Murray:

"I am truly happy Lord Byron's article meets your ideas of what may make some impression on his mind. In genius, poetry has seldom had his equal, and if he has acted very wrong in some respects, he has been no worse than half the men of his rank in London who have done the same, and are not spoken of because not worth being railed against. "

Lady Byron also wrote to Mr. Murray:

I am inclined to ask a question, which I hope you will not decline answering, if not contrary to your engagements. Who is the author of the review of "Childe Harold" in the *Quarterly*? Your faithful Servant, A. I. BYRON.

Among other ladies who wrote on the subject of Lord Byron's works was Lady Caroline Lamb, who had caricatured him (as he supposed) in her "Glenarvon. " Her letter is dated Welwyn, franked by William Lamb:

Lady Caroline Lamb to John Murray.

November 5, 1816.

"You cannot need my assuring you that if you will entrust me with the new poems, none of the things you fear shall occur, in proof of which I ask you to enquire with yourself, whether, if a person in constant correspondence and friendship with another, yet keeps a perfect silence on one subject, she cannot do so when at enmity and at a distance. "

This letter, to which no reply seems to have been sent, is followed by another, in which her Ladyship says:

I wish to ask you one question: are you offended with me or my letter? If so, I am sorry, but depend upon it if after seven years' acquaintance you choose to cut off what you ever termed your left hand, I have too much gratitude towards you to allow of it. Accept therefore every apology for every supposed fault. I always write eagerly and in haste, I never read over what I have written. If therefore I said anything I ought not, pardon it—it was not intended; and let me entreat you to remember a maxim I have found very useful to me, that there is nothing in this life worth quarrelling about, and that half the people we are offended with never intended to give us cause.

Thank you for Holcroft's "Life, " which is extremely curious and interesting. I think you will relent and send me "Childe Harold" before any one has it—this is the first time you have not done so— and the *Quarterly Review*; and pray also any other book that is curious.... I quite pine to see the *Quarterly Review* and "Childe Harold. " Have mercy and send them, or I shall gallop to town to see you. Is 450 guineas too dear for a new barouche? If you know this let me know, as we of the country know nothing.

Yours sincerely, C.L.

In sending home the MS. of the first act of "Manfred, " Lord Byron wrote, giving but unsatisfactory accounts of his own health. Mr. Murray replied:

John Murray to Lord Byron.

March 20, 1817.

My Lord,

I have to acknowledge your kind letter, dated the 3rd, received this hour; but I am sorry to say that it has occasioned, me great anxiety about your health. You are not wont to cry before you are hurt; and I am apprehensive that you are worse even than you allow. Pray keep quiet and take care of yourself. My *Review* shows you that you are worth preserving and that the world yet loves you. If you become seriously worse, I entreat you to let me know it, and I will fly to you with a physician; an Italian one is only a preparation for the anatomist. I will not tell your sister of this, if you will tell me true. I had hopes that this letter would have confirmed my expectations of your speedy return, which has been stated by Mr. Kinnaird, and repeated to me by Mr. Davies, whom I saw yesterday, and who promises to write. We often indulge our recollections of you, and he allows me to believe that I am one of the few who really know you.

Gifford gave me yesterday the first act of "Manfred" with a delighted countenance, telling me it was wonderfully poetical, and desiring me to assure you that it well merits publication. I shall send proofs to you with his remarks, if he have any; it is a wild and delightful thing, and I like it myself hugely....

I have just received, in a way perfectly unaccountable, a MS. from St. Helena—with not a word. I suppose it to be originally written by Buonaparte or his agents. —It is very curious—his life, in which each event is given in almost a word—a battle described in a short sentence. I call it therefore simply *Manuscrit venu de Ste. Helene d'une maniere inconnue.* [Footnote: This work attracted a considerable amount of attention in London, but still more in Paris, as purporting to be a chapter of autobiography by Napoleon, then a prisoner in St. Helena. It was in all probability the work of some of the deposed Emperor's friends and adherents in Paris, issued for the purpose of keeping his name prominently before the world. M. de Meneval, author of several books on Napoleon's career, has left it on record that the "M. S. venu de Sainte Helene" was written by M. Frederic Lullin de Chateauvieux, "genevois deja connu dans le monde savant. Cet ecrivain a avoue, apres vingt cinq ans de silence, qu'il avait compose l'ouvrage en 1816, qu'il avait porte lui-meme a Londres, et l'avait mis a la poste, a l'adresse du Libraire Murray. "] Lord Holland has a motion on our treatment of Buonaparte at St. Helena for Wednesday next; and on Monday I shall publish. You will have seen Buonaparte's Memorial on this subject, complaining bitterly of all; pungent but very injudicious, as it must offend all the other allied powers to be reminded of their former prostration.

April 12, 1817.

Our friend Southey has got into a confounded scrape. Some twenty years ago, when he knew no better and was a Republican, he wrote a certain drama, entitled, "Wat Tyler, " in order to disseminate wholesome doctrine amongst the *lower* orders. This he presented to a friend, with a fraternal embrace, who was at that time enjoying the cool reflection generated by his residence in Newgate. This friend, however, either thinking its publication might prolong his durance, or fancying that it would not become profitable as a speculation, quietly put it into his pocket; and now that the author has most manfully laid about him, slaying Whigs and Republicans by the million, this cursed friend publishes; but what is yet worse, the author, upon sueing for an injunction, to proceed in which he is obliged to swear that he is the author, is informed by the Chancellor that it is seditious—and that for sedition there is no copyright. I will inclose either now or in my next a second copy, for as there is no copyright, everyone has printed it, which will amuse you.

On July 15th and 20th Lord Byron wrote to Mr. Murray that the fourth canto of "Childe Harold" was completed, and only required to be "copied and polished, " but at the same time he began to "barter" for the price of the canto, so completely had his old scruples on this score disappeared. Mr. Murray replied, offering 1,500 guineas for the copyright.

Mr. Hobhouse spent a considerable part of the year 1817 travelling about in Italy, whither he had gone principally to see Lord Byron. He wrote to Mr. Murray on the subject of Thorwaldsen's bust of the poet:

"I shall conclude with telling you about Lord B. 's bust. It is a masterpiece by Thorwaldsen [Footnote: The bust was made for Mr. Hobhouse, at his expense. Lord Byron said, "I would not pay the price of a Thorwaldsen bust for any head and shoulders, except Napoleon's or my children's, or some 'absurd womankind's, ' as Monkbarns calls them, or my sister's. "] who is thought by most judges to surpass Canova in this branch of sculpture. The likeness is perfect: the artist worked *con amore*, and told me it was the finest head he had ever under his hand. I would have had a wreath round the brows, but the poet was afraid of being mistaken for a king or a conqueror, and his pride or modesty made him forbid the band. However, when the marble comes to England I shall place a golden laurel round it in the ancient style, and, if it is thought good enough, suffix the following inscription, which may serve at least to tell the name of the portrait and allude to the excellence of the artist, which very few lapidary inscriptions do;

'In vain would flattery steal a wreath from fame, And Rome's best sculptor only half succeed, If England owned no share in Byron's name Nor hailed the laurel she before decreed. '

Of course you are very welcome to a copy—I don't mean of the verses, but of the bust. But, with the exception of Mr. Kinnaird, who has applied, and Mr. Davies, who may apply, no other will be granted. Farewell, dear Sir. "

The fourth canto duly reached London in Mr. Hobhouse's portmanteau, and was published in the spring of 1818.

CHAPTER XV

LORD BYRON'S DEALINGS WITH MR. MURRAY—*continued*—
THE DEATH OF ALLEGRA, ETC.

Lord Byron informed Mr. Murray, on October 12, 1817, that he had
written "a poem in or after the excellent manner of Mr. Whistlecraft
(whom I take to be Frere)"; and in a subsequent letter he said, "Mr.
Whistlecraft has no greater admirer than myself. I have written a
story in eighty-nine stanzas in imitation of him, called 'Beppo, ' the
short name for Giuseppe, that is the Joe of the Italian Joseph. " Lord
Byron required that it should be printed anonymously, and in any
form that Mr. Murray pleased. The manuscript of the poem was not,
however, sent off until the beginning of 1818; and it reached the
publisher about a month later.

Meanwhile the friendly correspondence between the poet and his
publisher continued:

John Murray to Lord Byron.

September 22, 1818.

"I was much pleased to find, on my arrival from Edinburgh on
Saturday night, your letter of August 26. The former one of the 21st I
received whilst in Scotland. The Saturday and Sunday previous I
passed most delightfully with Walter Scott, who was incessant in his
inquiries after your welfare. He entertains the noblest sentiments of
regard towards you, and speaks of you with the best feelings. I
walked about ten miles with him round a very beautiful estate,
which he has purchased by degrees, within two miles of his
favourite Melrose. He has nearly completed the centre and one wing
of a castle on the banks of the Tweed, where he is the happiness as
well as pride of the whole neighbourhood. He is one of the most
hospitable, merry, and entertaining of mortals. He would, I am
confident, do anything to serve you; and as the Paper [Footnote: The
review of the fourth canto of "Childe Harold, " *Q. R.,* No. 37.]
which I now enclose is a second substantial proof of the interest he
takes in your literary character, perhaps it may naturally enough
afford occasion for a letter from you to him. I sent you by Mr.
Hanson four volumes of a second series of 'Tales of my Landlord, '
and four others are actually in the press. Scott does not yet avow

them, but no one doubts his being their author.... I sent also by Mr. Hanson a number or two of *Blackwood's Edinburgh Magazine*, and I have in a recent parcel sent the whole. I think that you will find in it a very great share of talent, and some most incomparable fun.... John Wilson, who wrote the article on Canto IV. of 'Childe Harold' (of which, by the way, I am anxious to know your opinion), has very much interested himself in the journal, and has communicated some most admirable papers. Indeed, he possesses very great talents and a variety of knowledge. I send you a very well-constructed kaleidoscope, a newly-invented toy which, if not yet seen in Venice, will I trust amuse some of your female friends. "

The following letter is inserted here, as it does not appear in Moore's "Biography":

Lord Byron to John Murray.

VENICE, *November* 24, 1818,

DEAR. MR. MURRAY,

Mr. Hanson has been here a week, and went five days ago. He brought nothing but his papers, some corn-rubbers, and a kaleidoscope. "For what we have received the Lord make us thankful"! for without His aid I shall not be so. He—Hanson-left everything else in *Chancery Lane* whatever, except your copy-papers for the last Canto, [Footnote: Of "Childe Harold. "] etc., which having a degree of parchment he brought with him. You may imagine his reception; he swore the books were a "waggon-load"; if they were, he should have come in a waggon; he would in that case have come quicker than he did.

Lord Lauderdale set off from hence twelve days ago accompanied by a cargo of Poesy directed to Mr. Hobhouse, all spick and span, and in MS. ; you will see what it is like. I have given it to Master Southey, and he shall have more before I have done with him.

You may make what I say here as public as you please, more particularly to Southey, whom I look upon—and will say so publicly-to be a dirty, lying rascal, and will prove it in ink—or in his blood, if I did not believe him to be too much of a poet to risk it! If he has forty reviews at his back, as he has the *Quarterly*, I would have at him in his scribbling capacity now that he has begun with me; but I will do nothing underhand; tell him what I say from *me* and every one else you please.

You will see what I have said, if the parcel arrives safe. I understand Coleridge went about repeating Southey's lie with pleasure. I can believe it, for I had done him what is called a favour.... I can understand Coleridge's abusing me—but how or why *Southey,* whom I had never obliged in any sort of way, or done him the remotest service, should go about fibbing and calumniating is more than I readily comprehend. Does he think to put me down with his *Canting,* not being able to do it with his poetry? We will try the question. I have read his review of Hunt, where he has attacked Shelley in an oblique and shabby manner. Does he know what that review has done? I will tell you; it has *sold* an edition of the "Revolt of Islam" which otherwise nobody would have thought of reading, and few who read can understand, I for one.

Southey would have attacked me too there, if he durst, further than by hints about Hunt's friends in general, and some outcry about an "Epicurean System" carried on by men of the most opposite habits and tastes and opinions in life and poetry (I believe) that ever had their names in the same volume—Moore, Byron, Shelley, Hazlitt, Haydon, Leigh Hunt, Lamb. What resemblance do ye find among all or any of these men? And how could any sort of system or plan be carried on or attempted amongst them? However, let Mr. Southey look to himself; since the wine is tapped, he shall drink it.

I got some books a few weeks ago—many thanks. Amongst them is Israeli's new edition; it was not fair in you to show him my copy of his former one, with all the marginal notes and nonsense made in Greece when I was not two-and-twenty, and which certainly were not meant for his perusal, nor for that of his readers.

I have a great respect for Israeli and his talents, and have read his works over and over and over repeatedly, and been amused by them greatly, and instructed often. Besides, I hate giving pain, unless provoked; and he is an author, and must feel like his brethren; and although his Liberality repaid my marginal flippancies with a compliment—the highest compliment—that don't reconcile me to myself—nor to *you.* It was a breach of confidence to do this without my leave; I don't know a living man's book I take up so often or lay down more reluctantly than Israeli's, and I never will forgive you— that is, for many weeks. If he had got out of humour I should have been less sorry; but even then I should have been sorry; but really he has heaped his "coals of fire" so handsomely upon my head that they burn unquenchably.

You ask me of the two reviews [Footnote: Of "Childe Harold" in the *Quarterly* and *Blackwood.*]—I will tell you. Scott's is the review of one poet on another—his friend; Wilson's, the review of a poet too, on another—his *Idol*; for he likes me better than he chooses to avow to the public with all his eulogy. I speak judging only from the article, for I don't know him personally.

Here is a long letter—can you read it?

Yours ever,

B.

In the course of September 1818 Lord Byron communicated to Mr. Moore that he had finished the first canto of a poem in the style and manner of "Beppo. " "It is called, " he said, "'Don Juan, ' and is meant to be a little quietly facetious upon everything; but, " he added, "I doubt whether it is not—at least so far as it has yet gone—too free for these very modest days. " In January 1819 Lord Byron requested Mr. Murray to print for private distribution fifty copies of "Don Juan. " Mr. Murray urged him to occupy himself with some great work worthy of his reputation. "This you have promised to Gifford long ago, and to Hobhouse and Kinnaird since. " Lord Byron, however, continued to write out his "Don Juan, " and sent the second canto in April 1819, together with the "Letter of Julia, " to be inserted in the first canto.

Mr. Murray, in acknowledging the receipt of the first and second cantos, was not so congratulatory as he had formerly been. The verses contained, no doubt, some of the author's finest poetry, but he had some objections to suggest. "I think, " he said, "you may modify or substitute other words for the lines on Romilly, whose death should save him. " But Byron entertained an extreme detestation for Romilly, because, he said, he had been "one of my assassins, " and had sacrificed him on "his legal altar"; and the verse [Footnote: St. 16, First Canto.] was allowed to stand over. "Your history, " wrote Murray, "of the plan of the progress of 'Don Juan' is very entertaining, but I am clear for sending him to hell, because he may favour us with a description of some of the characters whom he finds there. " Mr. Murray suggested the removal of some offensive words in Canto II. "These, " he said, "ladies may not read; the Shipwreck is a little too particular, and out of proportion to the rest of the picture. But if you do anything it must be done with extreme caution; think of the effects of such seductive poetry! It probably surpasses in talent anything that you ever wrote. Tell me if you think seriously of completing this work, or if you have sketched the story. I am very sorry to have occasioned you the trouble of writing again the "Letter of Julia"; but you are always very forgiving in such cases. " The lines in which the objectionable words appeared were obliterated by Lord Byron.

From the following letter we see that Mr. Murray continued his remonstrances:

John Murray to Lord Byron.

May 3, 1819.

"I find that 'Julia's Letter' has been safely received, and is with the printer. The whole remainder of the second canto will be sent by Friday's post. The inquiries after its appearance are not a few. Pray use your most tasteful discretion so as to wrap up or leave out certain approximations to indelicacy. "

Mr. Douglas Kinnaird, who was entrusted with the business portion of this transaction, wrote to Mr. Murray:

Mr. Douglas Kinnaird to John Murray.

June 7, 1819.

My Dear Sir,

Since I had the pleasure of seeing you, I have received from Lord Byron a letter in which he expresses himself as having left to Mr. Hobhouse and myself the sole and whole discretion and duty of settling with the publisher of the MSS. which are now in your hands the consideration to be given for them. Observing that you have advertised "Mazeppa, " I feel that it is my duty to request you will name an early day—of course previous to your publishing that or any other part of the MSS. —when we may meet and receive your offer of such terms as you may deem proper for the purchase of the copyright of them. The very liberal footing on which Lord Byron's intercourse with you in your character of publisher of his Lordship's works has hitherto been placed, leaves no doubt in my mind that our interview need be but very short, and that the terms you will propose will be met by our assent.

The parties met, and Mr. Murray agreed to give £525 for "Mazeppa," and £1,575 for the first and second cantos of "Don Juan, " with "The Ode to Venice" thrown in.

In accordance with Lord Byron's directions to his publisher to "keep the anonymous, " Cantos I. and II. of "Don Juan" appeared in London, in quarto, in July 1819, without the name of either author, publisher, or bookseller. The book was immediately pounced upon by the critics; but it is unnecessary to quote their reviews, as they are impartially given in the latest accredited editions of Lord Byron's poems. A few criticisms from Mr. Murray's private correspondence may be given.

Mr. Gifford to John Murray.

RYDE, *July* 1, 1819.

"Lord B. 's letter is shockingly amusing. [Footnote: Probably that written in May; printed in the "Life. "] He must be mad; but then there's method in his madness. I dread, however, the end. He is, or rather might be, the most extraordinary character of his age. I have lived to see three great men—men to whom none come near in their respective provinces—Pitt, Nelson, Wellington. Morality and religion would have placed our friend among them as the fourth boast of the time; even a decent respect for the good opinion of mankind might have done much now; but all is tending to displace him. "

Mr. Murray, who was still in communication with Mr. Blackwood, found that he refused to sell "Don Juan" because it contained personalities which he regarded as even more objectionable than those of which Murray had complained in the *Magazine*.

When the copyright of "Don Juan" was infringed by other publishers, it became necessary to take steps to protect it at law, and Mr. Sharon Turner was consulted on the subject. An injunction was applied for in Chancery, and the course of the negotiation will be best ascertained from the following letters:

Mr. Sharon Turner to John Murray.

October 21, 1819.

DEAR MURRAY,

... on "Don Juan" I have much apprehension. I had from the beginning, and therefore advised the separate assignment. The counsel who is settling the bill also doubts if the Chancellor will sustain the injunction. I think, when Mr. Bell comes to town, it will be best to have a consultation with him on the subject. The counsel, Mr. Loraine, shall state to him his view on the subject, and you shall hear what Mr. Bell feels upon it. Shall I appoint the consultation? The evil, if not stopped, will be great. It will circulate in a cheap form very extensively, injuring society wherever it spreads. Yet one consideration strikes me. You could wish Lord Byron to write less objectionably. You may also wish him to return you part of the £1,625. If the Chancellor should dissolve the injunction on this ground, that will show Lord B. that he must expect no more copyright money for such things, and that they are too bad for law to uphold. Will not this affect his mind and purify his pen? It is true that to get this good result you must encounter the risk and expense of the injunction and of the argument upon it. Will you do this? If I laid the case separately before three of our ablest counsel, and they concurred in as many opinions that it could not be supported, would this equally affect his Lordship's mind, and also induce him to return you an adequate proportion of the purchase money? Perhaps nothing but the Court treating him as it treated Southey [Footnote: In the case of "Wat Tyler, " see Murray's letter to Byron in preceding chapter, April 12, 1817.] may sufficiently impress Lord B. After the consultation with Bell you will better judge. Shall I get it appointed as soon as he comes to town?

Ever yours faithfully,

SHARON TURNER.

Mr. Bell gave his opinion that the Court would not afford protection to the book. He admitted, however, that he had not had time to study it.

The next letter relates to the opinion of Mr. Shadwell, afterwards Vice-Chancellor:

Mr. Sharon Turner to John Murray.

November 12, 1819.

Dear Murray,

I saw Mr. Shadwell to-day on "Don Juan. " He has gone through the book with more attention than Mr. Bell had time to do. He desires me to say that he does not think the Chancellor would refuse an injunction, or would overturn it if obtained....

Yours most faithfully,

SHARON TURNER.

In the event the injunction to restrain the publication of "Don Juan" by piratical publishers was granted.

Towards the end of 1819 Byron thought of returning to England. On November 8 he wrote to Mr. Murray:

"If she [the Countess Guiccioli] and her husband make it up, you will perhaps see me in England sooner than you expect. If not, I will retire with her to France or America, change my name, and lead a quiet provincial life. If she gets over this, and I get over my Tertian ague, I will perhaps look in at Albemarle Street *en passant* to Bolivar."

When Mr. Hobhouse, then living at Ramsbury, heard of Byron's intention to go to South America, he wrote to Mr. Murray as follows:

"... To be sure it is impossible that Lord B. should seriously contemplate, or, if he does, he must not expect us to encourage, this mad scheme. I do not know what in the world to say, but presume some one has been talking nonsense to him. Let Jim Perry go to Venezuela if he will—he may edit his 'Independent Gazette' amongst the Independents themselves, and reproduce his stale puns and politics without let or hindrance. But our poet is too good for a planter—too good to sit down before a fire made of mare's legs, to a dinner of beef without salt and bread. It is the wildest of all his meditations—pray tell him. The plague and Yellow Jack, and famine and free quarter, besides a thousand other ills, will stare him in the face. No tooth-brushes, no corn-rubbers, no *Quarterly Reviews*. In short, plenty of all he abominates and nothing of all he loves. I shall write, but you can tell facts, which will be better than my arguments."

Byron's half-formed intention was soon abandoned, and the Countess Guiccioli's serious illness recalled him to Ravenna, where he remained for the next year and a half.

Hobhouse's next letter to Murray (January 1820), in which he reported "Bad news from Ravenna—a great pity indeed, " is dated *Newgate*, where he had been lodged in consequence of his pamphlet entitled "A Trifling Mistake in Thomas Lord Erskine's Recent Pamphlet, " containing several very strong reflections on the House of Commons as then constituted.

During his imprisonment, Mr. Hobhouse was visited by Mr. Murray and Ugo Foscolo, as well as by many of his political friends.

Lady Caroline Lamb also wrote to Mr. Murray from Brockett Hall, asking for information about Byron and Hobhouse.

Lady Caroline Lamb to John Murray.

You have never written to tell me about him. Now, did you know the pain and agony this has given me, you had not been so remiss. If you could come here on Wednesday for one night, I have a few people and a supper. You could come by the Mail in two hours, much swifter than even in your swift carriage; and I have one million of things to say and ask also. Do tell me how that dear Radical Hob is, and pray remember me to him. I really hope you will be here at dinner or supper on Wednesday. Your bedroom shall be ready, and you can be back in Town before most people are up, though I rise here at seven.

Yours quite disturbed my mind, for want of your telling me how he [Byron] looks, what he says, if he is grown fat, if he is no uglier than he used to be, if he is good-humoured or cross-grained, putting his brows down—if his hair curls or is straight as somebody said, if he has seen Hobhouse, if he is going to stay long, if you went to Dover as you intended, and a great deal more, which, if you had the smallest tact or aught else, you would have written long ago; for as to me, I shall certainly not see him, neither do I care he should know that I ever asked after him. It is from mere curiosity I should like to hear all you can tell me about him. Pray come here immediately.

Yours,

C. L.

Notwithstanding the remarkable sale of "Don Juan, " Murray hesitated about publishing any more of the cantos. After the fifth canto was published, Lord Byron informed Murray that it was "hardly the beginning of the work, " that he intended to take Don Juan through the tour of Europe, put him through the Divorce Court, and make him finish as Anacharsis Clootz in the French Revolution. Besides being influenced by his own feelings, it is possible that the following letter of Mr. Croker may have induced Mr. Murray to have nothing further to do with the work:

Mr. Croker to John Murray.

MUNSTER HOUSE, *March* 26, 1820.

A rainy Sunday.

DEAR MURRAY,

I have to thank you for letting me see your two new cantos [the 3rd and 4th], which I return. What sublimity! what levity! what boldness! what tenderness! what majesty! what trifling! what variety! what *tediousness*! — for tedious to a strange degree, it must be confessed that whole passages are, particularly the earlier stanzas of the fourth canto. I know no man of such general powers of intellect as Brougham, yet I think *him* insufferably tedious; and I fancy the reason to be that he has such *facility* of expression that he is never recalled to a *selection* of his thoughts. A more costive orator would be obliged to choose, and a man of his talents could not fail to choose the best; but the power of uttering all and everything which passes across his mind, tempts him to say all. He goes on without thought — I should rather say, without pause. His speeches are poor from their richness, and dull from their infinite variety. An impediment in his speech would make him a perfect Demosthenes. Something of the same kind, and with something of the same effect, is Lord Byron's wonderful fertility of thought and facility of expression; and the Protean style of "Don Juan, " instead of checking (as the fetters of rhythm generally do) his natural activity, not only gives him wider limits to range in, but even generates a more roving disposition. I dare swear, if the truth were known, that his digressions and repetitions generate one another, and that the happy jingle of some of his comical rhymes has led him on to episodes of which he never originally thought; and thus it is that, with the most extraordinary merit, *merit of all kinds*, these two cantos have been to *me*, in several points, tedious and even obscure.

As to the PRINCIPLES, all the world, and you, Mr. Murray, *first of all*, have done this poem great injustice. There are levities here and there, more than good taste approves, but nothing to make such a terrible rout about—nothing so bad as "Tom Jones, " nor within a hundred degrees of "Count Fathom. "

The writer goes on to remark that the personalities in the poem are more to be deprecated than "its imputed looseness of principle":

I mean some expressions of political and personal feelings which, I believe, he, in fact, never felt, and threw in wantonly and *de gaieté de coeur*, and which he would have omitted, advisedly and *de bonté de coeur*, if he had not been goaded by indiscreet, contradictory, and urgent *criticisms*, which, in some cases, were dark enough to be called *calumnies*. But these are blowing over, if not blown over; and I cannot but think that if Mr. Gifford, or some friend in whose taste and disinterestedness Lord Byron could rely, were to point out to him the cruelty to individuals, the injury to the national character, the offence to public taste, and the injury to his own reputation, of such passages as those about Southey and Waterloo and the British Government and the head of that Government, I cannot but hope and believe that these blemishes in the first cantos would be wiped away in the next edition; and that some that occur in the two cantos (which you sent me) would never see the light. What interest can Lord Byron have in being the poet of a party in politics?... In politics, he cannot be what he appears, or rather what Messrs. Hobhouse and Leigh Hunt wish to make him appear. A man of his birth, a man of his taste, a man of his talents, a man of his habits, can have nothing in common with such miserable creatures as we now call *Radicals*, of whom I know not that I can better express the illiterate and blind ignorance and vulgarity than by saying that the best informed of them have probably never heard of Lord Byron. No, no, Lord Byron may be indulgent to these jackal followers of his; he may connive at their use of his name—nay, it is not to be denied that he has given them too, too much countenance—but he never can, I should think, now that he sees not only the road but the rate they are going, continue to take a part so contrary to all his own interests and feelings, and to the feelings and interests of all the respectable part of his country.... But what is to be the end of all this rigmarole of mine? To conclude, this—to advise you, for your own sake as a tradesman, for Lord Byron's sake as a poet, for the sake of good literature and good principles, which ought to be united, to take such measures as you may be able to venture upon to get Lord Byron to revise these two cantos, and not to make another step in the odious path which Hobhouse beckons him to pursue....

Yours ever,

J. W. CROKER.

But Byron would alter nothing more in his "Don Juan. " He accepted the corrections of Gifford in his "Tragedies, " but "Don Juan" was never submitted to him. Hobhouse was occasionally applied to, because he knew Lord Byron's handwriting; but even his suggestions of alterations or corrections of "Don Juan" were in most cases declined, and moreover about this time a slight coolness had sprung up between him and Byron. When Hobhouse was standing for Westminster with Sir Francis Burdett, Lord Byron sent a song about him in a letter to Mr. Murray. It ran to the tune of "My Boy Tammy? O! "

"Who are now the People's men? My boy Hobby O! Yourself and Burdett, Gentlemen, And Blackguard Hunt and Cobby O!

"When to the mob you make a speech, My boy Hobby O! How do you keep without their reach The watch without your fobby O? " [Footnote: The rest of the song is printed in *Murray's Magazine*, No.3.]

Lord Byron asked Murray to show the song not only to some of his friends—who got it by heart and had it printed in the newspapers— but also to Hobhouse himself. "I know, " said his Lordship, "that he will never forgive me, but I really have no patience with him for letting himself be put in quod by such a set of ragamuffins. " Mr. Hobhouse, however, was angry with Byron for his lampoon and with Murray for showing it to his friends. He accordingly wrote the following letter, which contains some interesting particulars of the Whig Club at Cambridge in Byron's University days:

Mr. Hobhouse to John Murray.

2, HANOVER SQUARE, *November*, 1820.

I have received your letter, and return to you Lord Byron's. I shall tell you very frankly, because I think it much better to speak a little of a man to his face than to say a great deal about him behind his back, that I think you have not treated me as I deserved, nor as might have been expected from that friendly intercourse which has subsisted between us for so many years. Had Lord Byron transmitted to me a lampoon on you, I should, if I know myself at all, either have put it into the fire without delivery, or should have sent it at once to you. I should not have given it a circulation for the gratification of all the small wits at the great and little houses, where no treat is so agreeable as to find a man laughing at his friend. In this case, the whole coterie of the very shabbiest party that ever disgraced and divided a nation—I mean the Whigs—are, I know, chuckling over that silly charge made by Mr. Lamb on the hustings, and now confirmed by Lord Byron, of my having belonged to a Whig club at Cambridge. Such a Whig as I then was, I am now. I had no notion that the name implied selfishness and subserviency, and desertion of the most important principles for the sake of the least important interest. I had no notion that it implied anything more than an attachment to the principles the ascendency of which expelled the Stuarts from the Throne. Lord Byron belonged to this Cambridge club, and desired me to scratch out his name, on account of the criticism in the *Edinburgh Review* on his early poems; but, exercising my discretion on the subject, I did not erase his name, but reconciled him to the said Whigs.

The members of the club were but few, and with those who have any marked politics amongst them, I continue to agree at this day. They were but ten, and you must know most of them—Mr. W. Ponsonby, Mr. George O'Callaghan, the Duke of Devonshire, Mr. Dominick Browne, Mr. Henry Pearce, Mr. Kinnaird, Lord Tavistock, Lord Ellenborough, Lord Byron, and myself. I was not, as Lord Byron says in the song, the founder of this Club; [Footnote:

"But when we at Cambridge were
My boy Hobbie O!
If my memory do not err,
You founded a Whig Clubbie O!"

] on the contrary, thinking myself of mighty importance in those days, I recollect very well that some difficulty attended my consenting to belong to the club, and I have by me a letter from Lord Tavistock, in which the distinction between being a Whig *party* man and a Revolution Whig is strongly insisted upon.

I have troubled you with this detail in consequence of Lord Byron's charge, which he, who despises and defies, and has lampooned the Whigs all round, only invented out of wantonness, and for the sake of annoying me—and he has certainly succeeded, thanks to your circulating this filthy ballad. As for his Lordship's vulgar notions about the *mob*, they are very fit for the Poet of the *Morning Post*, and for nobody else. Nothing in the ballad annoyed me but the charge about the Cambridge club, because nothing else had the semblance of truth; and I own it has hurt me very much to find Lord Byron playing into the hands of the Holland House sycophants, for whom he has himself the most sovereign contempt, and whom in other days I myself have tried to induce him to tolerate.

I shall say no more on this unpleasant subject except that, by a letter which I have just received from Lord Byron, I think he is ashamed of his song. I shall certainly speak as plainly to him as I have taken the liberty to do to you on this matter. He was very wanton and you very indiscreet; but I trust neither one nor the other meant mischief, and there's an end of it. Do not aggravate matters by telling how much I have been annoyed. Lord Byron has sent me a list of his new poems and some prose, all of which he requests me to prepare for the press for him. The monied arrangement is to be made by Mr. Kinnaird. When you are ready for me, the materials may be sent to me at this place, where I have taken up my abode for the season.

I remain, very truly yours, JOHN CAM HOBHOUSE.

Towards the end of 1820 Lord Byron wrote a long letter to Mr. Murray on Mr. Bowles's strictures on the "Life and Writings of Pope." It was a subject perhaps unworthy of his pen, but being an ardent admirer of Pope, he thought it his duty to "bowl him [Bowles]

down." "I mean to lay about me, " said Byron, "like a dragon, till I make manure of Bowles for the top of Parnassus. "
After some revision, the first and second letters to Bowles were published, and were well received.

The tragedy of "Sardanapalus, " the last three acts of which had been written in a fortnight, was despatched to Murray on May 30, 1821, and was within a few weeks followed by "The Two Foscari: an Historical Tragedy"—which had been composed within a month— and on September 10 by "Cain, a Mystery. " The three dramas, "Sardanapalus, " "The Two Foscari, " and "Cain, a Mystery, " were published together in December 1821, and Mr. Murray paid Lord Byron for them the sum of £2,710.

"Cain" was dedicated, by his consent, to Sir Walter Scott, who, in writing to Mr. Murray, described it as "a very grand and tremendous drama. " On its first appearance it was reprinted in a cheap form by two booksellers, under the impression that the Court of Chancery would not protect it, and it therefore became necessary to take out an injunction to restrain these piratical publishers.

The case came before Lord Chancellor Eldon on February 9. Mr. Shadwell, Mr. Spence, and Sergeant Copley were retained by Mr. Murray, and after considerable discussion the injunction was refused, the Lord Chancellor intimating that the publisher must establish his right to the publication at law, and obtain the decision of a jury, on which he would grant the injunction required. This was done accordingly, and the copyright in "Cain" was thus secured.

On the death of Allegra, his natural daughter, Lord Byron entrusted to Mr. Murray the painful duty of making arrangements for the burial of the remains in Harrow Church. Mr. Cunningham, the clergyman of Harrow, wrote in answer to Mr. Murray:

Rev. J.W. Cunningham to John Murray.

August 20, 1822.

Sir,

Mr. Henry Drury was so good as to communicate to me a request conveyed to you by Lord Byron respecting the burial of a child in this church. Mr. H. Drury will probably have also stated to you my willingness to comply with the wish of Lord Byron. Will you forgive me, however, for so far trespassing upon you (though a stranger) as to suggest an inquiry whether it might not be practicable and desirable to fulfil for the *present* only a *part* of his Lordship's wish— by burying the child, and putting up a tablet with simply its name upon the tablet; and thus leaving Lord B. more leisure to reflect upon the character of the inscription he may wish to be added. It does seem to me that whatever he may wish in the moment of his distress about the loss of this child, he will afterwards regret that he should have taken pains to proclaim to the world what he will not, I am sure, consider as honourable to his name. And if this be probable, then it appears to me the office of a true friend not to suffer him to commit himself but to allow his mind an opportunity of calm deliberation. I feel constrained to say that the inscription he proposed will be felt by every man of refined taste, to say nothing of sound morals, to be an offence against taste and propriety. My correspondence with his Lordship has been so small that I can scarcely venture myself to urge these objections. You perhaps will feel no such scruple. I have seen no person who did not concur in the propriety of stating them. I would entreat, however, that should you think it right to introduce my name into any statement made to Lord Byron, you will not do it without assuring him of my unwillingness to oppose the smallest obstacle to his wishes, or give the slightest pain to his mind. The injury which, in my judgment, he is from day to day inflicting upon society is no justification for measures of retaliation and unkindness.

Your obedient and faithful Servant, J.W. CUNNINGHAM.

No communication having been received by the Rector, he placed the application from Lord Byron before the churchwardens.

Rev. J.W. Cunningham to John Murray.

"The churchwardens have been urged to issue their prohibition by several leading and influential persons, laymen, in the parish. You are aware that as to *ex-parishioners* the consent of the churchwardens is no less necessary than my own; and that therefore the enclosed prohibition is decisive as to the putting up of the monument. You will oblige me by making known to Lord Byron the precise circumstances of the case.

I am, your obedient Servant, J.W. CUNNINGHAM.

The prohibition was as follows:

HARROW, *September* 17, 1822.

Honored Sir,

I object on behalf of the parish to admit the tablet of Lord Byron's child into the church.

JAMES WINKLEY, *Churchwarden*.

The remains of Allegra, after long delay, were at length buried in the church, just under the present door mat, over which the congregation enter the church; but no memorial tablet or other record of her appears on the walls of Harrow Church.

CHAPTER XVI

BYRON'S DEATH AND THE DESTRUCTION OF HIS MEMOIRS

No attempt has here been made to present a strictly chronological record of Mr. Murray's life; we have sought only so to group his correspondence as to lay before our readers the various episodes which go to form the business life of a publisher. In pursuance of this plan we now proceed to narrate the closing incidents of his friendship with Lord Byron, reserving to subsequent chapters the various other transactions in which he was engaged.

During the later months of Byron's residence in Italy this friendship had suffered some interruption, due in part perhaps to questions which had arisen out of the publication of "Don Juan, " and in part to the interference of the Hunts. With the activity aroused by his expedition to Greece, Byron's better nature reasserted itself, and his last letter to his publisher, though already printed in Moore's Life, cannot be omitted from these pages:

Lord Byron to John Murray.

MISSOLONGHI, *February* 25, 1824.

I have heard from Mr. Douglas Kinnaird that you state "a report of a satire on Mr. Gifford having arrived from Italy, *said* to be written by *me*! but that *you* do not believe it. " I dare say you do not, nor any body else, I should think. Whoever asserts that I am the author or abettor of anything of the kind on Gifford lies in his throat. I always regarded him as my literary father, and myself as his prodigal son; if any such composition exists, it is none of mine. *You* know as well as anybody upon *whom* I have or have not written; and *you* also know whether they do or did not deserve that same. And so much for such matters. You will perhaps be anxious to hear some news from this part of Greece (which is the most liable to invasion); but you will hear enough through public and private channels. I will, however, give you the events of a week, mingling my own private peculiar with the public; for we are here jumbled a little together at present.

On Sunday (the 15th, I believe) I had a strong and sudden convulsive attack, which left me speechless, though not motionless-for some strong men could not hold me; but whether it was epilepsy, catalepsy, cachexy, or apoplexy, or what other *exy* or *epsy* the doctors have not decided; or whether it was spasmodic or nervous, etc. ; but it was very unpleasant, and nearly carried me off, and all that. On Monday, they put leeches to my temples, no difficult matter, but the blood could not be stopped till eleven at night (they had gone too near the temporal artery for my temporal safety), and neither styptic nor caustic would cauterise the orifice till after a hundred attempts.

On Tuesday a Turkish brig of war ran on shore. On Wednesday, great preparations being made to attack her, though protected by her consorts, the Turks burned her and retired to Patras. On Thursday a quarrel ensued between the Suliotes and the Frank guard at the arsenal: a Swedish officer was killed, and a Suliote severely wounded, and a general fight expected, and with some difficulty prevented. On Friday, the officer was buried; and Captain Parry's English artificers mutinied, under pretence that their lives were in danger, and are for quitting the country: —they may.

On Saturday we had the smartest shock of an earthquake which I remember (and I have felt thirty, slight or smart, at different periods; they are common in the Mediterranean), and the whole army discharged their arms, upon the same principle that savages beat drums, or howl, during an eclipse of the moon: —it was a rare scene altogether—if you had but seen the English Johnnies, who had never been out of a cockney workshop before! —or will again, if they can help it—and on Sunday, we heard that the Vizier is come down to Larissa, with one hundred and odd thousand men.

In coming here, I had two escapes; one from the Turks *(one* of my vessels was taken but afterwards released), and the other from shipwreck. We drove twice on the rocks near the Scrofes (islands near the coast).

I have obtained from the Greeks the release of eight-and-twenty Turkish prisoners, men, women, and children, and sent them to Patras and Prevesa at my own charges. One little girl of nine years old, who prefers remaining with me, I shall (if I live) send, with her mother, probably, to Italy, or to England, and adopt her. Her name is Hato, or Hatagée. She is a very pretty lively child. All her brothers were killed by the Greeks, and she herself and her mother merely spared by special favour and owing to her extreme youth, she being then but five or six years old.

My health is now better, and I ride about again. My office here is no sinecure, so many parties and difficulties of every kind; but I will do what I can. Prince Mavrocordato is an excellent person, and does all in his power; but his situation is perplexing in the extreme. Still we have great hopes of the success of the contest. You will hear, however, more of public news from plenty of quarters: for I have little time to write.

Believe me, yours, etc., etc.,

N. BN.

The fierce lawlessness of the Suliotes had now risen to such a height that it became necessary, for the safety of the European population, to get rid of them altogether; and, by some sacrifices on the part of Lord Byron, this object was at length effected. The advance of a month's pay by him, and the discharge of their arrears by the Government (the latter, too, with money lent for that purpose by the same universal paymaster), at length induced these rude warriors to depart from the town, and with them vanished all hopes of the expedition against Lepanto.

Byron died at Missolonghi on April 19, 1824, and when the body arrived in London, Murray, on behalf of Mr. Hobhouse, who was not personally acquainted with Dr. Ireland, the Dean of Westminster, wrote to him, conveying "the request of the executors and nearest relatives of the deceased for permission that his Lordship's remains may be deposited in Westminster Abbey, in the most private manner, at an early hour in the morning. "

Dr. *Ireland to John Murray*. ISLIP, OXFORD, *July* 8, 1824.

Dear Sir,

No doubt the family vault is the most proper place for the remains of Lord Byron. It is to be wished, however, that nothing had been said *publicly* about Westminster Abbey before it was known whether the remains could be received there. In the newspapers, unfortunately, it has been proclaimed by somebody that the Abbey was to be the spot, and, on the appearance of this article, I have been questioned as to the truth of it from Oxford. My answer has been that the proposal has been made, but civilly declined. I had also informed the members of the church at Westminster (after your first letter) that I could not grant the favour asked. I cannot, therefore, answer now that the case will not be mentioned (as it has happened) by some person or other who knows it. The best thing to be done, however, by the executors and relatives, is to carry away the body, and say as little about it as possible. Unless the subject is provoked by some injudicious parade about the remains, perhaps the matter will draw little or no notice.

Yours very truly,

J. IRELAND,

The death of Byron brought into immediate prominence the question of his autobiographical memoirs, the MS. of which he had given to Moore, who was at that time his guest at La Mira, near Venice, in 1819.

"A short time before dinner, " wrote Moore, "he left the room, and in a minute or two returned carrying in his hand a white-leather bag. 'Look here, ' he said, holding it up, 'this would be worth something to Murray, though *you*, I daresay, would not give sixpence for it. ' 'What is it? ' I asked. 'My Life and Adventures, ' he answered. On hearing this I raised my hands in a gesture of wonder. 'It is not a thing, ' he continued, 'that can be published during my lifetime, but you may have it if you like: there, do whatever you please with it. '"

Moore was greatly gratified by the gift, and said the Memoirs would make a fine legacy for his little boy. Lord Byron informed Mr. Murray by letter what he had done. "They are not, " he said, "for publication during my life, but when I am cold you may do what you please. " In a subsequent letter to Mr. Murray, Lord Byron said: "As you say my *prose* is good, why don't you treat with Moore for the reversion of my Memoirs? —conditionally recollect; not to be published before decease. He has the permission to dispose of them, and I advised him to do so. " Moore thus mentions the subject in his Memoirs:

"*May* 28, 1820. —Received a letter at last from Lord Byron, through Murray, telling me he had informed Lady B. of his having given me his Memoirs for the purpose of their being published after his death, and offering her the perusal of them in case she might wish to confute any of his statements. Her note in answer to this offer (the original of which he enclosed me) is as follows":

KIRKBY MALLORY, *March* 10, 1820.

I received your letter of January 1st, offering for my perusal a Memoir of part of my life. I decline to inspect it. I consider the publication or circulation of such a composition at any time is prejudicial to Ada's future happiness. For my own sake I have no reason to shrink from publication; but notwithstanding the injuries which I have suffered, I should lament more of the *consequences*.

A. BYRON.

To LORD BYRON. [Footnote: For Byron's reply to this letter, see Moore's Memoirs, iii. 115.]

Moore received the continuation of Lord Byron's Memoirs on December 26, 1820, the postage amounting to forty-six francs and a half. "He advises me, " said Moore in his Diary, "to dispose of the reversion of the MS. now. " Accordingly, Moore, being then involved in pecuniary responsibilities by the defalcations of his deputy in Bermuda, endeavoured to dispose of the "Memoirs of Lord Byron. " He first wrote to the Messrs. Longman, who did not offer him enough; and then to Mr. Murray, who offered him the sum of 2,000 guineas, on condition that he should be the editor of the Memoirs, and write the Life of Lord Byron.

John Murray to Lord Byron. July 24, 1821.

Dear Lord Byron,

I have just received a letter from Mr. Moore—the subject of it is every way worthy of your usual liberality—and I had not a moment's hesitation in acceding to a proposal which enabled me in any way to join in assisting so excellent a fellow. I have told him— which I suppose you will think fair—that he should give me all additions that you may from time to time make—and in case of survivorship edit the whole—and I will leave it as an heirloom to my son.

I have written to accede to Mr. Moore's proposal. I remain, dear Lord Byron, Your grateful and faithful Servant, JOHN MURRAY.

Mr. Moore accepted the proposal, and then proceeded to draw upon Mr. Murray for part of the money. It may be added that the agreement between Murray and Moore gave the former the right of publishing the Memoirs three months after his Lordship's death. When that event was authenticated, the manuscript remained at Mr. Murray's absolute disposal if Moore had not previously redeemed it by the repayment of the 2,000 guineas.

During the period that Mr. Moore had been in negotiation with the Longmans and Murray respecting the purchase of the Memoirs, he had given "Lady Holland the MS. to read. " Lord John Russell also states, in his "Memoirs of Moore, " that he had read "the greater part, if not the whole, " and that he should say that some of it was too gross for publication. When the Memoirs came into the hands of Mr. Murray, he entrusted the manuscript to Mr. Gifford, whose opinion coincided with that of Lord John Russell. A few others saw the Memoirs, amongst them Washington Irving and Mr. Luttrell. Irving says, in his "Memoirs, " that Moore showed him the Byron recollections and that they were quite unpublishable.

Mr. Moore himself seems to have been thrown into some doubt as to the sale of the manuscript by the opinion of his friends. "Lord Holland, " he said, "expressed some scruples as to the sale of Lord Byron's Memoirs, and he wished that I could have got the 2,000 guineas in any other way; he seemed to think it was in cold blood, depositing a sort of quiver of poisoned arrows for a future warfare upon private character. " [Footnote: Lord John Russell's "Memoirs, Journals, and Correspondence of Thomas Moore, " iii. p. 298.] Mr. Moore had a long conversation on the subject with Mr. J.C. Hobhouse, "who, " he says in his Journal, "is an upright and honest man. " When speaking of Lord Byron, Hobhouse said, "I know more about Lord Byron than any one else, and much more than I should wish any one else to know. "

Lady Byron offered, through Mr. Kinnaird, to advance 2,000 guineas for the redemption of the Memoirs from Mr. Murray, but the negotiation was not brought to a definite issue. Moore, when informed of the offer, objected to Lady Byron being consulted about the matter, "for this would be treachery to Lord Byron's intentions and wishes, " but he agreed to place the Memoirs at the disposal of Lord Byron's sister, Mrs. Leigh, "to be done with exactly as she thought proper. " Moore was of opinion that those parts of the manuscript should be destroyed which were found objectionable; but that those parts should be retained which were not, for his benefit and that of the public.

At the same time it must be remembered that Moore's interest in the Memoirs had now entirely ceased, for in consequence of the death of Lord Byron they had become Mr. Murray's absolute property, in accordance with the terms of his purchase. But although Mr. Murray had paid so large a sum for the manuscript, and would probably have made a considerable profit by its publication, he was nevertheless willing to have it destroyed, if it should be the deliberate opinion of his Lordship's friends and relatives that such a step was desirable.

Mr. Murray therefore put himself into communication with Lord Byron's nearest friends and relations with respect to the disposal of the Memoirs. His suggestion was at first strongly opposed by some of them; but he urged his objections to publication with increased zeal, even renouncing every claim to indemnification for what he had paid to Mr. Moore. A meeting of those who were entitled to act in the matter was at length agreed upon, and took place in Murray's drawing-room, on May 17, 1824. There were present Mr. Murray, Mr. Moore, Mr. J.C. Hobhouse, Colonel Doyle representing Lady Byron, Mr. Wilmot Horton representing Mrs. Leigh, and Mr. Luttrell, a friend of Moore's. Young Mr. Murray—then sixteen; the only person of those assembled now living [1891]—was also in the room. The discussion was long and stormy before the meeting broke up, and nearly led to a challenge between Moore and Hobhouse. A reference to the agreement between Moore and Murray became necessary, but for a long time that document could not be found; it was at length discovered, but only after the decision to commit the manuscript to the flames had been made and carried out, and the party remained until the last sheet of Lord Byron's Memoirs had vanished in smoke up the Albemarle Street chimney.

Immediately after the burning, Mrs. Leigh wrote the following account to her friend, the Rev. Mr. Hodgson, an old friend of Byron's:

The Hon. Mrs. Leigh to the Rev. f. Hodgson.

"The parties, Messrs. Moore, Murray, Hobhouse, Col. Doyle for Lady B., and Mr. Wilmot for me, and Mr. Luttrell, a friend of Mr. Moore's, met at Mr. Murray's; and after a long dispute and nearly quarrelling, upon Mr. Wilmot stating what was my wish and opinion, the MS. was burnt, and Moore paid Murray the 2,000 guineas. Immediately almost *after* this was done, the legal agreement between Moore and Murray (which had been mislaid), was found, and, strange to say, it appeared from it (what both had forgotten), that the property of the MS. was Murray's *bond fide*. Consequently *he* had the right to dispose of it as he pleased; and as he had behaved most handsomely upon the occasion... it was desired by our family that he should receive the 2,000 guineas back. " [Footnote: "Memoir of the Rev. F. Hodgson, " ii. 139-40.]

But the Byrons did not repay the money. Mr. Moore would not permit it. He had borrowed the 2,000 guineas from the Messrs. Longman, and before he left the room, he repaid to Mr. Murray the sum he had received for the Memoirs, together with the interest during the time that the purchase-money had remained in his possession.

The statements made in the press, as to Lord Byron's Memoirs having been burnt, occasioned much public excitement, and many applications were made to Mr. Murray for information on the subject. Amongst those who made particular inquiry was Mr. Jerdan, of the *Literary Gazette*, who inclosed to Mr. Murray the paragraph which he proposed to insert in his journal. Mr. Murray informed him that the account was so very erroneous, that he desired him either to condense it down to the smallest compass, or to omit it altogether. Mr. Jerdan, however, replied that the subject was of so much public interest, that he could not refuse to state the particulars, and the following was sent to him, prepared by Mr. Murray:

"A general interest having been excited, touching the fate of Lord Byron's Memoirs, written by himself, and reports, confused and incorrect, having got into circulation upon the subject, it has been deemed requisite to signify the real particulars. The manuscript of these Memoirs was purchased by Mr. Murray in the year 1821 for the sum of two thousand guineas, under certain stipulations which gave him the right of publishing them three months after his Lordship's demise. When that event was authenticated, the Manuscript consequently remained at Mr. Murray's absolute disposal; and a day or two after the melancholy intelligence reached London, Mr. Murray submitted to the near connections of the family that the MSS. should be destroyed. In consequence of this, five persons variously concerned in the matter were convened for discussion upon it. As these Memoirs were not calculated to augment the fame of the writer, and as some passages were penned in a spirit which his better feelings since had virtually retracted, Mr. Murray proposed that they should be destroyed, considering it a duty to sacrifice every view of profit to the noble author, by whose confidence and friendship he had been so long honoured. The result has been, that notwithstanding some opposition, he obtained the desired decision, and the Manuscript was forthwith committed to the flames. Mr. Murray was immediately reimbursed in the purchase-money by Mr. Moore, although Mr. Murray had previously renounced every claim to repayment. "

The particulars of the transaction are more fully expressed in the following letter written by Mr. Murray to Mr. (afterwards Sir) Robert Wilmot Horton, two days after the destruction of the manuscript. It seems that Mr. Moore had already made a representation to Mr. Horton which was not quite correct. [Footnote: Lord J. Russell's " Memoirs, etc., of Thomas Moore, " iv. p. 188.]

John Murray to Mr. R. Wilmot Horton. ALBEMARLE STREET, *May* 19, 1824.

Dear Sir,

On my return home last night I found your letter, dated the 17th, calling on me for a specific answer whether I acknowledged the accuracy of the statement of Mr. Moore, communicated in it. However unpleasant it is to me, your requisition of a specific answer obliges me to say that I cannot, by any means, admit the accuracy of that statement; and in order to explain to you how Mr. Moore's misapprehension may have arisen, and the ground upon which my assertion rests, I feel it necessary to trouble you with a statement of all the circumstances of the case, which will enable you to judge for yourself.

Lord Byron having made Mr. Moore a present of his Memoirs, Mr. Moore offered them for sale to Messrs. Longman & Co., who however declined to purchase them; Mr. Moore then made me a similar offer, which I accepted; and in November 1821, a joint assignment of the Memoirs was made to me by Lord Byron and Mr. Moore, with all legal technicalities, in consideration of a sum of 2,000 guineas, which, on the execution of the agreement by Mr. Moore, I paid to him. Mr. Moore also covenanted, in consideration of the said sum, to act as Editor of the Memoirs, and to supply an account of the subsequent events of Lord Byron's life, etc.

Some months after the execution of this assignment, Mr. Moore requested me, as a great personal favour to himself and to Lord Byron, to enter into a second agreement, by which I should resign the absolute property which I had in the Memoirs, and give Mr. Moore and Lord Byron, or any of their friends, a power of redemption *during the life of Lord Byron*. As the reason pressed upon me for this change was that their friends thought there were some things in the Memoirs that might be injurious to both, I did not hesitate to make this alteration at Mr. Moore's request; and, accordingly, on the 6th day of May, 1822, a second deed was executed, stating that, "Whereas Lord Byron and Mr. Moore are now inclined to wish the said work not to be published, it is agreed that, if either of them shall, *during the life of the said Lord Byron*, repay the 2,000 guineas to Mr. Murray, the latter shall redeliver the Memoirs; but that, if the sum be not repaid *during the lifetime of Lord Byron*, Mr. Murray shall be at full liberty to print and publish the said Memoirs within Three Months [Footnote: The words "within Three Months " were substituted for "immediately, " at Mr. Moore's request—and they appear in pencil, in his own handwriting, upon the original draft of the deed, which is still in existence.] after the death of the said Lord Byron. " I need hardly call your particular attention to the words, carefully inserted twice over in this agreement, which limited its existence to the *lifetime of Lord Byron*; the reason of such limitation was obvious and natural—namely that, although I consented to restore the work, *while Lord Byron should be alive* to direct the ulterior disposal of it, I would by no means consent to place it *after his death* at the disposal of any other person.

I must now observe that I had never been able to obtain possession of the original assignment, which was my sole lien on this property, although I had made repeated applications to Mr. Moore to put me into possession of the deed, which was stated to be in the hands of Lord Byron's banker. Feeling, I confess, in some degree alarmed at the withholding the deed, and dissatisfied at Mr. Moore's inattention to my interests in this particular, I wrote urgently to him in March 1823, to procure me the deed, and at the same time expressed my wish that the second agreement should either be cancelled or *at once executed*.

Finding this application unavailing, and becoming, by the greater lapse of time, still more doubtful as to what the intentions of the parties might be, I, in March 1824, repeated my demand to Mr. Moore in a more peremptory manner, and was in consequence at length put into possession of the original deed. But, not being at all satisfied with the course that had been pursued towards me, I repeated to Mr. Moore my uneasiness at the terms on which I stood under the second agreement, and renewed my request to him that he would either cancel it, or execute its provisions by the immediate redemption of the work, in order that I might exactly know what my rights in the property were. He requested time to consider this proposition. In a day or two he called, and told me that he would adopt the latter alternative—namely, the redemption of the Memoirs—as he had found persons who were ready to advance the money on *his injuring his life*; and he promised to conclude the business on the first day of his return to town, by paying the money and giving up the agreement. Mr. Moore did return to town, but did not, that I have heard of, take any proceedings for insuring his life; he positively neither wrote nor called upon me as he had promised to do (though he was generally accustomed to make mine one of his first houses of call); —nor did he take any other step, that I am aware of, to show that he had any recollection of the conversation which had passed between us previous to his leaving town, until *the death of Lord Byron* had, *ipso facto*, cancelled the agreement in question, and completely restored my absolute rights over the property of the Memoirs.

You will therefore perceive that there was no verbal agreement in existence between Mr. Moore and me, at the time I made a verbal agreement with you to deliver the Memoirs to be destroyed. Mr. Moore might undoubtedly, *during Lord Byron's life*, have obtained possession of the Memoirs, if he had pleased to do so; he however neglected or delayed to give effect to our verbal agreement, which, as well as the written instrument to which it related, being cancelled by the death of Lord Byron, there was no reason whatsoever why I was not at that instant perfectly at liberty to dispose of the MS. as I thought proper. Had I considered only my own interest as a tradesman, I would have announced the work for immediate publication, and I cannot doubt that, under all the circumstances, the public curiosity about these Memoirs would have given me a very considerable profit beyond the large sum I originally paid for them; but you yourself are, I think, able to do me the justice of bearing witness that I looked at the case with no such feelings, and that my regard for Lord Byron's memory, and my respect for his surviving family, made me more anxious that the Memoirs should be immediately destroyed, since it was surmised that the publication might be injurious to the former and painful to the latter.

As I myself scrupulously refrained from looking into the Memoirs, I cannot, from my own knowledge, say whether such an opinion of the contents was correct or not; it was enough for me that the friends of Lord and Lady Byron united in wishing for their destruction. Why Mr. Moore should have wished to preserve them I did not nor will I inquire; but, having satisfied myself that he had no right whatever in them, I was happy in having an opportunity of making, by a pecuniary sacrifice on my part, some return for the honour, and I must add, the profit, which I had derived from Lord Byron's patronage and friendship. You will also be able to bear witness that—although I could not presume to impose an obligation on the friends of Lord Byron or Mr. Moore, by refusing to receive the repayment of the 2,000 guineas advanced by me—yet I had determined on the destruction of the Memoirs without any previous agreement for such repayment: —and you know the Memoirs were actually destroyed without any stipulation on my part, but even with a declaration that I had destroyed my own private property— and I therefore had no claim upon any party for remuneration.

I remain, dear Sir,

Your faithful servant,

JOHN MURRAY.

After the burning of the manuscript Sir Walter Scott wrote in his diary: "It was a pity that nothing save the total destruction of Byron's Memoirs would satisfy his executors; but there was a reason—*premat nox alta.* "

Shortly after the burning of the Memoirs, Mr. Moore began to meditate writing a Life of Lord Byron; "the Longmans looking earnestly and anxiously to it as the great source of my means of repaying them their money. " [Footnote: Moore's Memoirs, iv. 253.] Mr. Moore could not as yet, however, proceed with the Life, as the most important letters of Lord Byron were those written to Mr. Murray, which were in his exclusive possession. Lord John Russell also was against his writing the Life of Byron.

"If you write, " he wrote to Moore, "write poetry, or, if you can find a good subject, write prose; but do not undertake to write the life of another reprobate [referring to Moore's "Life of Sheridan"]. In short, do anything but write the life of Lord Byron. " [Footnote: Moore's Memoirs, v. 51.]

Yet Moore grievously wanted money, and this opportunity presented itself to him with irresistible force as a means of adding to his resources. At length he became reconciled to Mr. Murray through the intercession of Mr. Hobhouse. Moore informed the Longmans of the reconciliation, and, in a liberal and considerate manner, they said to him, "Do not let us stand in the way of any arrangements you may make; it is our wish to see you free from debt; and it would be only in this one work that we should be separated. " It was in this way that Mr. Moore undertook to write for Mr. Murray the Life of Lord Byron. Mr. Murray agreed to repay Moore the 2,000 guineas he had given for the burned Memoirs and £2,000 extra for editing the letters and writing the Life, and Moore in his diary says that he considered this offer perfectly liberal. Nothing, he adds, could be more frank, gentleman-like, and satisfactory than the manner in which this affair had been settled on all sides.

CHAPTER XVII

SCOTT'S NOVELS—BLACKWOOD AND MURRAY

The account of Mr. Murray's dealings with Lord Byron has carried us considerably beyond the date at which we left the history of his general business transactions, and compels us to go back to the year 1814, when, as is related in a previous chapter, he had associated himself with William Blackwood as his Edinburgh agent.

Blackwood, like Murray, was anxious to have a share in the business of publishing the works of Walter Scott—especially the novels teeming from the press by "The Author of 'Waverley.'" Although Constable and the Ballantynes were necessarily admitted to the knowledge of their authorship, to the world at large they were anonymous, and the author still remained unknown. Mr. Murray had, indeed, pointed out to Mr. Canning that "Waverley" was by Walter Scott; but Scott himself trailed so many red herrings across the path, that publishers as well as the public were thrown off the scent, and both Blackwood and Murray continued to be at fault with respect to the authorship of the "Waverley Novels. "

In February 1816 Ballantyne assured Blackwood that in a very few weeks he would have something very important to propose. On April 12 following, Blackwood addressed the following letter to Murray, "most strictly confidential"; and it contained important proposals:

Mr. W. Blackwood to John Murray.

MY DEAR MURRAY,

Some time ago I wrote to you that James Ballantyne had dined with me, and from what then passed I expected that I would soon have something very important to communicate. He has now fully explained himself to me, with liberty to inform you of anything he has communicated. This, however, he entreats of us to keep most strictly to ourselves, trusting to our honour that we will not breathe a syllable of it to the dearest friends we have.

He began by telling me that he thought he had it now in his power to show me how sensible he was of the services I had done him, and how anxious he was to accomplish that union of interests which I had so long been endeavouring to bring about. Till now he had only made professions; now he would act. He said that he was empowered to offer me, along with you, a work of fiction in four volumes, such as Waverley, etc. ; that he had read a considerable part of it; and, knowing the plan of the whole, he could answer for its being a production of the very first class; but that he was not at liberty to mention its title, nor was he at liberty to 'give the author's name. I naturally asked him, was it by the author of "Waverley"? He said it was to have no reference to any other work whatever, and everyone would be at liberty to form their own conjectures as to the author. He only requested that, whatever we might suppose from anything that might occur afterwards, we should keep strictly to ourselves that we were to be the publishers. The terms he was empowered by the author to offer for it were:

1. The author to receive one-half of the profits of each edition; these profits to be ascertained by deducting the paper and printing from the proceeds of the book sold at sale price; the publishers to be at the whole of the expense of advertising. 2. The property of the book to be the publishers', who were to print such editions as they chose. 3. The only condition upon which the author would agree to these terms is, that the publisher should take £600 of John Ballantyne's stock, selected from the list annexed, deducting 25 per cent, from the affixed sale prices. 4. If these terms are agreed to, the stock to the above amount to be immediately delivered, and a bill granted at twelve months. 5. That in the course of six or eight weeks, J.B. expected to be able to put into my hands the first two volumes printed, and that if on perusal we did not like the bargain, we should be at liberty to give it up. This he considered to be most unlikely; but if it should be the case, he would bind himself to repay or redeliver the bill on the books being returned. 6. That the edition, consisting of 2,000 copies, should be printed and ready for delivery by the 1st of October next.

I have thus stated to you as nearly as I can the substance of what passed. I tried in various ways to learn something with regard to the author; but he was quite impenetrable. My own impression now is, that it must be Walter Scott, for no one else would think of burdening us with such trash as John B. 's wretched stock. This is such a burden, that I am puzzled not a little. I endeavoured every way I could to get him to propose other terms, but he told me they could not be departed from in a single part; and the other works had been taken on the same conditions, and he knew they would be greedily accepted again in the same quarter. Consider the matter seriously, and write to me as soon as you can. After giving it my consideration, and making some calculations. I confess I feel inclined to hazard the speculation; but still I feel doubtful until I hear what you think of it. Do not let my opinion, which may be erroneous, influence you, but judge for yourself. From the very strong terms in which Jas. B. spoke of the work, I am sanguine enough to expect it will equal if not surpass any of the others. I would not lay so much stress upon what he says if I were not assured that his great interest, as well as Mr. Scott's, is to stand in the very best way both with you and me. They are anxious to get out of the clutches of Constable, and Ballantyne is sensible of the favour I have done and may still do him by giving so much employment, besides what he may expect from you. From Constable he can expect nothing. I had almost forgotten to mention that he assured me in the most solemn manner that we had got the first offer, and he ardently hoped we would accept of it. If, however, we did not, he trusted to our honour that we would say nothing of it; that the author of this work would likely write more; and should we not take this, we might have it in our power afterwards to do something with him, provided we acted with delicacy in the transaction, as he had no doubt we would do. I hope you will be able to write to me soon, and as fully as you can. If I have time tomorrow, or I should rather say this day, as it is now near one o'clock, I will write you about other matters; and if I have no letter from you, will perhaps give you another scolding.

Yours most truly,

W. BLACKWOOD.

A long correspondence took place between Blackwood and Murray on Ballantyne's proposal. Blackwood was inclined to accept, notwithstanding the odd nature of the proposal, in the firm belief that "the heart's desire" of Ballantyne was to get rid of Constable. He sent Murray a list of Ballantyne's stock, from which the necessary value of books was to be selected. It appeared, however, that there was one point on which Blackwood had been mistaken, and that was, that the copyright of the new novel was not to be absolutely conveyed, and that all that Ballantyne meant, or had authority to offer, was an edition, limited to six thousand copies, of the proposed work. Although Murray considered it "a blind bargain, " he was disposed to accept it, as it might lead to something better. Blackwood accordingly communicated to Ballantyne that he and Murray accepted his offer.

Mr. Wm. Blackwood to John Murray.

April 27, 1816.

"Everything is settled, and on Tuesday Ballantyne is to give a letter specifying the whole terms of the transaction. He could not do it sooner, he said, as he had to consult the author. This, I think, makes it clear that it is Walter Scott, who is at Abbotsford just now. What surprised me a good deal was, James Ballantyne told me that his brother John had gone out there with Constable, and Godwin (author of 'Caleb Williams'), whom Scott was anxious to see. They are really a strange set of people.... I am not over fond of all these mysteries, but they are a mysterious set of personages, and we must manage with them in the best way that we can. "

A letter followed from James Ballantyne to Murray (May I, 1816), congratulating him upon concluding the bargain through Blackwood, and saying:

"I have taken the liberty of drawing upon you at twelve months for £300 for your share.... It will be a singularly great accommodation if you can return the bill in course of post. "

Although Ballantyne had promised that the first edition of the proposed work should be ready by October 1, 1816, Blackwood found that in June the printing of the work had not yet commenced. Ballantyne said he had not yet got any part of the manuscript from the author, but that he would press him again on the subject. The controversy still continued as to the authorship of the Waverley Novels. "For these six months past, " wrote Blackwood (June 6, 1816), "there have been various rumours with regard to Greenfield being the author of these Novels, but I never paid much attention to it; the thing appeared to me so very improbable.... But from what I have heard lately, and from what you state, I now begin to think that Greenfield may probably be the author. " On the other hand, Mr. Mackenzie called upon Blackwood, and informed him that "he was now quite convinced that Thomas Scott, Walter's brother in Canada, writes all the novels. " The secret, however, was kept for many years longer.

Blackwood became quite provoked at the delay in proceeding with the proposed work.

Mr. Wm. Blackwood to John Murray.

June 21, 1816.

"I begin to fear that S. B. and Cy. are a nest of — —. There is neither faith nor truth in them. In my last letter I mentioned to you that there was not the smallest appearance of the work being yet begun, and there is as little still. James Ballantyne shifts this off his own shoulders by saying that he cannot help it. Now, my own belief is that at the time he made such solemn promises to me that the first volume would be in my hands in a month, he had not the smallest expectation of this being the case; but he knew that he would not have got our bills, which he absolutely wanted, without holding this out. It is now seven weeks since the bills were granted, and it is five weeks since I gave him the list of books which were to be delivered. I have applied to him again and again for them, and on Tuesday last his man at length called on me to say that John Ballantyne & Co. could not deliver fifty sets of 'Kerr's Voyages'—that they had only such quantities of particular odd volumes of which he showed me a list. "

Blackwood called upon Ballantyne, but he could not see him, and instead of returning Blackwood's visit, he sent a note of excuse. Next time they met was at Hollingworth's Hotel, after which Ballantyne sent Blackwood a letter "begging for a loan of £50 till next week, but not a word of business in it. " Next time they met was at the same hotel, when the two dined with Robert Miller.

Mr. Wm. Blackwood to John Murray.

"After dinner I walked home with J. B. Perhaps from the wine he had drunk, he was very communicative, and gave me a great deal of very curious and interesting private history. Would you believe it, that about six weeks ago—at the very time our transaction was going on—these worthies, Scott, Ballantyne & Co., concluded a transaction with Constable for 10,000 copies of this said 'History of Scotland' [which had been promised to Blackwood and Murray] in 4 vols., and actually received bills for the profits expected to be realized from this large number! Yet, when I put James Ballantyne in mind on Tuesday of what he had formally proposed by desire of Mr. Scott, and assured us we were positively to get the work, and asked him if there was any truth in the rumour I had heard, and even that you had heard, about Mr. Scott being about to publish a 'History of Scotland' with his name, and further asked him if Mr. Scott was now ready to make any arrangements with us about it (for it never occurred to me that he could make arrangements with any one else), he solemnly assured me that he knew nothing about it! Now, after this, what confidence can we have in anything that this man will say or profess! I confess I am sadly mortified at my own credulousness. John I always considered as no better than a swindler, but James I put some trust and confidence in. You judged more accurately, for you always said that 'he was a damned cunning fellow! ' Well, there is every appearance of your being right; but his cunning (as it never does) will not profit him. Within these three years I have given him nearly £1,400 for printing, and in return have only received empty professions, made, to be sure, in the most dramatic manner. Trite as the saying is, honesty is always the best policy; and if we live a little longer, we shall see what will be the end of all their cunning, never-ending labyrinths of plots and schemes. Constable is the proper person for them; set a thief to catch a thief: Jonathan Wild will be fully a match for any of the heroes of the 'Beggar's Opera. ' My blood boils when I think of them, and still more when I think of my allowing myself so long to keep my eyes shut to what I ought to have seen long ago. But the only apology I make to myself is, that one does not wish to think so ill of human nature. There is an old Scotch proverb, 'He has need o' a lang spoon that sups wi' the De'il, ' and since we are engaged, let us try if we can partake of the broth without scalding ourselves. I still hope that we may; and however much my feelings revolt at having any connection in future with them, yet I shall endeavour to the best of my power to repress my bile, and to turn their own tricks against themselves. One in business must submit to many things, and swallow many a bitter pill, when such a man as Walter Scott is the object in view. You will see, by this day's Edinburgh papers, that the copartnery of John Ballantyne & Co. is formally dissolved. Miller told me that, before James Ballantyne could get his wife's friends to assent to the marriage, Walter Scott was obliged to grant bonds and securities, taking upon himself all the engagements of John Ballantyne & Co., as well as of James Ballantyne & Co. ; [Footnote: Lockhart says, in his "Life of Scott, " that "in Feb., 1816, when James Ballantyne married, it is clearly proved, by letters in his handwriting, that he owed to Scott more than £3,000 of personal debt. "] so that, if there was any difficulty on their part, he bound himself to fulfil the whole. When we consider the large sums of money Walter Scott has got for his works, the greater part of which has been thrown into the hands of the Ballantynes, and likewise the excellent printing business J. B. has had for so many years, it is quite incomprehensible what has become of all the money. Miller says, 'It is just a jaw hole which swallows up all, ' and from what he has heard he does not believe Walter Scott is worth anything. "

Murray was nevertheless willing to go on until the terms of his bargain with Ballantyne were fulfilled, and wrote to Blackwood that he was "resolved to swallow the pill, bitter though it was, " but he expressed his surprise that "Mr. Scott should have allowed his property to be squandered as it has been by these people. "

Blackwood, however, was in great anxiety about the transaction, fearing the result of the engagement which he and Murray had entered into.

Mr. Wm. Blackwood to John Murray.

July 2, 1816.

"This morning I got up between five and six, but instead of sitting down to write to you, as I had intended, I mounted my pony and took a long ride to collect my thoughts. Sitting, walking, or riding is all the same. I feel as much puzzled as ever, and undetermined whether or not to cut the Gordian knot. Except my wife, there is not a friend whom I dare advise with. I have not once ventured to mention the business at all to my brother, on account of the cursed mysteries and injunctions of secrecy connected with it. I know he would blame me for ever engaging in it, for he has a very small opinion of the Ballantynes. I cannot therefore be benefited by his advice. Mrs. Blackwood, though she always disliked my having any connection with the Ballantynes, rather thinks we should wait a few weeks longer, till we see what is produced. I believe, after all, this is the safest course to pursue. I would beg of you, however, to think maturely upon the affair, taking into account Mr. Scott's usefulness to the *Review.* Take a day or two to consider the matter fully, and then give me your best advice.... As to Constable or his triumphs, as he will consider them, I perfectly agree with you that they are not to be coveted by us, and that they should not give us a moment's thought. Thank God, we shall never desire to compass any of our ends by underhand practices. "

Meanwhile correspondence with Ballantyne about the work of fiction—the name of which was still unknown-was still proceeding. Ballantyne said that the author "promised to put the first volume in his hands by the end of August, and that the whole would be ready for publication by Christmas. " Blackwood thought this reply was "humbug, as formerly. " Nevertheless, he was obliged to wait. At last he got the first sight of the manuscript.

Mr. Wm. Blackwood to John Murray.

August 23, 1816. *Midnight.*

"MY DEAR MURRAY, —I have this moment finished the reading of 192 pages of our book—for ours it must be, —and I cannot go to bed without telling you what is the strong and most favourable impression it has made upon me. If the remainder be at all equal— which it cannot fail to be, from the genius displayed in what is now before me—we have been most fortunate indeed. The title as, TALKS OF MY LANDLORD; *collected and reported by Jedediah Cleishbotham, Pariah Clerk and Schoolmaster of Gandercleugh. "*

Mr. Blackwood then proceeds to give an account of the Introduction, the commencement of "The Black Dwarf, " the first of the tales, and the general nature of the story, to the end of the fourth chapter. His letter is of great length, and extends to nine quarto pages. He concludes:

"There cannot be a doubt as to the splendid merit of the work. It would never have done to have hesitated and higgled about seeing more volumes. In the note which accompanied the sheets, Ballantyne says, 'each volume contains a Tale, ' so there will be four in all. [Footnote: This, the original intention, was departed from.] The next relates to the period of the Covenanters. I have now neither doubts nor fears with regard to the whole being good, and I anxiously hope that you will have as little. I am so happy at the fortunate termination of all my pains and anxieties, that I cannot be in bad humour with you for not writing me two lines in answer to my last letters. I hope I shall hear from you to-morrow; but I entreat of you to write me in course of post, as I wish to hear from you before I leave this [for London], which I intend to do on this day se'nnight by the smack. "

At length the principal part of the manuscript of the novel was in the press, and, as both the author and the printer were in sore straits for money, they became importunate on Blackwood and Murray for payment on account. They had taken Ballantyne's "wretched stock" of books, as Blackwood styled them, and Lockhart, in his "Life of Scott, " infers that Murray had consented to anticipate the period of his payments. At all events, he finds in a letter of Scott's, written in August, these words to John Ballantyne: "Dear John, —I have the pleasure to enclose Murray's acceptances. I earnestly recommend you to push, realising as much as you can.

"Consider weel, gude mon,
  We hae but borrowed gear,
The horse that I ride on,
  It is John Murray's mear."

Scott was at this time sorely pressed for ready money. He was buying one piece of land after another, usually at exorbitant prices, and having already increased the estate of Abbotsford from 150 to nearly 1,000 acres, he was in communication with Mr. Edward Blore as to the erection of a dwelling adjacent to the cottage, at a point facing the Tweed. This house grew and expanded, until it became the spacious mansion of Abbotsford. The Ballantynes also were ravenous for more money; but they could get nothing from Blackwood and Murray before the promised work was finished.

At last the book was completed, printed, and published on December 1, 1816; but without the magical words, "by the Author of 'Waverley, '" on the title-page. All doubts as to the work being by the author of "Waverley, " says Lockhart, had worn themselves out before the lapse of a week.

John Murray to Mr. Wm. Blackwood.

December 13, 1816.

"Having now heard every one's opinion about our 'Tales of my Landlord, ' I feel competent to assure you that it is universally in their favour. There is only 'Meg Merrilies' in their way. It is even, I think, superior to the other three novels. You may go on printing as many and as fast as you can; for we certainly need not stop until we come to the end of our, unfortunately, limited 6,000.... My copies are

A Publisher and His Friends

more than gone, and if you have any to spare pray send them up instantly. "

On the following day Mr. Murray wrote to Mr. Scott:

John Murray to Mr. Scott.

December 14, 1816.

DEAR SIR,

Although I dare not address you as the author of certain Tales— which, however, must be written either by Walter Scott or the devil—yet nothing can restrain me from thinking that it is to your influence with the author of them that I am indebted for the essential honour of being one of their publishers; and I must intrude upon you to offer my most hearty thanks, not divided but doubled, alike for my worldly gain therein, and for the great acquisition of professional reputation which their publication has already procured me. As to delight, I believe I could, under any oath that could be proposed, swear that I never experienced such great and unmixed pleasure in all my life as the reading of this exquisite work has afforded me; and if you witnessed the wet eyes and grinning cheeks with which, as the author's chamberlain, I receive the unanimous and vehement praise of them from every one who has read them, or heard the curses of those whose needs my scanty supply would not satisfy, you might judge of the sincerity with which I now entreat you to assure the author of the most complete success. After this, I could throw all the other books which I have in the press into the Thames, for no one will either read them or buy. Lord Holland said, when I asked his opinion: "Opinion? we did not one of us go to bed all night, and nothing slept but my gout. " Frere, Hallam, and Boswell; Lord Glenbervie came to me with tears in his eyes. "It is a cordial, " he said, "which has saved Lady Glenbervie's life. " Heber, who found it on his table on his arrival from a journey, had no rest till he had read it. He has only this moment left me, and he, with many others, agrees that it surpasses all the other novels. Wm. Lamb also; Gifford never read anything like it, he says; and his estimate of it absolutely increases at each recollection of it. Barrow with great difficulty was forced to read it; and he said yesterday, "Very good, to be sure, but what powerful writing is *thrown away*. " Heber says

there are only two men in the world, Walter Scott and Lord Byron. Between you, you have given existence to a third.
Ever your faithful servant,

JOHN MURRAY.

This letter did not effectually "draw the badger. " Scott replied in the following humorous but Jesuitical epistle:

Mr. Scott to John Murray.

December 18, 1816.

MY DEAR SIR,

I give you hearty joy of the success of the Tales, although I do not claim that paternal interest in them which my friends do me the credit to assign to me. I assure you I have never read a volume of them till they were printed, and can only join with the rest of the world in applauding the true and striking portraits which they present of old Scottish manners.

I do not expect implicit reliance to be placed on my disavowal, because I know very well that he who is disposed not to own a work must necessarily deny it, and that otherwise his secret would be at the mercy of all who chose to ask the question, since silence in such a case must always pass for consent, or rather assent. But I have a mode of convincing you that I am perfectly serious in my denial— pretty similar to that by which Solomon distinguished the fictitious from the real mother—and that is by reviewing the work, which I take to be an operation equal to that of quartering the child.... Kind compliments to Heber, whom I expected at Abbotsford this summer; also to Mr. Croker and all your four o'clock visitors. I am just going to Abbotsford, to make a small addition to my premises there. I have now about seven hundred acres, thanks to the booksellers and the discerning public.

Yours truly,

WALTER SCOTT.

The happy chance of securing a review of the Tales by the author of "Waverley" himself exceeded Murray's most sanguine expectations, and filled him with joy. He suggested that the reviewer, instead of sending an article on the Gypsies, as he proposed, should introduce whatever he had to say about that picturesque race in his review of the Tales, by way of comment on the character of Meg Merrilies. The review was written, and appeared in No. 32 of the *Quarterly*, in January 1817, by which time the novel had already gone to a third edition. It is curious now to look back upon the author reviewing his own work. He adopted Murray's view, and besides going over the history of "Waverley, " and the characters introduced in that novel, he introduced a disquisition about Meg Merrilies and the Gypsies, as set forth in his novel of "Guy Mannering. " He then proceeded to review the "Black Dwarf" and "Old Mortality, " but with the utmost skill avoided praising them, and rather endeavoured to put his friends off the scent by undervaluing them, and finding fault. The "Black Dwarf, " for example, was full of "violent events which are so common in romance, and of such rare occurrence in real life. " Indeed, he wrote, "the narrative is unusually artificial; neither hero nor heroine excites interest of any sort, being just that sort of *pattern* people whom nobody cares a farthing about. "

"The other story, " he adds, "is of much deeper interest. " He describes the person who gave the title to the novel—Robert Paterson, of the parish of Closeburn, in Dumfriesshire—and introduces a good deal of historical knowledge, but takes exception to many of the circumstances mentioned in the story, at the same time quoting some of the best passages about Cuddie Headrigg and his mother. In respect to the influence of Claverhouse and General Dalzell, the reviewer states that "the author has cruelly falsified history, " and relates the actual circumstances in reference to these generals. "We know little, " he says, "that the author can say for himself to excuse these sophistications, and, therefore, may charitably suggest that he was writing a romance, and not a history." In conclusion, the reviewer observed, "We intended here to conclude this long article, when a strong report reached us of certain trans-Atlantic confessions, which, if genuine (though of this we know nothing), assign a different author to these volumes than the party suspected by our Scottish correspondents. Yet a critic may be excused seizing upon the nearest suspicious person, on the principle happily expressed by Claverhouse in a letter to the Earl of Linlithgow. He had been, it seems, in search of a gifted weaver who used to hold forth at conventicles. "I sent to seek the webster (weaver); they brought in his *brother* for him; though he maybe cannot preach like his brother, I doubt not but he is as well-principled as he, wherefore I thought it would be no great fault to give him the trouble to go to the jail with the rest. "

Mr. Murray seems to have accepted the suggestion and wrote in January 1817 to Mr. Blackwood:

"I can assure you, but *in the greatest confidence*, that I have discovered the author of all these Novels to be Thomas Scott, Walter Scott's brother. He is now in Canada. I have no doubt but that Mr. Walter Scott did a great deal to the first 'Waverley Novel, ' because of his anxiety to serve his brother, and his doubt about the success of the work. This accounts for the many stories about it. Many persons had previously heard from Mr. Scott, but you may rely on the certainty of what I have told you. The whole country is starving for want of a complete supply of the 'Tales of my Landlord, ' respecting the interest and merit of which there continues to be but one sentiment."

A few weeks later Blackwood wrote to Murray:

January 22, 1817.

"It is an odd story here, that Mr. and Mrs. Thomas Scott are the authors of all these Novels. I, however, still think, as Mr. Croker said to me in one of his letters, that if they were not by Mr. Walter Scott, the only alternative is to give them to the devil, as by one or the other they must be written. "

On the other hand, Bernard Barton wrote to Mr. Murray, and said that he had "heard that James Hogg, the Ettrick Shepherd, was the author of 'Tales of my Landlord, ' and that he had had intimation from himself to that effect, " by no means an improbable story considering Hogg's vanity. Lady Mackintosh also wrote to Mr. Murray: "Did you hear who this *new* author of 'Waverley' and 'Guy Mannering' is? Mrs. Thomas Scott, as Mr. Thomas Scott assured Lord Selkirk (who had been in Canada), and his lordship, like Lord Monboddo, believes it. " Murray again wrote to Blackwood (February 15, 1817): "What is your theory as to the author of 'Harold the Dauntless'? I will believe, till within an inch of my life, that the author of 'Tales of my Landlord' is Thomas Scott. "

Thus matters remained until a few years later, when George IV. was on his memorable visit to Edinburgh. Walter Scott was one of the heroes of the occasion, and was the selected cicerone to the King.

One day George IV., in the sudden and abrupt manner which is peculiar to our Royal Family, asked Scott point-blank: "By the way, Scott, are you the author of 'Waverley'? " Scott as abruptly answered: "No, Sire! " Having made this answer (said Mr. Thomas Mitchell, who communicated the information to Mr. Murray some years later), "it is supposed that he considered it a matter of honour to keep the secret during the present King's reign. If the least personal allusion is made to the subject in Sir Walter's presence, Matthews says that his head gently drops upon his breast, and that is a signal for the person to desist. "

With respect to the first series of the "Tales of my Landlord, " so soon as the 6,000 copies had been disposed of which the author, through Ballantyne, had covenanted as the maximum number to be published by Murray and Blackwood, the work reverted to Constable, and was published uniformly with the other works by the author of "Waverley. "

CHAPTER XVIII

ALLIANCE WITH BLACKWOOD—BLACKWOOD'S
"EDINBURGH MAGAZINE"—TERMINATION OF PARTNERSHIP

We have already seen that Mr. Murray had some correspondence with Thomas Campbell in 1806 respecting the establishment of a monthly magazine; such an undertaking had long been a favourite scheme of his, and he had mentioned the subject to many friends at home as well as abroad. When, therefore, Mr. Blackwood started his magazine, Murray was ready to enter into his plans, and before long announced to the public that he had become joint proprietor and publisher of Blackwood's *Edinburgh Magazine*.

There was nothing very striking in the early numbers of the *Magazine*, and it does not appear to have obtained a considerable circulation. The first editors were Thomas Pringle, who—in conjunction with a friend—was the author of a poem entitled "The Institute, " and James Cleghorn, best known as a contributor to the *Farmers' Magazine*. Constable, who was himself the proprietor of the *Scots Magazine* as well as of the *Farmers' Magazine*, desired to keep the monopoly of the Scottish monthly periodicals in his own hands, and was greatly opposed to the new competitor. At all events, he contrived to draw away from Blackwood Pringle and Cleghorn, and to start a new series of the *Scots Magazine* under the title of the *Edinburgh Magazine*. Blackwood thereupon changed the name of his periodical to that by which it has since been so well known. He undertook the editing himself, but soon obtained many able and indefatigable helpers.

There were then two young advocates walking the Parliament House in search of briefs. These were John Wilson (Christopher North) and John Gibson Lockhart (afterwards editor of the *Quarterly*). Both were West-countrymen—Wilson, the son of a wealthy Paisley manufacturer, and Lockhart, the son of the minister of Cambusnethan, in Lanarkshire—and both had received the best of educations, Wilson, the robust Christian, having carried off the Newdigate prize at Oxford, and Lockhart, having gained the Snell foundation at Glasgow, was sent to Balliol, and took a first class in classics in 1813. These, with Dr. Maginn—under the *sobriquet* of "Morgan O'Dogherty, "—Hogg—the Ettrick Shepherd, —De

Quincey—the Opium-eater, —Thomas Mitchell, and others, were the principal writers in *Blackwood*.

No. 7, the first of the new series, created an unprecedented stir in Edinburgh. It came out on October 1, 1817, and sold very rapidly, but after 10,000 had been struck off it was suppressed, and could be had neither for love nor money. The cause of this sudden attraction was an article headed "Translation from an Ancient Chaldee Manuscript, " purporting to be an extract from some newly discovered historical document, every paragraph of which contained a special hit at some particular person well known in Edinburgh society. There was very little ill-nature in it; at least, nothing like the amount which it excited in those who were, or imagined themselves to be, caricatured in it. Constable, the "Crafty, " and Pringle and Cleghorn, editors of the *Edinburgh Magazine*, as well as Jeffrey, editor of the *Edinburgh Review*, came in for their share of burlesque description.

Among the persons delineated in the article were the publisher of Blackwood's *Edinburgh Magazine*, whose name "was as it had been, the colour of Ebony": indeed the name of Old Ebony long clung to the journal. The principal writers of the article were themselves included in the caricature. Hogg, the Ettrick Shepherd, was described as "the great wild boar from the forest of Lebanon, and he roused up his spirit, and I saw him whetting his dreadful tusks for the battle. " Wilson was "the beautiful leopard, " and Lockhart "the scorpion, "—names which were afterwards hurled back at them with interest. Walter Scott was described as "the great magician who dwelleth in the old fastness, hard by the river Jordan, which is by the Border. " Mackenzie, Jameson, Leslie, Brewster, Tytler, Alison, M'Crie, Playfair, Lord Murray, the Duncans—in fact, all the leading men of Edinburgh were hit off in the same fashion.

Mrs. Garden, in her "Memorials of James Hogg, " says that "there is no doubt that Hogg wrote the first draft; indeed, part of the original is still in the possession of the family.... Some of the more irreverent passages were not his, or were at all events largely added to by others before publication. " [Footnote: Mrs. Garden's "Memorials of James Hogg, " p. 107.] In a recent number of *Blackwood* it is said that:

"Hogg's name is nearly associated with the Chaldee Manuscript. Of course he claimed credit for having written the skit, and undoubtedly he originated the idea. The rough draft came from his pen, and we cannot speak with certainty as to how it was subsequently manipulated. But there is every reason to believe that Wilson and Lockhart, probably assisted by Sir William Hamilton, went to work upon it, and so altered it that Hogg's original offspring was changed out of all knowledge. " [Footnote: *Blackwood's Magazine*, September 1882, pp. 368-9.]

The whole article was probably intended as a harmless joke; and the persons indicated, had they been wise, might have joined in the laugh or treated the matter with indifference. On the contrary, however, they felt profoundly indignant, and some of them commenced actions in the Court of Session for the injuries done to their reputation.

The same number of *Blackwood* which contained the "Translation from an Ancient Chaldee Manuscript, " contained two articles, one probably by Wilson, on Coleridge's "Biographia Literaria, " the other, signed "Z, " by Lockhart, being the first of a series on "The Cockney School of Poetry. " They were both clever, but abusive, and exceedingly personal in their allusions.

Murray expostulated with Blackwood on the personality of the articles. He feared lest they should be damaging to the permanent success of the journal. Blackwood replied in a long letter, saying that the journal was prospering, and that it was only Constable and his myrmidons who were opposed to it, chiefly because of its success.

In August 1818, Murray paid £1,000 for a half share in the magazine, and from this time he took a deep and active interest in its progress, advising Blackwood as to its management, and urging him to introduce more foreign literary news, as well as more scientific information. He did not like the idea of two editors, who seem to have taken the management into their own hands.

Subsequent numbers of *Blackwood* contained other reviews of "The Cockney School of Poetry": Leigh Hunt, "the King of the Cockneys, " was attacked in May, and in August it was the poet Keats who came under the critic's lash, four months after Croker's famous review of "Endymion" in the *Quarterly*. [Footnote: It was said that Keats was killed by this brief notice, of four pages, in the *Quarterly*; and Byron, in his "Don Juan, " gave credit to this statement:

"Poor Keats, who was killed off by one critique,

> Just as he really promised something great,...
> 'Tis strange, the mind, that very fiery particle,
> Should let itself be snuffed out by an article."

Leigh Hunt, one of Keats' warmest friends, when in Italy, told Lord Byron (as he relates in his Autobiography) the real state of the case, proving to him that the supposition of Keats' death being the result of the review was a mistake, and therefore, if printed, would be a misrepresentation. But the stroke of wit was not to be given up. Either Mr. Gifford, or "the poet-priest Milman, " has generally, but erroneously, been blamed for being the author of the review in the *Quarterly*, which, as is now well known, was written by Mr. Croker.]

The same number of *Blackwood* contained a short article about Hazlitt—elsewhere styled "pimpled Hazlitt. " It was very short, and entitled "Hazlitt cross-questioned. " Hazlitt considered the article full of abuse, and commenced an action for libel against the proprietors of the magazine. Upon this Blackwood sent Hazlitt's threatening letter to Murray, with his remarks:

Mr. Blackwood to John Murray.

September 22, 1818.

"I suppose this fellow merely means to make a little bluster, and try if he can pick up a little money. There is nothing whatever actionable in the paper.... The article on Hazlitt, which will commence next number, will be a most powerful one, and this business will not deprive it of any of its edge. "

September 25, 1818.

"What are people saying about that fellow Hazlitt attempting to prosecute? There was a rascally paragraph in the *Times* of Friday last mentioning the prosecution, and saying the magazine was a work filled with private slander. My friends laugh at the idea of his prosecution. "

Mr. Murray, however, became increasingly dissatisfied with this state of things; he never sympathised with the slashing criticisms of *Blackwood*, and strongly disapproved of the personalities, an opinion which was shared by most of his literary friends. At the same time his name was on the title-page of the magazine, and he was jointly responsible with Blackwood for the articles which appeared there.

In a long letter dated September 28, 1818, Mr. Murray deprecated the personality of the articles in the magazine, and entreated that they be kept out. If not, he begged that Blackwood would omit his name from the title-page of the work.

A long correspondence took place during the month of October between Murray and Blackwood: the former continuing to declaim against the personality of the articles; the latter averring that there was nothing of the sort in the magazine. If Blackwood would only keep out these personal attacks, Murray would take care to send him articles by Mr. Frere, Mr. Barrow, and others, which would enhance the popularity and respectability of the publication.

In October of this year was published an anonymous pamphlet, entitled "Hypocrisy Unveiled, " which raked up the whole of the joke contained in the "Translation from an Ancient Chaldee Manuscript, " published a year before. The number containing it had, as we have already seen, been suppressed, because of the offence it had given to many persons of celebrity, while the general tone of bitterness and personality had been subsequently modified, if not abandoned. Murray assured Blackwood that his number for October 1818 was one of the best he had ever read, and he desired him to "offer to his friends his very best thanks and congratulations upon the production of so admirable a number. " "With this number," he said, "you have given me a fulcrum upon which I will move heaven and earth to get subscribers and contributors. " Indeed, several of the contributions in this surpassingly excellent number had been sent to the Edinburgh publisher through the instrumentality of Murray himself.

"Hypocrisy Unveiled" was a lampoon of a scurrilous and commonplace character, in which the leading contributors to and the publishers of the magazine were violently attacked. Both Murray and Blackwood, who were abused openly, by name, resolved to take no notice of it; but Lockhart and Wilson, who were mentioned under the thin disguise of "the Scorpion" and "the Leopard, " were so nettled by the remarks on themselves, that they, in October 1818, both sent challenges to the anonymous author, through the publisher of the pamphlet. This most injudicious step only increased their discomfiture, as the unknown writer not only refused to proclaim his identity, but published and circulated the challenges, together with a further attack on Lockhart and Wilson.

This foolish disclosure caused bitter vexation to Murray, who wrote:

John Murray to Mr. Blackwood.

October 27, 1818.

My DEAR BLACKWOOD,

I really can recollect no parallel to the palpable absurdity of your two friends. If they had planned the most complete triumph to their adversaries, nothing could have been so successfully effective. They have actually given up their names, as the authors of the offences charged upon them, by implication only, in the pamphlet. How they could possibly conceive that the writer of the pamphlet would be such an idiot as to quit his stronghold of concealment, and allow his head to be chopped off by exposure, I am at a loss to conceive....

I declare to God that had I known what I had so incautiously engaged in, I would not have undertaken what I have done, or have suffered what I have in my feelings and character—which no man had hitherto the slightest cause for assailing—I would not have done so for any sum....

In answer to these remonstrances Blackwood begged him to dismiss the matter from his mind, to preserve silence, and to do all that was possible to increase the popularity of the magazine. The next number, he said, would be excellent and unexceptionable; and it proved to be so.

The difficulty, however, was not yet over. While the principal editors of the Chaldee Manuscript had thus revealed themselves to the author of "Hypocrisy Unveiled, " the London publisher of *Blackwood* was, in November 1818, assailed by a biting pamphlet, entitled "A Letter to Mr. John Murray, of Albemarle Street, occasioned by his having undertaken the publication, in London, of *Blackwood's Magazine.* " "The curse of his respectability, " he was told, had brought the letter upon him. "Your name stands among the very highest in the department of Literature which has fallen to your lot: the eminent persons who have confided in you, and the works you have given to the world, have conduced to your establishment in the public favour; while your liberality, your impartiality, and your private motives, bear testimony to the justice of your claims to that honourable distinction. "

Other criticisms of the same kind reached Mr. Murray's ear. Moore, in his Diary (November 4, 1818), writes: "Received two most civil and anxious letters from the great 'Bibliopola Tryphon' Murray, expressing his regret at the article in *Blackwood*, and his resolution to give up all concern in it if it contained any more such personalities. " [Footnote: "Memoirs, Journal, and Correspondence of Thomas Moore, " ii. 210. By Lord John Russell.]

Finally the Hazlitt action was settled. Blackwood gave to Murray the following account of the matter:

December 16, 1818.

"I have had two letters from Mr. Patmore, informing me that Mr. Hazlitt was to drop the prosecution. His agent has since applied to mine offering to do this, if the expenses and a small sum for some charity were paid. My agent told him he would certainly advise any client of his to get out of court, but that he would never advise me to pay anything to be made a talk of, as a sum for a charity would be. He would advise me, he said, to pay the expenses, and a trifle to Hazlitt himself privately. Hazlitt's agent agreed to this. " [Footnote: I have not been able to discover what sum, if any, was paid to Hazlitt privately.]

Notwithstanding promises of amendment, Murray still complained of the personalities, and of the way in which the magazine was edited. He also objected to the "echo of the *Edinburgh Review's* abuse of Sharon Turner. It was sufficient to give pain to me, and to my most valued friend. There was another ungentlemanly and uncalled-for thrust at Thomas Moore. That just makes so many more enemies, unnecessarily; and you not only deprive me of the communications of my friends, but you positively provoke them to go over to your adversary. "

It seemed impossible to exercise any control over the editors, and Murray had no alternative left but to expostulate, and if his expostulations were unheeded, to retire from the magazine. The last course was that which he eventually decided to adopt, and the end of the partnership in *Blackwood's Magazine*, which had long been anticipated, at length arrived. Murray's name appeared for the last time on No. 22, for January 1819; the following number bore no London publisher's name; but on the number for March the names of T. Cadell and W. Davies were advertised as the London agents for the magazine.

On December 17, 1819, £1,000 were remitted to Mr. Murray in payment of the sum which he had originally advanced to purchase his share, and his connection with *Blackwood's Magazine* finally ceased. He thereupon transferred his agency for Scotland to Messrs. Oliver & Boyd, with whose firm it has ever since remained. The friendly correspondence between Murray and Blackwood nevertheless continued, as they were jointly interested in several works of importance.

In the course of the following year, "Christopher North" made the following statement in *Blackwood's Magazine* in "An Hour's Tête-à-tête with the Public":

"The Chaldee Manuscript, which appeared in our seventh number, gave us both a lift and a shove. Nothing else was talked of for a long while; and after 10,000 copies had been sold, it became a very great rarity, quite a desideratum.... The sale of the *Quarterly* is about 14,000, of the *Edinburgh* upwards of 7,000.... It is not our intention, at present, to suffer our sale to go beyond 17,000.... Mr. Murray, under whose auspices our *magnum opus* issued for a few months from Albemarle Street, began to suspect that we might be eclipsing the *Quarterly Review*. No such eclipse had been foretold; and Mr. Murray, being no great astronomer, was at a loss to know whether, in the darkness that was but too visible, we were eclipsing the *Quarterly*, or the *Quarterly* eclipsing us. We accordingly took our pen, and erased his name from our title-page, and he was once more happy. Under our present publishers we carry everything before us in London. "

Mr. Murray took no notice of this statement, preferring, without any more words, to be quit of his bargain.

It need scarcely be added that when Mr. Blackwood had got his critics and contributors well in hand—when his journal had passed its frisky and juvenile life of fun and frolic—when the personalities had ceased to appear in its columns, and it had reached the years of judgment and discretion—and especially when its principal editor,

Mr. John Wilson (Christopher North), had been appointed to the distinguished position of Professor of Moral Philosophy in the University of Edinburgh—the journal took that high rank in periodical literature which it has ever since maintained.

CHAPTER XIX

WORKS PUBLISHED IN 1817-18—CORRESPONDENCE, ETC. —

Scott was now beginning to suffer from the terrible mental and bodily strain to which he had subjected himself, and was shortly after seized with the illness to which reference has been made in a previous chapter, and which disabled him for some time. Blackwood informed Murray (March 7, 1817) that Mr. Scott "has been most dangerously ill, with violent pain arising from spasmodic action in the stomach; but he is gradually getting better. "

For some time he remained in a state of exhaustion, unable either to stir for weakness and giddiness; or to read, for dazzling in his eyes; or to listen, for a whizzing sound in his ears—all indications of too much brain-work and mental worry. Yet, as soon as he was able to resume his labours, we find him characteristically employed in helping his poorer friends.

Mr. Blackwood to John Murray.

May 28, 1817.

"Mr. Scott and some of his friends, in order to raise a sum of money to make the poor Shepherd comfortable, have projected a fourth edition of "The Queen's Wake, " with a few plates, to be published by subscription. We have inserted your name, as we have no doubt of your doing everything you can for the poor poet. The advertisement, which is excellent, is written by Mr. Scott. "

Hogg was tempted by the Duke of Buccleuch's gift of a farm on Eltrive Lake to build himself a house, as Scott was doing, and applied to Murray for a loan of £50, which was granted. In acknowledging the receipt of the money he wrote:

Mr. James Hogg to John Murray.

August 11, 1818.

.... I am told Gifford has a hard prejudice against me, but I cannot believe it. I do not see how any man can have a prejudice against me. He may, indeed, consider me an intruder in the walks of literature, but I am only a saunterer, and malign nobody who chooses to let me pass.... I was going to say before, but forgot, and said quite another thing, that if Mr. Gifford would point out any light work for me to review for him, I'll bet a MS. poem with him that I'll write it better than he expects.

Yours ever most sincerely,

JAMES HOGG.

As Scott still remained the Great Unknown, Murray's correspondence with him related principally to his articles in the *Quarterly*, to which he continued an occasional contributor. Murray suggested to him the subjects of articles, and also requested him to beat up for a few more contributors. He wanted an article on the Gypsies, and if Scott could not muster time to do it, he hoped that Mr. Erskine might be persuaded to favour him with an essay.

Scott, however, in the midst of pain and distress, was now busy with his "Rob Roy, " which was issued towards the end of the year.

A short interruption of his correspondence with Murray occurred— Scott being busy in getting the long buried and almost forgotten "Regalia of Scotland" exposed to light; he was also busy with one of his best novels, the "Heart of Midlothian. " Murray, knowing nothing of these things, again endeavoured to induce him to renew his correspondence, especially his articles for the *Review*. In response Scott contributed articles on Kirkton's "History of the Church of Scotland, " on Military Bridges, and on Lord Orford's Memoirs.

Towards the end of the year, Mr. Murray paid a visit to Edinburgh on business, and after seeing Mr. Blackwood, made his way southward, to pay his promised visit to Walter Scott at Abbotsford, an account of which has already been given in the correspondence with Lord Byron.

James Hogg, who was present at the meeting of Scott and Murray at Abbotsford, wrote to Murray as follows:

James Hogg to John Murray.

EDINBURGH, *February* 20, 1819.

MY DEAR SIR,

I arrived here the day before yesterday for my spring campaign in literature, drinking whiskey, etc., and as I have not heard a word of you or from you since we parted on the top of the hill above Abbotsford, I dedicate my first letter from the metropolis to you. And first of all, I was rather disappointed in getting so little cracking with you at that time. Scott and you had so much and so many people to converse about, whom nobody knew anything of but yourselves, that you two got all to say, and some of us great men, who deem we know everything at home, found that we knew nothing. You did not even tell me what conditions you were going to give me for my "Jacobite Relics of Scotland, " the first part of which will make its appearance this spring, and I think bids fair to be popular....

Believe me, yours very faithfully,

JAMES HOGG.

After the discontinuance of Murray's business connection with Blackwood, described in the preceding chapter, James Hogg wrote in great consternation:

Mr. James Hogg to John Murray,

ELTRIVE, by SELKIRK, *December* 9, 1829.

MY DEAR SIR,

By a letter from Blackwood to-day, I have the disagreeable intelligence that circumstances have occurred which I fear will deprive me of you as a publisher—I hope never as a friend; for I here attest, though I have heard some bitter things against you, that I never met with any man whatever who, on so slight an acquaintance, has behaved to me so much like a gentleman. Blackwood asks to transfer your shares of my trifling works to his new agents. I answered, "Never! without your permission. " As the "Jacobite Relics" are not yet published, and as they would only involve you further with one with whom you are going to close accounts, I gave him liberty to transfer the shares you were to have in them to Messrs. Cadell & Davies. But when I consider your handsome subscription for "The Queen's Wake, " if you have the slightest inclination to retain your shares of that work and "The Brownie, " as your name is on them, *along with Blackwood*, I would much rather, not only from affection, but interest, that you should continue to dispose of them.

I know these books are of no avail to you; and that if you retain them, it will be on the same principle that you published them, namely, one of friendship for your humble poetical countryman. I'll never forget your kindness; for I cannot think that I am tainted with the general vice of authors' *ingratitude*; and the first house that I call at in London will be the one in Albemarle Street.

I remain, ever yours most truly,

JAMES HOGG.

Murray did not cease to sell the Shepherd's works, and made arrangements with Blackwood to continue his agency for them, and to account for the sales in the usual way.

The name of Robert Owen is but little remembered now, but at the early part of the century he attained some notoriety from his endeavours to reform society. He was manager of the Lanark Cotton Mills, but in 1825 he emigrated to America, and bought land on the Wabash whereon to start a model colony, called New Harmony. This enterprise failed, and he returned to England in 1827. The following letter is in answer to his expressed intention of adding Mr. Murray's name to the title-page of the second edition of his "New View of Society. "

John Murray to Mr. Robert Owen.

September 9, 1817.

DEAR SIR,

As it is totally inconsistent with my plans to allow my name to be associated with any subject of so much political notoriety and debate as your New System of Society, I trust that you will not consider it as any diminution of personal regard if I request the favour of you to cause my name to be immediately struck out from every sort of advertisement that is likely to appear upon this subject. I trust that a moment's reflection will convince which I understand you talked of sending to my house. I beg leave again to repeat that I retain the same sentiments of personal esteem, and that I am, dear Sir,

Your faithful servant,

JOHN MURRAY.

Among the would-be poets was a young Quaker gentleman of Stockton-on-Tees who sent Mr. Murray a batch of poems. The publisher wrote an answer to his letter, which fell into the hands of the poet's father, who bore the same name as his son. The father answered:

Mr. Proctor to Mr. Murray.

ESTEEMED FRIEND,

I feel very much obliged by thy refusing to *publish* the papers sent thee by my son. I was entirely ignorant of anything of the kind, or should have nipt it in the bud. On receipt of this, please burn the whole that was sent thee, and at thy convenience inform me that it has been done. With thanks for thy highly commendable care.

I am respectfully, thy friend,

JOHN PROCTOR.

The number of persons who desired to publish poetry was surprising, even Sharon Turner, Murray's solicitor, whose valuable historical works had been published by the Longmans, wrote to him about the publication of poems, which he had written "to idle away the evenings as well as he could. " Murray answered his letter:

John Murray to Mr. Sharon Turner.

November 17, 1817.

I do not think it would be creditable to your name, or advantageous to your more important works, that the present one should proceed from a different publisher. Many might fancy that Longman had declined it. Longman might suspect me of interference; and thus, in the uncertainty of acting with propriety myself, I should have little hope of giving satisfaction to you. I therefore refer the matter to your own feelings and consideration. It has afforded me great pleasure to learn frequently of late that you are so much better. I hope during the winter, if we have any, to send you many amusing books to shorten the tediousness of time, and charm away your indisposition. Mrs. Murray is still up and well, and desires me to send her best compliments to you and Mrs. Turner.

Ever yours faithfully,

J. MURRAY.

Mr. Turner thanked Mr. Murray for his letter, and said that if he proceeded with his intentions he would adopt his advice. "I have always found Longman very kind and honourable, but I will not offer him now what you think it right to decline. "

During Gifford's now almost incessant attacks of illness, Mr. Croker took charge of the *Quarterly Review.* The following letter embodies some of his ideas as to editing:

Mr. Croker to John Murray.

BRIGHTON, *March* 29, 1823.

DEAR MURRAY,

As I shall not be in Town in time to see you to-morrow, I send you some papers. I return the *Poor* article [Footnote: "On the Poor Laws, " by Mr. Gleig.] with its additions. Let the author's amendments be attended to, and let his termination be inserted *between* his former conclusion and that which I have written. It is a good article, not overdone and yet not dull. I return, to be set up, the article [by Captain Procter] on Southey's "Peninsular War. " It is very bad—a mere *abstracted history of the war itself*, and not in the least a *review of the book*. I have taken pains to remove some part of this error, but you must feel how impossible it is to change the whole frame of such an article. A touch thrown in here and there will give some relief, and the character of a *review* will be in some small degree preserved. This cursed system of writing dissertations will be the death of us, and if I were to edit another number, I should make a great alteration in that particular. But for this time I must be satisfied with plastering up what I have not time to rebuild. One thing I would do immediately if I were you. I would pay for articles of *one* sheet as much as for articles of two and three, and, in fact, I would *scarcely* permit an article to exceed one sheet. I would reserve such extension for matters of great and immediate interest and importance. I am delighted that W. [Footnote: Probably Blanco White.] undertakes one, he will do it well; but remember the necessity of *absolute secrecy* on this point, and indeed on all others. If you were to publish such names as Cohen and Croker and Collinson and Coleridge, the magical WE would have little effect, and your *Review* would be absolutely despised—*omne ignotum pro mirifico*. I suppose I shall see you about twelve on Tuesday. Could you not get me a gay light article or two? If I am to *edit* for you, I cannot find time to *contribute*. Madame Campan's poem will more than expend my leisure. I came here for a little recreation, and I am all day at the desk as if I were at the Admiralty. This Peninsular article has cost me two days' hard work, and is, after all, not worth the trouble; but we must have something about it, and it is, I suppose, too late to expect anything better. Mr. Williams's article on Sir W. Scott [Lord Stowell] is contemptible, and would expose your *Review* to the ridicule of the whole bar; but it may be made something of, and I like the subject. I had a long and amusing talk with the Chancellor the night before last, on his own and his brother's judgments; I wish I had time to embody our conversation in an article.

Yours ever,

J. W.C.

Southey is *very* long, but as good as he is long—I have nearly done with him. I write *very slowly*, and cannot write long. This letter is written at three sittings.

No sooner had Croker got No. 56 of the *Review* out of his hands than he made a short visit to Paris. On this Mr. Barrow writes to Murray;

Mr. Barrow to John Murray.

April 2, 1823.

"Croker has run away to Paris, and left poor Gifford helpless. What will become of the *Quarterly?* ... Poor Gifford told me yesterday that he felt he *must* give up the Editorship, and that the doctors had *ordered* him to do so. "

Some months later, Barrow wrote to Murray saying that he had seen Gifford that morning:

Mr. Barrow to John Murray.

August 18, 1823.

"I told him to look out for some one to conduct the *Review*, but he comes to no decision. I told him that you very naturally looked to him for naming a proper person. He replied he had—Nassau Senior—but that you had taken some dislike to him. [Footnote: This, so far as can be ascertained, was a groundless assumption on Mr. Gifford's part.] I then said, 'You are now well; go on, and let neither Murray nor you trouble yourselves about a future editor yet; for should you even break down in the midst of a number, I can only repeat that Croker and myself will bring it round, and a second number if necessary, to give him time to look out for and fix upon a proper person, but that the work should not stop. ' I saw he did not like to continue the subject, and we talked of something else. "

Croker also was quite willing to enter into this scheme, and jointly with Barrow to undertake the temporary conduct of the *Review*. They received much assistance also from Mr. J.T. Coleridge, then a young barrister. Mr. Coleridge, as will be noticed presently, became for a time editor of the *Quarterly*. "Mr. C. is too long, " Gifford wrote to Murray, "and I am sorry for it. But he is a nice young man, and should be encouraged. "

CHAPTER XX

HALLAM BASIL HALL—CRABBE—HOPE—HORACE AND
JAMES SMITH

In 1817 Mr. Murray published for Mr. Hallam his "View of the State
of Europe during the Middle Ages. " The acquaintance thus formed
led to a close friendship, which lasted unbroken till Mr. Murray's
death.

Mr. Murray published at this time a variety of books of travel. Some
of these were sent to the Marquess of Abercorn—amongst them Mr.
(afterwards Sir) Henry Ellis's "Proceedings of Lord Amherst's
Embassy to China, " [Footnote: "Journal of the Proceedings of the
late Embassy to China, comprising a Correct Narrative of the Public
Transactions of the Embassy, of the Voyage to and from China, and
of the Journey from the Mouth of the Peiho to the Return to Canton."
By Henry Ellis, Esq., Secretary of the Embassy, and Third
Commissioner.] about which the Marchioness, at her husband's
request, wrote to the publisher as follows:

Marchioness of Abercorn to John Murray,

December 4, 1817.

"He returns Walpole, as he says since the age of fifteen he has read
so much Grecian history and antiquity that he has these last ten
years been sick of the subject. He does not like Ellis's account of 'The
Embassy to China, ' [Footnote: Ellis seems to have been made very
uncomfortable by the publication of his book. It was severely
reviewed in the *Times*, where it was said that the account (then in the
press) by Clark Abel, M.D., Principal Medical Officer and Naturalist
to the Embassy, would be greatly superior. On this Ellis wrote to
Murray (October 19, 1817): "An individual has seldom committed an
act so detrimental to his interests as I have done in this unfortunate
publication; and I shall be too happy when the lapse of time will
allow of my utterly forgetting the occurrence. I am already
indifferent to literary criticism, and had almost forgotten Abel's
approaching competition. " The work went through two editions.]
but is pleased with Macleod's [Footnote: "Narrative of a Voyage in
His Majesty's late ship *Alceste* to the Yellow Sea, along the Coast of
Corea, and through its numerous hitherto undiscovered Islands to

225

the Island of Lewchew, with an Account of her Shipwreck in the Straits of Gaspar. " By John MacLeod, surgeon of the *Alceste.*] narrative. He bids me tell you to say the best and what is least obnoxious of the [former] book. The composition and the narrative are so thoroughly wretched that he should be ashamed to let it stand in his library. He will be obliged to you to send him Leyden's 'Africa. ' Leyden was a friend of his, and desired leave to dedicate to him while he lived. "

Mr. Murray, in his reply, deprecated the severity of the Marquess of Abercorn's criticism on the work of Sir H. Ellis, who had done the best that he could on a subject of exceeding interest.

John Murray to Lady Abercorn.

"I am now printing Captain Hall's account (he commanded the *Lyra*), and I will venture to assure your Ladyship that it is one of the most delightful books I ever read, and it is calculated to heal the wound inflicted by poor Ellis. I believe I desired my people to send you Godwin's novel, which is execrably bad. But in most cases book readers must balance novelty against disappointment.

And in reply to a request for more books to replace those condemned or dull, he asks dryly:

"Shall I withhold 'Rob Roy' and 'Childe Harold' from your ladyship until their merits have been ascertained? Even if an indifferent book, it is something to be amongst the first to *say* that it is bad. You will be alarmed, I fear, at having provoked so many reasons for sending you dull publications.... I am printing two short but very clever novels by poor Miss Austen, the author of 'Pride and Prejudice. ' I send Leyden's 'Africa' for Lord Abercorn, who will be glad to hear that the 'Life and Posthumous Writings' will be ready soon. "

The Marchioness, in her answer to the above letter, thanked Mr. Murray for his entertaining answer to her letter, and said:

Marchioness of Abercorn to John Murray.

"Lord Abercorn says he thinks your conduct with respect to sending books back that he does not like is particularly liberal. He bids me tell you how very much he likes Mr. Macleod's book; we had seen some of it in manuscript before it was published. We are very anxious for Hall's account, and I trust you will send it to us the moment you can get a copy finished.

"No, indeed! you must not (though desirous you may be to punish us for the severity of the criticism on poor Ellis) keep back for a moment 'Rob Roy' or the fourth canto of 'Childe Harold. ' I have heard a good deal from Scotland that makes me continue *surmising* who is the author of these novels. Our friend Walter paid a visit last summer to a gentleman on the banks of Loch Lomond—the scene of Rob Roy's exploits—and was at great pains to learn all the traditions of the country regarding him from the clergyman and old people of the neighbourhood, of which he got a considerable stock. I am very glad to hear of a 'Life of Leyden. ' He was a very surprising young man, and his death is a great loss to the world. Pray send us Miss Austen's novels the moment you can. Lord Abercorn thinks them next to W. Scott's (if they are by W. Scott); it is a great pity that we shall have no more of hers. Who are the *Quarterly Reviewers*? I hear that Lady Morgan suspects Mr. Croker of having reviewed her 'France, ' and intends to be revenged, etc.

"Believe me to be yours, with great regard,

"A. J. ABERCORN. "

From many communications addressed to Mr. Murray about the beginning of 1818, it appears that he had proposed to start a *Monthly Register*, [Footnote: The announcement ran thus: "On the third Saturday in January, 1818, will be published the first number of a NEW PERIODICAL JOURNAL, the object of which will be to convey to the public a great variety of new, original, and interesting matter; and by a methodical arrangement of all Inventions in the Arts, Discoveries in the Sciences, and Novelties in Literature, to enable the reader to keep pace with human knowledge. To be printed uniformly with the QUARTERLY REVIEW. The price by the year will be £2 2s. "] and he set up in print a specimen copy. Many of his correspondents offered to assist him, amongst others Mr. J. Macculloch, Lord Sheffield, Dr. Polidori, then settled at St. Peter's, Norwich, Mr. Bulmer of the British Museum, and many other contributors. He sent copies of the specimen number to Mr. Croker and received the following candid reply:

Mr. Croker to John Murray.

January 11, 1818.

MY DEAR MURRAY,

Our friend Sepping [Footnote: A naval surveyor.] says, "Nothing is stronger than its weakest part, " and this is as true in book-making as in shipbuilding. I am sorry to say your *Register* has, in my opinion, a great many weak parts. It is for nobody's use; it is too popular and trivial for the learned, and too abstruse and plodding for the multitude. The preface is not English, nor yet Scotch or Irish. It must have been written by Lady Morgan. In the body of the volume, there is not *one* new nor curious article, unless it be Lady Hood's "Tiger Hunt. " In your Mechanics there is a miserable want of information, and in your Statistics there is a sad superabundance of American hyperbole and dulness mixed together, like the mud and gunpowder which, when a boy, I used to mix together to make a fizz. Your Poetry is so bad that I look upon it as your personal kindness to me that you did not put my lines under that head. Your criticism on Painting begins by calling West's very pale horse "an extraordinary effort of human *genius*. " Your criticism on Sculpture begins by applauding *beforehand* Mr. Wyatt's *impudent* cenotaph. Your criticism on the Theatre begins by *denouncing* the best production of its kind, 'The Beggar's Opera. ' Your article on Engraving puts under the head of Italy a stone drawing made in Paris. Your own engraving of the Polar Regions is confused and dirty; and your article on the Polar Seas sets out with the assertion of a fact of which I was profoundly ignorant, namely, that the Physical Constitution of the Globe is subject to *constant changes* and revolution. Of *constant changes* I never heard, except in one of Congreve's plays, in which the fair sex is accused of *constant inconstancy*; but suppose that for *constant* you read *frequent*. I should wish you, for my own particular information, to add in a note a few instances of the Physical Changes in the Constitution of the Globe, which have occurred since the year 1781, in which I happened to be born. I know of none, and I should be sorry to go out of the world ignorant of what has passed in my own time. You send me your proof "for my boldest criticism. " I have hurried over rather than read through the pages, and I give you honestly, and as plainly as an infamous pen (the same, I presume, which drew your polar chart) will permit, my hasty impression. If you will call here to-morrow between twelve and one, I will talk with you on the subject.

Yours,

J. W. C.

The project was eventually abandoned. Murray entered into the arrangement, already described, with Blackwood, of the *Edinburgh Magazine*. The article on the "Polar Ice" was inserted in the *Quarterly*.

Towards the end of 1818, Mr. Crabbe called upon Mr. Murray and offered to publish through him his "Tales of the Hall, " consisting of about twelve thousand lines. He also proposed to transfer to him from Mr. Colburn his other poems, so that the whole might be printed uniformly. Mr. Crabbe, who up to this period had received very little for his writings, was surprised when Mr. Murray offered him no less than £3,000 for the copyright of his poems. It seemed to him a mine of wealth compared to all that he had yet received. The following morning (December 6) he breakfasted with Mr. Rogers, and Tom Moore was present. Crabbe told them of his good fortune, and of the magnificent offer he had received. Rogers thought it was not enough, and that Crabbe should have received £3,000 for the "Tales of the Hall" alone, and that he would try if the Longmans would not give more. He went to Paternoster Row accordingly, and tried the Longmans; but they would not give more than £1,000 for the new work and the copyright of the old poems—that is, only one-third of what Murray had offered. [Footnote: "Memoirs, Journals, Correspondence, of Thomas Moore, " by Lord John Russell, ii. 237.]

When Crabbe was informed of this, he was in a state of great consternation. As Rogers had been bargaining with another publisher for better terms, the matter seemed still to be considered open; and in the meantime, if Murray were informed of the event, he might feel umbrage and withdraw his offer. Crabbe wrote to Murray on the subject, but received no answer. He had within his reach a prize far beyond his most sanguine hopes, and now, by the over-officiousness of his friends, he was in danger of losing it. In this crisis Rogers and Moore called upon Murray, and made enquiries on the subject of Crabbe's poems. "Oh, yes, " he said, "I have heard from Mr. Crabbe, and look upon the matter as settled. " Crabbe was thus released from all his fears. When he received the bills for £3,000, he insisted on taking them with him to Trowbridge to show them to his son John.

It proved after all that the Longmans were right in their offer to Rogers; Murray was far too liberal. Moore, in his Diary (iii. 332), says, "Even if the whole of the edition (3,000) were sold, Murray would still be £1,900 minus. " Crabbe had some difficulty in getting his old poems out of the hands of his former publisher, who wrote to him in a strain of the wildest indignation, and even threatened him with legal proceedings, but eventually the unsold stock, consisting of 2,426 copies, was handed over by Hatchard & Colburn to Mr. Murray, and nothing more was heard of this controversy between them and the poet.

"Anastasius, or Memoirs of a Modern Greek, written at the Close of the 18th Century, " was published anonymously, and was confidently asserted to be the work of Lord Byron, as the only person capable of having produced it. When the author was announced to be Mr. Thomas Hope, of Deepdene, some incredulity was expressed by the *literati*.

The Countess of Blessington, in her "Conversations with Lord Byron, " says: "Byron spoke to-day in terms of high commendation of Hope's 'Anastasius'; said he had wept bitterly over many pages of it, and for two reasons—first, that he had not written it; and, secondly, that Hope had; for that it was necessary to like a man excessively to pardon his writing such a book—a book, he said, excelling all recent productions as much in wit and talent as in true pathos. He added that he would have given his two most approved poems to have been the author of 'Anastasius. '" The work was greatly read at the time, and went through many large editions.

The refusal of the "Rejected Addresses, " by Horace and James Smith, was one of Mr. Murray's few mistakes. Horace was a stockbroker, and James a solicitor. They were not generally known as authors, though they contributed anonymously to the *New Monthly Magazine*, which was conducted by Campbell the poet. In 1812 they produced a collection purporting to be "Rejected Addresses, presented for competition at the opening of Drury Lane Theatre. " They offered the collection to Mr. Murray for £20, but he declined to purchase the copyright. The Smiths were connected with Cadell the publisher, and Murray, thinking that the MS. had been offered to and rejected by him, declined to look into it. The "Rejected

Addresses" were eventually published by John Miller, and excited a great deal of curiosity. They were considered to be the best imitations of living poets ever made. Byron was delighted with them. He wrote to Mr. Murray that he thought them "by far the best thing of the kind since the 'Rolliad. '" Crabbe said of the verses in imitation of himself, "In their versification they have done me admirably. " When he afterwards met Horace Smith, he seized both hands of the satirist, and said, with a good-humoured laugh, "Ah! my old enemy, how do you do? " Jeffrey said of the collection, "I take them, indeed, to be the very best imitations (and often of difficult originals) that ever were made, and, considering their extent and variety, to indicate a talent to which I do not know where to look for a parallel. " Murray had no sooner read the volume than he spared no pains to become the publisher, but it was not until after the appearance of the sixteenth edition that he was able to purchase the copyright for £131.

Towards the end of 1819, Mr. Murray was threatened with an action on account of certain articles which had appeared in Nos. 37 and 38 of the *Quarterly* relative to the campaign in Italy against Murat, King of Naples. The first was written by Dr. Reginald (afterwards Bishop) Heber, under the title of "Military and Political Power of Russia, by Sir Robert Wilson"; the second was entitled "Sir Robert Wilson's Reply. " Colonel Macirone occupied a very unimportant place in both articles. He had been in the service of Murat while King of Naples, and acted as his aide-de-camp, which post he retained after Murat became engaged in hostilities with Austria, then in alliance with England. Macirone was furnished with a passport for *himself* as envoy of the Allied Powers, and provided with another passport for Murat, under the name of Count Lipona, to be used by him in case he abandoned his claim to the throne of Naples. Murat indignantly declined the proposal, and took refuge in Corsica. Yet Macirone delivered to Murat the passport. Not only so, but he deliberately misled Captain Bastard, the commander of a small English squadron which had been stationed at Bastia to intercept Murat in the event of his embarking for the purpose of regaining his throne at Naples. Murat embarked, landed in Italy without interruption, and was soon after defeated and taken prisoner. He thereupon endeavoured to use the passport which Macirone had given him, to secure his release, but it was too late; he was tried and shot at Pizzo. The reviewer spoke of Colonel Macirone in no very measured terms. "For Murat, " he said, "we cannot feel respect, but we feel very considerable pity. Of Mr. Macirone we are tempted to predict that he has little reason to apprehend the honourable mode of death which was inflicted on his master. *His* vocation seems to be another kind of exit. "

Macirone gave notice of an action for damages, and claimed no less than £10,000. Serjeant Copley (afterwards Lord Lyndhurst), then Solicitor-General, and Mr. Gurney, were retained for Mr. Murray by his legal adviser Mr. Sharon Turner.

The case came on, and on the Bench were seated the Duke of Wellington, Lord Liverpool, and other leading statesmen, who had been subpoenaed as witnesses for the defence. One of the Ridgways, publishers, had also been subpoenaed with an accredited copy of Macirone's book; but it was not necessary to produce him as a witness, as Mr. Ball, the counsel for Macirone, *quoted* passages from it, and thus made the entire book available as evidence for the defendant, a proceeding of which Serjeant Copley availed himself with telling effect. He substantiated the facts stated in the *Quarterly* article by passages quoted from Colonel Macirone's own "Memoirs. " Before he had concluded his speech, it became obvious that the Jury had arrived at the conclusion to which he wished to lead them; but he went on to drive the conclusion home by a splendid peroration. [Footnote: Given in Sir Theodore Martin's "Life of Lord Lyudhurst, " p. 170.] The Jury intimated that they were all agreed; but the Judge, as a matter of precaution, proceeded to charge them on the evidence placed before them; and as soon as he had concluded, the Jury, without retiring from the box, at once returned their verdict for the defendant.

Although Mr. Murray had now a house in the country, he was almost invariably to be found at Albemarle Street. We find, in one of his letters to Blackwood, dated Wimbledon, May 22, 1819, the following: "I have been unwell with bile and rheumatism, and have come to a little place here, which I have bought lately, for a few days to recruit. "

The following description of a reception at Mr. Murray's is taken from the "Autobiography" of Mrs. Bray, the novelist. She relates that in the autumn of 1819 she made a visit to Mr. Murray, with her first husband, Charles Stothard, son of the well-known artist, for the purpose of showing him the illustrations of his "Letters from Normandy and Brittany. "

A Publisher and His Friends

"We did not know, " she says, "that Mr. Murray held daily from about three to five o'clock a literary levée at his house. In this way he gathered round him many of the most eminent men of the time. On calling, we sent up our cards, and finding he was engaged, proposed to retreat, when Mr. Murray himself appeared and insisted on our coming up. I was introduced to him by my husband, and welcomed by him with all the cordiality of an old acquaintance. He said Sir Walter Scott was there, and he thought that we should like to see him, and to be introduced to him. 'You will know him at once, ' added Mr. Murray, 'he is sitting on the sofa near the fire-place. ' We found Sir Walter talking to Mr. Gifford, then the Editor of the *Quarterly Review*. The room was filled with men and women, and among them several of the principal authors and authoresses of the day; but my attention was so fixed on Sir Walter and Mr. Gifford that I took little notice of the rest. Many of those present were engaged in looking at and making remarks upon a drawing, which represented a Venetian Countess (Guiccioli), the favourite, but not very respectable friend of Lord Byron. Mr. Murray made his way through the throng in order to lead us up to Sir Walter. We were introduced. Mr. Murray, anxious to remove the awkwardness of a first introduction, wished to say something which would engage a conversation between ourselves and Sir Walter Scott, and asked Charles if he happened to have about him his drawing of the Bayeux tapestry to show to Sir Walter. Charles smiled and said 'No'; but the saying answered the desired end; something had been said that led to conversation, and Sir Walter, Gifford, Mr. Murray, and Charles chatted on, and I listened.

"Gifford looked very aged, his face much wrinkled, and he seemed to be in declining health; his dress was careless, and his cravat and waistcoat covered with snuff. There was an antique, philosophic cast about his head and countenance, better adapted to exact a feeling of curiosity in a stranger than the head of Sir Walter Scott; the latter seemed more a man of this world's mould. Such, too, was his character; for, with all his fine genius, Sir Walter would never have been so successful an author, had he not possessed so large a share of common sense, united to a business-like method of conducting his affairs, even those which perhaps I might venture to call the affairs of imagination. We took our leave; and before we got further than the first landing, we met Mr. Murray conducting Sir Walter downstairs; they were going to have a private chat before the departure of the latter. " [Footnote: "Mrs. Bray's Autobiography, " pp. 145-7.]

233

CHAPTER XXI

MEMOIRS OF LADY HERVEY AND HORACE WALPOLE—
BELZONI—MILMAN—SOUTHEY —MRS. RUNDELL, ETC.

About the beginning of 1819 the question of publishing the letters and reminiscences of Lady Hervey, grandmother of the Earl of Mulgrave, was brought under the notice of Mr. Murray. Lady Hervey was the daughter of Brigadier-General Lepel, and the wife of Lord Hervey of Ickworth, author of the "Memoirs of the Court of George II. and Queen Caroline. " Her letters formed a sort of anecdotal history of the politics and literature of her times. A mysterious attachment is said to have existed between her and Lord Chesterfield, who, in his letters to his son, desired him never to mention her name when he could avoid it, while she, on the other hand, adopted all Lord Chesterfield's opinions, as afterwards appeared in the aforesaid letters. Mr. Walter Hamilton, author of the "Gazetteer of India, " an old and intimate friend of Mr. Murray, who first brought the subject under Mr. Murray's notice, said, "Lady Hervey writes more like a man than a woman, something like Lady M. W. Montagu, and in giving her opinion she never minces matters." Mr. Hamilton recommended that Archdeacon Coxe, author of the "Lives of Sir Robert and Horace Walpole, " should be the editor. Mr. Murray, however, consulted his *fidus Achates*, Mr. Croker; and, putting the letters in his hands, asked him to peruse them, and, if he approved, to edit them. The following was Mr. Croker's answer:

Mr. Croker to John Murray.

November 22, 1820.

DEAR MURRAY,

I shall do more than you ask. I shall give you a biographical sketch— sketch, do you hear? —of Lady Hervey, and notes on her letters, in which I shall endeavour to enliven a little the *sameness* of my author. Don't think that I say *sameness* in derogation of dear Mary Lepel's *powers* of entertainment. I have been *in love* with her a long time; which, as she was dead twenty years before I was born, I may without indiscretion avow; but all these letters being written in a journal style and to one person, there is a want of that variety which

Lady Hervey's mind was capable of giving. I have applied to her family for a little assistance; hitherto without success; and I think, as a *lover* of Lady Hervey's, I might reasonably resent the little enthusiasm I find that her descendants felt about her. In order to enable me to do this little job for you, I wish you would procure for me a file, if such a thing exists, of any newspaper from about 1740 to 1758, at which latter date the *Annual Register* begins, as I remember. So many little circumstances are mentioned in letters, and forgotten in history, that without some such guide, I shall make but blind work of it. If it be necessary, I will go to the Museum and *grab* them, as my betters have done before me. My dear little Nony [Footnote: Mr. Croker's adopted daughter, afterwards married to Sir George Barrow.] was worse last night, and not better all to-day; but this evening they make me happy by saying that she is decidedly improved.

Yours ever,

J. W. CROKER.

Send me "Walpoliana, " I have lost or mislaid mine. Are there any memoirs about the date of 1743, or later, beside Bubb's?

That Mr. Croker made all haste and exercised his usual painstaking industry in doing "this little job" for Mr. Murray will be evident from the following letters:

Mr. Croker to John Murray.

December 27, 1820.

DEAR MURRAY,

I have done "Lady Hervey. " I hear that there is a Mr. Vincent in the Treasury, the son of a Mr. and Mrs. Vincent, to whom the late General Hervey, the favourite son of Lady Hervey, left his fortune and his papers. Could you find out who they are? Nothing is more surprising than the ignorance in which I find all Lady Hervey's descendants about her. Most of them never heard her maiden name. It reminds one of Walpole writing to George Montagu, to tell him who his grandmother was! I am anxious to knock off this task whilst what little I know of it is fresh in my recollection; for I foresee that much of the entertainment of the work must depend on the elucidations in the Notes.

Yours,

J. W.C.

The publication of Lady Hervey's letters in 1821 was so successful that Mr. Croker was afterwards induced to edit, with great advantage, letters and memorials of a similar character. [Footnote: As late as 1848, Mr. Croker edited Lord Hervey's "Memoirs of the Court of George II. and Queen Caroline, " from the family archives at Ickworth. The editor in his preface said that Lord Hervey was almost the Boswell of George II. and Queen Caroline.]

The next important *mémoires pour servir* were brought under Mr. Murray's notice by Lord Holland, in the following letter:

Lord Holland to John Murray.

HOLLAND HOUSE, *November* 1820.

SIR,

I wrote a letter to you last week which by some accident Lord Lauderdale, who had taken charge of it, has mislaid. The object of it was to request you to call here some morning, and to let me know the hour by a line by two-penny post. I am authorized to dispose of two historical works, the one a short but admirably written and interesting memoir of the late Lord Waldegrave, who was a favourite of George II., and governor of George III. when Prince of Wales. The second consists of three close-written volumes of "Memoirs by Horace Walpole" (afterwards Lord Orford), which comprise the last nine years of George II. 's reign. I am anxious to give you the refusal of them, as I hear you have already expressed a wish to publish anything of this kind written by Horace Walpole, and had indirectly conveyed that wish to Lord Waldegrave, to whom these and many other MSS. of that lively and laborious writer belong. Lord Lauderdale has offered to assist me in adjusting the terms of the agreement, and perhaps you will arrange with him; he lives at Warren's Hotel, Waterloo Place, where you can make it convenient to meet him. I would meet you there, or call at your house; but before you can make any specific offer, you will no doubt like to look at the MSS., which are here, and which (not being mine) I do not like to expose unnecessarily to the risk even of a removal to London and back again.

I am, Sir, your obedient humble Servant, etc.,

VASSALL HOLLAND.

It would appear that Mr. Murray called upon Lord Holland and looked over the MSS., but made no proposal to purchase the papers. The matter lay over until Lord Holland again addressed Mr. Murray.

Lord Holland to John Murray.

"It appears that you are either not aware of the interesting nature of the MSS. which I showed you, or that the indifference produced by the present frenzy about the Queen's business [Footnote: The trial of Queen Caroline was then occupying public attention.] to all literary publications, has discouraged you from an undertaking in which you would otherwise engage most willingly. However, to come to the point. I have consulted Lord Waldegrave on the subject, and we agree that the two works, viz. his grandfather, Lord Waldegrave's "Memoirs, " and Horace Walpole's "Memoirs of the Last Nine Years of George II., " should not be sold for less than 3,000 guineas. If that sum would meet your ideas, or if you have any other offer to make, I will thank you to let me know before the second of next month. "

Three thousand guineas was certainly a very large price to ask for the Memoirs, and Mr. Murray hesitated very much before acceding to Lord Holland's proposal. He requested to have the MSS. for the purpose of consulting his literary adviser—probably Mr. Croker, though the following remarks, now before us, are not in his handwriting.

"This book of yours, " says the critic, "is a singular production. It is ill-written, deficient in grammar, and often in English; and yet it interests and even amuses. Now, the subjects of it are all, I suppose, gone *ad plures*; otherwise it would be intolerable. The writer richly deserves a licking or a cudgelling to every page, and yet I am ashamed to say I have travelled unwearied with him through the whole, divided between a grin and a scowl. I never saw nor heard of such an animal as a splenetic, bustling kind of a poco-curante. By the way, if you happen to hear of any plan for making me a king, be so good as to say that I am deceased; or tell any other good-natured lie to put the king-makers off their purpose. I really cannot submit to be the only slave in the nation, especially when I have a crossing to sweep within five yards of my door, and may gain my bread with less ill-usage than a king is obliged to put up with. If half that is here told be true, Lord Holland seems to me to tread on

> 'ignes
> Suppositos cineri doloso'

in retouching any part of the manuscript. He is so perfectly kind and good-natured, that he will feel more than any man the complaints of partiality and injustice; and where he is to stop, I see not. There is so much abuse that little is to be gained by an occasional erasure, while suspicion is excited. He would have consulted his quiet more by leaving the author to bear the blame of his own scandal. "

Notwithstanding this adverse judgment, Mr. Murray was disposed to buy the Memoirs. Lord Holland drove a very hard bargain, and endeavoured to obtain better terms from other publishers, but he could not, and eventually Mr. Murray paid to Lord Waldegrave, through Lord Holland, the sum of £2,500 on November 1, 1821, for the Waldegrave and Walpole Memoirs. They were edited by Lord Holland, who wrote a preface to each, and were published in the following year, but never repaid their expenses. After suffering considerable loss by this venture, Mr. Murray's rights were sold, after his death, to Mr. Colburn.

The last of the *mémoires pour servir* to which we shall here refer was the Letters of the Countess of Suffolk, bedchamber woman to the Princess of Wales (Caroline of Anspach), and a favourite of the Prince of Wales, afterwards George II. The Suffolk papers were admirably edited by Mr. Croker. Thackeray, in his "Lecture on George the Second, " says of his work: "Even Croker, who edited her letters, loves her, and has that regard for her with which her sweet graciousness seems to have inspired almost all men, and some women, who came near her. " The following letter of Croker shows the spirit in which he began to edit the Countess's letters:

Mr. Croker to John Murray.

May 29, 1822.

DEAR MURRAY,

As you told me that you are desirous of publishing the Suffolk volume by November, and as I have, all my life, had an aversion to making any one wait for me, I am anxious to begin my work upon them, and, if we are to be out by November, I presume it is high time. I must beg of you to answer me the following questions.

1st. What shape will you adopt? I think the correspondence of a nature rather too light for a quarto, and yet it would look well on the same shelf with Horace Walpole's works. If you should prefer an octavo, like Lady Hervey's letters, the papers would furnish two volumes. I, for my part, should prefer the quarto size, which is a great favourite with me, and the letters of such persons as Pope, Swift, and Gay, the Duchesses of Buckingham, Queensberry, and Marlbro', Lords Peterborough, Chesterfield, Bathurst, and Lansdowne, Messrs. Pitt, Pulteney, Pelham, Grenville, and Horace Walpole, seem to me almost to justify the magnificence of the quarto; though, in truth, all their epistles are, in its narrowest sense, *familiar*, and treat chiefly of tittle-tattle.

Decide, however, on your own view of your interests, only recollect that these papers are not to cost you more than "Belshazzar, " [Footnote: Mr. Milman's poem, for which Mr. Murray paid 500 guineas.] which I take to be of about the intrinsic value of the *writings on the walls*, and not a third of what you have given Mr. Crayon for his portrait of Squire Bracebridge.

2nd. Do you intend to have any portraits? One of Lady Suffolk is almost indispensable, and would be enough. There are two of her at Strawberry Hill; one, I think, a print, and neither, if I forget not, very good. There is also a print, an unassuming one, in Walpole's works, but a good artist would make something out of any of these, if even we can get nothing better to make our copy from. If you were to increase your number of portraits, I would add the Duchess of Queensberry, from a picture at Dalkeith which is alluded to in the letters; Lady Hervey and her beautiful friend, Mary Bellenden. They are in Walpole's works; Lady Hervey rather mawkish, but the Bellenden charming. I dare say these plates could now be bought cheap, and retouched from the originals, which would make them better than ever they were. Lady Vere (sister of Lady Temple, which latter is engraved in Park's edition of the "Noble Authors") was a lively writer, and is much distinguished in this correspondence. Of the men, I should propose Lord Peterborough, whose portraits are little known; Lord Liverpool has one of him, not, however, very characteristic. Mr. Pulteney is also little known, but he has been lately re-published in the Kit-cat Club. Of *our Horace* there is not a decent engraving anywhere. I presume that there must be a good original of him somewhere. Whatever you mean to do on this point, you should come to an early determination and put the works in hand.

3rd. I mean, if you approve, to prefix a biographical sketch of Mrs. Howard and two or three of those beautiful characters with which, in prose and verse, the greatest wits of the last century honoured her and themselves. To the first letter of each remarkable correspondent I would also affix a slight notice, and I would add, at the foot of the page, notes in the style of those on Lady Hervey. Let me know whether this plan suits your fancy.

4th. All the letters of Swift, except one or two, in this collection are printed (though not always accurately) in Scott's edition of his works. Yet I think it would be proper to reprint them from the originals, because they elucidate much of Lady Suffolk's history, and her correspondence could not be said to be complete without them. Let me know your wishes on this point.

5th. My materials are numerous, though perhaps the pieces of great merit are not many. I must therefore beg of you to set up, in the form and type you wish to adopt, the sheet which I send you, and you must say about how many pages you wish your volume, or volumes, to be. I will then select as much of the most interesting as will fill the space which you may desire to occupy.

Yours truly,

J. W. CROKER.

Mr. Croker also consented to edit the letters of Mrs. Delany to Mr. Hamilton, 1779-88, containing many anecdotes relating to the Royal Family.

Mr. Croker to John Murray.

"I have shown Mrs. Delany's MS. letters to the Prince Regent; he was much entertained with this revival of old times in his recollection, and *he says that every word of it is true*. You know that H. R.H. has a wonderful memory, and particularly for things of that kind. His certificate of Mrs. Delany's veracity will therefore be probably of some weight with you. As to the letter-writing powers of Mrs. Delany, the specimen inclines me to doubt. Her style seems stiff and formal, and though these two letters, which describe a peculiar kind of scene, have a good deal of interest in them, I do not hope for the same amusement from the rest of the collection. Poverty, obscurity, general ill-health, and blindness are but unpromising qualifications for making an agreeable volume of letters. If a shopkeeper at Portsmouth were to write his life, the extracts of what relates to the two days of the Imperial and Royal visit of 1814 would be amusing, though all the rest of the half century of his life would be intolerably tedious. I therefore counsel you not to buy the pig in Miss Hamilton's bag (though she is a most respectable lady), but ask to see the whole collection before you bid. "

The whole collection was obtained, and, with some corrections and elucidations, the volume of letters was given to the world by Mr. Murray in 1821.

In May 1820 Mr. Murray requested Mr. Croker to edit Horace Walpole's "Reminiscences. " Mr. Croker replied, saying: "I should certainly like the task very well if I felt a little better satisfied of my ability to perform it. Something towards such a work I would certainly contribute, for I have always loved that kind of tea-table history. " Not being able to undertake the work himself, Mr. Croker recommended Mr. Murray to apply to Miss Berry, the editor of Lady Russell's letters. "The Life, " he said, "by which those letters were preceded, is a beautiful piece of biography, and shows, besides higher qualities, much of that taste which a commentator on the 'Reminiscences' ought to have. " The work was accordingly placed in the hands of Miss Berry, who edited it satisfactorily, and it was published by Mr. Murray in the course of the following year.

Dr. Tomline, while Bishop of Winchester, entered into a correspondence with Mr. Murray respecting the "Life of William Pitt. " In December 1820, Dr. Tomline said he had brought the Memoirs down to the Declaration of War by France against Great

Britain on February I, 1793, and that the whole would make two volumes quarto. Until he became Bishop of Lincoln, Dr. Tomline had been Pitt's secretary, and from the opportunities he had possessed, there was promise here of a great work; but it was not well executed, and though a continuation was promised, it never appeared. When the work was sent to Mr. Gifford, he wrote to Mr. Murray that it was not at all what he expected, for it contained nothing of Pitt's private history. "He seems to be uneasy until he gets back to his Parliamentary papers. Yet it can hardly fail to be pretty widely interesting; but I would not have you make yourself too uneasy about these things. Pitt's name, and the Bishop's, will make the work sell. " Gifford was right. The "Life" went to a fourth edition in the following year.

Among Mr. Murray's devoted friends and adherents was Giovanni Belzoni, who, born at Padua in 1778, had, when a young man at Rome, intended to devote himself to the monastic life, but the French invasion of the city altered his purpose, and, instead of being a monk, he became an athlete. He was a man of gigantic physical power, and went from place to place, gaining his living in England, as elsewhere, as a posture-master, and by exhibiting at shows his great feats of strength. He made enough by this work to enable him to visit Egypt, where he erected hydraulic machines for the Pasha, and, through the influence of Mr. Salt, the British Consul, was employed to remove from Thebes, and ship for England, the colossal bust commonly called the Young Memnon. His knowledge of mechanics enabled him to accomplish this with great dexterity, and the head, now in the British Museum, is one of the finest specimens of Egyptian sculpture.

Belzoni, after performing this task, made further investigations among the Egyptian tombs and temples. He was the first to open the great temple of Ipsambul, cut in the side of a mountain, and at that time shut in by an accumulation of sand. Encouraged by these successes, he, in 1817, made a second journey to Upper Egypt and Nubia, and brought to light at Carnac several colossal heads of granite, now in the British Museum. After some further explorations among the tombs and temples, for which he was liberally paid by Mr. Salt, Belzoni returned to England with numerous drawings, casts, and many important works of Egyptian art. He called upon Mr. Murray, with the view of publishing the results of his investigations, which in due course were issued under the title of

"Narrative of the Operations and recent Discoveries within the Pyramids, Temples, Tombs, and Excavations in Egypt and Nubia. "

It was a very expensive book to arrange and publish, but nothing daunted Mr. Murray when a new and original work was brought under his notice. Although only 1,000 copies were printed, the payments to Belzoni and his translators, as well as for plates and engravings, amounted to over £2,163. The preparation of the work gave rise to no little difficulty, for Belzoni declined all help beyond that of the individual who was employed to copy out or translate his manuscript and correct the press. "As I make my discoveries alone, " he said, "I have been anxious to write my book by myself, though in so doing the reader will consider me, with great propriety, guilty of temerity; but the public will, perhaps, gain in the fidelity of my narration what it loses in elegance. " Lord Byron, to whom Mr. Murray sent a copy of his work, said: "Belzoni *is* a grand traveller, and his English is very prettily broken. "

Belzoni was a very interesting character, and a man of great natural refinement. After the publication of his work, he became one of the fashionable lions of London, but was very sensitive about his early career, and very sedulous to sink the posture-master in the traveller. He was often present at Mr. Murray's receptions; and on one particular occasion he was invited to join the family circle in Albemarle Street on the last evening of 1822, to see the Old Year out and the New Year in. All Mr. Murray's young people were present, as well as the entire D'Israeli family and Crofton Croker. After a merry game of Pope Joan, Mr. Murray presented each of the company with a pocket-book as a New Year's gift. A special bowl of punch was brewed for the occasion, and, while it was being prepared, Mr. Isaac D'Israeli took up Crofton Croker's pocket-book, and with his pencil wrote the following impromptu words:

"Gigantic Belzoni at Pope Joan and tea. What a group of mere puppets we seem beside thee; Which, our kind host perceiving, with infinite zest, Gives us Punch at our supper, to keep up the jest. "

The lines were pronounced to be excellent, and Belzoni, wishing to share in the enjoyment, desired to see the words. He read the last line twice over, and then, his eyes flashing fire, he exclaimed, "I am betrayed! " and suddenly left the room. Crofton Croker called upon Belzoni to ascertain the reason for his abrupt departure from Mr. Murray's, and was informed that he considered the lines to be an insulting allusion to his early career as a showman. Croker assured him that neither Murray nor D'Israeli knew anything of his former life; finally he prevailed upon Belzoni to accompany him to Mr. Murray's, who for the first time learnt that the celebrated Egyptian explorer had many years before been an itinerant exhibitor in England.

In 1823 Belzoni set out for Morocco, intending to penetrate thence to Eastern Africa; he wrote to Mr. Murray from Gibraltar, thanking him for many acts of kindness, and again from Tangier.

M. G. Belzoni to John Murray.

April 10, 1823.

"I have just received permission from H. M. the Emperor of Morocco to go to Fez, and am in hopes to obtain his approbation to enter the desert along with the caravan to Soudan. The letter of introduction from Mr. Wilmot to Mr. Douglas has been of much importance to me; this gentleman fortunately finds pleasure in affording me all the assistance in his power to promote my wishes, a circumstance which I have not been accustomed to meet in some other parts of Africa. I shall do myself the pleasure to acquaint you of my further progress at Fez, if not from some other part of Morocco. "

Belzoni would appear to have changed his intention, and endeavoured to penetrate to Timbuctoo from Benin, where, however, he was attacked by dysentery, and died a short time after the above letter was written.

Like many other men of Herculean power, he was not eager to exhibit his strength; but on one occasion he gave proof of it in the following circumstances. Mr. Murray had asked him to accompany him to the Coronation of George IV. They had tickets of admittance to Westminster Hall, but on arriving there they found that the sudden advent of Queen Caroline, attended by a mob claiming admission to the Abbey, had alarmed the authorities, who caused all the doors to be shut. That by which they should have entered was held close and guarded by several stalwart janitors. Belzoni thereupon advanced to the door, and, in spite of the efforts of these guardians, including Tom Crib and others of the pugilistic corps who had been engaged as constables, opened it with ease, and admitted himself and Mr. Murray.

In 1820 Mr. Murray was invited to publish "The Fall of Jerusalem, a Sacred Tragedy, " by the Rev. H.H. Milman, afterwards Dean of St. Paul's. As usual, he consulted Mr. Gifford, whose opinion was most favourable. "I have been more and more struck, " he said, "with the innumerable beauties in Milman's 'Fall of Jerusalem. '"

Mr. Murray requested the author to state his own price for the copyright, and Mr. Milman wrote:

"I am totally at a loss to fix one. I think I might decide whether an offer were exceedingly high or exceedingly low, whether a Byron or Scott price, or such as is given to the first essay of a new author. Though the 'Fall of Jerusalem' might demand an Israelitish bargain, yet I shall not be a Jew further than my poetry. Make a liberal offer, such as the prospect will warrant, and I will at once reply, but I am neither able nor inclined to name a price.... As I am at present not very far advanced in life, I may hereafter have further dealings with the Press, and, of course, where I meet with liberality shall hope to make a return in the same way. It has been rather a favourite scheme of mine, though this drama cannot appear on the boards, to show it before it is published to my friend Mrs. Siddons, who perhaps might like to read it, either at home or abroad. I have not even hinted at such a thing to her, so that this is mere uncertainty, and, before it is printed, it would be in vain to think of it, as the old lady's eyes and MS. could never agree together.

"P. S.—I ought to have said that I am very glad of Aristarchus' [Grifford's] approval. And, by the way, I think, if I help you in redeeming your character from 'Don Juan, ' the 'Hetaerse' in the *Quarterly*, [Footnote: Mitchell's article on "Female Society in Greece, " Q. R. No. 43.] etc., you ought to estimate that very highly. "

Mr. Murray offered Mr. Milman five hundred guineas for the copyright, to which the author replied: "Your offer appears to me very fair, and I shall have no scruple in acceding to it. "

Milman, in addition to numerous plays and poems, became a contributor to the *Quarterly*, and one of Murray's historians. He wrote the "History of the Jews" and the "History of Christianity"; he edited Gibbon and Horace, and continued during his lifetime to be one of Mr. Murray's most intimate and attached friends.

In 1820 we find the first mention of a name afterwards to become as celebrated as any of those with which Mr. Murray was associated. Owing to the warm friendship which existed between the Murrays and the D'Israelis, the younger members of both families were constantly brought together on the most intimate terms. Mr. Murray was among the first to mark the abilities of the boy, Benjamin Disraeli, and, as would appear from the subjoined letter, his confidence in his abilities was so firm that he consulted him as to the merits of a MS. when he had scarcely reached his eighteenth year.

Mr. Benjamin Disraeli to John Murray. August 1822.

Dear Sir,

I ran my eye over three acts of "Wallace, " [Footnote: "Wallace: a Historical Tragedy, " in five acts, was published in 1820. Joanna Baillie spoke of the author, C.E. Walker, as "a very young and promising dramatist. "] and, as far as I could form an opinion, I cannot conceive these acts to be as effective on the stage as you seemed to expect. However, it is impossible to say what a very clever actor like Macready may make of some of the passages. Notwithstanding the many erasures the diction is still diffuse, and sometimes languishing, though not inelegant. I cannot imagine it a powerful work as far as I have read. But, indeed, running over a part of a thing with people talking around is too unfair. I shall be anxious to hear how it succeeds. Many thanks, dear sir, for lending it to me. Your note arrives. If on so slight a knowledge of the play I could venture to erase either of the words you set before me, I fear it would be *Yes*, but I feel cruel and wicked in saying so. I hope you got your dinner in comfort when you got rid of me and that gentle pyramid [Belzoni].

Yours truly,

B. D.

Mr. Southey was an indefatigable and elaborate correspondent, and, as his letters have already been published, it is not necessary to quote them. He rarely wrote to Mr. Gifford, who cut down his articles, and, as Southey insisted, generally emasculated them by omitting the best portions. Two extracts may be given from those written to Mr. Murray in 1820, which do not seem yet to have been given to the world, the first in reference to a proposed Life of Warren Hastings:

"It appears to me that the proper plan will be to publish a selection from Warren Hastings's papers and correspondence, accompanying it with his Life. That Life requires a compendious view of our Indian history down to the time of his administration, and in its progress it embraces the preservation of our Indian empire and the establishment of the existing system. Something must be interwoven concerning the history of the native powers, Mahomedan, Moor, Mahratta, etc., and their institutions. I see how all this is to be introduced, and see also that no subject can afford materials more important or more various. And what a pleasure it will be to read the triumph of such a man as Hastings over the tremendous combination of his persecutors at home! I had a noble catastrophe in writing the Life of Nelson, but the latter days of Hastings afford a scene more touching, and perhaps more sublime, because it is more uncommon. Let me have the works of Orme and Bruce and Mill, and I will set apart a portion of every day to the course of reading, and begin my notes accordingly. "

The second touches on his perennial grievance against Gifford:

"You will really serve as well as oblige me, if you will let me have a duplicate set of proofs of my articles, that I may not *lose* the passages which Mr. Gifford, in spite of repeated promises, always will strike out. In the last paper, among many other mutilations, the most useful *fact* in the essay, for its immediate practical application, has been omitted, and for no imaginable reason (the historical fact that it was the reading a calumnious libel which induced Felton to murder the Duke of Buckingham). When next I touch upon public affairs for you, I will break the Whigs upon the wheel. "

Mrs. Graham, afterwards Lady Callcott, then the wife of Captain Graham, R.N., an authoress and friend of the Murray family, wrote to introduce Mr. (afterwards Sir) Charles Eastlake, who had translated Baron Bartholdy's "Memoirs of the Carbonari. "

Mrs. Graham to John Murray.

February 24, 1821.

All great men have to pay the penalty of their greatness, and you, *arch-bookseller* as you are, must now and then be entreated to do many things you only half like to do. I shall half break my heart if you and Bartholdy do not agree.

* * * * *

Now, whether you publish "The Carbonari" or not, I bespeak your acquaintance for the translator, Mr. Eastlake. I want him to see the sort of thing that one only sees in your house, at your morning *levées*—the traffic of mind and literature, if I may call it so. To a man who has lived most of his grown-up life out of England, it is both curious and instructive, and I wish for this advantage for my friend. And in return for what I want you to benefit him, by giving him the *entrée* to your rooms, I promise you great pleasure in having a gentleman of as much modesty as real accomplishment, and whose taste and talents as an artist must one day place him very high among our native geniuses. You and Mrs. Murray would, I am sure, love him as much as Captain Graham and I do. We met him at Malta on his return from Athens, where he had been with Lord Ruthven's party. Thence he went to Sicily with Lord Leven. In Rome, we lived in the same house. He was with us at Poli, and last summer at Ascoli with Lady Westmoreland. I have told him that, when he goes to London, he must show you two beautiful pictures he has done for Lord Guilford, views taken in Greece. You will see that his pictures and Lord Byron's poetry tell the same story of the "Land of the Unforgotten Brave. " I envy you your morning visitors. I am really hungry for a new book. If you are so good as to send me any *provision fresh from Murray's shambles*, as Mr. Rose says, address it to me, care of Wm. Eastlake, Esq., Plymouth. Love to Mrs. Murray and children.

Yours very gratefully and truly,

MARIA GRAHAM.

P. S.—If Graham has a ship given him at the time, and at the station promised, I shall be obliged to visit London towards the end of March or the beginning of April.

Mr. Murray accepted and published the book.

Lord Byron's works continued to be in great demand at home, and were soon pounced upon by the pirates in America and France. The Americans were beyond Murray's reach, but the French were, to a certain extent, in his power. Galignani, the Paris publisher, wrote to Lord Byron, requesting the assignment to him of the right of publishing his poetry in France. Byron replied that his poems belonged to Mr. Murray, and were his "property by purchase, right, and justice, " and referred Galignani to him, "washing his hands of the business altogether. " M. Galignani then applied to Mr. Murray, who sent him the following answer:

John Murray to M. Galignani.

January 16, 1821.

SIR,

I have received your letter requesting me to assign to you exclusively the right of printing Lord Byron's works in France. In answer I shall state what you do not seem to be aware of, that for the copyright of these works you are printing for nothing, I have given the author upwards of £10,000. Lord Byron has sent me the assignment, regularly made, and dated April 20, 1818; and if you will send me £250 I will make it over to you. I have just received a Tragedy by Lord Byron, for the copyright of which I have paid £1,050, and also three new cantos of "Don Juan, " for which I have paid £2,100. What can you afford to give me for the exclusive right of printing them in France upon condition that you receive them before any other bookseller? Your early reply will oblige.

Your obedient Servant,

J. MURRAY.

M. Galignani then informed Mr. Murray that a pirated edition of Lord Byron's works had been issued by another publisher, and was being sold for 10 francs; and that, if he would assign him the new Tragedy and the new cantos of "Don Juan, " he would pay him £100, and be at the expense of the prosecution of the surreptitious publisher. But nothing was said about the payment of £250 for the issue of Lord Byron's previous work.

Towards the end of 1821 Mr. Murray received a letter from Messrs. Longman & Co., intimating, in a friendly way, "you will see in a day or two, in the newspapers, an advertisement of Mrs. Rundell's improved edition of her 'Cookery Book, ' which she has placed in our hands for publication. " Now, the "Domestic Cookery, " as enlarged and improved by Mr. Murray, was practically a new work, and one of his best properties. When he heard of Mrs. Rundell's intention to bring out her Cookery Book through the Longmans, he consulted his legal adviser, Mr. Sharon Turner, who recommended that an injunction should at once be taken out to restrain the publication, and retained Mr. Littledale and Mr. Serjeant Copley for Mr. Murray. The injunction was duly granted.

After some controversy and litigation the matter was arranged. Mr. Murray voluntarily agreed to pay to Mrs. Rundell £2,000, in full of all claims, and her costs and expenses. The Messrs. Longman delivered to Mr. Murray the stereotype plates of the Cookery Book, and stopped all further advertisements of Mrs. Rundell's work. Mr. Sharon Turner, when writing to tell Mr. Murray the result of his negotiations, concludes with the recommendation: "As Home and Shadwell [Murray's counsel] took much pains, I think if you were to send them each a copy of the Cookery Book, and (as a novelty) of 'Cain, ' it would please them. "

Moore, in his Diary, notes: [Footnote: "Moore: Memoirs, Journal, and Correspondence, " v. p. 119.] "I called at Pickering's, in Chancery Lane, who showed me the original agreement between Milton and Symonds for the payment of five pounds for 'Paradise Lost. ' The contrast of this sum with the £2,000 given by Mr. Murray for Mrs. Rundell's 'Cookery' comprises a history in itself. Pickering, too, gave forty-five guineas for this agreement, nine times as much as the sum given for the poem. "

CHAPTER XXII

WASHINGTON IRVING—UGO FOSCOLO—LADY CAROLINE
LAMB—"HAJJI BABA"—MRS. MARKHAM'S HISTORIES.

The book trade between England and America was in its infancy at the, time of which we are now writing, and though Mr. Murray was frequently invited to publish American books, he had considerable hesitation in accepting such invitations.

Mr. Washington Irving, who was already since 1807 favourably known as an author in America, called upon Mr. Murray, and was asked to dine, as distinguished Americans usually were. He thus records his recollections of the event in a letter to his brother Peter at Liverpool:

Mr. Washington Irving to Mr. Peter Irving.

August 19, 1817.

"I had a very pleasant dinner at Murray's. I met there D'Israeli and an artist [Brockedon] just returned from Italy with an immense number of beautiful sketches of Italian scenery and architecture. D'Israeli's wife and daughter came in in the course of the evening, and we did not adjourn until twelve o'clock. I had a long *tête-à-tête* with old D'Israeli in a corner. He is a very pleasant, cheerful old fellow, curious about America, and evidently tickled at the circulation his works have had there, though, like most authors just now, he groans at not being able to participate in the profits. Murray was very merry and loquacious. He showed me a long letter from Lord Byron, who is in Italy. It is written with some flippancy, but is an odd jumble. His Lordship has written some 104 stanzas of the fourth canto ('Childe Harold'). He says it will be less metaphysical than the last canto, but thinks it will be at least equal to either of the preceding. Murray left town yesterday for some watering-place, so that I have had no further talk with him, but am to keep my eye on his advertisements and write to him when anything offers that I may think worth republishing in America. I shall find him a most valuable acquaintance on my return to London. "

A business in Liverpool, in which, with his brother, he was a partner, proved a failure, and in 1818 he was engaged on his famous "Sketch

Book, " which he wrote in England, and sent to his brother Ebenezer in New York to be published there. The work appeared in three parts in the course of the year 1819. Several of the articles were copied in English periodicals and were read with great admiration. A writer in *Blackwood* expressed surprise that Mr. Irving had thought fit to publish his "Sketch Book" in America earlier than in Britain, and predicted a large and eager demand for such a work. On this encouragement, Irving, who was still in England, took the first three numbers, which had already appeared in America, to Mr. Murray, and left them with him for examination and approval. Murray excused himself on the ground that he did not consider the work in question likely to form the basis of "satisfactory accounts, " and without this he had no "satisfaction" in undertaking to publish.

Irving thereupon sought (but did not take) the advice of Sir W. Scott, and entered into an arrangement with Miller of the Burlington Arcade, and in February 1820 the first four numbers were published in a volume. Miller shortly after became bankrupt, the sale of the book (of which one thousand had been printed) was interrupted, and Irving's hopes of profit were dashed to the ground. At this juncture, Walter Scott, who was then in London, came to his help.

"I called to him for help as I was sticking in the mire, and, more propitious than Hercules, he put his own shoulder to the wheel. Through his favourable representations Murray was quickly induced to undertake the future publication of the work which he had previously declined. A further edition of the first volume was put to press, and from that time Murray became my publisher, conducting himself in all his dealings with that fair, open, and liberal spirit which had obtained for him the well-merited appellation of the Prince of Booksellers. " [Footnote: Preface to the revised edition of "The Sketch Book. "]

Irving, being greatly in want of money, offered to dispose of the work entirely to the publisher, and Murray, though he had no legal protection for his purchase, not only gave him £200 for it, but two months later he wrote to Irving, stating that his volumes had succeeded so much beyond his commercial estimate that he begged he would do him the favour to draw on him at sixty-five days for one hundred guineas in addition to the sum agreed upon. And again, eight months later, Murray made Irving a second gratuitous contribution of a hundred pounds, to which the author replied, "I never knew any one convey so much meaning in so concise and agreeable a manner. " The author's "Bracebridge Hall" and other works were also published by Mr. Murray.

In 1822 Irving, who liked to help his literary fellow-countrymen, tried to induce Mr. Murray to republish James Fenimore Cooper's novels in England. Mr. Murray felt obliged to decline, as he found that these works were pirated by other publishers; American authors were then beginning to experience the same treatment in England which English authors have suffered in America. The wonder was that Washington Irving's works so long escaped the same doom.

In 1819 Mr. Murray first made the acquaintance of Ugo Foscolo. A native of Zante, descended from a Venetian family who had settled in the Ionian Islands, Foscolo studied at Padua, and afterwards took up his residence at Venice. The ancient aristocracy of that city had been banished by Napoleon Bonaparte, and the conqueror gave over Venice to Austria. Foscolo attacked Bonaparte in his "Lettere di Ortis. " After serving as a volunteer in the Lombard Legion through the disastrous campaign of 1799, Foscolo, on the capitulation of Genoa, retired to Milan, where he devoted himself to literary pursuits. He once more took service—under Napoleon—and in 1805 formed part of the army of England assembled at Boulogne; but soon left the army, went to Pavia (where he had been appointed Professor of Eloquence), and eventually at the age of forty took refuge in England. Here he found many friends, who supported him in his literary efforts. Among others he called upon Mr. Murray, who desired his co-operation in writing for the *Quarterly*. An article, on "The Poems of the Italians" was his first contribution. Mr. Thomas Mitchell, the translator of "Aristophanes, " desired Mr. Murray to give Foscolo his congratulations upon his excellent essay, as well as on his acquaintance with our language.

Mr. Thomas Mitchell to John Murray.

"The first time I had the pleasure of seeing M. Foscolo was at a *table d'h'te* at Berne. There was something in his physiognomy which very much attracted nay notice; and, for some reason or another, I thought that I seemed to be an object of his attention. At table, Foscolo was seated next to a young Hanoverian, between whom and me a very learned conversation had passed on the preceding evening, and a certain degree of acquaintance was cemented in consequence. The table was that day graced with the appearance of some of the Court ladies of Stuttgard, and all passed off with the decorum usually observed abroad, when suddenly, towards the conclusion of the feast a violent hubbub was heard between M. Foscolo and his Hanoverian neighbour, who, in angry terms and with violent gestures, respectively asserted the superior harmonies of Greek and Latin. This ended with the former's suddenly producing a card, accompanied with the following annunciation: 'Sir, my name is Ugo Foscolo; I am a native of Greece, and I have resided thirty years in Italy; I therefore think I ought to know something of the matter. This card contains my address, and if you have anything further to say, you know where I am to be found. ' Whether Foscolo's name or manner daunted the young Hanoverian, or whether he was only a bird of passage, I don't know, but we saw nothing more of him after that day. Foscolo, after the ladies had retired, made an apology, directed a good deal to me, who, by the forms of the place, happened to be at the head of the table; a considerable degree of intimacy took place between us, and an excellent man I believe him to be, in spite of these little ebullitions. "

Ugo Foscolo, who was eccentric to an excess, and very extravagant, had many attached friends, though he tried them sorely. To Mr. Murray he became one of the troubles of private as well as publishing life. He had a mania for building, and a mania for ornamentation, but he was very short of money for carrying out his freaks. He thought himself at the same time to be perfectly moderate, simple, and sweet-tempered. He took a house in South Bank, Regent's Park, which he named Digamma Cottage—from his having contributed to the *Quarterly Review* an article on the Digamma—and fitted it up in extravagant style.

Foscolo could scarcely live at peace with anybody, and, as the result of one of his numerous altercations, he had to fight a duel. "We are, " Lady Dacre wrote to Murray (December 1823), "to have the whole of Foscolo's duel to-morrow. He tells me that it is not about a 'Fair lady': thank heaven! "

Foscolo was one of Mr. Murray's inveterate correspondents—about lectures, about translations, about buildings, about debts, about loans, and about borrowings. On one occasion Mr. Murray received from him a letter of thirteen pages quarto. A few sentences of this may be worth quoting:

Mr. Foscolo to John Murray.

SOUTH BANK, *August* 20, 1822.

"During six years (for I landed in England the 10th September, 1816) I have constantly laboured under difficulties the most distressing; no one knows them so well as yourself, because no one came to my assistance with so warm a friendship or with cares so constant and delicate. My difficulties have become more perplexing since the Government both of the Ionian Islands and Italy have precluded even the possibility of my returning to the countries where a slender income would be sufficient, and where I would not be under the necessity of making a degrading use of my faculties. I was born a racehorse; and after near forty years of successful racing, I am now drawing the waggon—nay, to be the teacher of French to my copyists, and the critic of English to my translators! -to write sophistry about criticism, which I always considered a sort of literary quackery, and to put together paltry articles for works which I never read. Indeed, if I have not undergone the doom of almost all individuals whose situation becomes suddenly opposed to their feelings and habits, and if I am not yet a lunatic, I must thank the mechanical strength of my nerves. My nerves, however, will not withstand the threatenings of shame which I have always contemplated with terror. Time and fortune have taught me to meet all other evils with fortitude; but I grow every day more and more a coward at the idea of the approach of a stigma on my character; and as now I must live and die in England, and get the greater part of my subsistence from my labour, I ought to reconcile, if not labour with literary reputation, at least labour and life with a spotless name. "

He then goes on to state that his debts amount to £600 or thereabouts, including a sum of £20 which he owed to Mr. Murray himself. Then he must have the money necessary for his subsistence, and he "finds he cannot live on less than £400 per annum. "

"My apartments, " he continues, "decently furnished, encompass me with an atmosphere of ease and respectability; and I enjoy the illusion of not having fallen into the lowest circumstances.

I always declare that I will die like a gentleman, on a decent bed, surrounded by casts (as I cannot buy the marbles) of the Venuses, of the Apollos, and of the Graces, and the busts of great men; nay, even among flowers, and, if possible, with some graceful innocent girl playing an old pianoforte in an adjoining room. And thus dies the hero of my novel. Far from courting the sympathy of mankind, I would rather be forgotten by posterity than give it the gratification of ejaculating preposterous sighs because I died like Camoens and Tasso on the bed of an hospital. And since I must be buried in your country, I am happy in having insured for me the possession during the remains of my life of a cottage built after my plan, surrounded by flowering shrubs, almost within the tumpikes of the town, and yet as quiet as a country-house, and open to the free air. Whenever I can freely dispose of a hundred pounds, I will also build a small dwelling for my corpse, under a beautiful Oriental plane-tree, which I mean to plant next November, and cultivate *con amore*. So far I am indeed an epicure; in all other things I am the most moderate of men."

The upshot of the letter is, that he wishes Mr. Murray to let him have £1,000, to be repaid in five years, he meanwhile writing articles for the *Quarterly*—one-half of the payment to be left with the publisher, and the remaining half to be added to his personal income. He concludes:

"In seeking out a way of salvation, I think it incumbent on me to prevent the tyranny of necessity, that I might not be compelled by it to endanger my character and the interest of a friend whose kindness I have always experienced, and whose assistance I am once more obliged to solicit. "

Mr. Murray paid off some of his more pressing embarrassments— £30 to Messrs. Bentley for bills not taken up; £33 7*s*. to Mr. Kelly the printer; £14 to Mr. Antonini; and £50 to Foscolo's builder—besides becoming security for £300 to his bankers (with whom Foscolo did business), in order to ensure him a respite for six months. On the other hand, Foscolo agreed to insure his life for £600 as a sort of guarantee. "Was ever" impecunious author "so trusted before"? At this crisis in his affairs many friends came about him and took an interest in the patriot; Mr. Hallam and Mr. Wilbraham offered him money, but he would not accept "gratuities" from them, though he had no objection to accepting their "loans. " Arrangements were then made for Foscolo to deliver a series of lectures on Italian Literature. Everything was settled, the day arrived, the room was crowded with a distinguished assembly, when at the last moment Foscolo appeared without his MS., which he had forgotten.

The course of lectures, however, which had been designed to relieve him from the pressure of his debts, proved successful, and brought him in, it is said, as much as £1,000; whereupon he immediately set to work to squander his earnings by giving a public breakfast to his patrons, for which purpose he thought it incumbent on him, amongst other expenses, to make a new approach and a gravelled carriage road to Digamma Cottage.

Ugo Foscolo lived on credit to the end of his life, surrounded by all that was luxurious and beautiful. How he contrived it, no one knew, for his resources remained at the lowest ebb. Perhaps his friends helped him, for English Liberals of good means regarded him as a martyr in the cause of freedom, one who would never bow the knee to Baal, and who had dared the first Napoleon when his very word was law. But Foscolo's friends without doubt became tired of his extravagance and his licentious habits, and fell away from him. Disease at last found him out; he died of dropsy at Turnham Green, near Hammersmith, in 1827, when only in the fiftieth year of his age, and was buried in Chiswick churchyard; but in June 1871 his body was exhumed and conveyed to Florence, where he was buried in Santa Croce, between the tomb of Alfieri and the monument of Dante.

Lady Caroline Lamb had continued to keep up her intimacy with Mr. Murray; and now that she was preparing a new work for the press, her correspondence increased. While he was at Wimbledon during summer, she occasionally met literary friends at his house. She had already published "Glenarvon, " the hero of which was supposed to represent Lord Byron, and was now ready with "Penruddock. " "I am in great anxiety, " she wrote to Mr. Murray, "about your not informing me what Gifford says. I think it might be a civil way of giving me my death-warrant—if 'Penruddock' does not. "

Whether the criticism of Mr. Gifford was too severe, or whether Mr. Murray was so much engaged in business and correspondence as to take no notice of Lady Caroline Lamb's communication, does not appear; but she felt the neglect, and immediately followed it up with another letter as follows:

Lady Caroline Lamb to John Murray.

December 8, 1822.

MY DEAR AND MOST OBSTINATELY SILENT SIR,

From one until nine upon Tuesday I shall be at Melbourne House waiting for you; but if you wish to see the prettiest woman in England, —besides myself and William—be at Melbourne House at quarter to six, at which hour we dine; and if you will come at half-past one, or two, or three, to say you will dine and to ask me to forgive your inexorable and inhuman conduct, pray do, for I arrive at twelve in that said home and leave it at nine the ensuing morning. What can have happened to you that you will not write?

The following letter from William Lamb (afterwards Lord Melbourne), the long-suffering and generous husband of this wayward lady, refers to a novel entitled "Ada Reis. "

The Honble. William Lamb to John Murray.

December 20, 1822.

"The incongruity of, and objections to, the story of 'Ada Reis' can only be got over by power of writing, beauty of sentiment, striking and effective situation, etc. If Mr. Gifford thinks there is in the first two volumes anything of excellence sufficient to overbalance their manifest faults, I still hope that he will press upon Lady Caroline the absolute necessity of carefully reconsidering and revising the third volume, and particularly the conclusion of the novel.

"Mr. Gifford, I dare say, will agree with me that since the time of Lucian all the representations of the infernal regions, which have been attempted by satirical writers, such as 'Fielding's Journey from this World to the Next, ' have been feeble and flat. The sketch in "Ada Reis" is commonplace in its observations and altogether insufficient, and it would not do now to come with a decisive failure in an attempt of considerable boldness. I think, if it were thought that anything could be done with the novel, and that the faults of its design and structure can be got over, that I could put her in the way of writing up this part a little, and giving it something of strength, spirit, and novelty, and of making it at once more moral and more interesting. I wish you would communicate these my hasty suggestions to Mr. Gifford, and he will see the propriety of pressing Lady Caroline to take a little more time to this part of the novel. She will be guided by his authority, and her fault at present is to be too hasty and too impatient of the trouble of correcting and recasting what is faulty. "

"Ada Reis" was published in March 1823.

Another of England's Prime Ministers, Lord John Russell, had in contemplation a History of Europe, and consulted Mr. Murray on the subject. A first volume, entitled "The Affairs of Europe, " was published without the author's name on the title-page, and a few years later another volume was published, but it remained an unfinished work. Lord John was an ambitious and restless author; without steady perseverance in any branch of literature; he went from poems to tragedies, from tragedies to memoirs, then to history, tales, translations of part of the "Odyssey, " essays (by the Gentleman who left his Lodgings), and then to memoirs and histories again. Mr. Croker said of his "Don Carlos": "It is not easy to find any poetry, or even oratory, of the present day delivered with such cold and heavy diction, such distorted tropes and disjointed limbs of similes worn to the bones long ago. "

Another work that excited greater interest than Lord John Russell's anonymous history was Mr. James Morier's "Hajji Baba. " Mr. Morier had in his youth travelled through the East, especially in Persia, where he held a post under Sir Gore Ouseley, then English Ambassador. On his return to England, he published accounts of his travels; but his "Hajji Baba" was more read than any other of his works. Sir Walter Scott was especially pleased with it, and remarked that "Hajji Baba" might be termed the Oriental "Gil Bias. " Mr. Morier afterwards published "The Adventures of Hajji Baba in England, " as well as other works of an Eastern character. The following letter, written by the Persian Envoy in England, Miiza Abul Hassan, shows the impression created by English society on a foreigner in April 1824:

Letter from the Persian Envoy, Mirza Abul Hassan, to the London Gentleman without, who lately wrote letter to him and ask very much to give answer.

April 3, 1824.

SIR, MY LORD,

When you write to me some time ago to give my thought of what I see good and bad this country, that time I not speak English very well. Now I read, I write much little better. Now I give to you my think. In this country bad not too much, everything very good. But suppose I not tell something little bad, then you say I tell all flattery—therefore I tell most bad thing. I not like such crowd in evening party every night. In cold weather not very good, now hot weather, much too bad. I very much astonish every day now much hot than before, evening parties much crowd than before. Pretty beautiful ladies come sweat, that not very good. I always afraid some old lady in crowd come dead, that not very good, and spoil my happiness. I think old ladies after 85 years not come to evening party, that much better. Why for take so much trouble? Some other thing rather bad. Very beautiful young lady she got ugly fellow for husband, that not very good, very shocking. I ask Sr Gore [Sir Gore Ouseley] why for this. He says me—"perhaps he very good man, not handsome; no matter, perhaps he got too much money, perhaps got title. " I say I not like that, all very shocking. This all bad I know. Now I say good. English people all very good people. All very happy. Do what they like, say what like, write in newspaper what like. I love English people very much, they very civil to me. I tell my King English love Persian very much. English King best man in world, he love his people very good much; he speak very kind to me, I love him very much. Queen very best woman I ever saw. Prince of Wales such a fine elegant beautiful man. I not understand English enough proper to praise him, he too great for my language. I respect him same as my own King. I love him much better, his manner all same as talisman and charm. All the Princes very fine men, very handsome men, very sweet words, very affable. I like all too much. I think the ladies and gentlemen this country most high rank, high honour, very rich, except two or three most good, very kind to inferior peoples. This very good. I go to see Chelsea. All old men sit on grass in shade of fine tree, fine river run by, beautiful place, plenty to eat, drink, good coat, everything very good. Sir Gore he tell me King Charles and King Jame. I say Sir Gore, They not Musselman, but I think God love them very much. I think God he love the King very well for keeping up that charity. Then I see one small regiment of children go to dinner, one small boy he say thanks to God for eat, for drink, for clothes, other little boys they all answer

Amen. Then I cry a little, my heart too much pleased. This all very good for two things—one thing, God very much please; two things, soldiers fight much better, because see their good King take care of old wounded fathers and little children. Then I go to Greenwich, that too good place, such a fine sight make me a little sick for joy. All old men so happy, eat dinner, so well, fine house, fine beds—all very good. This very good country. English ladies very handsome, very beautiful. I travel great deal. I go Arabia, I go Calcutta, Hyderabad, Poonah, Bombay, Georgia, Armenia, Constantinople, Malta, Gibraltar. I see best Georgia, Circassian, Turkish, Greek ladies, but nothing not so beautiful as English ladies, all very clever, speak French, speak English, speak Italian, play music very well, sing very good. Very glad for me if Persian ladies like them. But English ladies speak such sweet words. I think tell a little story—that not very good.

One thing more I see but I not understand that thing good or bad. Last Thursday I see some fine horses, fine carriages, thousand people go to look that carriages. I ask why for? They say me, that gentleman on boxes they drive their own carriages. I say why for take so much trouble? They say me he drive very well; that very good thing. It rain very hard, some lord some gentleman he get very wet. I say why he not go inside? They tell me good coachman not mind get wet every day, will be much ashamed if go inside; that I not understand.

Sir, my Lord, good-night,

ABUL HASSAN.

Mr. Murray invariably consulted Mr. Barrow as to any works on voyages or travels he was required to publish, and found him a faithful adviser. The following expression of opinion, from one with so large an experience, is interesting:

Mr. J. Barrow to John Murray.

March 28, 1823.

"I need not tell you that caprice rather than merit governs the sale of a work. If instances are wanting, I might quote those of Belzoni and Hamilton. [Footnote: This reference probably refers to Walter Hamilton's "Description of Hindostan and adjacent Countries, " published a few years before.] The first absolute trumpery when put in competition with the second; yet the former, I believe, sold about ten times the number of the latter. "

Another little book published about this time has a curious history, and illustrates the lottery of book publishing. Mrs. Markham's [Footnote: This lady's real name was Mrs. Penrose.] "History of England" was first published by Constable, but it fell still-born from the press. Mr. Murray, discerning the merit of the work in 1824, bought the remainder of 333 copies from Constable, and had it revised, corrected, and enlarged, and brought out in an entirely new form. He placed it in his list of school books, and pushed it among the teachers throughout the country, until at length it obtained a very large and regular circulation. The book has subsequently undergone frequent revision, and down to the present date it continues to be a great favourite, especially in ladies' schools.

CHAPTER XXIII

GIFFORD'S RETIREMENT FROM THE EDITORSHIP OF THE
"QUARTERLY" — AND DEATH

It had for some time been evident, as has been shown in a previous chapter, that Gifford was becoming physically incapable of carrying on the Editorship of the *Quarterly Review*, but an occasional respite from the pressure of sickness, as well as his own unwillingness to abandon his connection with a work which he regarded with paternal affection, and Murray's difficulty in finding a worthy successor, combined to induce him to remain at his post.

He accordingly undertook to carry on his editorial duties till the publication of the 60th number, aided and supported by the active energy of Barrow and Croker, who, in conjunction with the publisher, did most of the necessary drudgery.

In December 1823 Canning had written to say that he was in bed with the gout; to this Gifford replied:

MY DEAR CANNING,

I wish you had a pleasanter bedfellow; but here am I on the sofa with a cough, and a very disagreeable associate I find it. Old Moore, I think, died all but his voice, and my voice is nearly dead before me; in other respects, I am much as I was when you saw me, and this weather is in my favour.... I have promised Murray to try to carry on the *Review* to the 60th number; the 58th is now nearly finished. This seems a desperate promise, and beyond it I will not, cannot go; for, at best, as the old philosopher said, I am dying at my ease, as my complaint has taken a consumptive turn. The vultures already scent the carcase, and three or four *Quarterly Reviews* are about to start. One is to be set up by Haygarth, whom I think I once mentioned to you as talked of to succeed me, but he is now in open hostility to Murray; another is to be called the *Westminster Quarterly Review*, and will, if I may judge from the professions of impartiality, be a decided Opposition Journal. They will all have their little day, perhaps, and then drop into the grave of their predecessors. The worst is that we cannot yet light upon a fit and promising successor.

Ever, my dear Canning,

Faithfully and affectionately yours,

WILLIAM GIFFORD.

This state of matters could not be allowed to go on much longer; sometimes a quarter passed without a number appearing; in 1824 only two *Quarterlies* appeared—No. 60, due in January, but only published in August; and No. 61, due in April, but published in December. An expostulation came from Croker to Murray (January 23, 1824):

"Have you made up *your mind* about an editor? Southey has written to me on the subject, as if you had, and as if he knew your choice; I do not like to answer him before I know what I am to say. Will you dine at Kensington on Sunday at 6? "

Southey had long been meditating about the editorship. It never appears to have been actually offered to him, but his name, as we have already seen, was often mentioned in connection with it. He preferred, however, going on with his own works and remaining a contributor only. Politics, too, may have influenced him, for we find him writing to Mr. Murray on December 15, 1824: "The time cannot be far distant when the *Q. R.* must take its part upon a most momentous subject, and choose between Mr. Canning and the Church. I have always considered it as one of the greatest errors in the management of the *Review* that it should have been silent upon that subject so long. " So far as regarded his position as a contributor, Southey expressed his opinion to Murray explicitly:

Mr. Southey to John Murray.

October 25, 1824.

"No future Editor, be he who he may, must expect to exercise the same discretion over my papers which Mr. Gifford has done. I will at any time curtail what may be deemed too long, and consider any objections that may be made, with a disposition to defer to them when it can be done without sacrificing my own judgment upon points which may seem to me important. But my age and (I may add without arrogance) the rank which I hold in literature entitle me to say that I will never again write under the correction of any one. "

Gifford's resignation is announced in the following letter to Canning (September 8, 1824):

Mr. W. Gifford to the Rt. Hon. G. Canning.

September 8, 1824.

MY DEAR CANNING,

I have laid aside my Regalia, and King Gifford, first of the name, is now no more, as Sir Andrew Aguecheek says, "than an ordinary mortal or a Christian. " It is necessary to tell you this, for, with the exception of a dark cloud which has come over Murray's brow, no prodigies in earth or air, as far as I have heard, have announced it.

It is now exactly sixteen years ago since your letter invited or encouraged me to take the throne. I did not mount it without a trembling fit; but I was promised support, and I have been nobly supported. As far as regards myself, I have borne my faculties soberly, if not meekly. I have resisted, with undeviating firmness, every attempt to encroach upon me, every solicitation of publisher, author, friend, or friend's friend, and turned not a jot aside for power or delight. In consequence of this integrity of purpose, the Review has long possessed a degree of influence, not only in this, but in other countries hitherto unknown; and I have the satisfaction, at this late hour, of seeing it in its most palmy state. No number has sold better than the sixtieth.

But there is a sad tale to tell. For the last three years I have perceived the mastery which disease and age were acquiring over a constitution battered and torn at the best, and have been perpetually urging Murray to look about for a successor, while I begged Coplestone, Blomfield, and others to assist the search. All has been ineffectual. Murray, indeed, has been foolishly flattering himself that I might be cajoled on from number to number, and has not, therefore, exerted himself as he ought to have done; but the rest have been in earnest. Do you know any one? I once thought of Robert Grant; but he proved timid, and indeed his saintly propensities would render him suspected. Reginald Heber, whom I should have preferred to any one, was snatched from me for a far higher object.

I have been offered a Doctor's Degree, and when I declined it, on account of my inability to appear in public, my own college (Exeter) most kindly offered to confer it on me in private; that is, at the Rector's lodgings. This, too, I declined, and begged the Dean of Westminster, who has a living in the neighbourhood, to excuse me as handsomely as he could. It might, for aught I know, be a hard race between a shroud and a gown which shall get me first; at any rate, it was too late for honours.

Faithfully and affectionately yours,

WILLIAM GIFFORD.

Mr. J.T. Coleridge had long been regarded as the most eligible successor to Mr. Gifford, and on him the choice now fell. Mr. Murray forwarded the reply of Mr. Coleridge which contained his acceptance of the editorship to Mr. Gifford, accompanied by the following note:

John Murray to Mr. Gifford.

WHITEHALL PLACE,

December 11, 1824.

MY DEAR SIR,

I shall not attempt to express the feelings with which I communicate the enclosed answer to the proposal which I suspect it would have been thought contemptible in me any longer to have delayed, and all that I can find to console myself with is the hope that I may be able to evince my gratitude to you during life, and to your memory, if it so please the Almighty that I am to be the survivor.

I am your obliged and faithful Servant,

JOHN MURRAY.

Mr. Murray lost no time in informing his friends of the new arrangement.

Gifford lived for about two years more, and continued to entertain many kind thoughts of his friends and fellow-contributors: his intercourse with his publisher was as close and intimate as ever to the end.

The last month of Gifford's life was but a slow dying. He was sleepless, feverish, oppressed by an extreme difficulty of breathing, which often entirely deprived him of speech; and his sight had failed. Towards the end of his life he would sometimes take up a pen, and after a vain attempt to write, would throw it down, saying, "No, my work is done! " Even thinking caused him pain. As his last hour drew near, his mind began to wander. "These books have driven me mad, " he once said, "I must read my prayers. " He passed gradually away, his pulse ceasing to beat five hours before his death. And then he slept out of life, on December 31, 1826, in his 68th year—a few months before the death of Canning.

Mr. Gifford desired that he should be buried in the ground attached to Grosvenor Chapel, South Audley Street, where he had interred Annie Davies, his faithful old housekeeper, but his friends made application for his interment in Westminster Abbey, which was acceded to, and he was buried there accordingly on January 8, 1827, immediately under the monuments of Camden and Garrick. He was much richer at the time of his death than he was at all aware of, for he was perfectly indifferent about money. Indeed, he several times returned money to Mr. Murray, saying that "he had been too liberal." He left £25,000 of personal property, a considerable part of which he left to the relatives of Mr. Cookesley, the surgeon of Ashburton, who had been to him so faithful and self-denying a friend in his early life. To Mr. Murray he left £100 as a memorial, and also 500 guineas, to enable him to reimburse a military gentleman, to whom, jointly with Mr. Cookesley, he appears to have been bound for that sum at a former period.

Gifford has earned, but it is now generally recognised that he has unjustly earned, the character of a severe, if not a bitter critic. Possessing an unusually keen discernment of genuine excellence, and a scathing power of denunciation of what was false or bad in literature, he formed his judgments in accordance with a very high standard of merit. Sir Walter Scott said of his "Baviad and Mæviad, that "he squashed at one blow a set of coxcombs who might have humbugged the world long enough. " His critical temper, however, was in truth exceptionally equable; regarding it as his duty to encourage all that was good and elevating, and relentlessly to denounce all that was bad or tended to lower the tone of literature, he conscientiously acted up to the standard by which he judged others, and never allowed personal feeling to intrude upon his official judgments.

It need scarcely be said that he proved himself an excellent editor, and that he entertained a high idea of the duties of that office. William Jerdan, who was introduced to Gifford by Canning, said: "I speak of him as he always was to me—full of gentleness, a sagacious adviser and instructor, upon so comprehensive a scale, that I never met his superior among the men of the age most renowned for vast information, and his captivating power in communicating it. " His sagacity and quickness of apprehension were remarkable, as was also the extraordinary rapidity with which he was able to eviscerate a work, and summarize its contents in a few pages.

The number of articles which he himself wrote was comparatively small, for he confined himself for the most part to revising and improving the criticisms of others, and though in thus dealing with articles submitted to him he frequently erased what the writers considered some of their best criticisms, he never lost their friendship and support. He disliked incurring any obligation which might in any degree shackle the expression of his free opinions. In conjunction with Mr. Murray, he laid down a rule, which as we have already seen was advocated by Scott, and to which no exception has ever been made, that every writer in the *Quarterly* should receive payment for his contribution. On one occasion, when a gentleman in office would not receive the money, the article was returned. "I am not more certain of many conjectures, " says Jerdan, "than I am of this, that he never propagated a dishonest opinion nor did a dishonest act. "

Gifford took no notice of the ferocious attacks made upon him by Hunt and Hazlitt. Holding, as he did, that inviolable secrecy was one of the prime functions of an editor—though the practice has since become very different—he never attempted to vindicate himself, or to reveal the secret as to the writers of the reviews. In accordance with his plan of secrecy, he desired Dr. Ireland, his executor, to destroy all confidential letters, especially those relating to the *Review*, so that the names of the authors, as well as the prices paid for each article, might never be known.

In society, of which he saw but little, except at Mr. Murray's, he was very entertaining. He told a story remarkably well; and had an inexhaustible supply; the archness of his eyes and countenance making them all equally good.

He had never been married; but although he had no children, he had an exceeding love for them. When well, he delighted in giving juvenile parties, and rejoiced at seeing the children frisking about in the happiness of youth—a contrast which threw the misery of his own early life into strange relief. His domestic favourites were his dog and his cat, both of which he dearly loved. He was also most kind and generous to his domestic servants; and all who knew him well, sorrowfully lamented his death.

Many years after Gifford's death, a venomous article upon him appeared in a London periodical. The chief point of this anonymous attack was contained in certain extracts from the writings of Sir W. Scott, Southey, and other eminent contemporaries of Mr. Gifford. Mr. R.W. Hay, one of the oldest contributors to the *Quarterly*, was at that time still living, and, in allusion to the article in question, he wrote to Mr. Murray's son:

Mr. R.W. Hay to Mr. Murray.

July 7, 1856.

It is wholly worthless, excepting as it contains strictures of Sir W. Scott, Southey, and John Wilson on the critical character of the late Wm. Gifford. I by no means subscribe to all that is said by these distinguished individuals on the subject, and I cannot help suspecting that the high station in literature which they occupied rendered them more than commonly sensitive to the corrections and erasures which were proposed by the editor. Sir Walter (great man as he was) was perfectly capable of writing so carelessly as to require correction, and both Southey and John Wilson might occasionally have brought forth opinions, on political and other matters, which were not in keeping with the general tone of the *Quarterly Review*. That poor Gifford was deformed in figure, feeble in health, unhappily for him there can be no denying, but that he had any pleasure in tormenting, as asserted by some, that he indulged in needless criticism without any regard to the feelings of those who were under his lash, I am quite satisfied cannot justly be maintained. In my small dealings with the *Review*, I only found the editor most kind and considerate. His amendments and alterations I generally at once concurred in, and I especially remember in one of the early articles, that he diminished the number of Latin quotations very much to its advantage; that his heart was quite in the right place I have had perfect means of knowing from more than one circumstance, *e. g.*, his anxiety for the welfare of his friend Hoppner the painter's children was displayed in the variety of modes which he adopted to assist them, and when John Gait was sorely maltreated in the *Review* in consequence of his having attributed to me, incorrectly, an article which occasioned his wrath and indignation, and afterwards was exposed to many embarrassments in life, Gifford most kindly took up his cause, and did all he could to further the promotion of his family. That our poor friend should have been exposed throughout the most part of his life to the strong dislike of the greatest part of the community is not unnatural. As the *redacteur* of the *Anti-Jacobin*, etc., he, in the latter part of the last century, drew upon himself the hostile attacks of all the modern philosophers of the age, and of all those who hailed with applause the dawn of liberty in the French Revolution; as editor of the *Quarterly Review*, he acquired in addition to the former hosts of enemies, the undisguised hatred of all the Whigs and Liberals, who were for making peace with Bonaparte, and for destroying the settled order of things in this country. In the present generation, when the feeling of national hatred against France has entirely subsided, and party feelings have so much gone by that no man can say to which party any public man belongs, it is impossible for anyone to comprehend the state of public feeling which prevailed during the great war of the Revolution, and for some years after its termination. Gifford was deeply imbued with all the sentiments on public matters which prevailed in his time, and, as some people have a hatred of a cat, and others of a toad, so our friend felt uneasy when a Frenchman was named; and buckled on his armour of criticism whenever a Liberal or even a Whig was brought under his notice; and although in the present day there appears to be a greater indulgence to crime amongst judges and juries, and perhaps a more lenient system of criticism is adopted by reviewers, I am not sure that any public advantage is gained by having Ticket of Leave men, who ought to be in New South Wales, let loose upon the English world by the unchecked appearance of a vast deal of spurious literature, which ought to have withered under the severe blasts of Criticism.

Believe yours very truly,

R. W. HAY.

CHAPTER XXIV

THE "REPRESENTATIVE"

Mr. Murray had for long been desirous of publishing a journal which should appear more frequently than once a quarter, more especially after the discontinuance of his interest in Blackwood's magazine. In 1825 he conceived the more ambitious design of publishing a daily morning paper, a project now chiefly interesting from the fact that in this venture he had the assistance of the future Lord Beaconsfield. The intimacy which existed between the Murrays and D'Israelis had afforded Mr. Murray exceptional opportunities of forming an opinion of Benjamin's character, and he saw with delight the rapidly developing capacities of his old friend's son. Even in his eighteenth year Benjamin was consulted by Mr. Murray as to the merits of a MS., and two years later he wrote a novel entitled "Aylmer Papillon," which did not see the light. He also edited a "History of Paul Jones, Admiral in the Russian Navy, " written by Theophilus Smart, an American, and originally published in the United States.

Young Disraeli was already gifted with a power of influencing others, unusual in a man of his age. He was eloquent, persuasive, and ingenious, and even then, as in future years, when he became a leading figure in the political world, he had the power of drawing others over to the views which he entertained, however different they might be from their own. Looking merely to his literary career as a successful novel writer, his correspondence with Mr. Murray about his proposed work of "Aylmer Papillon" is not without interest.

Mr. Benjamin Disraeli to John Murray.

May, 1824.

MY DEAR SIR,

Your very kind letter induces me to trouble you with this most trivial of trifles. My plan has been in these few pages so to mix up any observations which I had to make on the present state of society with the bustle and hurry of a story, that my satire should never be protruded on my reader. If you will look at the last chapter but one, entitled "Lady Modeley's, " you will see what I mean better than I can express it. The first pages of that chapter I have written in the same manner as I would a common novel, but I have endeavoured to put in *action* at the *end*, the present fashion of getting on in the world. I write no humbug about "candidly giving your opinion, etc., etc. " You must be aware that you cannot do me a greater favour than refusing to publish it, if you think *it won't do*; and who should be a better judge than yourself?

Believe me ever to be, my dear Sir,

Your most faithful and obliged,

B. DISRAELI. [Footnote: It will be observed that while the father maintained the older spelling of the name, the son invariably writes it thus.]

P. S.—The second and the last chapters are unfortunately mislaid, but they have no particular connection with the story. They are both very short, the first contains an adventure on the road, and the last Mr. Papillon's banishment under the Alien Act from a ministerial misconception of a metaphysical sonnet.

Thursday morn. : Excuse want of seal, as we're doing a bit of summer to-day, and there is not a fire in the house.

FREDERICK PLACE, *May* 25, 1824.

1/2 past 1 o'clock A. M.

MY DEAR SIR,

The travels, to which I alluded this morning, would not bind up with "Parry, " since a moderate duodecimo would contain the adventures of a certain Mr. Aylmer Papillon in a *terra incognita*. I certainly should never have mentioned them had I been aware that you were so very much engaged, and I only allude to them once more that no confusion may arise from the half-explanations given this morning. You will oblige me by not mentioning this to anybody.

Believe me to be, my dear Sir,

Your very faithful and obliged Servant,

B. DISRAELI.

FREDERICK PLACE, *June* 1824.

MY DEAR SIR,

Until I received your note this morning I had flattered myself that my indiscretion had been forgotten. It is to me a matter of great regret that, as appears by your letter, any more trouble should be given respecting this unfortunate MS., which will, most probably, be considered too crude a production for the public, and which, if it is even imagined to possess any interest, is certainly too late for this season, and will be obsolete in the next. I think, therefore, that the sooner it be put behind the fire the better, and as you have some small experience in burning MSS., [Footnote: Byron's Memoirs had been burnt at Albemarle Street during the preceding month.] you will be perhaps so kind as to consign it to the flames. Once more apologising for all the trouble I have given you, I remain ever, my dear Sir,

Yours very faithfully,

B. DISRAELI.

Murray had a special regard for the remarkable young man, and by degrees had thoroughly taken him into his confidence; had related to him his experiences of men and affairs, and ere long began to consult him about a variety of schemes and projects. These long confidential communications led eventually to the suggestion of a much more ambitious and hazardous scheme, the establishment of a daily paper in the Conservative interest. Daring as this must appear, Murray was encouraged in it by the recollection of the success which had attended the foundation of the *Quarterly*, and believed, rashly, that his personal energy and resources, aided by the abilities displayed by his young counsellor, would lead to equal success. He evidently had too superficially weighed the enormous difficulties of this far greater undertaking, and the vast difference between the conduct of a *Quarterly Review* and a daily newspaper.

Intent upon gaining a position in the world, Benjamin Disraeli saw a prospect of advancing his own interests-by obtaining the influential position of director of a Conservative daily paper, which he fully imagined was destined to equal the *Times*, and he succeeded in imbuing Murray with the like fallacious hopes.

The emancipation of the Colonies of Spain in South America in 1824-25 gave rise to much speculation in the money market in the expectation of developing the resources of that country, especially its mines. Shares, stocks, and loans were issued to an unlimited extent.

Mr. Benjamin Disraeli seems to have thrown himself into the vortex, for he became connected with at least one financial firm in the City, that of Messrs. Powles, and employed his abilities in writing several pamphlets on the subject. This led to his inducing Messrs. Powles to embark with him in the scheme of a daily paper. At length an arrangement was entered into, by which John Murray, J.D. Powles, and Benjamin Disraeli were to become the joint proprietors of the proposed new journal. The arrangement was as follows:

MEMORANDUM.

LONDON, *August* 3, 1825.

The undersigned parties agree to establish a Morning Paper, the property in which is to be in the following proportions, viz. :

Mr. Murray.... One-half. Mr. Powles.... One-quarter. Mr. Disraeli.... One-quarter.

Each party contributing to the expense, capital, and risk, in those proportions.

The paper to be published by, and be under the management of Mr. Murray.

JOHN MURRAY.

J. D. POWLES.

B. DISRAELI.

Such was the memorandum of agreement entered into with a view to the publication of the new morning paper, eventually called the *Representative*. As the first number was to appear in January 1826, there was little time to be lost in making the necessary arrangements for its publication. In the first place, an able editor had to be found; and, perhaps of almost equal importance, an able subeditor. Trustworthy reporters had to be engaged; foreign and home correspondents had also to be selected with care; a printing office had to be taken; all the necessary plant and apparatus had to be provided, and a staff of men brought together preliminary to the opening day.

The most important point in connection with the proposed journal was to find the editor. Mr. Murray had been so ably assisted by Sir Walter Scott in the projection of the *Quarterly Review*, that he resolved to consult him on the subject; and this mission was undertaken by Benjamin Disraeli, part proprietor of the intended daily journal, though he was then only twenty years old. It was hoped that Mr. Lockhart, Sir Walter Scott's son-in-law, might be induced to undertake the editorship. The following are Mr. Disraeli's letters to Mr. Murray, giving an account of the progress of his negotiations. It will be observed that he surrounds the subject with a degree of mystery, through the names which he gives to the gentlemen whom he interviewed. Thus the Chevalier is Sir Walter Scott; M. is Mr. Lockhart; X. is Mr. Canning; O. is the political Puck (could this be himself?); and Chronometer is Mr. Barrow.

On reaching Edinburgh, Mr. Disraeli wrote to Mr. Murray the following account of his first journey across the Border:

Mr. B. Disraeli to John Murray.

ROYAL HOTEL, EDINBURGH. *September* 21, 1825.

MY DEAR SIR,

I arrived in Edinburgh yesterday night at 11 o'clock. I slept at Stamford, York, and Newcastle, and by so doing felt quite fresh at the end of my journey. I never preconceived a place better than Edinburgh. It is exactly what I fancied it, and certainly is the most beautiful town in the world. You can scarcely call it a city; at least, it has little of the roar of millions, and at this time is of course very empty. I could not enter Scotland by the route you pointed out, and therefore was unable to ascertain the fact of the Chevalier being at his Castellum. I should in that case have gone by Carlisle. I called on the gentleman to whom Wright [Footnote: A solicitor in London, and friend of both parties, who had been consulted in the negotiations.] gave me a letter this morning. He is at his country house; he will get a letter from me this morning. You see, therefore, that I have lost little time.

I called at Oliver & Boyd's this morning, thinking that you might have written. You had not, however. When you write to me, enclose to them, as they will forward, wherever I may be, and my stay at an hotel is always uncertain. Mr. Boyd was most particularly civil. Their establishment is one of the completest I have ever seen. They are booksellers, bookbinders, and printers, all under the same roof; everything but making paper. I intend to examine the whole minutely before I leave, as it may be useful. I never thought of binding. Suppose you were to sew, etc., your own publications?

I arrived at York in the midst of the Grand [Musical] Festival. It was late at night when I arrived, but the streets were crowded, and continued so for hours. I never witnessed a city in such an extreme bustle, and so delightfully gay. It was a perfect carnival. I postponed my journey from five in the morning to eleven, and by so doing got an hour for the Minster, where I witnessed a scene which must have far surpassed, by all accounts, the celebrated commemoration in Westminster Abbey. York Minster baffles all conception. Westminster Abbey is a toy to it. I think it is impossible to conceive of what Gothic architecture is susceptible until you see York. I speak with cathedrals of the Netherlands and the Rhine fresh in my memory. I witnessed in York another splendid sight—the pouring in of all the nobility and gentry of the neighbourhood and the neighbouring counties. The four-in-hands of the Yorkshire squires, the splendid rivalry in liveries and outriders, and the immense quantity of gorgeous equipages—numbers with four horses—formed a scene which you can only witness in the mighty and aristocratic county of York. It beat a Drawing Room hollow, as much as an oratorio in York Minster does a concert in the Opera House. This delightful stay at York quite refreshed me, and I am not the least fatigued by my journey.

As I have only been in Edinburgh a few hours, of course I have little to say. I shall write immediately that anything occurs. Kindest remembrances to Mrs. Murray and all.

Ever yours,

B. D.

I find Froissart a most entertaining companion, just the fellow for a traveller's evening; and just the work too, for it needs neither books of reference nor accumulations of MS.

ROYAL HOTEL, EDINBURGH, *Sunday.*

September 22, 1825.

MY DEAR SIR,

I sent a despatch by Saturday night's post, directed to Mr. Barrow. You have doubtless received it safe. As I consider you are anxious to hear minutely of the state of my operations, I again send you a few lines. I received this morning a very polite letter from L[ockhart]. He had just received that morning (Saturday) Wright's letter. I enclose you a copy of L. 's letter, as it will be interesting to you to see or judge what effect was produced on his mind by its perusal. I have written to-day to say that I will call at Chiefswood [Footnote: Chiefswood, where Lockhart then lived, is about two miles distant from Abbotsford. Sir Walter Scott describes it as "a nice little cottage, in a glen belonging to this property, with a rivulet in front, and a grove of trees on the east side to keep away the cold wind. "] on Tuesday. I intend to go to Melrose tomorrow, but as I will not take the chance of meeting him the least tired, I shall sleep at Melrose and call on the following morning. I shall, of course, accept his offer of staying there. I shall call again at B[oyd]'s before my departure to-morrow, to see if there is any despatch from you.... I shall continue to give you advice of all my movements. You will agree with me that I have at least not lost any time, but that all things have gone very well as yet. There is of course no danger in our communications of anything unfairly transpiring; but from the very delicate nature of names interested, it will be expedient to adopt some cloak.

The Chevalier will speak for itself.

M., from Melrose, for Mr. L.

X. for a certain personage on whom we called one day, who lives a slight distance from town, and who was then unwell.

O. for the political Puck.

MR. CHRONOMETER will speak for itself, at least to all those who give African dinners.

I think this necessary, and try to remember it. I am quite delighted with Edinburgh, Its beauties become every moment more apparent.

The view from the Calton Hill finds me a frequent votary. In the present state of affairs, I suppose it will not be expedient to leave the letter for Mrs. Bruce. It will seem odd; p. p.c. at the same moment I bring a letter of introduction. If I return to Edinburgh, I can avail myself of it. If the letter contains anything which would otherwise make Mrs. Murray wish it to be left, let me know. I revel in the various beauties of a Scotch breakfast. Cold grouse and marmalade find me, however, constant.

Ever yours,

B. D.

The letter of Mr. Lockhart, to which Mr. Disraeli refers, ran as follows:

Mr. J.G. Lockhart to Mr. B. Disraeli.

"The business to which the letter [of Mr. Wright] refers entitles it to much consideration. As yet I have had no leisure nor means to form even an approximation towards any opinion as to the proposal Mr. W. mentions, far less to commit my friend. In a word, I am perfectly in the dark as to everything else, except that I am sure it will give Mrs. Lockhart and myself very great pleasure to see Mr. Disraeli under this roof.... If you had no other object in view, I flatter myself that this neighbourhood has, in Melrose and Abbotsford, some attractions not unworthy of your notice. "

Mr. Disraeli paid his promised visit to Chiefswood. It appeared that Mr. Lockhart expected to receive Mr. Isaac D'Israeli, the well-known author of "The Curiosities of Literature"; instead of which, the person who appeared before him was Mr. D'Israeli's then unknown son Benjamin.

Mr. B, Disraeli to John Murray.

CHIEFSWOOD, *September* 25, 1825.

MY DEAR SIR,

I arrived at Chiefswood yesterday. M. [Lockhart] had conceived that it was my father who was coming. He was led to believe this through Wright's letter. In addition, therefore, to his natural reserve, there was, of course, an evident disappointment at seeing me. Everything looked as black as possible. I shall not detain you now by informing you of fresh particulars. I leave them for when we meet. Suffice it to say that in a few hours we completely understood each other, and were upon the most intimate terms. M. enters into our views with a facility and readiness which were capital. He thinks that nothing can be more magnificent or excellent; but two points immediately occurred: First, the difficulty of his leaving Edinburgh without any ostensible purpose; and, secondly, the losing caste in society by so doing. He is fully aware that he may end by making his situation as important as any in the empire, but the primary difficulty is insurmountable.

As regards his interest, I mentioned that he should be guaranteed, for three years, £1,000 per annum, and should take an eighth of every paper which was established, without risk, his income ceasing on his so doing. These are much better terms than we had imagined we could have made. The agreement is thought extremely handsome, both by him and the Chevalier; but the income is not imagined to be too large. However, I dropped that point, as it should be arranged with you when we all meet.

The Chevalier breakfasted here to-day, and afterwards we were all three closeted together. The Chevalier entered into it excellently. He thought, however, that we could not depend upon Malcolm, Barrow, etc., *keeping to it*; but this I do not fear. He, of course, has no idea of your influence or connections. With regard to the delicate point I mentioned, the Chevalier is willing to make any sacrifice in his personal comforts for Lockhart's advancement; but he feels that his son-in-law will "lose caste" by going to town without anything ostensible. He agrees with me that M. cannot accept an official situation of any kind, as it would compromise his independence, but he thinks *Parliament for M. indispensable*, and also very much to *our interest*. I dine at Abbotsford to-day, and we shall most probably again discuss matters.

Now, these are the points which occur to me. When M. comes to town, it will be most important that it should be distinctly proved to him that he *will* be supported by the great interests I have mentioned to him. He must see that, through Powles, all America and the Commercial Interest is at our beck; that Wilmot H., etc., not as mere under-secretary, but as our private friend, is most staunch; that the Chevalier is firm; that the West India Interest will pledge themselves that such men and in such situations as Barrow, etc., etc., are *distinctly in our power*; and finally, that he is coming to London, not to be an Editor of a Newspaper, but the Director-General of an immense organ, and at the head of a band of high-bred gentlemen and important interests.

The Chevalier and M. have unburthened themselves to me in a manner the *most confidential* that you can possibly conceive. Of M. 's capability, *perfect complete capability*, there is no manner of doubt. Of his sound principles, and of his real views in life, I could in a moment satisfy you. Rest assured, however, that you are dealing with a *perfect gentleman*. There has been no disguise to me of what has been done, and the Chevalier had a private conversation with me on the subject, of a nature *the most satisfactory*. With regard to other plans of ours, if we could get him up, we should find him invaluable. I have a most singular and secret history on this subject when we meet.

Now, on the grand point—Parliament. M. cannot be a representative of a Government borough. It is impossible. He must be free as air. I am sure that if this could be arranged, all would be settled; but it is *"indispensable, "* without you can suggest anything else. M. was two days in company with X. this summer, as well as X. 's and our friend, but nothing transpired of our views. This is a most favourable time to make a parliamentary arrangement. What do you think of making a confidant of Wilmot H[orton]? He is the kind of man who would be right pleased by such conduct. There is no harm of Lockhart's coming in for a Tory borough, because he is a Tory; but a Ministerial borough is impossible to be managed.

If this point could be arranged, I have no doubt that I shall be able to organise, in the interest with which I am now engaged, a most *immense party*, and a *most serviceable one*. Be so kind as not to leave the vicinity of London, in case M. and myself come up *suddenly*; but I pray you, if you have any real desire to establish a mighty engine, to exert yourself at this present moment, and assist me to your very utmost. Write as soon as possible, to give me some idea of your movements, and direct to me here, as I shall then be sure to obtain your communication. The Chevalier and all here have the highest idea of Wright's *nous*, and think it most important that he should be at the head of the legal department. I write this despatch in the most extreme haste.

Ever yours,

B. D.

On receiving the above letter and the previous communications, Mr. Murray sent them to Mr. Isaac D'Israeli for his perusal.

Mr. Isaac D'Israeli to Mr. Murray.

HYDE HOUSE, AMERSHAM,

September 29, 1825.

MY DEAR FRIEND,

How deeply I feel obliged and gratified by your confidential communication! I read repeatedly the third letter of our young plenipotentiary. I know nothing against him but his youth—a fault which a few seasons of experience will infallibly correct; but I have observed that the habits and experience he has acquired as a lawyer often greatly serve him in matters o£ business. His views are vast, but they are baaed on good sense, and he is most determinedly serious when he sets to work. The Chevalier and M. seem to have received him with all the open confidence of men struck by a stranger, yet a stranger not wholly strange, and known enough to them to deserve their confidence if he could inspire it. I flatter myself he has fully—he must, if he has really had confidential intercourse with the Chevalier, and so confidently impresses you with so high and favourable a character of M. On your side, my dear Murray, no ordinary exertions will avail. You, too, have faith and confidence to inspire in them. You observe how the wary Northern Genius attempted to probe whether certain friends of yours would stand together; no doubt they wish to ascertain that point. Pardon me if I add, that in satisfying their cautious and anxious inquiries as to your influence with these persons, it may be wise to throw a little shade of mystery, and not to tell everything too openly at first; because, when objects are clearly defined, they do not affect our imaginations as when they are somewhat concealed.... Vast as the project seems, held up as it will be by personages of wealth, interests, politics, etc., whenever it is once set up, I should have no fears for the results, which are indeed the most important that one can well conceive.... Had the editor of "Paul Jones" consulted me a little, I could probably have furnished him with the account of the miserable end of his hero; and I am astonished it is not found, as you tell me, in your American biography. [Footnote: The last paragraph in Mr. D'Israeli's letter refers to "The Life of Paul Jones, " which has been already mentioned. As the novel "Aylmer Papillon, " written in 1824, was never published, the preface to "Paul Jones" was Benjamin's first appearance as an author.]

Meanwhile, young Disraeli still remained with Mr. Lockhart at Chiefswood.

Mr. B, Disraeli to John Murray.

September, 1825.

MY DEAR SIR,

I am quite sure, that upon the business I am upon now every line will be acceptable, and I therefore make no apology for this hurried despatch. I have just received a parcel from Oliver & Boyd. I transmitted a letter from M. to Wright, and which [Footnote: This is an ungrammatical construction which Lord Beaconsfield to the end of his days never abandoned. *Vide* letter on p. 318 and Lothair *passim*. —T. M.] was for your mutual consideration, to you, *viá Chronometer*, last Friday. I afterwards received a note from you, dated Chichester, and fearing from that circumstance that some confusion would arise, I wrote a few lines to you at Mr. Holland's. [Footnote: The Rev. W. Holland, Mr. Murray's brother-in-law, was a minor canon of Chichester.] I now find that you will be in town on Monday, on which day I rather imagine the said letter from M. to Wright will arrive. I therefore trust that the suspected confusion will not arise.

I am very much obliged to you for your letters; but I am very sorry that you have incurred any trouble, when it is most probable that I shall not use them. The Abbotsford and Chiefswood families have placed me on such a friendly and familiar footing, that it is utterly impossible for me to leave them while there exists any chance of M. 's going to England. M. has introduced me to most of the neighbouring gentry, and receives with a loud laugh any mention of my return to Edinburgh. I dined with Dr. Brewster the other day. He has a pretty place near Melrose. It is impossible for me to give to you any written idea of the beauty and unique character of Abbotsford. *Adio!*

B. D.

Mr. Murray continued to transmit the correspondence to Mr. Isaac D'Israeli, whose delight may be conceived from the following:

Mr. D'Israeli to John Murray.

October 9, 1825.

MY DEAR FRIEND,

Thanks! My warmest ones are poor returns for the ardent note you have so affectionately conveyed to me by him on whom we now both alike rest our hopes and our confidence. The more I think of this whole affair, from its obscure beginnings, the more I am quite overcome by what he has already achieved; never did the finest season of blossoms promise a richer gathering. But he has not the sole merit, for you share it with him, in the grand view you take of the capability of this new intellectual steam engine.

In the following letter Lockhart definitely declined the editorship of the *Representative*.

Mr. Lockhart to John Murray.

October 7, 1825.

"I am afraid, that in spite of my earnest desire to be clear and explicit, you have not after all fully understood the inexpressible feeling I entertain in regard to the *impossibility* of my ever entering into the career of London in the capacity of a newspaper editor. I confess that you, who have adorned and raised your own profession so highly, may feel inclined, and justly perhaps, to smile at some of my scruples; but it is enough to say that every hour that has elapsed since the idea was first started has only served to deepen and confirm the feeling with which I at the first moment regarded it; and, in short, that if such a game *ought* to be played, I am neither young nor poor enough to be the man that takes the hazard. "

Sir Walter Scott also expressed his views on the subject as follows:

Sir W. Scott to John Murray.

ABBOTSFORD, *Sunday,*

MY DEAR SIR,

Lockhart seems to wish that I would express my opinion of the plan which you have had the kindness to submit to him, and I am myself glad of an opportunity to express my sincere thanks for the great confidence you are willing to repose in one so near to me, and whom I value so highly. There is nothing in life that can be more interesting to me than his prosperity, and should there eventually appear a serious prospect of his bettering his fortunes by quitting Scotland, I have too much regard for him to desire him to remain, notwithstanding all the happiness I must lose by his absence and that of my daughter. The present state, however, of the negotiation leaves me little or no reason to think that I will be subjected to this deprivation, for I cannot conceive it advisable that he should leave Scotland on the speculation of becoming editor of a newspaper. It is very true that this department of literature may and ought to be rendered more respectable than it is at present, but I think this is a reformation more to be wished than hoped for, and should think it rash for any young man, of whatever talent, to sacrifice, nominally at least, a considerable portion of his respectability in society in hopes of being submitted as an exception to a rule which is at present pretty general. This might open the door to love of money, but it would effectually shut it against ambition.

To leave Scotland, Lockhart must make very great sacrifices, for his views here, though moderate, are certain, his situation in public estimation and in private society is as high as that of any one at our Bar, and his road to the public open, if he chooses to assist his income by literary resources. But of the extent and value of these sacrifices he must himself be a judge, and a more unprejudiced one, probably, than I am.

I am very glad he meets your wishes by going up to town, as this, though it should bear no further consequences, cannot but serve to show a grateful sense of the confidence and kindness of the parties concerned, and yours in particular.

I beg kind compliments to Mr. D'Israeli, and am, dear sir, with best wishes for the success of your great national plan.

Yours very truly,

WALTER SCOTT.

Although Mr. Lockhart hung back from the proposed editorship, he nevertheless carried out his intention of visiting Mr. Murray in London a few weeks after the date of the above letter. Mr. J.T. Coleridge had expressed his desire to resign the editorship of the *Quarterly*, in consequence of his rapidly increasing practice on the western circuit, and Mr. Lockhart was sounded as to his willingness to become his successor. Mr. Murray entertained the hope that he might be able to give a portion of his time to rendering some assistance in the management of the proposed newspaper. As Sir Walter Scott had been taken into their counsels, through the medium of Mr. Disraeli, Mr. Murray proceeded to correspond with him on the subject. From the draft of one of Mr. Murray's letters we extract the following:

John Murray to Sir Walter Scott.

October 13, 1825.

MY DEAR SIR WALTER,

I feel greatly obliged by the favour of your kind letter, and for the good opinion which you are disposed to entertain of certain plans, of which you will by degrees be enabled to form, I hope, a still more satisfactory estimate. At present, I will take the liberty of assuring you, that after your confidence in me, I will neither propose nor think of anything respecting Mr. Lockhart that has not clearly for its basis the honour of his family. With regard to our Great Plan—which really ought not to be designated a newspaper, as that department of literature has hitherto been conducted—Mr. Lockhart was never intended to have anything to do as editor: for we have already secured two most efficient and respectable persons to fill that department. I merely wished to receive his general advice and assistance. And Mr. Lockhart would only be known or suspected to be the author of certain papers of grave national importance. The more we have thought and talked over our plans, the more certain are we of their inevitable success, and of their leading us to certain power, reputation, and fortune. For myself, the heyday of my youth is passed, though I may be allowed certain experience in my profession. I have acquired a moderate fortune, and have a certain character, and move now in the first circles of society; and I have a family: these, I hope, may be some fair pledge to you that I would not engage in this venture with any hazard, when all that is dearest to man would be my loss.

In order, however, to completely obviate any difficulties which have been urged, I have proposed to Mr. Lockhart to come to London as the editor of the *Quarterly*—an appointment which, I verily believe, is coveted by many of the highest literary characters in the country, and which, of itself, would entitle its possessor to enter into and mix with the first classes of society. For this, and without writing a line, but merely for performing the duties of an editor, I shall have the pleasure of allowing him a thousand pounds a year; and this, with contributions of his own, might easily become £1,500, and take no serious portion of his time either. Then, for his connection with the paper, he will become permanently interested in a share we can guarantee to him for three years, and which, I am confident, will be worth, at the end of that period, at least £3,000; and the profits from that share will not be less than £1,500 per annum. I have lately heard, from good authority, that the annual profit of the *Times* is £40,000, and that a share in the *Courier* sold last week (wretchedly conducted, it seems) at the rate of £100,000 for the property.

But this is not all. You know well enough that the business of a publishing bookseller is not in his shop or even his connection, but in his brains; and we can put forward together a series of valuable literary works, and without, observe me, in any of these plans, the slightest risk to Mr. Lockhart. And I do most solemnly assure you that if I may take any credit to myself for possessing anything like sound judgment in my profession, the things which we shall immediately begin upon, as Mr. Lockhart will explain to you, are as perfectly certain of commanding a great sale as anything I ever had the good fortune to engage in.

Lockhart finally accepted the editorship of the *Quarterly*, after negotiations which brought Mr. Disraeli on a second visit to Scotland, but he undertook no formal responsibility for the new daily paper.

In London Disraeli was indefatigable. He visited City men, for the purpose of obtaining articles on commercial subjects. He employed an architect, Mr. G. Basevi, jun., his cousin, with a view to the planning of offices and printing premises. A large house was eventually taken in Great George Street, Westminster, and duly fitted up as a printing office.

He then proceeded, in common with Mr. Murray, to make arrangements for the foreign correspondence. In the summer of 1824—before the new enterprise was thought of—he had travelled in the Rhine country, and made some pleasant acquaintances, of whom he now bethought himself when making arrangements for the new paper. One of them was Mr. Maas, of the Trierscher Hof, Coblentz, and Mr. Disraeli addressed him as follows:

Mr. B. Disraeli to Mr. Maas.

October 25, 1825.

DEAR SIR,

Your hospitality, which I have twice enjoyed, convinces me that you will not consider this as an intrusion. My friend, Mr. Murray, of Albemarle Street, London, the most eminent publisher that we have, is about to establish a daily journal of the first importance. With his great influence and connections, there is no doubt that he will succeed in his endeavour to make it the focus of the information of the whole world. Among other places at which he wishes to have correspondents is the Rhine, and he has applied to me for my advice upon this point. It has struck me that Coblentz is a very good situation for intelligence. Its proximity to the Rhine and the Moselle, its contiguity to the beautiful baths of the Taunus, and the innumerable travellers who pass through it, and spread everywhere the fame of your admirable hotel, all conduce to make it a place from which much interesting intelligence might be procured.

The most celebrated men in Europe have promised their assistance to Mr. Murray in his great project. I wish to know whether you can point out any one to him who will occasionally write him a letter from your city. Intelligence as to the company at Wiesbaden and Ems, and of the persons of eminence, particularly English, who pass through Coblentz, of the travellers down the Rhine, and such topics, are very interesting to us. You yourself would make a most admirable correspondent. The labour would be very light and very agreeable; and Mr. Murray would take care to acknowledge your kindness by various courtesies. If you object to say anything about politics you can omit mentioning the subject. I wish you would undertake it, as I am sure you would write most agreeable letters. Once a month would be sufficient, or rather write whenever you have anything that you think interesting. Will you be so kind as to write me in answer what you think of this proposal? The communication may be carried on in any language you please.

Last year when I was at Coblentz you were kind enough to show me a very pretty collection of ancient glass. Pray is it yet to be purchased? I think I know an English gentleman who would be happy to possess it. I hope this will not be the last letter which passes between us.

I am, dear Sir,

Yours most truly,

B. DISRAELI.

Mr. Maas agreed to Mr. Disraeli's proposal, and his letter was handed to Mr. Murray, who gave him further instructions as to the foreign correspondence which he required. Mr. Murray himself wrote to correspondents at Hamburg, Maestricht, Genoa, Trieste, Gibraltar, and other places, with the same object.

The time for the publication of the newspaper was rapidly approaching, and Mr. B. Disraeli's correspondence on the subject of the engagement of a staff became fast and furious.

By the end of December Mr. Lockhart had arrived in London, for the purpose of commencing his editorship of the *Quarterly Review*. The name of the new morning paper had not then been yet fixed on; from the correspondence respecting it, we find that some spoke of it as the *Daily Review*, others as the *Morning News*, and so on; but that Mr. Benjamin Disraeli settled the matter appears from the following letter of Mr. Lockhart to Mr. Murray:

Mr. Lockhart to John Murray.

December 21, 1825.

MY DEAR SIR,

I am delighted, and, what is more, satisfied with Disraeli's title—the *Representative*. If Mr. Powles does not produce some thundering objection, let this be fixed, in God's name.

Strange to say, from this time forward nothing more is heard of Mr. Benjamin Disraeli in connection with the *Representative*. After his two Journeys to Scotland, his interviews with Sir Walter Scott and Mr. Lockhart, his activity in making arrangements previous to the starting of the daily paper, his communications with the architect as to the purchase and fitting up of the premises in Great George Street, and with the solicitors as to the proposed deed of partnership, he suddenly drops out of sight; and nothing more is heard of him in connection with the business.

It would appear that when the time arrived for the proprietors of the new paper to provide the necessary capital under the terms of the memorandum of agreement dated August 3, 1825, both Mr. Disraeli and Mr. Powles failed to contribute their several proportions. Mr. Murray had indeed already spent a considerable sum, and entered into agreements for the purchase of printing-offices, printing-machines, types, and all the paraphernalia of a newspaper establishment. He had engaged reporters, correspondents, printers, sub-editors, though he still wanted an efficient editor. He was greatly disappointed at not being able to obtain the services of Mr. Lockhart. Mr. Disraeli was too young—being then only twenty-one, and entirely inexperienced in the work of conducting a daily paper—to be entrusted with the editorship. Indeed, it is doubtful whether he ever contemplated occupying that position, though he had engaged himself most sedulously in the preliminary arrangements in one department, his endeavours to obtain the assistance of men of commerce in the City; however, he was by no means successful. Nevertheless, Mr. Murray was so far committed that he felt bound to go on with the enterprise, and he advertised the publication of the new morning paper. Some of his friends congratulated him on the announcement, trusting that they might see on their breakfast-table a paper which their wives and daughters might read without a blush.

The first number of the *Representative* accordingly appeared on January 25, 1826, price 7*d.* ; the Stamp Tax was then 4*d*. In politics it was a supporter of Lord Liverpool's Government; but public distress, the currency, trade and commerce were subjects of independent comment.

Notwithstanding the pains which had been taken, and the money which had been spent, the *Representative* was a failure from the beginning. It was badly organized, badly edited, and its contents— leading articles, home and foreign news—were ill-balanced. Failing Lockhart, an editor, named Tyndale, had been appointed on short notice, though he was an obscure and uninfluential person. He soon disappeared in favour of others, who were no better. Dr. Maginn [Footnote: Dr. Maginn's papers in *Blackwood* are or should be known to the reader. The Murray correspondence contains many characteristic letters from this jovial and impecunious Irishman. He is generally supposed to have been the prototype of Thackeray's Captain Shandon. —T. M.] had been engaged—the Morgan O'Doherty of *Blackwood's Magazine*—wit, scholar, and Bohemian. He was sent to Paris, where he evidently enjoyed himself; but the results, as regarded the *Representative*, were by no means satisfactory. He was better at borrowing money than at writing articles.

Mr. S.C. Hall, one of the parliamentary reporters of the paper, says, in his "Retrospect of a Long Life, " that:

"The day preceding the issue of the first number, Mr. Murray might have obtained a very large sum for a shore of the copyright, of which he was the sole proprietor; the day after that issue, the copyright was worth comparatively nothing.... Editor there was literally none, from the beginning to the end. The first number supplied conclusive evidence of the utter ignorance of editorial tact on the part of the person entrusted with the duty.... In short, the work was badly done; if not a snare, it was a delusion; and the reputation of the new journal fell below zero in twenty-four hours. " [Footnote: "Retrospect of a Long Life, from 1815 to 1883. " By S. C. Hall, F.S. A., i. p. 126.]

An inspection of the file of the *Representative* justifies Mr. Hall's remarks. The first number contained an article by Lockhart, four columns in length, on the affairs of Europe. It was correct and scholar-like, but tame and colourless. Incorrectness in a leading article may be tolerated, but dulness amounts to a literary crime. The foreign correspondence consisted of a letter from Valetta, and a communication from Paris, more than a column in length, relating to French opera. In the matter of news, for which the dailies are principally purchased, the first number was exceedingly defective. It is hard to judge of the merits of a new journal from the first number, which must necessarily labour under many disadvantages, but the *Representative* did not from the first exhibit any element of success.

Mr. Murray found his new enterprise an increasing source of annoyance and worry. His health broke down under the strain, and when he was confined to his bed by illness things went worse from day to day. The usual publishing business was neglected; letters remained unanswered, manuscripts remained unread, and some correspondents became excessively angry at their communications being neglected.

Mr. Murray's worries were increased by the commercial crisis then prevailing, and by the downfall of many large publishing houses. It was feared that Mr. Murray might be implicated in the failures. At the end of January, the great firm of Archibald Constable & Co., of Edinburgh publishers of Sir Walter Scott's novels, was declared bankrupt; shortly after, the failure was announced of James Ballantyne & Co., in which Sir Walter Scott was a partner; and with these houses, that of Hurst, Kobinson & Co., of London, was hopelessly involved. The market was flooded with the dishonoured paper of all these concerns, and mercantile confidence in the great publishing houses was almost at an end. We find Washington Irving communicating the following intelligence to A. H. Everett, United States Minister at Madrid (January 31, 1826):

"You will perceive by the papers the failure of Constable & Co., at Edinburgh, and Hurst, Robinson & Co., at London. These are severe shocks in the trading world of literature. Pray Heaven, Murray may stand unmoved, and not go into the *Gazette*, instead of publishing one! "

Mr. Murray held his ground. He was not only able to pay his way, but to assist some of the best-known London publishers through the pressure of their difficulties. One of these was Mr. Robert Baldwin, of Paternoster Row, who expressed his repeated obligations to Mr. Murray for his help in time of need. The events of this crisis clearly demonstrated the wisdom and foresight of Murray in breaking loose from the Ballantyne and Constable connection, in spite of the promising advantages which it had offered him.

Murray still went on with the *Representative*, though the result was increasing annoyance and vexation. Mr. Milman wrote to him, "Do get a new editor for the lighter part of your paper, and look well to the *Quarterly*. " The advice was taken, and Dr. Maginn was brought over from Paris to take charge of the lighter part of the paper at a salary of £700 a year, with a house. The result was, that a number of clever *jeux d'esprit* were inserted by him, but these were intermingled with some biting articles, which gave considerable offence.

At length the strain became more than he could bear, and he sought the first opportunity for stopping the further publication of the paper. This occurred at the end of the general election, and the *Representative* ceased to exist on July 29, 1826, after a career of only six months, during which brief period it had involved Mr. Murray in a loss of not less than £26,000. [Footnote: The *Representative* was afterwards incorporated with the *New Times*, another unfortunate paper.]

Mr. Murray bore his loss with much equanimity, and found it an inexpressible relief to be rid of the *Representative* even at such a sacrifice. To Washington Irving he wrote:

John Murray to Mr. Irving.

"One cause of my not writing to you during one whole year was my 'entanglement, ' as Lady G— — says, with a newspaper, which absorbed my money, and distracted and depressed my mind; but I have cut the knot of evil, which I could not untie, and am now, by the blessing of God, again returned to reason and the shop. "

One of the unfortunate results of the initiation and publication of the *Representative* was that it disturbed the friendship which had so long existed between Mr. Murray and Mr. Isaac D'Israeli. The real cause of Benjamin's sudden dissociation from an enterprise of which in its earlier stages he had been the moving spirit, can only be matter of conjecture. The only mention of his name in the later correspondence regarding the newspaper occurs in the following letter:

Mr. Lockhart to John Murray.

THURSDAY, *February* 14, 1826.

I think Mr. B. Disraeli ought to tell you what it is that he wishes to say to Mr. Croker on a business *of yours* ere he asks of you a letter to the Secretary. If there really be something worth saying, I certainly know nobody that would say it better, but I confess I think, all things considered, you have no need of anybody to come between you and Mr. Croker. What can it be?

Yours,

J. G.L.

But after the *Representative*, had ceased to be published, the elder D'Israeli thought he had a cause of quarrel with Mr. Murray, and proposed to publish a pamphlet on the subject. The matter was brought under the notice of Mr. Sharon Turner, the historian and solicitor, and the friend of both. Mr. Turner strongly advised Mr. Isaac D'Israeli to abstain from issuing any such publication.

Mr. Sharon Turner to Mr. D'Israeli.

October 6, 1826.

"Fame is pleasant, if it arise from what will give credit or do good. But to make oneself notorious only to be the football of all the dinner-tables, tea-tables, and gossiping visits of the country, will be so great a weakness, that until I see you actually committing yourself to it, I shall not believe that you, at an age like my own, can wilfully and deliberately do anything that will bring the evil on you. Therefore I earnestly advise that whatever has passed be left as it is.... If you give it any further publicity, you will, I think, cast a shade over a name that at present stands quite fair before the public eye. And nothing can dim it to you that will not injure all who belong to you. Therefore, as I have said to Murray, I say to you: Let Oblivion absorb the whole question as soon as possible, and do not stir a step to rescue it from her salutary power.... If I did not gee your words before me, I could not have supposed that after your experience of these things and of the world, you could deliberately intend to write—that is, to publish in print—anything on the differences between you, Murray, and the *Representative*, and your son.... If you do, Murray will be driven to answer. To him the worst that can befall will be the public smile that he could have embarked in a speculation that has cost him many thousand pounds, and a criticism on what led to it.... The public know it, and talk as they please about it, but in a short time will say no more upon it. It is now dying away. Very few at present know that you were in any way concerned about it. To you, therefore, all that results will be new matter for the public discussion and censure. And, after reading Benjamin's agreement of the 3rd August, 1825, and your letters to Murray on him and the business, of the 27th September, the 29th September, and the 9th October, my sincere opinion is that you cannot, with a due regard to your own reputation, *write* or *publish* anything about it. I send you hastily my immediate thoughts, that he whom I have always respected may not, by publishing what will be immediately contradicted, diminish or destroy in others that respect which at present he possesses, and which I hope he will continue to enjoy. "

Mr. D'Israeli did not write his proposed pamphlet. What Mr. Murray thought of his intention may be inferred from the following extract from his letter to Mr. Sharon Turner:

John Murray to Mr. Sharon Turner.

October 16, 1826.

"Mr. D'Israeli is totally wrong in supposing that my indignation against his son arises in the smallest degree from the sum which I have lost by yielding to that son's unrelenting excitement and importunity; this loss, whilst it was in weekly operation, may be supposed, and naturally enough, to have been sufficiently painful, [Footnote: See note at the end of the chapter.] but now that it has ceased, I solemnly declare that I neither care nor think about it, more than one does of the long-suffered agonies of an aching tooth the day after we have summoned resolution enough to have it extracted. On the contrary, I am disposed to consider this apparent misfortune as one of that chastening class which, if suffered wisely, may be productive of greater good, and I feel confidently that, as it has re-kindled my ancient ardour in business, a very few months will enable me to replace this temporary loss, and make me infinitely the gainer, if I profit by the prudential lesson which this whole affair is calculated to teach.... From me his son had received nothing but the most unbounded confidence and parental attachment; my fault was in having loved, not wisely, but too well. "

To conclude the story, as far as Mr. Disraeli was concerned, we may print here a letter written some time later. Mr. Powles had availed himself of Disraeli's literary skill to recommend his mining speculations to the public. In March 1825, Mr. Murray had published, on commission, "American Mining Companies, " and the same year "Present State of Mexico, " and "Lawyers and

Legislators," all of them written by, or under the superintendence of, Mr. Disraeli. Mr. Powles, however, again proved faithless, and although the money for the printing had been due for some time, he paid nothing; and at length Mr. Disraeli addressed Mr. Murray in the following letter:

Mr. Benjamin Disraeli to John Murray.

6 BLOOMSBURY SQUARE, *March* 19, 1827.

SIR,

I beg to enclose you the sum of one hundred and fifty pounds, which I believe to be the amount due to you for certain pamphlets published respecting the American Mining Companies, as stated in accounts sent in some time since. I have never been able to obtain a settlement of these accounts from the parties originally responsible, and it has hitherto been quite out of my power to exempt myself from the liability, which, I have ever been conscious, on their incompetency, resulted from the peculiar circumstances of the case to myself. In now enclosing you what I consider to be the amount, I beg also to state that I have fixed upon it from memory, having been unsuccessful in my endeavours to obtain even a return of the accounts from the original parties, and being unwilling to trouble you again for a second set of accounts, which had been so long and so improperly kept unsettled. In the event, therefore, of there being any mistake, I will be obliged by your clerk instantly informing me of it, and it will be as instantly rectified; and I will also thank you to enclose me a receipt, in order to substantiate my claims and enforce my demands against the parties originally responsible. I have to express my sense of your courtesy in this business, and

I am, sir, yours truly,

BENJAMIN DISRAELI.

Fortunately, the misunderstanding between the two old friends did not last long, for towards the end of the year we find Mr. Isaac D'Israeli communicating with Mr. Murray respecting Wool's "Life of Joseph Warton, " and certain selected letters by Warton which he thought worthy of republication; and with respect to his son, Mr. Benjamin Disraeli, although he published his first work, "Vivian Grey, " through Colburn, he returned to Albemarle Street a few years later, and published his "Contarini Fleming" through Mr. Murray.

NOTE. —It appears from the correspondence that Mr. Murray had been led by the "unrelenting excitement and importunity" of his young friend to make some joint speculation in South American mines. The same financial crisis which prevented Mr. Powles from fulfilling his obligations probably swept away all chance of profit from this investment. The financial loss involved in the failure of the *Representative* was more serious, but Mr. Murray's resentment against young Mr. Disraeli was not due to any such considerations. Justly or unjustly he felt bitterly aggrieved at certain personalities which, he thought, were to be detected in "Vivian Grey. " Mr. Disraeli was also suspected of being concerned in an ephemeral publication called *The Star Chamber*, to which he undoubtedly contributed certain articles, and in which paragraphs appeared giving offence in Albemarle Street. The story of Vivian Grey (as it appeared in the first edition) is transposed from the literary to the political key. It is undoubtedly autobiographical, but the identification of Mr. Murray with the Marquis of Carabas must seem very far-fetched. It is, at all times, difficult to say within what limits the novelist is entitled to resort to portraiture in order to build up the fabric of his romance. Intention of offence was vehemently denied by the D'Israeli family, which, as the correspondence shows, rushed with one accord to the defence of the future Lord Beaconsfield. It was really a storm in a teacup, and but for the future eminence of one of the friends concerned would call for no remark. Mr. Disraeli's bitter disappointment at the failure of his great journalistic combination sharpened the keen edge of his wit and perhaps magnified the irksomeness of the restraint which his older fellow-adventurer tried to put on his "unrelenting excitement, " and it is possible that his feelings found vent in the novel which he then was composing. It is pleasing to remark that at a later date his confidence and esteem for his father's old friend returned to him, and that the incident ended in a way honourable to all concerned. —T. M.

CHAPTER XXV

MR. LOCKHART AS EDITOR OF THE "QUARTERLY"—
HALLAM—WORDSWORTH—DEATH OF CONSTABLE

The appointment of a new editor naturally excited much interest among the contributors and supporters of the *Quarterly Review*. Comments were made, and drew from Scott the following letter:

Sir Walter Scott to John Murray.

ABBOTSFORD, *November* 17, 1825.

My Dear Sir,

I was much surprised to-day to learn from Lockhart by letter that some scruples were in circulation among some of the respectable among the supporters of the *Quarterly Review* concerning his capacity to undertake that highly responsible task. In most cases I might not be considered as a disinterested witness on behalf of so near a connection, but in the present instance I have some claim to call myself so. The plan (I need not remind you) of calling Lockhart to this distinguished situation, far from being favoured by me, or in any respect advanced or furthered by such interest as I might have urged, was not communicated to me until it was formed; and as it involved the removal of my daughter and of her husband, who has always loved and honoured me as a son, from their native country and from my vicinity, my private wish and that of all the members of my family was that such a change should not take place. But the advantages proposed were so considerable, that it removed all title on my part to state my own strong desire that he should remain in Scotland. Now I do assure you that if in these circumstances I had seen anything in Lockhart's habits, cast of mind, or mode of thinking or composition which made him unfit for the duty he had to undertake, I should have been the last man in the world to permit, without the strongest expostulation not with him alone but with you, his exchanging an easy and increasing income in his own country and amongst his own friends for a larger income perhaps, but a highly responsible situation in London. I considered this matter very attentively, and recalled to my recollection all I had known of Mr. Lockhart both before and since his connection with my family. I have no hesitation in saying that when he was paying his addresses in my family I fairly stated to him that however I might be pleased with his general talents and accomplishments, with his family, which is highly respectable, and his views in life, which I thought satisfactory, I did decidedly object to the use he and others had made of their wit and satirical talent in *Blackwood's Magazine*, which, though a work of considerable power, I thought too personal to be in good taste or to be quite respectable. Mr. Lockhart then pledged his word to me that he would withdraw from this species of warfare, and I have every reason to believe that he has kept his word with me. In particular I *know* that he had not the least concern with the *Beacon* newspaper, though strongly urged by his young friends at the Bar, and I also know that while he has sometimes contributed an essay to *Blackwood* on general literature, or politics, which can be referred to if necessary, he has no connection whatever with the satirical part of the work or with its general management, nor was he at any time the Editor of the publication.

It seems extremely hard (though not perhaps to be wondered at) that the follies of three—or four and twenty should be remembered against a man of thirty, who has abstained during the interval from giving the least cause of offence. There are few men of any rank in letters who have not at some time or other been guilty of some abuse of their satirical powers, and very few who have not seen reason to wish that they had restrained their vein of pleasantry. Thinking over Lockhart's offences with my own, and other men's whom either politics or literary controversy has led into such effusions, I cannot help thinking that five years' proscription ought to obtain a full immunity on their account. There were none of them which could be ascribed to any worse motive than a wicked wit, and many of the individuals against whom they were directed were worthy of more severe chastisement. The blame was in meddling with such men at all. Lockhart is reckoned an excellent scholar, and Oxford has said so. He is born a gentleman, has always kept the best society, and his personal character is without a shadow of blame. In the most unfortunate affair of his life he did all that man could do, and the unhappy tragedy was the result of the poor sufferer's after-thought to get out of a scrape. [Footnote: This refers, without doubt, to the unfortunate death of John Scott, the editor of the *London Magazine*, in a duel with Lockhart's friend Christie, the result of a quarrel in which Lockhart himself had been concerned.] Of his general talents I will not presume to speak, but they are generally allowed to be of the first order. This, however, I *will* say, that I have known the most able men of my time, and I never met any one who had such ready command of his own mind, or possessed in a greater degree the power of making his talents available upon the shortest notice, and upon any subject. He is also remarkably docile and willing to receive advice or admonition from the old and experienced. He is a fond husband and almost a doating father, seeks no amusement out of his own family, and is not only addicted to no bad habits, but averse to spending time in society or the dissipations connected with it. Speaking upon my honour as a gentleman and my credit as a man of letters, I do not know a person so well qualified for the very difficult and responsible task he has undertaken, and I think the distinct testimony of one who must know the individual well ought to bear weight against all vague rumours, whether arising from idle squibs he may have been guilty of when he came from College—and I know none of these which indicate a bad heart in the jester—or, as is much more likely, from those which have been rashly and falsely ascribed to him.

Had any shadow of this want of confidence been expressed in the beginning of the business I for one would have advised Lockhart to have nothing to do with a concern for which his capacity was called in question. But *now* what can be done? A liberal offer, handsomely made, has been accepted with the same confidence with which it was offered. Lockhart has resigned his office in Edinburgh, given up his business, taken a house in London, and has let, or is on the eve of letting, his house here. The thing is so public, that about thirty of the most respectable gentlemen in Edinburgh have proposed to me that a dinner should be given in his honour. The ground is cut away behind him for a retreat, nor can such a thing be proposed as matters now stand.

Upon what grounds or by whom Lockhart was first recommended to you I have no right or wish to inquire, having no access whatsoever to the negotiation, the result of which must be in every wise painful enough to me. But as their advice must in addition to your own judgment have had great weight with you, I conceive they will join with me in the expectation that the other respectable friends of this important work will not form any decision to Lockhart's prejudice till they shall see how the business is conducted. By a different conduct they may do harm to the Editor, Publisher, and the work itself, as far as the withdrawing of their countenance must necessarily be prejudicial to its currency. But if it shall prove that their suspicions prove unfounded, I am sure it will give pain to them to have listened to them for a moment.

It has been my lot twice before now to stand forward to the best of my power as the assistant of two individuals against whom a party run was made. The one case was that of Wilson, to whom a thousand idle pranks were imputed of a character very different and far more eccentric than anything that ever attached to Lockhart. We carried him through upon the fair principle that in the case of good morals and perfect talents for a situation, where vice or crimes are not alleged, the follies of youth should not obstruct the fair prospects of advanced manhood. God help us all if some such modification of censure is not extended to us, since most men have sown wild oats enough! Wilson was made a professor, as you know, has one of the fullest classes in the University, lectures most eloquently, and is much beloved by his pupils. The other was the case of John Williams, now Rector of our new Academy here, who was opposed most violently upon what on examination proved to be exaggerated rumours of old Winchester stories. He got the situation chiefly, I think, by my own standing firm and keeping others together. And the gentlemen who opposed him most violently have repeatedly told me that I did the utmost service to the Academy by bringing him in, for never was a man in such a situation so eminently qualified for the task of education.

I only mention these things to show that it is not in my son-in-law's affairs alone that I would endeavour to remove that sort of prejudice which envy and party zeal are always ready to throw in the way of rising talent. Those who are interested in the matter may be well assured that with whatever prejudice they may receive Lockhart at first, all who have candour enough to wait till he can afford them the means of judging will be of opinion that they have got a person possibly as well situated for the duties of such an office as any man that England could afford them.

I would rather have written a letter of this kind concerning any other person than one connected with myself, but it is every word true, were there neither son nor daughter in the case; but as such I leave it at your discretion to show it, not generally, but to such friends and patrons of the *Review* as in your opinion have a title to know the contents.

Believe me, dear Sir, Your most obedient Servant, WALTER SCOTT.

Mr. Lockhart himself addressed the two following letters to Mr. Murray:

Mr. Lockhart to John Murray.

Chiefswood, *November* 19, 1825.

My Dear Sir, I am deeply indebted to Disraeli for the trouble he has taken to come hither again at a time when he has so many matters of real importance to attend to in London. The sort of stuff that certain grave gentlemen have been mincing at, was of course thoroughly foreseen by Sir W. Scott and by myself from the beginning of the business. Such prejudices I cannot hope to overcome, except by doing well what has been entrusted to me, and after all I should like to know what man could have been put at the head of the *Quarterly Review* at my time of life without having the Doctors uttering doctorisms on the occasion. If you but knew it, you yourself personally could in one moment overcome and silence for ever the whole of these people. As for me, nobody has more sincere respect for them in their own different walks of excellence than myself; and if there be one thing that I may promise for myself, it is, that age, experience, and eminence, shall never find fair reason to accuse me of treating them with presumption. I am much more afraid of falling into the opposite error. I have written at some length on these matters to Mr. Croker, Mr. Ellis, and Mr. Rose—and to no one else; nor will I again put pen to paper, unless someone, having a right to put a distinct question to me, does put it.

Mr. Lockhart to John Murray.

Sunday, CHIEFSWOOD, *November* 27, 1825.

My Dear Murray,

I have read the letter I received yesterday evening with the greatest interest, and closed it with the sincerest pleasure. I think we now begin to understand each other, and if we do that I am sure *I* have no sort of apprehension as to the result of the whole business. But in writing one must come to the point, therefore I proceed at once to your topics in their order, and rely on it I shall speak as openly on every one of them as I would *to my brother*.

Mr. Croker's behaviour has indeed distressed me, for I had always considered him as one of those bad enemies who make excellent friends. I had not the least idea that he had ever ceased to regard you personally with friendship, even affection, until B. D. told me about his trafficking with Knight; for as to the little hints you gave me when in town, I set all that down to his aversion for the notion of your setting up a paper, and thereby dethroning him from his invisible predominance over the Tory daily press, and of course attached little importance to it. I am now satisfied, more particularly after hearing how he behaved himself in the interview with you, that there is some deeper feeling in his mind. The correspondence that has been passing between him and me may have been somewhat imprudently managed on my part. I may have *committed* myself to a certain extent in it in more ways than one. It is needless to regret what cannot be undone; at all events, I perceive that it is now over with us for the present. I do not, however, believe but that he will continue to do what he has been used to do for the *Review*; indeed, unless he makes the newspaper business his excuse, he stands completely pledged to me to adhere to that.

But with reverence be it spoken, even this does not seem to me a matter of very great moment. On the contrary, I believe that his papers in the *Review* have (with a few exceptions) done the work a great deal more harm than good. I cannot express what I feel; but there was always the bitterness of Gifford without his dignity, and the bigotry of Southey without his *bonne-foi.* His scourging of such poor deer as Lady Morgan was unworthy of a work of that rank. If we can get the same *information* elsewhere, no fear that we need equally regret the secretary's quill. As it is, we must be contented to watch the course of things and recollect the Roman's maxim, "quae casus obtullerint ad sapientiam vertenda. "

I an vexed not a little at Mr. Barrow's imprudence in mentioning my name to Croker and to Rose as in connection with the paper; and for this reason that I was most anxious to have produced at least one number of the *Review* ere that matter should have been at all suspected. As it is, I hope you will still find means to make Barrow, Rose, and Croker (at all events the two last) completely understand that you had, indeed, wished me to edit the paper, but that I had declined that, and that *then* you had offered me the *Review*.

No matter what you say as to the firm belief I have expressed that the paper *will* answer, and the resolutions I have made to assist you by writing political articles in it. It is of the highest importance that in our anxiety about a new affair one should not lose sight of the old and established one, and I *can* believe that if the real state of the case were known at the outset of my career in London, a considerable feeling detrimental to the *Quarterly might* be excited. We have enough of adverse feelings to meet, without unnecessarily swelling their number and aggravating their quality.

I beg you to have a serious conversation with Mr. Barrow on this head, and in the course of it take care to make him thoroughly understand that the prejudices or doubts he gave utterance to in regard to me were heard of by me without surprise, and excited no sort of angry feeling whatever. He could know nothing of me but from flying rumours, for the nature of which *he* could in no shape be answerable. As for poor Rose's well-meant hints about my "identifying myself perhaps in the mind of society with the scavengers of the press, " "the folly of *your* risking your name on a *paper*, " etc., etc., of course we shall equally appreciate all this. Rose is a timid dandy, and a bit of a Whig to boot. I shall make some explanation to him when I next have occasion to write to him, but that sort of thing would come surely with a better grace from you than from me. I have not a doubt that he will be a daily scribbler in your paper ere it is a week old.

To all these people—Croker as well as the rest—John Murray is of much more importance than they ever can be to him if he will only *believe* what I *know*, viz. that his own name in *society* stands miles above any of theirs. Croker *cannot* form the nucleus of a literary association which you have any reason to dread. He is hated by the higher Tories quite as sincerely as by the Whigs: besides, he has not *now-a-days* courage to strike an effective blow; he will not come forward.

I come to pleasanter matters. Nothing, indeed, can be more handsome, more generous than Mr. Coleridge's whole behaviour. I beg of you to express to him the sense I have of the civility with which he has been pleased to remember and allude to *me*, and assure him that I am most grateful for the assistance he offers, and accept of it to any extent he chooses.

In this way Mr. Lockhart succeeded to the control of what his friend John Wilson called "a National Work"; and he justified the selection which Mr. Murray had made of him as editor: not only maintaining and enhancing the reputation of the *Review*, by securing the friendship of the old contributors, but enlisting the assistance of many new ones. Sir Walter Scott, though "working himself to pieces" to free himself from debt, came to his help, and to the first number which Lockhart edited he contributed an interesting article on "Pepys' Memoirs. "

Lockhart's literary taste and discernment were of the highest order; and he displayed a moderation and gentleness, even in his adverse criticism, for which those who knew him but slightly, or by reputation only, scarce gave him credit. There soon sprang up between him and his publisher an intimacy and mutual confidence which lasted till Murray's death; and Lockhart continued to edit the *Quarterly* till his own death in 1854. In truth there was need of mutual confidence between editor and publisher, for they were called upon to deal with not a few persons whose deep interest in the *Quarterly* tempted them at times to assume a somewhat dictatorial tone in their comments on and advice for the management of the *Review*. When an article written by Croker, on Lamennais' "Paroles d'un Croyant, " [Footnote: The article by J. W. Croker was afterwards published in No. 104 of the *Quarterly*.] was under consideration, Lockhart wrote to the publisher:

Mr. Lockhart to John Murray.

November 8, 1826.

My Dear Murray,

It is always agreeable and often useful for us to hear what you think of the articles in progress. Croker and I both differ from you as to the general affair, for this reason simply, that Lamennais is to Paris what Benson or Lonsdale is to London. His book has produced and is producing a very great effect. Even religious people there applaud him, and they are re-echoed here by old Jerdan, who pronounces that, be he right or wrong, he has produced "a noble sacred poem. " It is needful to caution the English against the course of France by showing up the audacious extent of her horrors, political, moral, and religious; and you know what *was* the result of our article on those vile tragedies, the extracts of which were more likely to offend a family circle than anything in the "Paroles d'un Croyant, " and which even I was afraid of. Mr. Croker, however, will modify and curtail the paper so as to get rid of your specific objections. It had already been judged advisable to put the last and only blasphemous extract in French in place of English. Depend upon it, if we were to lower our scale so as to run no risk of offending any good people's delicate feelings, we should soon lower ourselves so as to rival "My

Grandmother the British" in want of interest to the world at large, and even (though they would not say so) to the saints themselves. — *Verb. sap.*

Like most sagacious publishers, Murray was free from prejudice, and was ready to publish for all parties and for men of opposite opinions. For instance, he published Malthus's "Essay on Population, " and Sadler's contradiction of the theory. He published Byron's attack on Southey, and Southey's two letters against Lord Byron. He published Nugent's "Memorials of Hampden, " and the *Quarterly Review's* attack upon it. Southey's "Book of the Church" evoked a huge number of works on the Roman Catholic controversy, most of which were published by Mr. Murray. Mr. Charles Butler followed with his "Book on the Roman Catholic Church. " And the Rev. Joseph Blanco White's "Practical and Internal Evidence against Catholicism, " with occasional strictures on Mr. Butler's "Book on the Roman Catholic Church. " Another answer to Mr. Butler came from Dr. George Townsend, in his "Accusations of History against the Church of Rome. " Then followed the Divines, of whom there were many: the Rev. Dr. Henry Phillpotts (then of Stanhope Rectory, Durham, but afterwards Bishop of Exeter), in his "Letter to Charles Butler on the Theological Parts of his Book on the Roman Catholic Church"; the Rev. G.S. Faber's "Difficulties of Romanism"; and many others.

While most authors are ready to take "cash down" for their manuscripts, there are others who desire to be remunerated in proportion to the sale of their works. This is especially the case with works of history or biography, which are likely to have a permanent circulation. Hence, when the judicious Mr. Hallam—who had sold the first three editions of "Europe during the Middle Ages" to Mr. Murray for £1,400—had completed his "Constitutional History of England, " he made proposals which resulted in Mr. Murray's agreeing to print and publish at his own cost and risk the "Constitutional History of England, " and pay to the author two-thirds of the net profits. And these were the terms on which Mr. Murray published all Mr. Hallam's subsequent works.

Mr. Wordsworth about this time desired to republish his Poems, and made application with that object to Mr. Murray, who thereupon consulted Lockhart.

Mr. Lockhart to John Murray. July 9, 1826.

"In regard to Wordsworth I certainly cannot doubt that it must be creditable to any publisher to publish the works *of* one who is and must continue to be a classic Poet of England. Your adventure with Crabbe, however, ought to be a lesson of much caution. On the other hand, again, W.'s poems *must* become more popular, else why so many editions in the course of the last few years. There have been *two* of the 'Excursion' alone, and I know that those have not satisfied the public. Everything, I should humbly say, depends on the terms proposed by the great Laker, whose vanity, be it whispered, is nearly as remarkable as his genius. "

The following is the letter in which Mr. Wordsworth made his formal proposal to Mr. Murray to publish his collected poems:

Mr. Wordsworth to John Murray.

RYDAL MOUNT, NEAR AMBLESIDE

December 4, 1826.

Dear Sir,

I have at last determined to go to the Press with my Poems as early as possible. Twelve months ago the were to have been put into the hands of Messrs. Robinson & Hurst, upon the terms of payment of a certain sum, independent of expense on my part; but the failure of that house prevented the thing going forward. Before I offer the publication to any one but yourself, upon the different principle agreed on between you and me, as you may recollect, viz. ; the author to meet two-thirds of the expenses and risk, and to share two-thirds of the profit, I think it proper to renew that proposal to you. If you are not inclined to accept it, I shall infer so from your silence; if such an arrangement suits you, pray let me *immediately* know; and all I have to request is, that without loss of time, when I have informed you of the intended quantity of letter-press, you will then let me know what my share of the expense will amount to.

I am, dear Sir,

Your obedient servant,

WM. WORDSWORTH.

As Mr. Murray did not answer this letter promptly, Mr. H. Crabb Robinson called upon him to receive his decision, and subsequently wrote:

Mr. H.G. Robinson to John Murray.

February 1827.

"I wrote to Mr. Wordsworth the day after I had the pleasure of seeing you. I am sorry to say that my letter came too late. Mr. Wordsworth interpreted your silence into a rejection of his offer; and his works will unfortunately lose the benefit of appearing under you auspices. They have been under the press some weeks. "

For about fifteen years there had been no business transactions between Murray and Constable. On the eve of the failure of the Constables, the head of the firm, Mr. Archibald Constable (October 1825), was paying a visit at Wimbledon, when Mr. Murray addressed his host—Mr. Wright, whose name has already occurred in the *Representative* correspondence—as follows:

My Dear Wright,

Although I intend to do myself the pleasure of calling upon Mr. Constable at your house tomorrow immediately after church (for it is our charity sermon at Wimbledon, and I must attend), yet I should be most happy, if it were agreeable to you and to him, to favour us with your company at dinner at, I will say, five tomorrow. Mr. Constable is godfather to my son, who will be at home, and I am anxious to introduce him to Mr. C., who may not be long in town.

Mr. Constable and his friend accordingly dined with Murray, and that the meeting was very pleasant may be inferred from Mr. Constable's letter of a few days later, in which he wrote to Murray, "It made my heart glad to be once more happy together as we were the other evening. " The rest of Mr. Constable's letter referred to Hume's Philosophical Writings, which were tendered to Murray, but which he declined to publish.

Constable died two years later, John Ballantyne, Scott's partner, a few years earlier; and Scott entered in his diary, "It is written that nothing shall flourish under my shadow. "

CHAPTER XXVI

SIR WALTER'S LAST YEARS

Owing to the intimate relations which were now established between Murray and Lockhart, the correspondence is full of references to Sir Walter Scott and to the last phases of his illustrious career.

Lockhart had often occasion to be at Abbotsford to see Sir Walter Scott, who was then carrying on, single-handed, that terrible struggle with adversity, which has never been equalled in the annals of literature. His son-in-law went down in February 1827 to see him about further articles, but wrote to Murray: "I fear we must not now expect Sir W. S.'s assistance ere 'Napoleon' be out of hand. " In the following month of June Lockhart wrote from Portobello: "Sir W. Scott has got 'Napoleon' out of his hands, and I have made arrangements for three or four articles; and I think we may count for a paper of his every quarter. " Articles accordingly appeared from Sir Walter Scott on diverse subjects, one in No. 71, June 1827, on the "Works of John Home "; another in No. 72, October 1827, on "Planting Waste Lands "; a third in No. 74, March 1828, on "Plantation and Landscape Gardening "; and a fourth in No. 76, October 1828, on Sir H. Davy's "Salmonia, or Days of Fly-Fishing. " The last article was cordial and generous, like everything proceeding from Sir Walter's pen. Lady Davy was greatly pleased with it. "It must always be a proud and gratifying distinction, " she said, "to have the name of Sir Walter Scott associated with that of my husband in the review of 'Salmonia. ' I am sure Sir Humphry will like his bairn the better for the public opinion given of it by one whose immortality renders praise as durable as it seems truly felt. "

With respect to "Salmonia" the following anecdote may be mentioned, as related to Mr. Murray by Dr. Gooch, a valued contributor to the *Quarterly*.

"At page 6 of Salmonia, " said Dr. Gooch, "it is stated that 'Nelson was a good fly-fisher, and continued the pursuit even with his left hand. ' I can add that one of his reasons for regretting the loss of his right arm was that it deprived him of the power of pursuing this amusement efficiently, as is shown by the following incident, which is, I think, worth preserving in that part of his history which relates to his talents as a fly-fisher. I was at the Naval Hospital at Yarmouth on the morning when Nelson, after the battle of Copenhagen (having sent the wounded before him), arrived in the Roads and landed on the Jetty. The populace soon surrounded him, and the military were drawn up in the marketplace ready to receive him; but making his way through the crowd, and the dust and the clamour, he went straight to the Hospital. I went round the wards with him, and was much interested in observing his demeanour to the sailors. He stopped at every bed, and to every man he had something kind and cheering to say. At length he stopped opposite a bed in which a sailor was lying who had lost his right arm close to the shoulder joint, and the following short dialogue passed between them. *Nelson*: 'Well, Jack, what's the matter with you? ' *Sailor*: 'Lost my right arm, your Honour. ' Nelson paused, looked down at his own empty sleeve, then at the sailor, and then said playfully, 'Well, Jack, then you and I are spoiled for fishermen; but cheer up, my brave fellow. ' He then passed quickly on to the next bed, but these few words had a magical effect upon the poor fellow, for I saw his eyes sparkle with delight as Nelson turned away and pursued his course through the wards. This was the only occasion on which I ever saw Lord Nelson."

In the summer of 1828 Mr. Lockhart went down to Brighton, accompanied by Sir Walter Scott, Miss Scott, Mrs. Lockhart and her son John—the Littlejohn to whom Scott's charming "Tales of a Grandfather, " which were at that time in course of publication, had been addressed. It was on the boy's account the party went to Brighton; he was very ill and gradually sinking.

While at Brighton, Lockhart had an interview with the Duke of Wellington, and wrote to Murray on the subject.

Mr. Lockhart to John Murray. May 18, 1828.

"I have a message from the D. of W. to say that he, on the whole, highly approves the paper on foreign politics, but has some criticisms to offer on particular points, and will send for me some day soon to hear them. I have of course signified my readiness to attend him any time he is pleased to appoint, and expect it will be next week. "

That the Duke maintained his interest in the *Quarterly* is shown by a subsequent extract:

Mr. Lockhart to John Murray.

AUCHENRAITH, *January* 19, 1829.

"Sir Walter met me here yesterday, and he considered the Duke's epistle as an effort of the deepest moment to the *Quarterly* and all concerned. He is sure no minister ever gave a more distinguished proof of his feeling than by this readiness to second the efforts of a literary organ. Therefore, no matter about a week sooner or later, let us do the thing justice. "

Before his departure for Brighton, Mr. Lockhart had been commissioned by Murray to offer Sir Walter Scott £1,250 for the copyright of his "History of Scotland, " a transaction concerning which some informal communications had already passed.

Mr. Lockhart to John Murray.

MY DEAR *SIR,*

Sir W. Scott has already agreed to furnish Dr. Lardner's "Cyclopaedia" with one vol. —"History of Scotland"—for £1,000, and he is now at this work. This is grievous, but you must not blame me, for he has acted in the full knowledge of my connection with and anxiety about the Family Library. I answered him, expressing my great regret and reminding him of Peterborough. I suppose, as I never mentioned, nor well could, *money*, that Dr. Lardner's matter appeared more a piece of business. Perhaps you may think of something to be done. It is a great loss to us and gain to them.

Yours truly,

J. G.L.

After the failure of Ballantyne and Constable, Cadell, who had in former years been a partner in Constable's house, became Scott's publisher, and at the close of 1827 the principal copyrights of Scott's works, including the novels from "Waverley" to "Quentin Durward, " and most of the poems, were put up to auction, and purchased by Cadell and Scott jointly for £8,500. At this time the "Tales of a Grandfather" were appearing by instalments, and Murray wrote to the author, begging to be allowed to become the London publisher of this work. Scott replied:

Sir W. Scott to John Murray.

6, Shandwick Place, Edinburgh,

November 26, 1828.

My Dear Sir,

I was favoured with your note some time since, but could not answer it at the moment till I knew whether I was like to publish at Edinburgh or not. The motives for doing so are very strong, for I need not tell you that in literary affairs a frequent and ready communication with the bookseller is a very necessary thing.

As we have settled, with advice of those who have given me their assistance in extricating my affairs, to publish in Edinburgh, I do not feel myself at liberty to dictate to Cadell any particular selection of a London publisher. If I did so, I should be certainly involved in any discussions or differences which might occur between my London and Edinburgh friends, which would be adding an additional degree of perplexity to my affairs. I feel and know the value of your name as a publisher, but if we should at any time have the pleasure of being connected with you in that way, it must be when it is entirely on your own account. The little history designed for Johnnie Lockhart was long since promised to Cadell.

I do not, in my conscience, think that I deprive you of anything of consequence in not being at present connected with you in literary business. My reputation with the world is something like a high-pressure engine, which does very well while all lasts stout and tight, but is subject to sudden explosion, and I would rather that another than an old friend stood the risk of suffering by the splinters.

I feel all the delicacy of the time and mode of your application, and you cannot doubt I would greatly prefer you personally to men of whom I know nothing. But they are not of my choosing, nor are they in any way responsible to me. I transact with the Edinburgh bookseller alone, and as I must neglect no becoming mode of securing myself, my terms are harder than I think you, in possession of so well established a trade, would like to enter upon, though they may suit one who gives up his time to them as almost his sole object of expense and attention. I hope this necessary arrangement will make no difference betwixt us, being, with regard,

Your faithful, humble Servant,

Walter Scott.

On his return to London, Lockhart proceeded to take a house, No. 24, Sussex Place, Regent's Park; for he had been heretofore living in the furnished apartments provided for him in Pall Mall. Mr. Murray wrote to him on the subject:

John Murray to Mr. Lockhart.

July 31, 1828.

As you are about taking or retaking a house, I think it right to inform you now that the editor's dividend on the *Quarterly Review* will be in future £325 on the publication of each number; and I think it very hard if you do not get £200 or £300 more for your own contributions.

Most truly yours,

JOHN MURRAY.

At the beginning of the following year Lockhart went down to Abbotsford, where he found his father-in-law working as hard as ever.

Mr. Lockhart to John Murray.

January 4, 1820.

"I have found Sir Walter Scott in grand health and spirits, and have had much conversation with him on his hill-side about all our concerns. I shall keep a world of his hints and suggestions till we meet; but meanwhile he has agreed to write *almost immediately* a one volume biography of the great Earl of Peterborough, and I think you will agree with me in considering the choice of this, perhaps the last of our romantic heroes, as in all respects happy.... He will also write *now* an article on some recent works of Scottish History (Tytler's, etc.) giving, he promises, a complete and gay summary of all that controversy; and next Nov. a general review of the Scots ballads, whereof some twenty volumes have been published within these ten years, and many not published but only printed by the Bannatyne club of Edinburgh, and another club of the same order at Glasgow.... I am coaxing him to make a selection from Crabbe, with a preface, and think he will be persuaded. "

January 8, 1829.

"Sir Walter Scott suggests overhauling Caulfield's portraits of remarkable characters (3 vols., 1816), and having roughish woodcuts taken from that book and from others, and the biographies newly done, whenever they are not in the words of the old original writers. He says the march of intellect will never put women with beards and men with horns out of fashion—Old Parr, Jenkins, Venner, Muggleton, and Mother Souse, are immortal, all in their several ways. "

By 1829 Scott and Cadell had been enabled to obtain possession of all the principal copyrights, with the exception of two one-fourth shares of "Marmion, " held by Murray and Longman respectively. Sir Walter Scott applied to Murray through Lockhart, respecting this fourth share. The following was Murray's reply to Sir Walter Scott:

John Murray to Sir Walter Scott.

June 8, 1829.

My Dear Sir,

Mr. Lockhart has at this moment communicated to me your letter respecting my fourth share of the copyright of "Marmion. " I have already been applied to by Messrs. Constable and by Messrs. Longman, to know what sum I would sell this share for; but so highly do I estimate the honour of being, even in so small a degree, the publisher of the author of the poem, that no pecuniary consideration whatever can induce me to part with it. But there is a consideration of another kind, which, until now, I was not aware of, which would make it painful to me if I were to retain it a moment longer. I mean, the knowledge of its being required by the author, into whose hands it was spontaneously resigned in the same instant that I read his request. This share has been profitable to me fifty-fold beyond what either publisher or author could have anticipated; and, therefore, my returning it on such an occasion, you will, I trust, do me the favour to consider in no other light than as a mere act of grateful acknowledgment for benefits already received by, my dear sir,

Your obliged and faithful Servant,

JOHN MURRAY.

P. S.—It will be proper for your man of business to prepare a regular deed to carry this into effect, which I will sign with the greatest self-satisfaction, as soon as I receive it.

Sir W. Scott to John Murray.

EDINBURGH, *June* 12, 1829.

My Dear Sir,

Nothing can be more obliging or gratifying to me than the very kind manner in which you have resigned to me the share you held in "Marmion, " which, as I am circumstanced, is a favour of real value and most handsomely rendered. I hope an opportunity may occur in which I may more effectually express my sense of the obligation than by mere words. I will send the document of transference when it can be made out. In the meantime I am, with sincere regard and thanks,

Your most obedient and obliged Servant,

WALTER SCOTT.

At the end of August 1829 Lockhart was again at Abbotsford; and sending the slips of Sir Walter's new article for the next *Quarterly*. He had already written for No. 77 the article on "Hajji Baba, " and for No. 81 an article on the "Ancient History of Scotland. " The slips for the new article were to be a continuation of the last, in a review of Tytler's "History of Scotland. " The only other articles he wrote for the *Quarterly* were his review of Southey's "Life of John Bunyan, " No. 86, in October 1830; and his review—the very last—of Pitcairn's "Criminal Trials of Scotland, " No. 88, in February 1831.

His last letter to Mr. Murray refers to the payment for one of these articles:

Sir W. Scott to John Murray.

ABBOTSFORD, *Monday,* 1830.

My Dear Sir,

I acknowledge with thanks your remittance of £100, and I will be happy to light on some subject which will suit the *Review*, which may be interesting and present some novelty. But I have to look forward to a very busy period betwixt this month and January, which may prevent my contribution being ready before that time. You may be assured that for many reasons I have every wish to assist the *Quarterly*, and will be always happy to give any support which is in my power.

I have inclosed for Moore a copy of one of Byron's letters to me. I received another of considerable interest, but I do not think it right to give publicity without the permission of a person whose name is repeatedly mentioned. I hope the token of my good wishes will not come too late. These letters have been only recovered after a long search through my correspondence, which, as usual with literary folks, is sadly confused.

I beg my kind compliments to Mrs. Murray and the young ladies, and am, yours truly,

WALTER SCOTT.

Scott now began to decline rapidly, and was suffering much from his usual spasmodic attacks; yet he had Turner with him, making drawings for the new edition of his poems. Referring to his last article in the *Quarterly* on Pitcairn's "Criminal Trials, " he bids Lockhart to inform Mr. Murray that "no one knows better your liberal disposition, and he is aware that £50 is more than his paper is worth. " Scott's illness increased, and Lockhart rarely left his side.

Mr. Lockhart to John Murray.

CHIEFSWOOD, *September* 16, 1831.

"Yesterday determined Sir W. Scott's motions. He owes to Croker the offer of a passage to Naples in a frigate which sails in about a fortnight. He will therefore proceed southwards by land next week, halting at Rokeby, and with his son at Notts, by the way. We shall leave Edinburgh by next Tuesday's steamer, so as to be in town before him, and ready for his reception. We are all deeply obliged to Croker on this occasion, for Sir Walter is quite unfit for the fatigues of a long land journey, and the annoyances innumerable of Continental inns; and, above all, he will have a good surgeon at hand, in case of need. The arrangement has relieved us all of a great burden of annoyances and perplexities and fears. "

Another, and the last of Lockhart's letters on this subject, may be given:

Mr. Lockhart to John Murray.

CHIEFSWOOD, *September* 19, 1831.

DEAR MURRAY,

In consequence of my sister-in-law, Annie Scott, being taken unwell, with frequent fainting fits, the result no doubt of over anxieties of late, I have been obliged to let my wife and children depart by tomorrow's steamer without me, and I remain to attend to Sir Walter thro' his land progress, which will begin on Friday, and end, I hope well, on Wednesday. If this should give any inconvenience to you, God knows I regret it, and God knows also I couldn't do otherwise without exposing Sir W. and his daughter to a feeling that I had not done my duty to them. On the whole, public affairs seem to be so dark, that I am inclined to think our best course, in the *Quarterly*, may turn out to have been and to be, that of not again appearing until the fate of this Bill has been quite settled. My wife will, if you are in town, be much rejoiced with a visit; and if you write to me, so as to catch me at Rokeby Park, Greta Bridge, next Saturday, 'tis well.

Yours,

J. G. LOCKHART.

P. S.—But I see Rokeby Park would not do. I shall be at Major Scott's, 15th Hussars, Nottingham, on Monday night.

It would be beyond our province to describe in these pages the closing scenes of Sir Walter Scott's life: his journey to Naples, his attempt to write more novels, his failure, and his return home to

Abbotsford to die. His biography, by his son-in-law Lockhart, one of the best in the whole range of English literature, is familiar to all our readers; and perhaps never was a more faithful memorial erected, in the shape of a book, to the beauty, goodness, and faithfulness of a noble literary character.

In this work we are only concerned with Sir Walter's friendship and dealings with Mr. Murray, and on these the foregoing correspondence, extending over nearly a quarter of a century, is sufficient comment. When a committee was formed in Sir Walter's closing years to organize and carry out some public act of homage and respect to the great genius, Mr. Murray strongly urged that the money collected, with which Abbotsford was eventually redeemed, should be devoted to the purchase of all the copyrights for the benefit of Scott and his family: it cannot but be matter of regret that this admirable suggestion was not adopted.

During the year 1827 Mr. Murray's son, John Murray the Third, was residing in Edinburgh as a student at the University, and attended the memorable dinner at which Scott was forced to declare himself the author of the "Waverley Novels. "

His account of the scene, as given in a letter to his father, forms a fitting conclusion to this chapter.

"I believe I mentioned to you that Mr. Allan had kindly offered to take me with him to a Theatrical Fund dinner, which took place on Friday last. There were present about 300 persons—a mixed company, many of them not of the most respectable order. Sir Walter Scott took the chair, and there was scarcely another person of any note to support him except the actors. The dinner, therefore, would have been little better than endurable, had it not been remarkable for the confession of Sir Walter Scott that he was the author of the 'Waverley Novels. '

"This acknowledgment was forced from him, I believe, contrary to his own wish, in this manner. Lord Meadowbank, who sat on his left hand, proposed his health, and after paying him many compliments, ended his speech by saying that the clouds and mists which had so long surrounded the Great Unknown were now revealed, and he appeared in his true character (probably alluding to the *expose* made before Constable's creditors, for I do not think there was any preconcerted plan). Upon this Sir Walter rose, and said, 'I did not expect on coming here today that I should have to disclose before 300 people a secret which, considering it had already been made known to about thirty persons, had been tolerably well kept. I am not prepared to give my reasons for preserving it a secret, caprice had certainly a great share in the matter. Now that it is out, I beg leave to observe that I am sole and undivided author of those novels. Every part of them has originated with me, or has been suggested to me in the course of my reading. I confess I am guilty, and am almost afraid to examine the extent of my delinquency. "Look on't again, I dare not! " The wand of Prospero is now broken, and my book is buried, but before I retire I shall propose the health of a person who has given so much delight to all now present, The Bailie Nicol Jarvie.'

"I report this from memory. Of course it is not quite accurate in words, but you will find a tolerable report of it in the *Caledonian Mercury* of Saturday. This declaration was received with loud and long applause. As this was gradually subsiding, a voice from the end of the room was heard [Footnote: The speaker on this occasion was the actor Mackay, who had attained considerable celebrity by his representation of Scottish characters, and especially of that of the famous Bailie in "Rob Roy. "] exclaiming in character, ' Ma conscience! if my father the Bailie had been alive to hear that ma health had been proposed by the Author of Waverley, ' etc., which, as you may suppose, had a most excellent effect. "

CHAPTER XXVII

NAPIER'S "PENINSULAR WAR" — CHOKER'S "BOSWELL" —
"THE FAMILY LIBRARY, " ETC.

The public has long since made up its mind as to the merits of Colonel Napier's "History of the Peninsular War. " It is a work which none but a soldier who had served through the war as he had done, and who, moreover, combined with practical experience a thorough knowledge of the science of war, could have written.

At the outset of his work he applied to the Duke of Wellington for his papers. This rather abrupt request took the Duke by surprise. The documents in his possession were so momentous, and the great part of them so confidential in their nature, that he felt it to be impossible to entrust them indiscriminately to any man living. He, however, promised Napier to put in his hands any specified paper or document he might ask for, provided no confidence would be broken by its examination. He also offered to answer any question Napier might put to him, and with this object invited him to Stratfieldsaye, where the two Generals discussed many points connected with the campaign.

Colonel W. Napier to John Murray.

BROMHAM, WILTS,

December 5, 1828.

Dear Sir,

My first volume is now nearly ready for the press, and as I think that in matters of business a plain straightforward course is best, I will at once say what I conceive to be the valuable part of my work, and leave you to make a proposition relative to publication of the single volume, reserving further discussion about the whole until the other volumes shall be in a more forward state.

The volume in question commences with the secret treaty of Fontainebleau concluded in 1809, and ends with the battle of Corunna. It will have an appendix of original documents, many of

319

which are extremely interesting, and there will also be some plans of the battles. My authorities have been:

1. All the original papers of Sir Hew Dalrymple.

2. Those of Sir John Moore.

3. King Joseph's correspondence taken at the battle of Vittoria, and placed at my disposal by the Duke of Wellington. Among other papers are several notes and detailed instructions by Napoleon which throw a complete light upon his views and proceedings in the early part of the war.

4. Notes of conversations held with the Duke of Wellington for the especial purpose of connecting my account of his operations.

5. Notes of conversation with officers of high rank in the French, English, and Spanish services.

6. Original journals, and the most unreserved communications with Marshal Soult.

7. My own notes of affairs in which I have been present.

8. Journals of regimental officers of talent, and last but not least, copies taken by myself from the original muster rolls of the French army as they were transmitted to the Emperor.

Having thus distributed all my best wares in the bow window, I shall leave you to judge for yourself; and, as the diplomatists say, will be happy to treat upon a suitable basis. In the meantime,

I remain, your very obedient Servant,

W. NAPIER.

About a fortnight later (December 25, 1827) he again wrote that he would have the pleasure of putting a portion of his work into Mr. Murray's hands in a few days; but that "it would be disagreeable to him to have it referred to Mr. Southey for an opinion. " Murray, it should be mentioned, had published Southey's "History of the War in Spain. " Some negotiations ensued, in the course of which Mr.

Murray offered 500 guineas for the volume. This proposal, however, was declined by Colonel Napier.

Murray after fuller consideration offered a thousand guineas, which Colonel Napier accepted, and the volume was accordingly published in the course of 1828. Notwithstanding the beauty of its style and the grandeur of its descriptions, the book gave great offence by the severity of its criticism, and called forth a multitude of replies and animadversions. More than a dozen of these appeared in the shape of pamphlets bearing their authors' names, added to which the *Quarterly Review*, departing from the general rule, gave no less than four criticisms in succession. This innovation greatly disgusted the publisher, who regarded them as so much lead weighing down his *Review*, although they proceeded from the pen of the Duke's right-hand man, the Rt. Hon. Sir George Murray. They were unreadable and produced no effect. It is needless to add the Duke had nothing to do with them.

Mr. Murray published no further volumes of the "History of the Peninsular War, " but at his suggestion Colonel Napier brought out the second and succeeding volumes on his own account. In illustration of the loss which occurred to Mr. Murray in publishing the first volume of the history, the following letter may be given, as addressed to the editor of the *Morning Chronicle*:

John Murray to the Editor of the Morning Chronicle.

ALBEMARLE STREET, *February* 13, 1837.

SIR,

My attention has been called to an article in your paper of the 14th of January, containing the following extract from Colonel Napier's reply to the third article in the *Quarterly Review*, on his "History of the Peninsular War. " [Footnote: The article appeared in No. 111 of *Quarterly*, April 1836.]

"Sir George Murray only has thrown obstacles in my way, and if I am rightly informed of the following circumstances, his opposition has not been confined to what I have stated above. Mr. Murray, the bookseller, purchased my first volume, with the right of refusal for the second volume. When the latter was nearly ready, a friend informed me that he did not think Murray would purchase, because he had heard him say that Sir George Murray had declared it was not 'The Book. ' He did not point out any particular error, but it was not 'The Book, ' meaning, doubtless, that his own production, when it appeared, would be 'The Book. ' My friend's prognostic was not false. I was offered just half of the sum given for the first volume. I declined it, and published on my own account, and certainly I have had no reason to regret that Mr. Bookseller Murray waited for 'The Book, ' indeed, he has since told me very frankly that he had mistaken his own interest. "

In answer to the first part of this statement, I beg leave to say, that I had not, at the time to which Colonel Napier refers, the honour of any acquaintance with Sir George Murray, nor have I held any conversation or correspondence with him on the subject of Colonel Napier's book, or of any other book on the Peninsular War. In reply to the second part of the statement, regarding the offer for Colonel Napier's second volume of half the sum (viz. 500 guineas) that I gave for the first volume (namely, 1,000 guineas), I have only to beg the favour of your insertion of the following letter, written by me to Colonel Napier, upon the occasion referred to.

ALBEMARLE STREET, *May* 13, 1829.

MY DEAR SIR,

Upon making up the account of the sale of the first volume of "The History of the War in the Peninsula" I find that I am at this time minus £545 12s. At this loss I do by no means in the present instance repine, for I have derived much gratification from being the publisher of a work which is so intrinsically valuable, and which has been so generally admired, and it is some satisfaction to me to find by this result that my own proposal to you was perfectly just. I will not, however, venture to offer you a less sum for the second volume, but recommend that you should, in justice to yourself, apply to some other publishers; if you should obtain from them the sum which you are right in expecting, it will afford me great pleasure, and, if you do not, you will find me perfectly ready to negotiate; and in any case I shall continue to be, with the highest esteem, dear Sir,

Your obliged and faithful servant,

JOHN MURRAY.

I am confident you will do me the justice to insert this letter, and have no doubt its contents will convince Colonel Napier that his recollection of the circumstances has been incomplete.

I have the honour to be, sir,

Your obedient humble Servant,

JOHN MURRAY.

It may not be generally known that we owe to Colonel Napier's work the publication of the Duke of Wellington's immortal "Despatches. " The Duke, upon principle, refused to read Napier's work; not wishing, as he said, to quarrel with its author. But he was made sufficiently acquainted with the contents from friends who had perused it, and who, having made the campaigns with him, could point to praise and blame equally undeserved, to designs misunderstood and misrepresented, as well as to supercilious criticism and patronizing approval, which could not but be painful to the great commander. His nature was too noble to resent this; but he resolved, in self-defence, to give the public the means of ascertaining the truth, by publishing all his most important and secret despatches, in order, he said, to give the world a correct account not only of what he did, but of what he intended to do.

Colonel Gurwood was appointed editor of the "Despatches" and, during their preparation, not a page escaped the Duke's eye, or his own careful revision. Mr. Murray, who was honoured by being chosen as the publisher, compared this wonderful collection of documents to a watch: hitherto the general public had only seen in the successful and orderly development of his campaigns, as it were the hands moving over the dial without fault or failure, but now the Duke opened the works, and they were enabled to inspect the complicated machinery—the wheels within wheels—which had produced this admirable result. It is enough to state that in these despatches the *whole* truth relating to the Peninsular War is fully and elaborately set forth.

At the beginning of 1829 Croker consulted Murray on the subject of an annotated edition of "Boswell's Johnson. " Murray was greatly pleased with the idea of a new edition of the work by his laborious friend, and closing at once with Croker's proposal, wrote, "I shall be happy to give, as something in the way of remuneration, the sum of one thousand guineas. " Mr. Croker accepted the offer, and proceeded immediately with the work.

Mr. Murray communicated to Mr. Lockhart the arrangement he had made with Croker. His answer was:

Mr. Lockhart to John Murray.

January 19, 1829.

"I am heartily rejoiced that this 'Johnson, ' of which we had so often talked, is in such hands at whatever cost. Pray ask Croker whether Boswell's account of the Hebridean Tour ought not to be melted into the book. Sir Walter has many MS. annotations in his 'Boswell, ' both 'Life' and 'Tour, ' and will, I am sure, give them with hearty good will.... He will write down all that he has heard about Johnson when in Scotland; and, in particular, about the amusing intercourse between him and Lord Auchinleck—Boswell's father—if Croker considers it worth his while. "

Sir Walter Scott's offer of information, [Footnote: Sir Walter's letter to Croker on the subject will be found in the "Croker Correspondence, " ii. 28.] to a certain extent, delayed Croker's progress with the work. He wrote to Mr. Murray (November 17, 1829): "The reference to Sir Walter Scott delays us a little as to the revises, but his name is well worth the delay. My share of the next volume (the 2nd) is quite done; and I could complete the other two in a fortnight. "

While the work was passing through the press Lockhart again wrote:

Mr. Lockhart to John Murray.

"I am reading the new 'Boswell' with great pleasure, though, I think, the editor is often wrong. A prodigious flood of light is thrown on the book assuredly; and the incorporation of the 'Tour' is a great advantage. Now, do have a really good Index. That to the former edition I have continually found inadequate and faulty. The book is a dictionary of wisdom and wit, and one should know exactly where to find the *dictum magistri*. Many of Croker's own remarks and little disquisitions will also be hereafter among the choicest of *quotabilia*. "

Croker carried out the work with great industry and vigour, and it appeared in 1831. It contained numerous additions, notes, explanations, and memoranda, and, as the first attempt to explain the difficulties and enigmas which lapse of time had created, it may not unfairly be said to have been admirably edited; and though Macaulay, according to his own account, "smashed" it in the *Edinburgh*, [Footnote: The correspondence on the subject, and the criticism on the work by Macaulay, will be found in the "Croker Correspondence, " vol. ii. pp. 24-49.] some fifty thousand of the "Life" have been sold.

It has been the fashion with certain recent editors of "Boswell's Johnson" to depreciate Croker's edition; but to any one who has taken the pains to make himself familiar with that work, and to study the vast amount of information there collected, such criticism cannot but appear most ungenerous. Croker was acquainted with, or sought out, all the distinguished survivors of Dr. Johnson's own generation, and by his indefatigable efforts was enabled to add to the results of his own literary research, oral traditions and personal reminiscences, which but for him would have been irrevocably lost.

The additions of subsequent editors are but of trifling value compared with the information collected by Mr. Croker, and one of his successors at least has not hesitated slightly to transpose or alter many of Mr. Croker's notes, and mark them as his own.

Mrs. Shelley, widow of the poet, on receiving a present of Croker's "Boswell, " from Mr. Murray, said:

Mrs. Shelley to John Murray.

"I have read 'Boswell's Journal' ten times: I hope to read it many more. It is the most amusing book in the world. Beside that, I do love the kind-hearted, wise, and gentle Bear, and think him as lovable and kind a friend as a profound philosopher. "

Mr. Henry Taylor submitted his play of "Isaac Comnenus"—his first work—to Mr. Murray, in February 1827. Lockhart was consulted, and, after perusing the play, he wrote to Mr. Murray:

Mr. Lockhart to John Murray.

"There can be no sort of doubt that this play is everyway worthy of coming out from Albemarle Street. That the author might greatly improve it by shortening its dialogue often, and, once at least, leaving out a scene, and by dramatizing the scene at the Synod, instead of narrating it, I think sufficiently clear: but, probably, the author has followed his own course, upon deliberation, in all these matters. I am of opinion, certainly, that *no poem* has been lately published of anything like the power or promise of this. "

Lockhart's suggestion was submitted to Mr. Taylor, who gratefully acknowledged his criticism, and amended his play.

Mr. Taylor made a very unusual request. He proposed to divide the loss on his drama with the publisher! He wrote to Mr. Murray:

"I have been pretty well convinced, for some time past, that my book will never sell, and, under these circumstances, I cannot think it proper that you should be the sole sufferer. Whenever, therefore, you are of opinion that the book has had a fair trial, I beg you to understand that I shall be ready to divide the loss equally with you, that being, I conceive, the just arrangement in the case. "

Though Mr. Lockhart gave an interesting review of "Isaac Comnenus" in the *Quarterly*, it still hung fire, and did not sell. A few years later, however, Henry Taylor showed what he could do, as a poet, by his "Philip van Artevelde, " which raised his reputation to the highest point. Moore, after the publication of this drama, wrote in his "Diary": "I breakfasted in the morning at Rogers's, to meet the new poet, Mr. Taylor, author of 'Philip van Artevelde': our company, besides, being Sydney Smith and Southey. 'Van Artevelde' is a tall, handsome young fellow. Conversation chiefly about the profits booksellers make of us scribblers. I remember Peter Pindar saying, one of the few times I ever met him, that the booksellers drank their wine in the manner of the heroes in the hall of Odin, out of authors' skulls. " This was a sharp saying; but Rogers, if he had chosen to relate his own experiences when he negotiated with Mr. Murray about the sale of Crabbe's works, and the result of that negotiation, might have proved that the rule was not of universal application.

"The Family Library" has already been mentioned. Mr. Murray had long contemplated a serial publication, by means of which good literature and copyright works might be rendered cheaper and accessible to a wider circle of readers than they had hitherto been.

The Society for the Diffusion of Useful Knowledge was established in 1828, with Henry Brougham as Chairman. Mr. Murray subscribed £10 to this society, and agreed to publish their "Library of Entertaining Knowledge. " Shortly afterwards, however, he withdrew from this undertaking, which was transferred to Mr. Knight, and reverted to his own proposed publication of cheap works.

The first volume of "The Family Library" appeared in April 1829. Murray sent a copy to Charles Knight, who returned him the first volume of the "Library of Entertaining Knowledge. "

Mr. Charles Knight to John Murray.

"We each launch our vessels on the same day, and I most earnestly hope that both will succeed, for good must come of that success. We have plenty of sea-room and need never run foul of each other. My belief is that, in a very few years, scarcely any other description of books will be published, and in that case we that are first in the field may hope to win the race. "

Mr. Murray's intention was to include in the Library works on a variety of subjects, including History, Biography, Voyages and Travels, Natural History, Science, and general literature. They were to be written by the best-known authors of the day—Sir Walter Scott, Southey, Milman, Lockhart, Washington Irving, Barrow, Allan Cunningham, Dr. Brewster, Captain Head, G.R. Gleig, Palgrave, and others. The collection was headed by an admirable "Life of Napoleon, " by J. G. Lockhart, partly condensed from Scott's "Life of Napoleon Bonaparte, " and illustrated by George Cruikshank. When Lockhart was first invited to undertake this biography he consulted Sir Walter Scott as to the propriety of his doing so. Sir Walter replied:

Sir W. Scott to Mr. Lockhart.

October 30, 1828.

"Your scruples about doing an epitome of the 'Life of Boney' for the Family Library that is to be, are a great deal over delicate. My book in nine thick volumes can never fill the place which our friend

Murray wants you to fill, and which if you don't some one else will right soon. Moreover, you took much pains in helping me when I was beginning my task, and I afterwards greatly regretted that Constable had no means of remunerating you, as no doubt he intended when you were giving him so much good advice in laying down his grand plans about the Miscellany. By all means do what the Emperor [Footnote: From the time of his removal to Albemarle Street, Mr. Murray was universally known among "the Trade" as "The Emperor of the West. "] asks. He is what the Emperor Napoleon was not, much a gentleman, and knowing our footing in all things, would not have proposed anything that ought to have excited scruples on your side. " [Footnote: Lockhart's "Life of Scott."]

The book met with a warm reception from the public, and went through many editions.

Among other works published in "The Family Library" was the Rev. H.H. Milman's "History of the Jews, " in three vols., which occasioned much adverse criticism and controversy. It is difficult for us who live in such different times to understand or account for the tempest of disapprobation with which a work, which now appears so innocent, was greeted, or the obloquy with which its author was assailed. The "History of the Jews" was pronounced *unsound*; it was alleged that the miracles had been too summarily disposed of; Abraham was referred to as an Arab sheik, and Jewish history was too sacred to be submitted to the laws of ordinary investigation. Hence Milman was preached against, from Sunday to Sunday, from the University and other pulpits. Even Mr. Sharon Turner expostulated with Mr. Murray as to the publication of the book. He said he had seen it in the window of Carlile, the infidel bookseller,"as if he thought it suited his purpose. " The following letter is interesting as indicating what the Jews themselves thought of the history.

Mr. Magnus to John Murray. March 17, 1834.

Sir,

Will you have the goodness to inform me of the Christian name of the Rev. Mr. Milman, and the correct manner of spelling his name; as a subscription is about to be opened by individuals of the Jewish nation for the purpose of presenting him with a piece of plate for the liberal manner in which he has written their history.

The piece of plate was duly subscribed for and presented, with every demonstration of acknowledgment and thanks. Milman's "History of the Jews" did not prevent his preferment, as he was promoted from the vicarage of St. Mary's, Reading, to the rectorship of St. Margaret's, Westminster, and a canonry in the Collegiate Church of St. Peter; after which, in 1849, he was made Dean of St. Paul's.

CHAPTER XXVIII

MOORE'S "LIFE OF BYRON"

In 1827 or 1828 Mr. Hanson, the late Lord Byron's solicitor, wrote to Murray, enquiring, on behalf of the executors, whether he would be willing to dispose of his interest in the first five cantos of "Don Juan." Mr. Murray, however, had long been desirous of publishing a complete edition of the works of Lord Byron, "for the public, " he wrote, "are absolutely indignant at not being able to obtain a complete edition of Lord Byron's works in this country; and at least 15,000 copies have been brought here from France. " Murray proposed that those copyrights of Lord Byron, which were the property of his executors, should be valued by three respectable publishers, and that he should purchase them at their valuation. Mr. Hobhouse, to whom as one of the executors this proposal was made, was anxious that the complete edition should be published in England with as little delay as possible, but he stated that "some obstacles have arisen in consequence of the Messrs. Hunt having upon hand some hundred copies of their two volumes, which they have asked a little time to get rid of, and for which they are now accounting to the executors. "

Murray requested Mr. Hanson to apply to the executors, and inform him what sum they required for the works of Lord Byron, the copyrights of which were in their possession. This they refused to state, but after considerable delay, during which the Hunts were disposing of the two volumes, the whole of the works of Lord Byron which were not in Mr. Murray's possession were put up to auction, and bought by him for the sum of £3,885. These included the "Hours of Idleness, " eleven cantos of "Don Juan, " the "Age of Bronze, " and other works—all of which had already been published.

Notwithstanding the destruction of Lord Byron's Memoirs, described in a previous chapter, Murray had never abandoned the intention of bringing out a Biography of his old friend the poet, for which he possessed plenteous materials in the mass of correspondence which had passed between them. Although his arrangement with Thomas Moore had been cancelled by that event, his eye rested on him as the fittest person, from his long intimacy with the poet, to be entrusted with the task, for which, indeed, Lord Byron had himself selected him.

Accordingly in 1826 author and publisher seem to have drawn together again, and begun the collection of materials, which was carried on in a leisurely way, until Leigh Hunt's scandalous attack on his old patron and benefactor [Footnote: "Recollections of Lord Byron and some of his Contemporaries, " 1828. 4to.] roused Murray's ardour into immediate action.

It was eventually resolved to publish the Life and Correspondence together; and many letters passed between Murray and Moore on the subject.

From the voluminous correspondence we retain the following extract from a letter from Moore to Murray:

"One of my great objects, as you will see in reading me, is to keep my style down to as much simplicity as I am capable of; for nothing could be imagined more discordant than the mixture of any of our Asiatico-Hibernian eloquence with the simple English diction of Byron's letters. "

Murray showed the early part of "Byron's Life" to Lockhart, who replied to him at once:

Mr. Lockhart to John Murray.

February 23, 1829.

"I can't wait till tomorrow to say that I think the beginning of 'Byron' quite perfect in every way—the style simple, and unaffected, as the materials are rich, and how sad. It will be Moore's greatest work—at least, next to the 'Melodies, ' and will be a fortune to you. My wife says it is divine. By all means engrave the early miniature. Never was anything so drearily satisfactory to the imagination as the whole picture of the lame boy's start in life. "

Moore was greatly touched by this letter. He wrote from Sloperton:

Mr. Moore to John Murray.

"Lockhart's praise has given me great pleasure, and his wife's even still greater; but, after all, the merit is in my subject—in the man, not in me. He must be a sad bungler who would spoil such a story. "

As the work advanced, Sir Walter Scott's opinion also was asked.

Mr. Lockhart to John Murray.

September 29, 1829.

"Sir Walter has read the first 120 pages of Moore's 'Life of Byron'; and he says they are charming, and not a syllable *de trop*. He is now busy at a grand rummage among his papers, and has already found one of Lord Byron's letters which shall be at Mr. Moore's service forthwith. He expects to find more of them. This is curious, as being the first of 'Byron' to Scott. "

The first volume of "Lord Byron's Life and Letters, " published on January 1, 1830, was read with enthusiasm, and met with a very favourable reception. Moore says in his Diary that "Lady Byron was highly pleased with the 'Life, '" but among the letters received by Mr. Murray, one of the most interesting was from Mrs. Shelley, to whom a presentation copy had been sent.

Mrs. Shelley to John Murray.

January 19, 1830.

Except the occupation of one or two annoyances, I have done nothing but read, since I got "Lord Byron's Life. " I have no pretensions to being a critic, yet I know infinitely well what pleases me. Not to mention the judicious arrangement and happy *tact* displayed by Mr. Moore, which distinguish the book, I must say a word concerning the style, which is elegant and forcible. I was particularly struck by the observations on Lord Byron's character before his departure to Greece, and on his return. There is strength and richness, as well as sweetness.

The great charm of the work to me, and it will have the same to you, is that the Lord Byron I find there is *our* Lord Byron—the fascinating, faulty, philosophical being—daring the world, docile to a private circle, impetuous and indolent, gloomy, and yet more gay than any other. I live with him again in these pages—getting reconciled (as I used in his lifetime) to those waywardnesses which annoyed me when he was away, through the delightful tone of his conversation and manners.

His own letters and journals mirror himself as he was, and are invaluable. There is something cruelly kind in this single volume. When will the next come? Impatient before, how tenfold more so am I now. Among its many other virtues, this book is accurate to a miracle. I have not stumbled on one mistake with regard either to time, place, or feeling.

I am, dear Sir,

Your obedient and obliged Servant,

MARY SHELLEY.

The preparation of the second volume proceeded more rapidly than the first, for Lord Byron's letters to Murray and Moore during the later years of his life covered the whole period, and gave to the record an almost autobiographical character. It appeared in January 1831, and amongst many other readers of it Mrs. Somerville, to whom Mr. Murray sent a present of the book, was full of unstinted praise.

Mrs. Somerville to John Murray.

January 13, 1831.

You have kindly afforded me a source of very great interest and pleasure in the perusal of the second volume of Moore's "Life of Byron. " In my opinion, it is very superior to the first; there is less repetition of the letters; they are better written, abound more in criticism and observation, and make the reader better acquainted with Lord Byron's principles and character. His morality was certainly more suited to the meridian of Italy than England; but with all his faults there is a charm about him that excites the deepest interest and admiration. His letter to Lady Byron is more affecting and beautiful than anything I have read; it must ever be a subject of regret that it was not sent; it seems impossible that it should not have made a lasting impression, and might possibly have changed the destinies of both. With kind remembrances to Mrs. Murray and the young people,

Believe me, truly yours,

MARY SOMERVILLE.

Mr. Croker's opinion was as follows:

"As to what you say of Byron's volume, no doubt there are *longueurs*, but really not many. The most teasing part is the blanks, which perplex without concealing. I also think that Moore went on a wrong principle, when, publishing *any* personality, he did not publish *all*. It is like a suppression of evidence. When such horrors are published of Sir S. Romilly, it would have been justice to his memory to show that, on the *slightest* provocation, Byron would treat his dearest friend in the same style. When his sneers against Lady Byron and her mother are recorded, it would lessen their effect if it were shown that he sneered at all man and womankind in turn; and that the friend of his choicest selection, or the mistress of his maddest love, were served no better, when the maggot (selfishness) bit, than his wife or his mother-in-law. "

The appearance of the Life induced Captain Medwin to publish his "Conversations with Lord Byron, " a work now chiefly remembered as having called forth from Murray, who was attacked in it, a reply which, as a crashing refutation of personal charges, has seldom been surpassed. [Footnote: Mr. Murray's answer to Medwin's fabrications is published in the Appendix to the 8vo edition of "Lord Byron's Poems. "]

Amongst the reviews of the biography was one by Lockhart in the *Quarterly* (No. 87), which was very favourable; but an article, by Mr. Croker in No. 91, on another of Moore's works—the "Life of Lord Edward Fitzgerald"—was of a very different character. Murray told Moore of the approaching appearance of the article in the next number, and Moore enters in his Diary, "Saw my 'Lord Edward Fitzgerald' announced as one of the articles in the *Quarterly*, to be abused of course; and this too immediately after my dinings and junketings with both author and publisher. "

Mr. Moore to John Murray.

October 25, 1831.

... I see that what I took for a joke of yours is true, and that you are *at* me in this number of the *Quarterly*. I have desired Power to send you back my copy when it comes, not liking to read it just now for reasons. In the meantime, here's some *good*-humoured doggerel for you:

THOUGHTS ON EDITORS.

Editur et edit.

No! Editors don't care a button,
  What false and faithless things they do;
They'll let you come and cut their mutton,
  And then, they'll have a cut at you.

With Barnes I oft my dinner took,
  Nay, met e'en Horace Twiss to please him:
Yet Mister Barnes traduc'd my Book,
  For which may his own devils seize him!

With Doctor Bowring I drank tea,
  Nor of his cakes consumed a particle;
And yet th' ungrateful LL.D.
  Let fly at me, next week, an article!

John Wilson gave me suppers hot,
  With bards of fame, like Hogg and Packwood;
A dose of black-strap then I got,
  And after a still worse of Blackwood.

Alas! and must I close the list
  With thee, my Lockhart of the *Quarterly?*
So kind, with bumper in thy fist, —
  With pen, so very gruff and tartarly.

Now in thy parlour feasting me,
  Now scribbling at me from your garret, —
Till, 'twixt the two, in doubt I be,
  Which sourest is, thy wit or claret?

Should you again see the Noble Scott before he goes, remember me most affectionately to him. Ever yours,

Thomas Moore.

Mr. Murray now found himself at liberty to proceed with his cherished scheme of a complete edition of Lord Byron's works.

John Murray to Mr. Moore.

February 28, 1832.

When I commenced this complete edition of Byron's works I was so out of heart by the loss upon the first edition of the "Life, " and by the simultaneous losses from the failure of three booksellers very largely in my debt, that I had little if any hopes of its success, and I felt myself under the necessity of declining your kind offer to edit it, because I did not think that I should have had it in my power to offer you an adequate remuneration. But now that the success of this speculation is established, if you will do me the favour to do what you propose, I shall have great satisfaction in giving you 500 guineas for your labours.

Most sincerely yours,

John Murray.

In 1837, the year in which the work now in contemplation was published, the Countess Guiccioli was in London, and received much kindness from Mr. Murray. After her return to Rome, she wrote to him a long letter, acknowledging the beautifully bound volume of the landscape and portrait illustrations of Lord Byron's works. She complained, however, of Brockedon's portrait of herself.

Countess Guiccioli to John Murray.

"It is not resembling, and to tell you the truth, my dear Mr. Murray, I wish it was so; not on account of the ugliness of features (which is also remarkable), but particularly for having this portrait an expression of *stupidity*, and for its being *molto antipatico*, as we say in our language. But perhaps it is not the fault of the painter, but of the original, and I am sorry for that. What is certain is that towards such a creature nobody may feel inclined to be indulgent; and if she has faults and errors to be pardoned for, she will never be so on account of her *antipatia*! But pray don't say that to Mr. Brockedon. "

A copy was likewise sent to Sir R. Peel with the following letter:

ALBEMARLE STREET, *April* 17, 1837.

DEAR SIR,

As the invaluable instructions which you addressed to the students of the University of Glasgow have as completely associated your name with the literature of this country, as your political conduct has with its greatest statesmen, I trust that I shall be pardoned for having inscribed to you (without soliciting permission) the present edition of the works of one of our greatest poets, "your own school-and form-fellow, " *Byron*.

I have the honour to be, etc.,

JOHN MURRAY.

The Right Hon. Sir R. Peel to John Murray.

WHITEHALL, *April* 18, 1837.

MY DEAR SIR,

I am much flattered by the compliment which you have paid to me in dedicating to me a beautiful edition of the works of my distinguished "school-and form-fellow. "

I was the next boy to Lord Byron at Harrow for three or four years, and was always on very friendly terms with him, though not living in particular intimacy out of school.

I do not recollect ever having a single angry word with him, or that there ever was any the slightest jealousy or coldness between us.

It is a gratification to me to have my name associated with his in the manner in which you have placed it in friendly connection; and I do not believe, if he could have foreseen, when we were boys together at school, this continuance of a sort of amicable relation between us after his death, the idea would have been otherwise than pleasing to him.

Believe me,

My dear Sir,

Very faithfully yours,

ROBERT PEEL.

A few words remain to be added respecting the statue of Lord Byron, which had been so splendidly executed by Thorwaldsen at Rome. Mr. Hobhouse wrote to Murray: "Thorwaldsen offers the completed work for £1,000, together with a bas-relief for the pedestal, suitable for the subject of the monument. " The sculptor's offer was accepted, and the statue was forwarded from Rome to London. Murray then applied to the Dean of Westminster, on behalf of the subscribers, requesting to know "upon what terms the statue now completed could be placed in some suitable spot in Westminster Abbey. " The Dean's answer was as follows:

The Dean of Westminster to John Murray.

DEANERY, WESTMINSTER, *December* 17, 1834.

DEAR SIR,

I have not had the opportunity, till this morning, of consulting with the Chapter on the subject of your note. When you formerly applied to me for leave to inter the remains of Lord Byron within this Abbey, I stated to you the principle on which, as Churchmen, we were compelled to decline the proposal. The erection of a monument in honour of his memory which you now desire is, in its proportion, subject to the same objection. I do indeed greatly wish for a figure by Thorwaldsen here; but no taste ought to be indulged to the prejudice of a duty.

With my respectful compliments to the Committee, I beg you to believe me,

Yours truly,

JOHN IRELAND.

The statue was for some time laid up in a shed on a Thames wharf. An attempt was made in the House of Commons to alter the decision of the Dean and Chapter, but it proved of no avail. "I would do my best, " said Mr. Hobhouse, "to prevail upon Sir Robert Peel to use his influence with the Dean. It is a national disgrace that the statue should lie neglected in a carrier's ware-house, and it is so felt by men of all parties. I have had a formal application from Trinity College, Cambridge, for leave to place the monument in their great library, and it has been intimated to me that the French Government desire to have it for the Louvre. " The result was that the subscribers, in order to retain the statue in England, forwarded it to Trinity College, Cambridge, whose noble library it now adorns.

The only memorial to Byron in London is the contemptible leaning bronze statue in Apsley House Gardens, nearly opposite the statue of Achilles. Its pedestal is a block of Parian marble, presented by the Greek Government as a national tribute to the memory of Byron.

CHAPTER XXIX

BENJAMIN DISRAELI—THOMAS CARLYLE—AND OTHERS

Me. Disraeli's earliest appearance as an author had been with the novel of "Vivian Grey, " published after a brief visit to Germany while he was still in his eighteenth year. Two volumes were published in 1826, and a third volume, or continuation, in the following year. The work brought the author some notoriety, but, as already noticed, it contained matter which gave offence in Albemarle Street. After the publication of the first part, which was contemporaneous with the calamitous affair of the *Representative*, Mr. Murray saw but little of the Disraeli family, but at the commencement of 1830, Mr. Benjamin Disraeli once more applied to him for an interview. Mr. Murray, however, in whose mind the former episode was still fresh, was unwilling to accede to this request, and replied in the third person.

John Murray to Mr. B. Disraeli.

"Mr. Murray is obliged to decline at present any personal interview; but if Mr. Benjamin Disraeli is disposed to confide his MS. to Mr. Murray as a man of business, Mr. Disraeli is assured that the proposal will be entertained in every respect with the strictest honour and impartiality. "

Mr. B. Disraeli to John Murray.

UNION HOTEL, COCKSPUR STREET, 1830.

The object of my interview with you is *purely literary*. It has always been my wish, if it ever were my fate to write anything calculated to arrest public attention, that you should be the organ of introducing it to public notice. A letter I received this morning from my elected critic was the reason of my addressing myself to you.

I am sorry that Mr. Mitchell is out of town, because he is a person in whom you rightly have confidence; but from some observations he made to me the other day it is perhaps not to be regretted that he does not interfere in this business. As he has overrated some juvenile indiscretions of mine, I fear he is too friendly a critic.

I am thus explicit because I think that candour, for all reasons, is highly desirable. If you feel any inclination to pursue this affair, act as you like, and fix upon any critic you please. I have no objection to Mr. Lockhart, who is certainly an able one, and is, I believe, influenced by no undue partiality towards me.

At all events, this is an affair of no great importance—and whatever may be your determination, it will not change the feelings which, on my part, influenced this application. I have the honour to be, Sir,

Your obedient Servant,

BENJ. DISRAELI.

P. S.—I think it proper to observe that I cannot crudely deliver my MS. to any one. I must have the honour of seeing you or your critic. I shall keep this negotiation open for a couple of days—that is, I shall wait for your answer till Tuesday morning, although, from particular circumstances, time is important to me.

Mr. Disraeli was about to make a prolonged journey abroad. Before he set out he again wrote to Mr. Murray:

Mr. Disraeli to John Murray.

BRADENHAM, BERKS, *May* 27, 1830.

SIR,

I am unwilling to leave England, which I do on Saturday, without noticing your last communication, because I should regret very much if you were to misconceive the motives which actuated me in not complying with the suggestion therein contained. I can assure you I leave in perfect confidence both in your "honour" and your "impartiality, " for the first I have never doubted, and the second it is your interest to exercise.

The truth is, my friend and myself differed in the estimate of the MS. alluded to, and while I felt justified, from his opinion, in submitting it to your judgment, I felt it due to my own to explain verbally the contending views of the case, for reasons which must be obvious.

As you forced me to decide, I decided as I thought most prudently. The work is one which, I dare say, would neither disgrace you to publish, nor me to write; but it is not the kind of production which should recommence our connection, or be introduced to the world by the publisher of Byron and Anastasius.

I am now about to leave England for an indefinite, perhaps a long period. When I return, if I do return, I trust it will be in my power for the *third time* to endeavour that you should be the means of submitting my works to the public. For this I shall be ever ready to make great sacrifices, and let me therefore hope that when I next offer my volumes to your examination, like the Sibylline books, their inspiration may at length be recognised.

I am, Sir,

Your obedient Servant,

B. DISRAELI.

John Murray to Mr. Disraeli.

May 29, 1830.

Mr. Murray acknowledges the receipt of Mr. Benjamin Disraeli's polite letter of the 27th. Mr. Murray will be ready at all times to receive any MS. which Mr. B. Disraeli may think proper to confide to him. Mr. Murray hopes the result of Mr. Disraeli's travels will complete the restoration of his health, and the gratification of his expectations. "

Nearly two years passed before Mr. Disraeli returned to England from those travels in Spain, the Mediterranean and the Levant, which are so admirably described in his "Home Letters, " [Footnote: "Home Letters, " written by the late Earl of Beaconsfield in 1830 and 1831. London, 1885.] and which appear to have exercised so powerful an influence on his own character, and his subsequent career. Shortly after his return, he wrote to Mr. Murray:

Mr. Disraeli to John Murray.

BRADENHAM HOUSE, WYCOMBE,

February 10, 1832.

Sir,

I have at length completed a work which I wish to submit to your consideration. In so doing, I am influenced by the feelings I have already communicated to you.

If you retain the wish expressed in a note which I received at Athens in the autumn of 1830, I shall have the honour of forwarding the MS, to you. Believe me, Sir, whatever may be the result,

Very cordially yours,

BENJ. DISRAELI.

The MS. of the work was at once forwarded to Mr. Murray, who was, however, averse to publishing it without taking the advice of his friends. He first sent it to Mr. Lockhart, requesting him to read it and pronounce his opinion.

Mr. Lockhart to John Murray.

March 3, 1832.

"I can't say what ought to be done with this book. To me, knowing whose it is, it is full of interest; but the affectations and absurdities are such that I can't but think they would disgust others more than the life and brilliancy of many of the descriptions would please them. You should send it to Milman without saying who is the author. —J. G.L. "

The MS. was accordingly sent to Mr. Milman, but as he was very ill at the time, and could not read it himself, but transferred it to his wife, much delay occurred in its perusal. Meanwhile, Mr. Disraeli became very impatient about the publication, and again wrote:

Mr. Disraeli to John Murray.

March 4, 1832.

MY DEAR SIR,

I wish that I could simplify our arrangements by a stroke by making you a present of "The Psychological Romance"; but at present you must indeed take the will for the deed, although I hope the future will allow us to get on more swimmingly. That work has, in all probability, cost me more than I shall ever obtain by it, and indeed I may truly say that to write that work I have thrown to the winds all the obvious worldly prospects of life.

I am ready to make every possible sacrifice on my part to range myself under your colours. I will willingly give up the immediate and positive receipt of a large sum of money for the copyright, and by publishing the work anonymously renounce that certain sale which, as a successful, although I confess not very worthy author, I can command. But in quitting my present publisher, I incur, from the terms of our last agreement, a *virtual penalty*, which I have no means to pay excepting from the proceeds of my pen. Have you, therefore, any objection to advance me a sum on the anticipated profits of the edition, not exceeding two hundred pounds?

It grieves me much to appear exacting to you, but I frankly tell you the reason, and, as it will enable me to place myself at your disposal, I hope you will not consider me mercenary, when I am indeed influenced by the most sincere desire to meet your views.

If this modification of your arrangement will suit you, as I fervently trust it will, I shall be delighted to accede to your wishes. In that case let me know without loss of time, and pray let us meet to talk over minor points, as to the mode of publication, etc. I shall be at home all the morning; my time is very much occupied, and on Thursday or Friday I must run down, for a day or two, to Wycombe to attend a public meeting. [Footnote: Mr. Disraeli was then a candidate, on the Radical side, for the borough of Wycombe.]

Fervently trusting that this arrangement will meet your wishes,

Believe me, yours,

BENJ. DISRAELI.

While the MS. was still in Mr. Milman's hands, Mr. Disraeli followed this up with another letter:

Mr. Disraeli to John Murray

35 DUKE STREET, ST. JAMES'S.

MY DEAR SIR, I am very sensible that you have conducted yourself, with regard to my MS., in the most honourable, kind, and judicious manner; and I very much regret the result of your exertions, which neither of us deserve.

I can wait no longer. The delay is most injurious to me, and in every respect very annoying. I am therefore under the painful necessity of requesting you to require from your friend the return of my work without a moment's delay, but I shall not deny myself the gratification of thanking you for your kindness and subscribing myself, with regard,

Your faithful Servant,

BENJ. DISRAELI.

At length Mr. Milman's letter arrived, expressing his judgment on the work, which was much more satisfactory than that of Mr. Lockhart.

The Rev. H.H. Milman to John Murray.

READING, *March* 5, 1832.

MY DEAR SIR,

I have been utterly inefficient for the last week, in a state of almost complete blindness; but am now, I trust, nearly restored. Mrs. Milman, however, has read to me the whole of the MS. It is a very remarkable production—very wild, very extravagant, very German, very powerful, very poetical. It will, I think, be much read—as far as one dare predict anything of the capricious taste of the day—much admired, and much abused. It is much more in the Macaulay than in the Croker line, and the former is evidently in the ascendant. Some passages will startle the rigidly orthodox; the phrenologists will be in rapture. I tell you all this, that you may judge for yourself. One thing insist upon, if you publish it-that the title be changed. The whole beauty, of the latter part especially, is its truth. It is a rapid volume of travels, a "Childe Harold" in prose; therefore do not let it be called "a Romance" on any account. Let those who will, believe it to be a real history, and those who are not taken in, dispute whether it is truth or fiction. If it makes any sensation, this will add to its notoriety. "A Psychological Auto-Biography" would be too sesquipedalian a title; but "My Life Psychologically Related, " or "The Psychology of my Life, " or some such title, might be substituted.

H. H. MILMAN.

Before Mr. Milman's communication had been received, another pressing letter arrived from Mr. Disraeli.

Mr. Disraeli to John Murray.

MY DEAR SIR,

It is with deep regret and some mortification that I appear to press you. It is of the highest importance to me that the "P. R." should appear without loss of time. I have an impending election in the country, which a single and not improbable event may precipitate. It is a great object with me, that my work should be published before that election.

Its rejection by you will only cause me sorrow. I have no desire that you should become its publisher, unless you conceive it may be the first of a series of works, which may support your name, and sustain your fortunes. There is no question of pecuniary matters between us; I leave all these with you, with illimitable trust.

Pray, pray, my dear Sir, do not let me repent the feelings which impel me to seek this renewal of our connection. I entreat therefore your attention to this subject, and request that you will communicate your decision.

Believe me, as I have already said, that whatever that decision may be, I shall not the less consider myself,

Very cordially yours,

B. DISRAELI.

And again, in a subsequent letter, Mr. Disraeli said:

"There is no work of fiction on whose character I could not decide in four-and-twenty hours, and your critic ought not to be less able than your author. Pray, therefore, to communicate without loss of time to your obedient faithful servant.

"B. D."

On receiving Mr. Milman's approval, Mr. Murray immediately made up his mind to publish the work. He wrote to Mr. Disraeli:

John Murray to Mr. Disraeli.

March 6, 1832.

MY DEAR SIR,

Your MS. has this moment been returned to me, accompanied by a commendation which enables me to say that I should be proud of being its publisher. But in these times I am obliged to refrain from speculation, and I cannot offer any sum for it that is likely to be equal to its probable value.

I would, however, if it so please you, print at my expense an edition of 1,200 or 1,500 copies, and give you half the profits; and after the sale of this edition, the copyright shall be entirely your own; so that if the work prove as successful as I anticipate, you will ensure all the advantages of it without incurring any risque. If this proposal should not suit you, I beg to add that I shall, for the handsome offer of your work in the first instance, still remain,

Your obedient Servant,

JOHN MURRAY.

Some further correspondence took place as to the title of the work. "What do you think, " said Mr. Disraeli, "of the 'Psychological Memoir'? I hesitate between this and 'Narrative, ' but discard 'History' or 'Biography. ' On survey, I conceive the MS. will make four Byronic tomes, according to the pattern you were kind enough to show me. " The work was at length published in 4 vols., foolscap

8vo, with the title of "Contarini Fleming: a Psychological Biography."

Before the appearance of the work, Mr. Disraeli wrote to Mr. Murray as follows:

Mr. Disraeli to John Murray.

BRADENHAM HOUSE, *May* 6, 1832.

DEAR SIR,

From the notice of "C. F." in the *Literary Gazette,* which I received this morning, I imagine that Jerdan has either bribed the printer, or purloined some sheets. It is evident that he has only seen the last volume. It is unnecessary for me to observe that such premature notice, written in such complete ignorance of the work, can do no good. I think that he should be reprimanded, and his petty larceny arrested. I shall be in town on Tuesday.

Yours, B.D.

The work, when it appeared in 1833, excited considerable sensation, and was very popular at the time of its publication. It is now included in the uniform edition of Lord Beaconsfield's works.

During his travels in the East, Mr. Disraeli was attended by Lord Byron's faithful gondolier, who had accompanied his master to Missolonghi, and remained with him till his death.

Mr. Disraeli to John Murray.

DUKE STREET, *July 5,* 1832.

DEAR SIR,

I have just returned to town, and will call in Albemarle Street as soon as I can. Tita, Lord Byron's faithful servant, and [Footnote: See note,

p. 259.] who was also my travelling companion in the East, called upon me this morning. I thought you might wish to see one so intimately connected with the lost bard, and who is himself one of the most deserving creatures in the world.

Yours faithfully,

B. DISRAELI.

At the same time that Mr. Disraeli was engaged on his novel, he was busy with another, but this time a political work entitled "England and France: a Cure for the Ministerial Gallomania, " dedicated to Lord Grey. The first letter on the subject—after Mr. Murray had agreed to publish the work—appears to have been the following, from Bradenham, Monday night, but without date:

Mr. Disraeli to John Murray.

DEAR SIR,

By to-morrow's coach, at your desire, I send you one-half of the volume, which, however, is not in the finished state I could have wished. I have materials for any length, but it is desirable to get out without a moment's loss of time. It has been suggested to publish a volume periodically, and let this come out as No. 1; so as to establish a journal of general foreign politics, for which there are ample means of first-rate information. I have not been able even to revise what is sent, but it will sufficiently indicate the work.

I am to meet a personage on Thursday evening in town, and read over the whole to him. It is therefore absolutely necessary that the MS. should be returned to you on Thursday morning, and I will call in Albemarle Street the moment of my arrival, which will be about four o'clock. If in time, acknowledge the receipt by return of post.

The remaining portion of the volume consists of several more dramatic scenes in Paris, a view of the character and career of L. P., [Footnote: Louis Philippe.] a most curious chapter on the conduct of the Diplomatists, and a general view of the state of Europe at the moment of publication. Pray be cautious, and above all let me depend upon your having the MS. on Thursday, otherwise, as Liston says in "Love, Law and Physic, " "*we shall get all shot. "*

B. D.

Mr. Disraeli to John Murray,

Friday, 11 o'clock.

MY DEAR SIR,

I much regret that I missed you yesterday, but I called upon you the instant I arrived. I very much wish to talk over the "Gallomania, " and will come on to you, if it be really impossible for you to pay me a visit. I have so much at this moment on my hands, that I should esteem such an incident, not only an honour, but a convenience.

B. D.

There seems to have been a difference of opinion between the author and the publisher respecting the title of the book:

Mr. Disraeli to John Murray.

DEAR SIR,

I have a great respect for your judgment, especially on the subject of titles, as I have shown in another instance, one which I shall ever regret. In the present, I shall be happy to receive from you any suggestion, but I can offer none. To me the *Gallomania* (or *mania* for what is French) appears to be one of the most felicitous titles ever devised. It is comprehensive, it is explicit, it is poignant and intelligible, as I should suppose, to learned and unlearned. The word *Anglomania* is one of the commonest on the other side of the channel, is repeated daily in almost every newspaper; has been the title of one or two works; and of the best farce in the French language. It is here also common and intelligible.

There is no objection to erasing the epithet "New, " if you think it loads the title.

Yours truly,

B. D.

The three following letters were written on the same day:

Mr. Disraeli to John Murray. DUKE STREET, *March* 30, 1832.

DEAR SIR,

I am going to dine with Baron D'Haussez, Baron de Haber, *et hoc genus*, today, and must report progress, otherwise they will think I am trifling with them. Have you determined on a title? What think you of "A Cure for the Ministerial Gallomania, " and advertise, dedicated to Lord Grey? Pray decide. You are aware I have not yet received a proof. Affairs look awkward in France. Beware lest we are a day after the fair, and only annalists instead of prophets.

Your very faithful Servant, B. DISRAELI.

March 30.

DEAR SIR,

I think it does very well, and I hope you are also satisfied. I shall send you the rest of the MS. tomorrow morning. There is a very remarkable chapter on Louis Philippe which is at present with Baron D'Haussez; and this is the reason I have not forwarded it to you. I keep the advertisement to show them.

B. D.

MY DEAR SIR,

In further answer to your note received this evening, I think it proper to observe that I entirely agree with you that I "am bound to make as few alterations as possible, " coming as they do from such a quarter; and I have acted throughout in such a spirit. All alterations and omissions of consequence are in this first sheet, and I have retained in the others many things of which I do not approve, merely on account of my respect for the source from whence they are derived.

While you remind me of what I observed to your son, let me also remind you of the condition with which my permission was accompanied, viz. : that everything was to be submitted to my approval, and subject to my satisfaction. On this condition I have placed the proofs in the hands of several persons not less distinguished than your friend, [Footnote: Mr. Croker, with Mr. B. Disraeli's knowledge, revised the proofs.] and superior even in rank and recent office. Their papers are on my table, and I shall be happy to show them to you. I will mention one: the chapter on Belgium was originally written by the Plenipotentiary of the King of Holland to the Conference, Baron Van Zuylen. Scarcely a line of the original composition remains, although a very able one, because it did not accord with the main design of the book.

With regard to the omission, pp. 12, 13, I acknowledge its felicity; but it is totally at variance with every other notice of M. de Talleyrand in the work, and entirely dissonant with the elaborate mention of him in the last chapter. When the reviser introduced this pungent remark, he had never even read the work he was revising.

With regard to the authorship of this work, I should never be ashamed of being considered the author, I should be *proud to be*; but I am not. It is written by Legion, but I am one of them, and I bear the responsibility. If it be supposed to be written by a Frenchman, all its good effects must be marred, as it seeks to command attention and interest by its purely British spirit.

I have no desire to thrust my acquaintance on your critic. More than once, I have had an opportunity to form that acquaintance, and more than once I have declined it, but I am ready to bear the *brunt of explanation,* if you desire me.

It is quite impossible that anything adverse to the general measure of Reform can issue from my pen or from anything to which I contribute. Within these four months I have declined being returned for a Tory borough, and almost within these four hours, to mention slight affairs, I have refused to inscribe myself a member of "The Conservative Club. " I cannot believe that you will place your critic's feelings for a few erased passages against my permanent interest.

But in fact these have nothing to do with the question. To convenience you, I have no objection to wash my hands of the whole business, and put you in direct communication with my coadjutors. I can assure you that it is from no regard for my situation that Reform was omitted, but because they are of opinion that its notice would be unwise and injurious. For myself, I am ready to do anything that you can desire, except entirely change my position in life.

I will see your critic, if you please, or you can give up the publication and be reimbursed, which shall make no difference in our other affairs. All I ask in this and all other affairs, are candour and decision.

The present business is most pressing. At present I am writing a chapter on Poland from intelligence just received, and it will be ready for the printer tomorrow morning, as I shall finish it before I retire. I await your answer with anxiety.

Yours truly,

B. D.

Mr. Disraeli was evidently intent upon the immediate publication of his work. On the following day he wrote again to Mr. Murray:

Mr. Disraeli to John Murray.

March 31, 1832.

MY DEAR SIR,

We shall have an opportunity of submitting the work to Count Orloff tomorrow morning, in case you can let me have a set of the proofs tonight, I mean as far as we have gone. I do not like to send mine, which are covered with corrections.

Yours truly, B.D.

Mr. Disraeli to John Murray. Monday morning, 9 *o'clock [April* 2].

DEAR SIR,

Since I had the honour of addressing you the note of last night, I have seen the Baron. Our interview was intended to have been a final one, and it was therefore absolutely necessary that I should apprize him of all that had happened, of course concealing the name of your friend. The Baron says that the insertion of the obnoxious passages is fatal to all his combinations; that he has devoted two months of the most valuable time to this affair, and that he must hold me personally responsible for the immediate fulfilment of my agreement, viz. : to ensure its publication when finished.

We dine at the same house today, and I have pledged myself to give him a categorical reply at that time, and to ensure its publication by some mode or other.

Under these principal circumstances, my dear sir, I can only state that the work must be published at once, and with the omission of all passages hostile to Reform; and that if you are unwilling to introduce it in that way, I request from your friendliness such assistance as you can afford me about the printer, etc., to occasion its immediate publication in some other quarter.

After what took place between myself and my coadjutor last night, I really can have for him only one answer or one alternative, and as I wish to give him the first, and ever avoid the second, I look forward with confidence to your answer.

B. D.

Mr. Disraeli next desires to have a set of the proofs to put into the hands of the Duke of Wellington:

Mr. Disraeli to John Murray,

April 6, 1832.

MY DEAR SIR,

I have just received a note, that if I can get a set of clean proofs by Sunday, they will be put in the Duke's hands preliminary to the debate. I thought you would like to know this. Do you think it impossible? Let this be between us. I am sorry to give you all this trouble, but I know your zeal, and the interest you take in these affairs. I myself will never keep the printer, and engage when the proofs are sent me to prepare them for the press within an hour.

Yours,

B. D.

Mr. Disraeli to John Murray.

MY DEAR SIR,

I am very glad to receive the copy. I think that one should be sent to the editor of the *Times* as quickly as possible; that at least he should not be anticipated in the receipt, even if in the *notice*, by a Sunday paper. But I leave all this to your better judgment. You will send copies to Duke Street as soon as you have them.

B. D.

After the article in the *Times* had appeared, Baron de Haber, a mysterious German gentleman of Jewish extraction, who had taken part in the production of "Gallomania, " wrote to Mr. Murray:

Baron de Haber to John Murray.

2 *Mai*, 1832.

MON CHER MONSIEUR,

J'espère que vous serez content de l'article de *Times* sur la "Gallomania. " C'est un grand pas de fait. Il serait utile que le *Standard* et le *Morning Post* le copie en entier, avec des observations dans son sens. C'est a vous, mon cher Monsieur Murray, de soigner cet objet. J'ai infiniment regrette de ne m'etre pas trouve chez moi hier, lorsque vous etes venu me voir, avec l'aimable Mr. Lockhart.

Tout a vous,

DE H.

Baron de Haber to John Murray.

Vendredi.

MON CHER MONSIEUR MURRAY,

Vous desirez dans l'intèrêt de l'ouvrage faire mentionner dans le *Standard* que le *Times* d'aujourd'hui paroît etre assez d'accord avec l'auteur de la "Gallomania" sur M. Thiers, espérant que de jour en jour il reviendra aux idees de cet auteur.

Il seroit aussi convenable de dire que la *prophétie* dans la lettre à *My Lord Grey* était assez juste: Allusion—"In less than a month we shall no doubt hear of their *warm* reception in the Provinces, and of some gratifying, perhaps startling, demonstrations of national gratitude. " Voyez, mon cher Monsieur, comme depuis 8 jours ces pauvres Députés qui ont voté pour le Ministre sont traités, Si vous étes à la maison ce soir, dites-le-moi, je désire vous parler. Dinez-vous chez-vous?

Votre dévoué,

DE H.

The following announcement was published by Mr. Disraeli in reply to certain criticisms of his work:

"I cannot allow myself to omit certain observations of my able critic without remarking that those omissions are occasioned by no insensibility to their acuteness.

"Circumstances of paramount necessity render it quite impossible that anything can proceed from my pen hostile to the general question of *Reform*.

"Independent however of all personal considerations, and viewing the question of Reform for a moment in the light in which my critic evidently speculates, I would humbly suggest that the cause which he advocates would perhaps be more united in the present pages by being passed over *in silence*. It is important that this work should be a work not of *party* but of national interest, and I am induced to believe that a large class in this country, who think themselves bound to support the present administration from a superficial sympathy with their domestic measures, have long viewed their foreign policy with distrust and alarm.

"If the public are at length convinced that Foreign Policy, instead of being an abstract and isolated division of the national interests, is in fact the basis of our empire and present order, and that this basis shakes under the unskilful government of the Cabinet, the public may be induced to withdraw their confidence from that Cabinet altogether.

"With this exception, I have adopted all the additions and alterations that I have yet had the pleasure of seeing without reserve, and I seize this opportunity of expressing my sense of their justness and their value.

"*The Author of 'Gallomania.* '" [Footnote: Several references are made to "Contarini Fleming" and "Gallomania" in "Lord Beaconsfield's Letters to his Sister, " published in 1887.]

The next person whom we shall introduce to the reader was one who had but little in common with Mr. Benjamin Disraeli, except that, like him, he had at that time won little of that world-wide renown which he was afterwards to achieve. This "writer of books, " as he described himself, was no other than Thomas Carlyle, who, when he made the acquaintance of Mr. Murray, had translated Goethe's "Wilhelm Meister, " written the "Life of Schiller, " and several articles in the Reviews; but was not yet known as a literary man of mark. He was living among the bleak, bare moors of Dumfriesshire at Craigenputtock, where he was consoled at times by visits from Jeffrey and Emerson, and by letters from Goethe, and where he wrote that strange and rhapsodical book "Sartor Resartus, " containing a considerable portion of his own experience. After the MS. was nearly finished, he wrapt it in a piece of paper, put in it his pocket, and started for Dumfries, on his way to London.

Mr. Francis Jeffrey, then Lord Advocate, recommended Carlyle to try Murray, because, "in spite of its radicalism, he would be the better publisher. " Jeffrey wrote to Mr. Murray on the subject, without mentioning Carlyle's name:

Mr. Jeffrey to John Murray. May I, 1831.

"Lord Jeffrey [Footnote: Jeffrey writes thus, although he did not become a Lord of Session till 1834.] understands that the earlier chapters of this work (which is the production of a friend of his) were shown some months ago to Mr. Murray (or his reader), and were formally judged of; though, from its incomplete state, no proposal for its publication could then be entertained. What is now sent completes it; the earlier chapters being now under the final perusal of the author.

"Lord Jeffrey, who thinks highly of the author's abilities, ventures to beg Mr. Murray to look at the MS. now left with him, and to give him, as soon as possible, his opinion as to its probable success on publication; and also to say whether he is willing to undertake it, and on what terms. "

Carlyle, who was himself at the time in London, called upon Mr. Murray, and left with him a portion of the manuscript, and an outline of the proposed volume.

Mr. Carlyle to John Murray.

6 WOBURN BUILDINGS, TAVISTOCK SQUARE,

Wednesday, August 10, 1831.

DEAR SIR,

I here send you the MS. concerning which I have, for the present, only to repeat my urgent request that no time may be lost in deciding on it. At latest, next Wednesday I shall wait upon you, to see what further, or whether anything further is to be done.

In the meanwhile, it is perhaps unnecessary to say, that the whole business is strictly confidential; the rather, as I wish to publish anonymously.

I remain, dear Sir, yours truly,

THOMAS CARLYLE.

Be so kind as to write, by the bearer, these two words, "MS. received."

When Carlyle called a second time Murray was not at home, but he found that the parcel containing the MS. had not been opened. He again wrote to the publisher on the following Friday:

Mr. Carlyle to John Murray.

DEAR SIR,

As I am naturally very anxious to have this little business that lies between us off my hands—and, perhaps, a few minutes' conversation would suffice to settle it all—I will again request, in case I should be so unlucky as to miss you in Albemarle Street, that you would have the goodness to appoint me a short meeting at any, the earliest, hour that suits your convenience.

I remain, dear Sir, yours truly,

THOMAS CARLYLE.

This was followed up by a letter from Mr. Jeffrey:

Mr. Jeffrey to John Murray.

Sunday, August 28, 1831.

MY DEAR SIR,

Will you favour me with a few minutes' conversation, any morning of this week (the early part of it, if possible), on the subject of my friend Carlyle's projected publication. I have looked a little into the MS. and can tell you something about it. Believe me, always, very faithfully yours,

F. JEFFREY.

The interview between Jeffrey and Murray led to an offer for the MS.

Mr. Carlyle to John Murray.

TUESDAY.

DEAR SIR,

I have seen the Lord Advocate [Jeffrey], who informs me that you are willing to print an edition of 750 copies of my MS., at your own cost, on the principle of what is called "half profits"; the copyright of the book after that to belong to myself. I came down at present to say that, being very anxious to have you as a publisher, and to see my book put forth soon, I am ready to accede to these terms; and I should like much to meet you, or hear from you, at your earliest convenience, that the business might be actually put in motion. I much incline to think, in contrasting the character of my little speculation with the character of the times, that *now* (even in these months, say in November) were the best season for emitting it. Hoping soon to see all this pleasantly settled,

I remain, dear Sir, yours truly,

THOMAS CARLYLE.

Mr. Murray was willing to undertake the risk of publishing 750 copies, and thus to allow the author to exhibit his literary wares to the public. Even if the whole edition had sold, the pecuniary results to both author and publisher would have been comparatively trifling, but as the copyright was to remain in the author's possession, and he would have been able to make a much better bargain with the future editions, the terms may be considered very liberal, having regard to the exceptional nature of the work. Mr. Carlyle, however, who did not know the usual custom of publishers, had in the meantime taken away his MS. and offered it to other publishers in London, evidently to try whether he could not get a better bid for his book. Even Jeffrey thought it "was too much of the nature of a rhapsody, to command success or respectful attention. " The publishers thought the same. Carlyle took the MS. to Fraser of Regent Street, who offered to publish it if Carlyle would *give him* a sum not exceeding £150 sterling. He had already been to Longmans & Co., offering them his "German Literary History, " but they declined to publish the work, and he now offered them his "Sartor Resartus, " with a similar result. He also tried Colburn and Bentley, but without success. When Murray, then at Ramsgate, heard that Carlyle had been offering his book to other publishers, he wrote to him:

John Murray to Mr. Carlyle.

September 17, 1831.

DEAR SIR,

Your conversation with me respecting the publication of your MS. led me to infer that you had given me the preference, and certainly not that you had already submitted it to the greatest publishers in

London, who had declined to engage in it. Under these circumstances it will be necessary for me also to get it read by some literary friend, before I can, in justice to myself, engage in the printing of it.

I am, dear Sir, your faithful servant,

JOHN MURRAY.

To this Mr. Carlyle replied:

September 19, 1831

SIR,

I am this moment favoured with your note of the 17th, and beg to say, in reply, :

First. —That your idea, derived from conversation with me, of my giving you the preference to all other Publishers, was perfectly correct. I had heard you described as a man of honour, frankness, and even generosity, and knew you to have the best and widest connexions; on which grounds, I might well say, and can still well say, that a transaction with you would please me better than a similar one with any other member of the Trade.

Secondly. —That your information, of my having submitted my MS. to the greatest publishers in London, if you mean that, after coming out of your hands, it lay two days in those of Messrs. Longman & Rees, and was from them delivered over to the Lord Advocate, is also perfectly correct: if you mean anything else, incorrect.

Thirdly. —That if you wish the Bargain, which I had understood myself to have made with you, unmade, you have only to cause your Printer, who is now working on my MS., to return the same, without damage or delay, and consider the business as finished. I remain, Sir, your obedient servant,

THOMAS CARLYLE.

In the meantime Murray submitted the MS. to one of his literary advisers, probably Lockhart, whose report was not very encouraging. Later, as Mr. Carlyle was unwilling to entertain the idea of taking his manuscript home with him, and none of the other publishers would accept it, he urgently requested Mr. Murray again to examine it, and come to some further decision. "While I, with great readiness, " he said, "admit your views, and shall cheerfully release you from all engagement, or shadow of engagement, with me in regard to it: the rather, as it seems reasonable for me to expect some higher remuneration for a work that has cost me so much effort, were it once fairly examined, such remuneration as was talked of between *us* can, I believe, at all times, be procured. " He then proposed "a quite new negotiation, if you incline to enter on such"; and requested his decision. "If not, pray have the goodness to cause my papers to be returned with the least possible delay. " The MS. was at once returned; and Carlyle acknowledged its receipt:

Mr. Carlyle to John Murray.

October 6, 1831.

MY DEAR SIR,

I have received the MS., with your note and your friend's criticism, and I find it all safe and right. In conclusion, allow me to thank you for your punctuality and courtesy in this part of the business; and to join cordially in the hope you express that, in some fitter case, a closer relation may arise between us. I remain, my dear Sir, faithfully yours,

T. CARLYLE.

Mr. Carlyle returned to Craigenputtock with his manuscript in his pocket; very much annoyed and disgusted by the treatment of the London publishers. Shortly after his arrival at home, he wrote to Mr. Macvey Napier, then editor of the *Edinburgh Review*:

"All manner of perplexities have occurred in the publishing of my poor book, which perplexities I could only cut asunder, not unloose; so the MS., like an unhappy ghost, still lingers on the wrong side of Styx: the Charon of Albemarle Street durst not risk it in his *sutilis cymba*, so it leaped ashore again. Better days are coming, and new trials will end more happily. "

A little later (February 6, 1832) he said:

"I have given up the notion of hawking my little manuscript book about any further. For a long time it has lain quiet in its drawer, waiting for a better day. The bookselling trade seems on the edge of dissolution; the force of puffing can go no further; yet bankruptcy clamours at every door: sad fate! to serve the Devil, and get no wages even from him! The poor bookseller Guild, I often predict to myself, will ere long be found unfit for the strange part it now plays in our European World; and give place to new and higher arrangements, of which the coming shadows are already becoming visible. "

The "Sartor Resartus" was not, however, lost. Two years after Carlyle's visit to London, it came out, bit by bit, in *Fraser's Magazine*. Through the influence of Emerson, it was issued, as a book, at Boston, in the United States, and Carlyle got some money for his production. It was eventually published in England, and, strange to say, has had the largest sale in the "People's Edition of Carlyle's Works. " Carlyle, himself, created the taste to appreciate "Sartor Resartus. "

CHAPTER XXX

MR. GLADSTONE AND OTHERS

In July 1838 Mr. W.E. Gladstone, then Tory member of Parliament for Newark-upon-Trent, wrote to Mr. Murray from 6 Carlton Gardens, informing him that he has written and thinks of publishing some papers on the subject of the relationship of the "Church and the State, " which would probably fill a moderate octavo volume, and that he would be glad to know if Mr. Murray would be inclined to see them. Mr. Murray saw the papers, and on August 9 he agreed with Mr. Gladstone to publish 750 or 1,000 copies of the work on "Church and State, " on half profits, the copyright to remain with the author after the first edition was sold. The work was immediately sent to press, and proofs were sent to Mr. Gladstone, about to embark for Holland. A note was received by Mr. Murray from the author (August 17, 1838):

"I write a line from Rotterdam to say that sea-sickness prevented my correcting the proofs on the passage. "

This was Mr. Gladstone's first appearance in the character of an author, and the work proved remarkably successful, four editions being called for in the course of three years. It was reviewed by Macaulay in the *Edinburgh* for April 1839, and in the *Quarterly* by the Rev. W. Sewell in December. "Church Principles, " published in 1840, did not meet with equal success. Two years later we find a reference to the same subject.

Mr. W.E. Gladstone to John Murray.

13 CARLTON HOUSE TERRACE, *April* 6, 1842.

My DEAR SIR,

I thank you very much for your kindness in sending me the new number of the *Quarterly*. As yet I have only read a part of the article on the Church of England, which seems to be by a known hand, and to be full of very valuable research: I hope next to turn to Lord Mahon's "Joan of Arc. "

Amidst the pressure of more urgent affairs, I have held no consultation with you regarding my books and the sale or no sale of them. As to the third edition of the "State in its Relations, " I should think the remaining copies had better be got rid of in whatever summary or ignominious mode you may deem best. They must be dead beyond recall. As to the others, I do not know whether the season of the year has at all revived the demand; and would suggest to you whether it would be well to advertise them a little. I do not think they find their way much into the second-hand shops.

With regard to the fourth edition, I do not know whether it would be well to procure any review or notice of it, and I am not a fair judge of its merits even in comparison with the original form of the work; but my idea is, that it is less defective both in the theoretical and in the historical development, and ought to be worth the notice of those who deemed the earlier editions worth their notice and purchase: that it would really put a reader in possession of the view it was intended to convey, which I fear is more than can with any truth be said of its predecessors.

I am not, however, in any state of anxiety or impatience: and I am chiefly moved to refer these suggestions to your judgment from perceiving that the Fourth Edition is as yet far from having cleared itself.

I remain always,

Very faithfully yours,

W. E. GLADSTONE.

In the same year another author of different politics and strong anti-slavery views appeared to claim Mr. Murray's assistance as a publisher. It was Mr. Thomas Fowell Buxton, M.P., who desired him to publish his work upon the "Slave Trade and its Remedy. "

Mr. Buxton to John Murray.

December 31, 1837.

"The basis of my proposed book has already been brought before the Cabinet Ministers in a confidential letter addressed to Lord Melbourne.... It is now my purpose to publish a portion of the work, on the nature, extent, and horrors of the slave trade, and the failure of the efforts hitherto made to suppress it, [Footnote: See "Life of W. E. Forster, " ch. iv.] reserving the remainder for another volume to be published at a future day. I should like to have 1,500 copies of the first volume thrown off without delay. "

The book was published, and was followed by a cheaper volume in the following year, of which a large number was sold and distributed.

The following letter illustrates the dangerous results of reading sleepy books by candle-light in bed:

Mr. Longman to John Murray.

2 HANOVER TERRACE, 1838.

MY DEAR MURRAY,

Can you oblige me by letting me have a third volume of "Wilberforce"? The fact is, that in reading that work, my neighbour, Mr. Alexander, fell fast asleep from exhaustion, and, setting himself on fire, burnt the volume and his bed, to the narrow escape of the whole Terrace. Since that book has been published, premiums of fire assurance are up, and not having already insured my No. 2, now that the fire has broken out near my own door, no office will touch my house nor any others in the Terrace until it is ascertained that Mr. Alexander has finished with the book. So pray consider our position, and let me have a third volume to make up the set as soon as possible.

Mr. Murray had agreed with the Bishop of Llandaff to publish Lord Dudley's posthumous works, but the Bishop made certain complaints which led to the following letter from Mr. Murray:

John Murray to the Bishop of Llandaff.

December 31, 1839.

MY LORD,

I am told that your Lordship continues to make heavy complaints of the inconvenience you incur by making me the publisher of "Lord

Dudley's Letters, " in consequence of the great distance between St. Paul's Churchyard and Albemarle Street, and that you have discovered another cause for dissatisfaction in what you consider the inordinate profits of a publisher.

My Lord, when I had the honour to publish for Sir Walter Scott and Lord Byron, the one resided in Edinburgh, the other in Venice; and, with regard to the supposed advantages of a publisher, they were only such as custom has established, and experience proved to be no more than equivalent to his peculiar trouble and the inordinate risque which he incurs.

My long acquaintance with Lord Dudley, and the kindness and friendship with which he honoured me to the last, made me, in addition to my admiration of his talents, desire, and, indeed, expect to become the publisher of his posthumous works, being convinced that he would have had no other. After what has passed on your Lordship's side, however, I feel that it would be inconsistent with my own character to embarrass you any longer, and I therefore release your Lordship at once from any promise or supposed understanding whatever regarding this publication, and remain, my Lord,

Your Lordship's humble Servant,

JOHN MURRAY.

The Bishop of Llandaff seems to have thought better of the matter, and in Mr. Murray's second letter to him (January 1, 1840) he states that, after his Lordship's satisfactory letter, he "renews his engagement as publisher of Lord Dudley's 'Letters' with increased pleasure. " The volume was published in the following year, but was afterwards suppressed; it is now very scarce.

Mrs. Jameson proposed to Mr. Murray to publish a "Guide to the Picture-Galleries of London. " He was willing to comply with her request, provided she submitted her manuscript for perusal and approval. But as she did not comply with his request, Mr. Murray wrote to her as follows:

John Murray to Mrs. Jameson.

July 14, 1840

MY DEAR MADAM,

It is with unfeigned regret that I perceive that you and I are not likely to understand each other. The change from a Publisher, to whose mode of conducting business you are accustomed, to another of whom you have heard merely good reports, operates something like second marriages, in which, whatever occurs that is different from that which was experienced in the first, is always considered wrong by the party who has married a second time. If, for a particular case, you have been induced to change your physician, you should not take offence, or feel even surprise, at a different mode of treatment.

My rule is, never to engage in the publication of any work of which I have not been allowed to form a judgment of its merits and chances of success, by having the MSS. left with me a reasonable time, in order to form such opinion; and from this habit of many years' exercise, I confess to you that it will not, even upon the present occasion, suit me to deviate.

I am well aware that you would not wish to publish anything derogatory to the high reputation which you have so deservedly acquired; but Shakespeare, Byron, and Scott have written works that do not sell; and, as you expect money for the work which you wish to allow me the honour of publishing, how am I to judge of its value if I am not previously allowed to read it?

Mrs. Jameson at length submitted her work for Mr. Murray's inspection; and after some negotiation, her Guide-Book was purchased for £400.

Mr. Murray, it may here be mentioned, had much communication with Sir Robert Peel during his parliamentary career. He published many of Peel's speeches and addresses—his Address to the Students of Glasgow University; his Speeches on the Irish Disturbances Bill, the Coercion Bill, the Repeal of the Union, and the Sugar Bills—all of which were most carefully revised before being issued. Sugar had become so cloying with Sir Robert, that he refused to read his speeches on the subject. "I am so sick of Sugar, " he wrote to Murray, "and of the eight nights' debate, that I have not the courage to look at any report of my speech—at least at present. " A later letter shows that the connection continued.

The Rt. Hon. Sir R. Peel to John Murray.

July or *August,* 1840.

DEAR SIR,

Your printer must be descended from him who omitted *not* from the seventh Commandment, and finding a superfluous "not" in his possession, is anxious to find a place for it.

I am sorry he has bestowed it upon me, and has made me assure my constituents that I do *not* intend to support my political principles. Pray look at the 4th line of the second page of the enclosed.

Faithfully yours,

ROBERT PEEL.

No account of Mr. Murray's career would be complete without some mention of the "Handbooks, " with which his name has been for sixty years associated; for though this series was in reality the invention of his son, it was Mr. Murray who provided the means and encouragement for the execution of the scheme, and by his own experience was instrumental in ensuring its success.

As early as 1817 Hobhouse had remarked on the inadequate character of most books of European travel. In later years Mrs. Starke made a beginning, but her works were very superficial and inadequate, and after personally testing them on their own ground, Mr. John Murray decided that something better was needed.

Of the origin of the Guide-books Mr. John Murray the Third has given the following account in Murray's Magazine for November 1889.

"Since so many thousands of persons have profited by these books, it may be of some interest to the public to learn their origin, and the cause which led me to prepare them. Having from my early youth been possessed by an ardent desire to travel, my very indulgent father acceded to my request, on condition that I should prepare myself by mastering the language of the country I was to travel in. Accordingly, in 1829, having brushed up my German, I first set foot on the Continent at Rotterdam, and my 'Handbook for Holland' gives the results of my personal observations and private studies of that wonderful country.

"At that time such a thing as a Guide-book for Germany, France, or Spain did not exist. The only Guides deserving the name were: Ebel, for Switzerland; Boyce, for Belgium; and Mrs. Starke, for Italy. Hers was a work of real utility, because, amidst a singular medley of classical lore, borrowed from Lemprière's Dictionary, interwoven with details regulating the charges in washing-bills at Sorrento and Naples, and an elaborate theory on the origin of *Devonshire Cream*, in which she proves that it was brought by Phoenician colonists from Asia Minor into the West of England, it contained much practical information gathered on the spot. But I set forth for the North of Europe unprovided with any guide, excepting a few manuscript notes about towns and inns, etc., in Holland, furnished me by my good friend Dr. Somerville, husband of the learned Mrs. Somerville. These were of the greatest use. Sorry was I when, on landing at Hamburg, I found myself destitute of such friendly aid. It was this that impressed on my mind the value of practical information gathered on the spot, and I set to work to collect for myself all the facts, information, statistics, etc., which an English tourist would be likely to require or find useful.

The first of Mr. John Murray's Handbooks to the Continent, published 1836, included Holland, Belgium, and North Germany, and was followed at short intervals by South Germany, Switzerland—in which he was assisted by his intimate friend and fellow-traveller, William Brockedon, the artist, who was then engaged in preparing his own splendid work on "The Peaks, Passes, and Glaciers of the Alps"—and France. These were all written by Mr. Murray himself; but, as the series proceeded, it was necessary to call in the aid of other writers and travellers. Switzerland, which appeared in 1838, was followed in 1839 by Norway, Sweden, and Denmark, and in 1840 by the Handbook to the East, the work of Mr. H. Parish, aided by Mr. Godfrey Levinge. In 1842 Sir Francis Palgrave completed the Guide to Northern Italy, while Central and Southern Italy were entrusted to Mr. Octavian Blewitt, for many years Secretary of the Royal Literary Fund.

In later years, as well as at the earlier period, the originator of the Handbooks was fortunate enough to secure very able colleagues, among whom it is sufficient to mention Richard Ford for Spain, Sir Gardner Wilkinson for Egypt, Dr. Porter for Palestine, Sir George Bowen for Greece, Sir Lambert Playfair for Algiers and the Mediterranean, and Mr. George Dennis for Sicily.

CHAPTER XXXI

GEORGE BORROW—RICHARD FORD—HORACE TWISS—JOHN STERLING—MR. GLADSTONE—DEATH OF SOUTHEY, ETC.

In November 1840 a tall athletic gentleman in black called upon Mr. Murray offering a MS. for perusal and publication. George Borrow had been a travelling missionary of the Bible Society in Spain, though in early life he had prided himself on being an athlete, and had even taken lessons in pugilism from Thurtell, who was a fellow-townsman. He was a native of Dereham, Norfolk, but had wandered much in his youth, first following his father, who was a Captain of Militia. He went from south to north, from Kent to Edinburgh, where he was entered as pupil in the High School, and took part in the "bickers" so well described by Sir Walter Scott. Then the boy followed the regiment to Ireland, where he studied the Celtic dialect. From early youth he had a passion, and an extraordinary capacity, for learning languages, and on reaching manhood he was appointed agent to the Bible Society, and was sent to Russia to translate and introduce the Scriptures. While there he mastered the language, and learnt besides the Solavonian and the gypsy dialects. He translated the New Testament into the Tartar Mantchow, and published versions from English into thirty languages. He made successive visits into Russia, Norway, Turkey, Bohemia, Spain and Barbary. In fact, the sole of his foot never rested. While an agent for the Bible Society in Spain, he translated the New Testament into Spanish, Portuguese, Romany, and Basque—which language, it is said, the devil himself never could learn—and when he had learnt the Basque he acquired the name of Lavengro, or word-master.

Such was George Borrow when he called upon Murray to offer him the MSS. of his first book, "The Gypsies in Spain. " Mr. Murray could not fail to be taken at first sight with this extraordinary man. He had a splendid physique, standing six feet two in his stockings, and he had brains as well as muscles, as his works sufficiently show. The book now submitted was of a very uncommon character, and neither the author nor the publisher was very sanguine about its success. Mr. Murray agreed, after perusal, to print and publish 750 copies of "The Gypsies in Spain, " and divide the profits with the author. But this was only the beginning, and Borrow reaped much better remuneration from future editions of the volume. Indeed, the book was exceedingly well received, and met with a considerable sale; but not so great as his next work, "The Bible in Spain, " which he was now preparing.

Mr. George Borrow to John Murray. August 23, 1841.

"A queer book will be this same 'Bible in Spain, ' containing all my queer adventures in that queer country whilst engaged in distributing the Gospel, but neither learning, nor disquisition, fine writing, or poetry. A book with such a Bible and of this description can scarcely fail of success. It will make two nice foolscap octavo volumes of about 500 pages each. I have not heard from Ford since I had last the pleasure of seeing you. Is his book out? I hope that he will not review the 'Zincali' until the Bible is forthcoming, when he may, if he please, kill two birds with one stone. I hear from Saint Petersburg that there is a notice of the 'Zincali' in the *Revue Britannique*; it has been translated into Russian. Do you know anything about it? "

Mr. George Borrow to John Murray. OULTON HALL, LOWESTOFT, *January* 1842.

MY DEAR SIR,

We are losing time. I have corrected seven hundred consecutive pages of MS., and the remaining two hundred will be ready in a fortnight. I do not think there will be a dull page in the whole book, as I have made one or two very important alterations; the account of my imprisonment at Madrid cannot fail, I think, of being particularly interesting.... During the last week I have been chiefly engaged in horse-breaking. A most magnificent animal has found his way to this neighbourhood—a half-bred Arabian. He is at present in the hands of a low horse-dealer, and can be bought for eight pounds, but no one will have him. It is said that he kills everybody who mounts him. I have been *charming* him, and have so far succeeded that he does not fling me more than once in five minutes. What a contemptible trade is the author's compared with that of the jockey's!

Mr. Borrow prided himself on being a horse-sorcerer, an art he learned among the gypsies, with whose secrets he claimed acquaintance. He whispered some unknown gibberish into their ears, and professed thus to tame them.

He proceeded with "The Bible in Spain. " In the following month he sent to Mr. Murray the MS. of the first volume. To the general information as to the contents and interest of the volume, he added these words:

Mr. George Borrow to John Murray.

February, 1842.

"I spent a day last week with our friend Dawson Turner at Yarmouth. What capital port he keeps! He gave me some twenty years old, and of nearly the finest flavour that I ever tasted. There are few better things than old books, old pictures, and old port, and he seems to have plenty of all three. "

May 10, 1842.

"I am coming up to London tomorrow, and intend to call at Albemarle Street.... I make no doubt that we shall be able to come to terms; I like not the idea of applying to second-rate people. I have been dreadfully unwell since I last heard from you—a regular nervous attack; at present I have a bad cough, caught by getting up at night in pursuit of poachers and thieves. A horrible neighbourhood this—not a magistrate that dares to do his duty.

"P. S.—Ford's book not out yet? "

There seems to have been some difficulty about coming to terms. Borrow had promised his friends that his book should be out by October 1, and he did not wish them to be disappointed:

Mr. George Borrow to John Murray.

July 4, 1842.

Why this delay? Mr. Woodfall [the printer] tells me that the state of trade is wretched. Well and good! But you yourself told me so two months ago, when you wrote requesting that I would give you the preference, provided I had not made arrangements with other publishers. Between ourselves, my dear friend, I wish the state of the trade were ten times worse than it is, and then things would find their true level, and an original work would be properly appreciated, and a set of people who have no pretensions to write, having nothing to communicate but tea-table twaddle, could no longer be palmed off upon the public as mighty lions and lionesses. But to the question: What are your intentions with respect to "The Bible in Spain"? I am a frank man, and frankness never offends me. Has anybody put you out of conceit with the book? There is no lack of critics, especially in your neighbourhood. Tell me frankly, and I will drink your health in Rommany. Or, would the appearance of "The Bible" on the first of October interfere with the Avatar, first or second, of some very Lion or Divinity, to whom George Borrow, who is neither, must, of course, give place? Be frank with me, my dear sir, and I will drink your health in Rommany and Madeira.

In case of either of the above possibilities being the fact, allow me to assure you that I am quite willing to release you from your share of the agreement into which we entered. At the same time, I do not intend to let the work fall to the ground, as it has been promised to the public. Unless you go on with it, I shall remit Woodfall the necessary money for the purchase of paper, and when it is ready offer it to the world. If it be but allowed fair play, I have no doubt of its success. It is an original book, on an original subject. Tomorrow, July 5, I am thirty-nine. Have the kindness to drink my health in Madeira.

Ever most sincerely yours,

GEORGE BORROW.

Terms were eventually arranged to the satisfaction of both parties. Borrow informed Murray that he had sent the last proofs to the printer, and continued:

Mr. George Borrow to John Murray.

November 25, 1842.

Only think, poor Allan Cunningham dead! A young man, only fifty-eight, strong and tall as a giant, might have lived to a hundred and one; but he bothered himself about the affairs of this world far too much. That statue shop [of Chantrey's] was his bane! Took to bookmaking likewise—in a word, was too fond of Mammon. Awful death—no preparation—came literally upon him like a thief in the dark. I'm thinking of writing a short life of him; old friend of twenty years' standing. I know a good deal about him; "Traditional Tales, " his best work, first appeared in *London Magazine*, Pray send Dr. Bowring a copy of the Bible-another old friend. Send one to Ford, a capital fellow. God bless you—feel quite melancholy.

Ever yours,

G. BORROW.

"The Bible in Spain" was published towards the end of the year, and created a sensation. It was praised by many critics, and condemned by others, for Borrow had his enemies in the press.

Mr. George Borrow to John Murray, Junior.

LOWESTOFT, *December* 1, 1842.

MY DEAR SIR,

I received your kind letter containing the bills. It was very friendly of you, and I thank you, though, thank God, I have no Christmas bills to settle. Money, however, always acceptable. I dare say I shall be in London with the entrance of the New Year; I shall be most happy to see you, and still more your father, whose jokes do one good. I wish all the world were as gay as he; a gentleman drowned himself last week on my property, I wish he had gone somewhere else. I can't get poor Allan out of my head. When I come up, intend to go and see his wife. What a woman! I hope our book will be successful. If so, shall put another on the stocks. Capital subject; early life, studies, and adventures; some account of my father, William Taylor, Whiter, Big Ben, etc., etc. Had another letter from Ford; wonderful fellow; seems in high spirits. Yesterday read "Letters from the Baltic"; much pleased with it; very clever writer; critique in *Despatch* harsh and unjust; quite uncalled for; blackguard affair altogether.

I remain, dear Sir, ever yours,

GEORGE BORROW.

December 31, 1842.

MY DEAR SIR,

I have great pleasure in acknowledging your very kind letter of the 28th, and am happy to hear that matters are going on so prosperously. It is quite useless to write books unless they sell, and the public has of late become so fastidious that it is no easy matter to please it. With respect to the critique in the *Times*, I fully agree with you that it was harsh and unjust, and the passages selected by no means calculated to afford a fair idea of the contents of the work. A book, however, like "The Bible in Spain" can scarcely be published without exciting considerable hostility, and I have been so long used to receiving hard knocks that they make no impression upon me. After all, the abuse of the *Times* is better than its silence; it would scarcely have attacked the work unless it had deemed it of some importance, and so the public will think. All I can say is, that I did my best, never writing but when the fit took me, and never delivering anything to my amanuensis but what I was perfectly satisfied with. You ask me my opinion of the review in the *Quarterly*. Very good, very clever, very neatly done. Only one fault to find—too laudatory. I am by no means the person which the reviewer had the kindness to represent me. I hope you are getting on well as to health; strange weather this, very unwholesome, I believe, both for man and beast: several people dead, and great mortality amongst the cattle. Am tolerably well myself, but get but little rest—disagreeable dreams—digestion not quite so good as I could wish; been on the water system—won't do; have left it off, and am now taking lessons in singing. I hope to be in London towards the end of next month, and reckon much upon the pleasure of seeing you. On Monday I shall mount my horse and ride into Norwich to pay a visit to a few old friends. Yesterday the son of our excellent Dawson Turner rode over to see me; they are all well, it seems. Our friend Joseph Gurney, however, seems to be in a strange way—diabetes, I hear. I frequently meditate upon "The Life, " and am arranging the scenes in my mind. With best remembrances to Mrs. M. and all your excellent family,

Truly and respectfully yours,

GEORGE BORROW.

Mr. Richard Ford's forthcoming work—"The Handbook for Spain"—about which Mr. Borrow had been making so many enquiries, was the result of many years' hard riding and constant investigation throughout Spain, one of the least known of all European countries at that time. Mr. Ford called upon Mr. Murray, after "The Bible in Spain" had been published, and a copy of the work was presented to him. He was about to start on his journey to Heavitree, near Exeter. A few days after his arrival Mr. Murray received the following letter from him:

Mr. Richard Ford to John Murray.

"I read Borrow with great delight all the way down per rail, and it shortened the rapid flight of that velocipede. You may depend upon it that the book will sell, which, after all, is the rub. It is the antipodes of Lord Carnarvon, and yet how they tally in what they have in common, and that is much—the people, the scenery of Galicia, and the suspicions and absurdities of Spanish Jacks-in-office, who yield not in ignorance or insolence to any kind of red-tapists, hatched in the hot-beds of jobbery and utilitarian mares-nests... Borrow spares none of them. I see he hits right and left, and floors his man wherever he meets him. I am pleased with his honest sincerity of purpose and his graphic abrupt style. It is like an old Spanish ballad, leaping in *res medias*, going from incident to incident, bang, bang, bang, hops, steps, and jumps like a cracker, and leaving off like one, when you wish he would give you another touch or *coup de grâce*... He really sometimes puts me in mind of Gil Blas; but he has not the sneer of the Frenchman, nor does he gild the bad. He has a touch of Bunyan, and, like that enthusiastic tinker, hammers away, *à la Gitano*, whenever he thinks he can thwack the Devil or his man-of-all-work on earth—the Pope. Therein he resembles my friend and everybody's friend—*Punch*—who, amidst all his adventures, never spares the black one. However, I am not going to review him now; for I know that Mr. Lockhart has expressed a wish that I should do it for the *Quarterly Review*. Now, a wish from my liege master is a command. I had half engaged myself elsewhere, thinking that he did not quite appreciate such a *trump* as I know Borrow to be. He is as full of meat as an egg, and a fresh laid one—not one of your Inglis breed, long addled by over-bookmaking. Borrow will lay you golden eggs, and hatch them after the ways of Egypt; put salt on his tail and secure him in your coop, and beware how any poacher coaxes him with 'raisins' or reasons out of the Albemarle preserves. When you see Mr. Lockhart tell him that I will do the paper. I owe my entire allowance to the *Q. R.* flag... Perhaps my understanding the *full force* of this 'gratia' makes me over partial to this wild Missionary; but I have ridden over the same tracks without the tracts, seen the same people, and know that *he* is true, and I believe that he believes all that he writes to be true. "

Mr. Lockhart himself, however, wrote the review for the *Quarterly* (No. 141, December 1842). It was a temptation that he could not resist, and his article was most interesting. "The Gypsies in Spain" and "The Bible in Spain" went through many editions, and there is still a large demand for both works. Before we leave George Borrow we will give a few extracts from his letters, which, like his books, were short, abrupt, and graphic. He was asked to become a member of the Royal Institution.

Mr. George Borrow to John Murray.

February 26, 1843.

"I should like to become a member. The thing would just suit me, more especially as they do not want *clever* men, but *safe* men. Now, I am safe enough; ask the Bible Society, whose secrets I have kept so much to their satisfaction, that they have just accepted at my hands an English Gypsy Gospel gratis. What would the Institution expect me to write? I have exhausted Spain and the Gypsies, though an essay on Welsh language and literature might suit, with an account of the Celtic tongue. Or, won't something about the ancient North and its literature be more acceptable? I have just received an invitation to join the Ethnological Society (who are they?), which I have declined. I am at present in great demand; a bishop has just requested me to visit him. The worst of these bishops is that they are skin-flints, saving for their families. Their cuisine is bad, and their port wine execrable, and as for their cigars! —I say, do you remember those precious ones of the Sanctuary? A few days ago one of them turned up again. I found it in my great-coat pocket, and thought of you. I have seen the article in the *Edinburgh* about the Bible—exceedingly brilliant and clever, but rather too epigrammatic, quotations scanty and not correct. Ford is certainly a most astonishing fellow; he quite flabbergasts me—handbooks, review's, and I hear that he has just been writing a 'Life of Velasquez' for the 'Penny Cyclopaedia'! "

OULTON HALL, LOWESTOFT, *March* 13, 1843.

"So the second edition is disposed of. Well and good. Now, my dear friend, have the kindness to send me an account of the profits of it and let us come to a settlement. Up to the present time do assure you I have not made a penny by writing, what with journeys to London and tarrying there. Basta! I hate to talk of money matters.

"Let them call me a nonentity if they will; I believe that some of those who say I am a phantom would alter their tone provided they were to ask me to a good dinner; bottles emptied and fowls devoured are not exactly the feats of a phantom: no! I partake more of the nature of a Brownie or Robin Goodfellow—goblins, 'tis true, but full of merriment and fun, and fond of good eating and drinking. Occasionally I write a page or two of my life. I am now getting my father into the Earl of Albemarle's regiment, in which he was captain for many years. If I live, and my spirits keep up tolerably well, I hope that within a year I shall be able to go to press with something which shall beat the 'Bible in Spain. '"

And a few days later:

"I have received your account for the two editions. I am perfectly satisfied. We will now, whenever you please, bring out a third edition.

"The book which I am at present about will consist, if I live to finish it, of a series of Rembrandt pictures, interspersed here and there with a Claude. I shall tell the world of my parentage, my early thoughts and habits, how I become a *sap-engro*, or viper-catcher: my wanderings with the regiment in England, Scotland, and Ireland, in which last place my jockey habits first commenced: then a great deal about Norwich, Billy Taylor, Thurtell, etc. : how I took to study and became a *lav-engro*. What do you think of this for a bill of fare? I am now in a blacksmith's shop in the south of Ireland taking lessons from the Vulcan in horse charming and horse-shoe making. By the bye, I wish I were acquainted with Sir Robert Peel. I could give him many a useful hint with respect to Ireland and the Irish. I know both tolerably well. Whenever there's a row, I intend to go over with Sidi Habesmith and put myself at the head of a body of volunteers. "

During the negotiations for the publication of Mr. Horace Twiss's "Life of the Earl of Eldon, " Mr. Murray wrote to Mr. Twiss:

John Murray to Mr. Twiss.

May 11, 1842.

"I am very sorry to say that the publishing of books at this time involves nothing but loss, and that I have found it absolutely necessary to withdraw from the printers every work that I had in the press, and to return to the authors any MS. for which they required immediate publication. "

Mr. Murray nevertheless agreed to publish the "Life of Eldon" on commission, and it proved very successful, going through several editions.

Another work offered to Mr. Murray in 1841 was "The Moor and the Loch, " by John Colquhoun, of Luss. He had published the first edition at Edinburgh through Mr. Blackwood; and, having had some differences with that publisher, he now proposed to issue the second edition in London. He wrote to Mr. Murray desiring him to undertake the work, and received the following reply:

John Murray to Mr. Colquhoun.

March 16, 1841.

SIR,

I should certainly have had much pleasure in being the original publisher of your very interesting work "The Moor and the Loch, " but I have a very great dislike to the *appearance even* of interfering with any other publisher. Having glass windows, I must not throw stones. With Blackwood, indeed, I have long had particular relations, and they for several years acted as my agents in Edinburgh; so pray have the kindness to confide to me the cause of your misunderstanding with that house, and let me have the satisfaction of at least trying in the first place to settle the matter amicably. In any case, however, you may rely upon all my means to promote the success of your work, the offer of which has made me, dear Sir,

Your obliged and faithful Servant,

JOHN MURRAY.

Mr. Colquhoun to John Murray.

March 20, 1841.

DEAR SIR,

I am much obliged by your note which I received yesterday. I shall endeavour to see you directly, and when I explain the cause of my dissatisfaction with Messrs. Blackwood, I am sure you will at once see that it would be impossible for us to go on comfortably together with my second edition; and even if any adjustment was brought about, I feel convinced that the book would suffer. I do not mean to imply anything against the Messrs. Blackwood as men of business, and should be sorry to be thus understood; but this case has been a peculiar one, and requires too long an explanation for a letter. In the meantime I have written to you under the strictest confidence, as the Messrs. B. are not aware of my intention of bringing out a second edition at the present time, or of my leaving them. My reasons, however, are such that my determination cannot be altered; and I hope, after a full explanation with you, that we shall at once agree to publish the book with the least possible delay. I shall be most happy to return your note, which you may afterwards show to Messrs. B., and I may add that had you altogether refused to publish my book, it could in no way have affected my decision of leaving them.

I remain, dear Sir, faithfully yours,

JOHN COLQUHOUN.

Mr. Colquhoun came up expressly to London, and after an interview with Mr. Murray, who again expressed his willingness to mediate with the Edinburgh publishers, Mr. Colquhoun repeated his final decision, and Mr. Murray at length agreed to publish the second edition of "The Moor and the Loch. " It may be added that in the end Mr. Colquhoun did, as urged by Murray, return to the Blackwoods, who still continue to publish his work.

Allan Cunningham ended his literary life by preparing the "Memoirs" of his friend Sir David Wilkie. Shortly before he undertook the work he had been prostrated by a stroke of paralysis, but on his partial recovery he proceeded with the memoirs, and the enfeebling effects of his attack may be traced in portions of the work. Towards the close of his life Wilkie had made a journey to the East, had painted the Sultan at Constantinople, and afterwards made his way to Smyrna, Rhodes, Beyrout, Jaffa, and Jerusalem. He returned through Egypt, and at Alexandria he embarked on board the *Oriental* steamship for England. While at Alexandria, he had complained of illness, which increased, partly in consequence of his intense sickness at sea, and he died off Gibraltar on June 1, 1841, when his body was committed to the deep. Turner's splendid picture of the scene was one of Wilkie's best memorials. A review of Allan Cunningham's work, by Mr. Lockhart, appeared in the *Quarterly*, No. 144. Previous to its appearance he wrote to Mr. Murray as follows:

Mr. Lockhart to John Murray.

February 25, 1843.

DEAR MURRAY,

I don't know if you have read much of "The Life of Wilkie. " All Cunningham's part seems to be wretched, but in the "Italian and Spanish Journals and Letters" Wilkie shines out in a comparatively new character. He is a very eloquent and, I fancy, a deep and instructive critic on painting; at all events, Vol. ii. is full of very high interest.... Is there anywhere a good criticism on the alteration that Wilkie's style exhibited after his Italian and Spanish tours? The general impression always was, and I suppose will always be, that the change was for the worse. But it will be a nice piece of work to account for an unfortunate change being the result of travel and observation, which we now own to have produced such a stock of admirable theoretical disquisition on the principles of the Art. I can see little to admire or like in the man Wilkie. Some good homely Scotch kindness for kith and kin, and for some old friends too perhaps; but generally the character seems not to rise above the dull prudentialities of a decent man in awe of the world and the great, and awfully careful about No. 1. No genuine enjoyment, save in study of Art, and getting money through that study. He is a fellow that you can't suppose ever to have been drunk or in love—too much a Presbyterian Elder for either you or me.

Mr. Murray received a communication (December 16, 1841), from Mr. John Sterling, Carlyle's friend, with whom he had had transactions on his own account. "Not, " he said, "respecting his own literary affairs, but those of a friend. " The friend was Mr. John Stuart Mill, son of the historian of British India. He had completed his work on Logic, of which Mr. Sterling had the highest opinion. He said it had been the "labour of many years of a singularly subtle, patient, and comprehensive mind. It will be our chief speculative monument of this age. " Mr. Mill himself addressed Mr. Murray, first on December 20, 1841, while he was preparing the work for the press, and again in January and February, 1842, when he had forwarded the MS. to the publisher, and requested his decision. We find, however, that Mr. Murray was very ill at the time; that he could not give the necessary attention to the subject; and that the MS. was eventually returned.

When Copyright became the subject of legislation in 1843, Mr. Murray received a letter from Mr. Gladstone.

Mr. Gladstone to John Murray.

WHITEHALL, *February* 6, 1843.

MY DEAR SIR,

I beg leave to thank you for the information contained in and accompanying your note which reached me on Saturday. The view with which the clauses relating to copyright in the Customs Act were framed was that those interested in the exclusion of pirated works would take care to supply the Board of Customs from time to time with lists of all works under copyright which were at all likely to be reprinted abroad, and that this would render the law upon the whole much more operative and more fair than an enormous catalogue of all the works entitled to the privilege, of which it would be found very difficult for the officers at the ports to manage the use.

Directions in conformity with the Acts of last Session will be sent to the Colonies.

But I cannot omit to state that I learn from your note with great satisfaction, that steps are to be taken here to back the recent proceedings of the Legislature. I must not hesitate to express my conviction that what Parliament has done will be fruitless, unless the *law* be seconded by the adoption of such modes of publication, as will allow the public here and in the colonies to obtain possession of new and popular English works at moderate prices. If it be practicable for authors and publishers to make such arrangements, I should hope to see a great extension of our book trade, as well as much advantage to literature, from the measures that have now been taken and from those which I trust we shall be enabled to take in completion of them; but unless the proceedings of the trade itself adapt and adjust themselves to the altered circumstances, I can feel no doubt that we shall relapse into or towards the old state of things; the law will be first evaded and then relaxed.

I am, my dear Sir,

Faithfully yours,

W. E. GLADSTONE.

Here it is fitting that a few paragraphs should be devoted to the closing years of Robert Southey, who for so many years had been the friend and coadjutor of the publisher of the *Quarterly*.

Between 1808 and 1838, Southey had written ninety-four articles for the *Quarterly*; the last was upon his friend Thomas Telford, the engineer, who left him a legacy. He had been returned Member of Parliament for Downton (before the Reform Bill passed), but refused the honour—a curious episode not often remembered in the career of this distinguished man of letters. When about fifty-five years old, his only certain source of income was from his pension, from which he received £145, and from his laureateship, which was £90. But the larger portion of these sums went in payment for his life insurance, so that not more than £100 could be calculated on as available. His works were not always profitable. In one year he only received £26 for twenty-one of his books, published by Longman.

Murray gave him £1,000 for the copyright of the "Peninsular War"; but his "Book of the Church" and his "Vindiciae" produced nothing.

Southey's chief means of support was the payments (generally £100 for each article) which he received for his contributions to the *Quarterly*; but while recognizing this, as he could not fail to do, as well as Murray's general kindness towards him, he occasionally allowed a vein of discontent to show itself even in his acknowledgment of favours received.

In 1835 Southey received a pension of £300 from the Government of Sir Robert Peel. He was offered a Baronetcy at the same time, but he declined it, as his circumstances did not permit him to accept the honour.

Mr. Southey to John Murray.

June 17, 1835.

"What Sir Robert Peel has done for me will enable me, when my present engagements are completed, to employ the remainder of my life upon those works for which inclination, peculiar circumstances, and long preparation, have best qualified me. They are "The History of Portugal, " "The History of the Monastic Orders, " and "The History of English Literature, " from the time when Wharton breaks off. The possibility of accomplishing three such works at my age could not be dreamt of, if I had not made very considerable progress with one, and no little, though not in such regular order, with the others. "

Shortly after his second marriage, Southey's intellect began to fail him, and he soon sank into a state of mental imbecility. He would wander about his library, take down a book, look into it, and then put it back again, but was incapable of work. When Mr. Murray sent him the octavo edition of the "Peninsular War, " his wife answered:

Mrs. Southey to John Murray.

GRETA HALL, *May* 15, 1840.

If the word *pleasure* were not become to me as a *dead letter, I* should tell you with how much I took possession of your kind gift. But I *may* tell you truly that it gratified, and more than gratified me, by giving pleasure to my dear husband, as a token of your regard for him, so testified towards myself. The time is not far passed when we should have rejoiced together like children over such an acquisition.

Yours very truly and thankfully,

CAR. SOUTHEY.

May 23, 1840.

DEAR SIR,

Very cordially I return your friendly salutations, feeling, as I do, that every manifestation of kindness for my husband's sake is more precious to me than any I could receive for my own exclusively. Two-and-twenty years ago, when he wished to put into your hands, as publisher, a first attempt of mine, of which he thought better than it deserved, he little thought in that so doing he was endeavouring to forward the interests of his future wife; of her for whom it was appointed (a sad but honoured lot) to be the companion of his later days, over which it has pleased God to cast the "shadow before" of that "night in which no man can work. " But twelve short months ago he was cheerfully anticipating (in the bright buoyancy of his happy nature) a far other companionship for the short remainder of our earthly sojourn; never forgetting, however, that ours must be short at the longest, and that "in the midst of life we are in death. " He desires me to thank you for your kind expressions towards him, and to be most kindly remembered to you. Your intimation of the favourable progress of his 8vo "Book of the Church" gave him pleasure, and he thanks you for so promptly attending to his wishes about a neatly bound set of his "Peninsular War. " Accept my assurances of regard, and believe me to be, dear Sir,

Yours very truly,

CAROLINE SOUTHEY.

On September 17, 1840, Mr. Murray sent to Mr. Southey a draft for £259, being the balance for his "Book of the Church, " and informed him that he would be pleased to know that another edition was called for. Mrs. Southey replied:

Mrs. Southey to John Murray.

"He made no remark on your request to be favoured with any suggestions he might have to offer. *My* sad persuasion is that Robert Southey's works have received their last revision and correction from his mind and pen. "

GRETA HALL, *October 5*, 1840.

DEAR SIR,

I will not let another post go out, without conveying to you my thanks for your very kind letter last night received. It will gratify you to know that its contents (the copy of the critique included), aroused and fixed Mr. Southey's attention more than anything that has occurred for months past—gratifying him, I believe, far more than anything more immediately concerning himself could have done. "Tell Murray, " he said, "I am very much obliged to him. " It is long since he has sent a message to friend or relation.

Now let me say for myself that I am very thankful to *you*—very thankful to my indulgent reviewer—and that if I could yet feel interest about anything of my own writing, I should be pleased and encouraged by his encomium—as well as grateful for it. But if it did *not sound thanklessly*, I should say, "too late—too late—it comes too late! " and that bitter feeling came upon me so suddenly, as my eyes fell upon the passage in question, that they overflowed with tears before it was finished.

But he *did take interest in* it, at least for a few moments, and so it was not *quite* too late; and (doing as I *know he would have me*), I shall act upon your most *kind* and *friendly* advice, and transmit it to Blackwood, who will, I doubt not, be willingly guided by it.

It was one of my husband's pleasant visions before our marriage, and his favourite prospect, to publish a volume of poetry conjointly with me, not weighing the disproportion of talent.

I must tell you that immediately on receiving the *Review*, I should have written to express my sense of your kindness, and of the flattering nature of the critique; but happening to *tell* Miss Southey and her brother that you had sent it me, as I believed, as an obliging personal attention, they assured me I was mistaken, and that the numbers were only intended for "their set. " Fearing, therefore, to arrogate to myself more than was designed for me, I kept silence; and now expose *my simplicity* rather than *leave* myself *open* to the imputation of unthankfulness. Mr. Southey desires to be very kindly remembered to you, and I am, my dear Sir,

Very thankfully and truly yours, Car. Southey.

P. S.—I had almost forgotten to thank you for so kindly offering to send the *Review* to any friends of mine, I may wish to gratify. I *will* accept the proffered favour, and ask you to send one addressed to Miss Burnard, Shirley, Southampton, Hants. The other members of my family and most of my friends take the Q. R., or are sure of seeing it. This last number is an excellent one.

Southey died on March 21, 1843. The old circle of friends was being sadly diminished. "Disease and death, " his old friend Thomas Mitchell, one of the survivors of the early contributors to the *Quarterly*, wrote to Murray, "seem to be making no small havoc among our literary men—Maginn, Cunningham, Basil Hall, and poor Southey, worst of all. Lockhart's letters of late have made me very uneasy, too, about him. Has he yet returned from Scotland, and is he at all improved? " Only a few months later Mr. Murray himself was to be called away from the scene of his life's activity. In the autumn of 1842 his health had already begun to fail rapidly, and he had found it necessary to live much out of London, and to try various watering-places; but although he rallied at times sufficiently to return to his business for short periods, he never recovered, and passed away in sleep on June 27, 1843, at the age of sixty-five.

CHAPTER XXXII

JOHN MURRAY AS A PUBLISHER

In considering the career of John Murray, the reader can hardly fail to be struck with the remarkable manner in which his personal qualities appeared to correspond with the circumstances out of which he built his fortunes.

When he entered his profession, the standard of conduct in every department of life connected with the publishing trade was determined by aristocratic ideas. The unwritten laws which regulated the practice of bookselling in the eighteenth century were derived from the Stationers' Company. Founded as it had been on the joint principles of commercial monopoly and State control, this famous organization had long lost its old vitality. But it had bequeathed to the bookselling community a large portion of its original spirit, both in the practice of cooperative publication which produced the "Trade Books, " so common in the last century, and in that deep-rooted belief in the perpetuity of copyright, which only received its death-blow from the celebrated judgment of the House of Lords in the case of Donaldson *v.* Becket in 1774. Narrow and exclusive as they may have been in their relation to the public interest, there can be no doubt that these traditions helped to constitute, in the dealings of the booksellers among themselves, a standard of honour which put a certain curb on the pursuit of private gain. It was this feeling which provoked such intense indignation in the trade against the publishers who took advantage of their strict legal rights to invade what was generally regarded as the property of their brethren; while the sense of what was due to the credit, as well as to the interest, of a great organized body, made the associated booksellers zealous in the promotion of all enterprises likely to add to the fame of English literature.

Again, there was something, in the best sense of the word, aristocratic in the position of literature itself. Patronage, indeed, had declined. The patron of the early days of the century, who, like Halifax, sought in the Universities or in the London Coffee-houses for literary talent to strengthen the ranks of political party, had disappeared, together with the later and inferior order of patron, who, after the manner of Bubb Dodington, nattered his social pride by maintaining a retinue of poetical clients at his country seat. The nobility themselves, absorbed in politics or pleasure, cared far less for letters than their fathers in the reigns of Anne and the first two Georges. Hence, as Johnson said, the bookseller had become the Maecenas of the age; but not the bookseller of Grub Street. To be a man of letters was no longer a reproach. Johnson himself had been rewarded with a literary pension, and the names of almost all the distinguished scholars of the latter part of the eighteenth century — Warburton, the two Wartons, Lowth, Burke, Hume, Gibbon, Robertson—belong to men who either by birth or merit were in a position which rendered them independent of literature as a source of livelihood. The author influenced the public rather than the public the author, while the part of the bookseller was restricted to introducing and distributing to society the works which the scholar had designed.

Naturally enough, from such conditions arose a highly aristocratic standard of taste. The centre of literary judgment passed from the half-democratic society of the Coffee-house to the dining-room of scholars like Cambridge or Beauclerk; and opinion, formed from the brilliant conversation at such gatherings as the Literary Club; afterwards circulated among the public either in the treatises of individual critics, or in the pages of the two leading Monthly Reviews. The society from which it proceeded, though not in the strict sense of the word fashionable, was eminently refined and widely representative; it included the politician, the clergyman, the artist, the connoisseur, and was permeated with the necessary leaven of feminine intuition, ranging from the observation of Miss Burney or the vivacity of Mrs. Thrale, to the stately morality of Mrs. Montagu and Mrs. Hannah More.

On the other hand, the whole period of Murray's life as a publisher, extending, to speak broadly, from the first French Revolution to almost the eve of the French Revolution of 1848, was characterized in a marked degree by the advance of Democracy. In all directions there was an uprising of the spirit of individual liberty against the prescriptions of established authority. In Politics the tendency is apparent in the progress of the Reform movement. In Commerce it was marked by the inauguration of the Free Trade movement. In Literature it made itself felt in the great outburst of poetry at the beginning of the century, and in the assertion of the superiority of individual genius to the traditional laws of form.

The effect produced by the working of the democratic spirit within the aristocratic constitution of society and taste may without exaggeration be described as prodigious. At first sight, indeed, there seems to be a certain abruptness in the transition from the highly organized society represented in Boswell's "Life of Johnson, " to the philosophical retirement of Wordsworth and Coleridge. It is only when we look beneath the surface that we see the old traditions still upheld by a small class of Conservative writers, including Campbell, Rogers, and Crabbe, and, as far as style is concerned, by some of the romantic innovators, Byron, Scott, and Moore. But, generally speaking, the age succeeding the first French Revolution exhibits the triumph of individualism. Society itself is penetrated by new ideas; literature becomes fashionable; men of position are no longer ashamed to be known as authors, nor women of distinction afraid to welcome men of letters in their drawing-rooms. On all sides the excitement and curiosity of the times is reflected in the demand for poems, novels, essays, travels, and every kind of imaginative production, under the name of *belles lettres*.

A certain romantic spirit of enterprise shows itself in Murray's character at the very outset of his career. Tied to a partner of a petty and timorous disposition, he seizes an early opportunity to rid himself of the incubus. With youthful ardour he begs of a veteran author to be allowed the privilege of publishing, as his first undertaking, a work which he himself genuinely admired. He refuses to be bound by mere trading calculations. "The business of a publishing bookseller, " he writes to a correspondent, "is not in his shop, or even in his connections, but in his brains. " In all his professional conduct a largeness of view is apparent. A new conception of the scope of his trade seems early to have risen in his mind, and he was perhaps the first member of the Stationers' craft to separate the business of bookselling from that of publishing. When Constable in Edinburgh sent him "a miscellaneous order of books from London, " he replied: "Country orders are a branch of business which I have ever totally declined as incompatible with my more serious plans as a publisher. "

With ideas of this kind, it may readily be imagined that Murray was not what is usually called "a good man of business, " a fact of which he was well aware, as the following incident, which occurred in his later years, amusingly indicates.

The head of one of the larger firms with which he dealt came in person to Albemarle Street to receive payment of his account. This was duly handed to him in bills, which, by some carelessness, he lost on his way home, He thereupon wrote to Mr. Murray, requesting him to advertise in his own name for the lost property. Murray's reply was as follows:

TWICKENHAM, *October* 26, 1841.

MY DEAR— —-,

I am exceedingly sorry for the vexatious, though, I hope, only temporary loss which you have met with; but I have so little character for being a man of business, that if the bills were advertised in *my* name it would be publicly confirming the suspicion—but in your own name, it will be only considered as a very extraordinary circumstance, and I therefore give my impartial opinion in favour of the latter mode. Remaining, my dear— —-,

Most truly yours,

JOHN MURRAY.

The possession of ordinary commercial shrewdness, however, was by no means the quality most essential for successful publishing at the beginning of the nineteenth century. Both Constable and Ballantyne were men of great cleverness and aptitude for business; but, wanting certain higher endowments, they were unable to resist the whirl of excitement accompanying an unprecedented measure of financial success. Their ruin was as rapid as their rise. To Murray, on the other hand, perhaps their inferior in the average arts of calculation, a vigorous native sense, tempering a genuine enthusiasm for what was excellent in literature, gave precisely that mixture of dash and steadiness which was needed to satisfy the complicated requirements of the public taste.

A high sense of rectitude is apparent in all his business transactions; and Charles Knight did him no more than justice in saying that he had "left an example of talent and honourable conduct which would long be a model for those who aim at distinction in the profession. " He would have nothing to do with what was poor and shabby. When it was suggested to him, as a young publisher, that his former partner was ready to bear part of the risk in a contemplated undertaking, he refused to associate his fortunes with a man who conducted his business on methods that he did not approve. "I cannot allow my name to stand with his, because he undersells all other publishers at the regular and advertised prices. " Boundless as was his admiration for the genius of Scott and Byron, he abandoned one of the most cherished objects of his ambition-to be the publisher of new works by the author of "Waverley"—rather than involve himself further in transactions which he foresaw must lead to discredit and disaster; and, at the risk of a quarrel, strove to recall Byron to the ways of sound literature, when through his wayward genius he seemed to be drifting into an unworthy course.

In the same way, when the disagreement between the firms of Constable and Longmans seemed likely to turn to his own advantage, instead of making haste to seize the golden opportunity, he exerted himself to effect a reconciliation between the disputants, by pointing out what he considered the just and reasonable view of their mutual interests. The letters which, on this occasion, he addressed respectively to Mr. A.G. Hunter, to the Constables, and to the Longmans, are models of good sense and manly rectitude. Nor was his conduct to Constable, after the downfall of the latter, less worthy of admiration. Deeply as Constable had injured him by the reckless conduct of his business, Murray not only retained no ill-feeling against him, but, anxious simply to help a brother in misfortune, resigned in his favour, in a manner full of the most delicate consideration, his own claim to a valuable copyright. The same warmth of heart and disinterested friendship appears in his efforts to re-establish the affairs of the Robinsons after the failure of that firm. Yet, remarkable as he was for his loyalty to his comrades, he was no less distinguished by his spirit and independence. No man without a very high sense of justice and self-respect could have conducted a correspondence on a matter of business in terms of such dignified propriety as Murray employed in addressing Benjamin Disraeli after the collapse of the *Representative*. It is indeed a proof of power to appreciate character, remarkable in so young a man, that Disraeli should, after all that had passed between them, have approached Murray in his capacity of publisher with complete confidence. He knew that he was dealing with a man at once shrewd and magnanimous, and he gave him credit for understanding how to estimate his professional interest apart from his sense of private injury.

Perhaps his most distinguishing characteristic as a publisher was his unfeigned love of literature for its own sake. His almost romantic admiration for genius and its productions raised him above the atmosphere of petty calculation. Not unfrequently it of course led him into commercial mistakes, and in his purchase of Crabbe's "Tales" he found to his cost that his enthusiastic appreciation of that author's works and the magnificence of his dealings with him were not the measure of the public taste. Yet disappointments of this kind in no way embittered his temper, or affected the liberality with which he treated writers like Washington Irving, of whose powers he had himself once formed a high conception. The mere love of money indeed was never an absorbing motive in Murray's commercial career, otherwise it is certain that his course in the suppression of Byron's Memoirs would have been something very different to that which he actually pursued. On the perfect letter which he wrote to Scott, presenting him with his fourth share in "Marmion, " the best comment is the equally admirable letter in which Scott returned his thanks. The grandeur—for that seems the appropriate word—of his dealings with men of high genius, is seen in his payments to Byron, while his confidence in the solid value of literary excellence appears from the fact that, when the *Quarterly* was not paying its expenses, he gave Southey for his "Life of Nelson" double the usual rate of remuneration. No doubt his lavish generosity was politic as well as splendid. This, and the prestige which he obtained as Byron's publisher, naturally drew to him all that was vigorous and original in the intellect of the day, so that there was a general desire among young authors to be introduced to the public under his auspices. The relations between author and publisher which had prevailed in the eighteenth century were, in his case, curiously inverted, and, in the place of a solitary scholar like Johnson, surrounded by an association of booksellers, the drawing-room of Murray now presented the remarkable spectacle of a single publisher acting as the centre of attraction to a host of distinguished writers.

In Murray the spirit of the eighteenth century seemed to meet and harmonize with the spirit of the nineteenth. Enthusiasm, daring, originality, and freedom from conventionality made him eminently a man of his time, and, in a certain sense, he did as much as any of his contemporaries to swell that movement in his profession towards complete individual liberty which had been growing almost from the foundation of the Stationers' Company. On the other hand, in his temper, taste, and general principles, he reflected the best and most ancient traditions of his craft. Had his life been prolonged, he would have witnessed the disappearance in the trade of many institutions which he reverenced and always sought to develop. Some of them, indeed, vanished in his own life-time. The old association of booksellers, with its accompaniment of trade-books, dwindled with the growth of the spirit of competition and the greater facility of communication, so that, long before his death, the co-operation between the booksellers of London and Edinburgh was no more than a memory. Another institution which had his warm support was the Sale dinner, but this too has all but succumbed, of recent years, to the existing tendency for new and more rapid methods of conducting business. The object of the Sale dinner was to induce the great distributing houses and the retail booksellers to speculate, and buy an increased supply of books on special terms. Speculation has now almost ceased in consequence of the enormous number of books published, which makes it difficult for a bookseller to keep a large stock of any single work, and renders the life of a new book so precarious that the demand for it may at any moment come to a sudden stop.

The country booksellers—a class in which Murray was always deeply interested—are dying out. Profits on books being cut down to a minimum, these tradesmen find it almost impossible to live by the sale of books alone, and are forced to couple this with some other kind of business.

The apparent risk involved in Murray's extraordinary spirit of adventure was in reality diminished by the many checks which in his day operated on competition, and by the high prices then paid for ordinary books. Men were at that time in the habit of forming large private libraries, and furnishing them with the sumptuous editions of travels and books of costly engraving issued from Murray's press. The taste of the time has changed. Collections of books have been superseded, as a fashion, by collections of pictures, and the circulating library encourages the habit of reading books without buying them. Cheap bookselling, the characteristic of the age, has been promoted by the removal of the tax on paper, and by the fact that paper can now be manufactured out of refuse at a very low cost. This cheapness, the ideal condition for which Charles Knight sighed, has been accompanied by a distinct deterioration in the taste and industry of the general reader. The multiplication of reviews, magazines, manuals, and abstracts has impaired the love of, and perhaps the capacity for, study, research, and scholarship on which the general quality of literature must depend. Books, and even knowledge, like other commodities, may, in proportion to the ease with which they are obtained, lose at once both their external value and their intrinsic merit.

Murray's professional success is sufficient evidence of the extent of his intellectual powers. The foregoing Memoir has confined itself almost exclusively to an account of his life as a publisher, and it has been left to the reader's imagination to divine from a few glimpses how much of this success was due to force of character and a rare combination of personal qualities. A few concluding words on this point may not be inappropriate.

Quick-tempered and impulsive, he was at the same time warm-hearted and generous to a fault, while a genuine sense of humour, which constantly shows itself in his letters, saved him many a time from those troubles into which the hasty often fall. "I wish, " wrote George Borrow, within a short time of the publisher's death, "that all the world were as gay as he. "

He was in some respects indolent, and not infrequently caused serious misunderstandings by his neglect to answer letters; but when he did apply himself to work, he achieved results more solid than most of his compeers. He had, moreover, a wonderful power of attraction, and both in his conversation and correspondence possessed a gift of felicitous expression which rarely failed to arouse a sympathetic response in those whom he addressed. Throughout "the trade" he was beloved, and he rarely lost a friend among those who had come within his personal influence.

He was eager to look for, and quick to discern, any promise of talent in the young. "Every one, " he would say, "has a book in him, or her, if one only knew how to extract it, " and many was the time that he lent a helping hand to those who were first entering on a literary career.

To his remarkable powers as a host, the many descriptions of his dinner parties which have been preserved amply testify; he was more than a mere entertainer, and took the utmost pains so to combine and to place his guests as best to promote sympathetic conversation and the general harmony of the gathering. Among the noted wits and talkers, moreover, who assembled round his table he was fully able to hold his own in conversation and in repartee.

On one occasion Lady Bell was present at one of these parties, and wrote: "The talk was of wit, and Moore gave specimens. Charles thought that our host Murray said the best things that brilliant night."

Many of the friends whose names are most conspicuous in these pages had passed away before him, but of those who remained there was scarcely one whose letters do not testify to the general affection with which he was regarded. We give here one or two extracts from letters received during his last illness.

Thomas Mitchell wrote to Mr. Murray's son:

"Give my most affectionate remembrances to your father. More than once I should have sunk under the ills of life but for his kind support and countenance, and so I believe would many others say besides myself. Be his maladies small or great, assure him that he has the earnest sympathies of one who well knows and appreciates his sterling merits. "

Sir Francis Palgrave, who had known Mr. Murray during the whole course of his career, wrote to him affectionately of "the friendship and goodwill which, " said he, "you have borne towards me during a period of more than half my life. I am sure, " he added, "as we grow older we find day by day the impossibility of finding *any* equivalent for old friends. " Sharon Turner also, the historian, was most cordial in his letters.

"Our old friends, " he said, "are dropping off so often that it becomes more and more pleasing to know that some still survive whom we esteem and by whom we are not forgotten.... Certainly we can look back on each other now for forty years, and I can do so as to you with great pleasure and satisfaction, when, besides the grounds of private satisfaction and esteem, I think of the many works of great benefit to society which you have been instrumental in publishing, and in some instances of suggesting and causing. You have thus made your life serviceable to the world as well as honourable to yourself.... You are frequently in my recollections, and always with those feelings which accompanied our intercourse in our days of health and activity. May every blessing accompany you and yours, both here and hereafter. "

It was not only in England that his loss was felt, for the news of his death called forth many tokens of respect and regard from beyond the seas, and we will close these remarks with two typical extracts from the letters of American correspondents.

To Mr. Murray's son, Dr. Robinson of New York summed up his qualities in these words:

"I have deeply sympathised with the bereaved family at the tidings of the decease of one of whom I have heard and read from childhood, and to whose kindness and friendship I had recently been myself so much indebted. He has indeed left you a rich inheritance, not only by his successful example in business and a wide circle of friends, but also in that good name which is better than all riches. He lived in a fortunate period—his own name is inseparably connected with one of the brightest eras of English literature—one, too, which, if not created, was yet developed and fostered by his unparalleled enterprise and princely liberality. I counted it a high privilege to be connected with him as a publisher, and shall rejoice in continuing the connection with his son and successor. "

Mrs. L.H. Sigourney wrote from Hartford, Connecticut, U.S. :

"Your father's death is a loss which is mourned on this side of the Atlantic. His powerful agency on the patronage of a correct literature, which he was so well qualified to appreciate, has rendered him a benefactor in that realm of intellect which binds men together in all ages, however dissevered by political creed or local prejudice. His urbanity to strangers is treasured with gratitude in many hearts. To me his personal kindness was so great that I deeply regretted not having formed his acquaintance until just on the eve of my leaving London. But his parting gifts are among the chief ornaments of my library, and his last letter, preserved as a sacred autograph, expresses the kindness of a friend of long standing, and promises another 'more at length, ' which, unfortunately, I had never the happiness of receiving. "

THE END